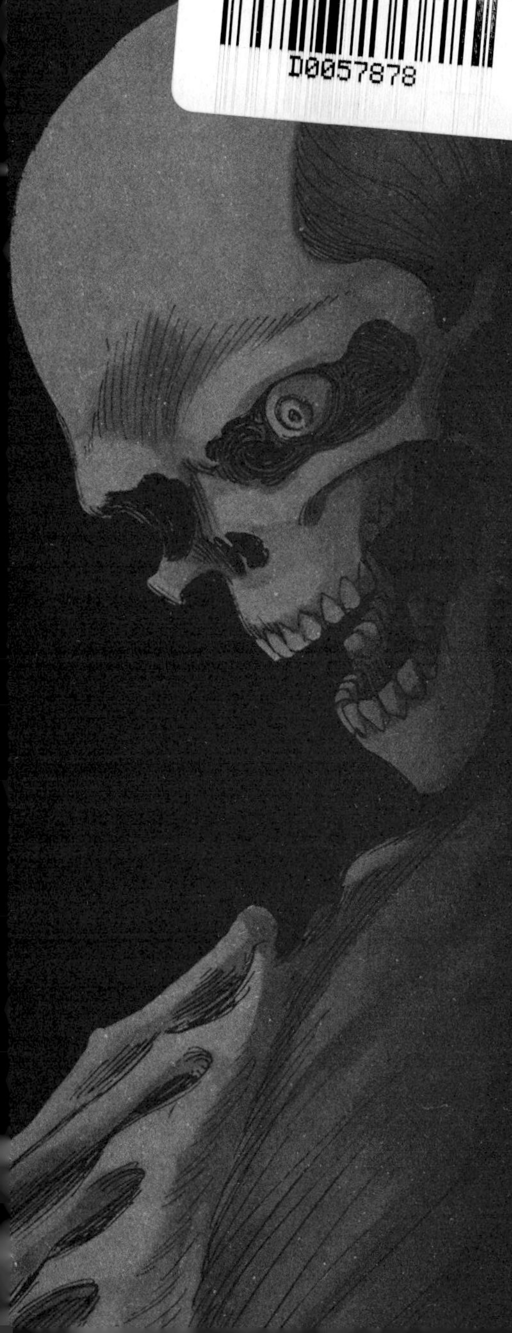

ATTACK ON TITAN 3

HAJIME ISAYAMA

The World of "Attack on Titan"

Armin Arlert
Eren and Mikasa's childhood friend, he is physically weak and feels that he has gone through life with them protecting him.

Mikasa Ackerman
Mikasa graduated at the top of her training corps. She lost her parents before her eyes. Afterward she becomes committed to protecting Eren, who was raised alongside her.

Eren Yeager
Longing for the world outside the wall, Eren aimed to join the Survey Corps. He was swallowed by a Titan, but was later discovered inside a Titan.

Grisha Yeager
A doctor and Eren's father. He went missing after the Titan attack five years ago.

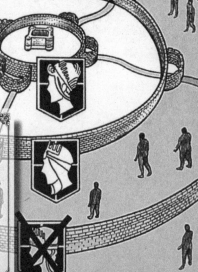

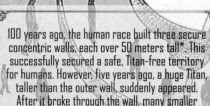

100 years ago, the human race built three secure concentric walls, each over 50 meters tall*. This successfully secured a safe, Titan-free territory for humans. However, five years ago, a huge Titan, taller than the outer wall, suddenly appeared.

After it broke through the wall, many smaller Titans found their way in, forcing the humans to abandon their outer wall. Currently, the sphere of activity of the human race has been reduced to the area behind the second wall, "Wall Rose."

* 164 feet

TITANS

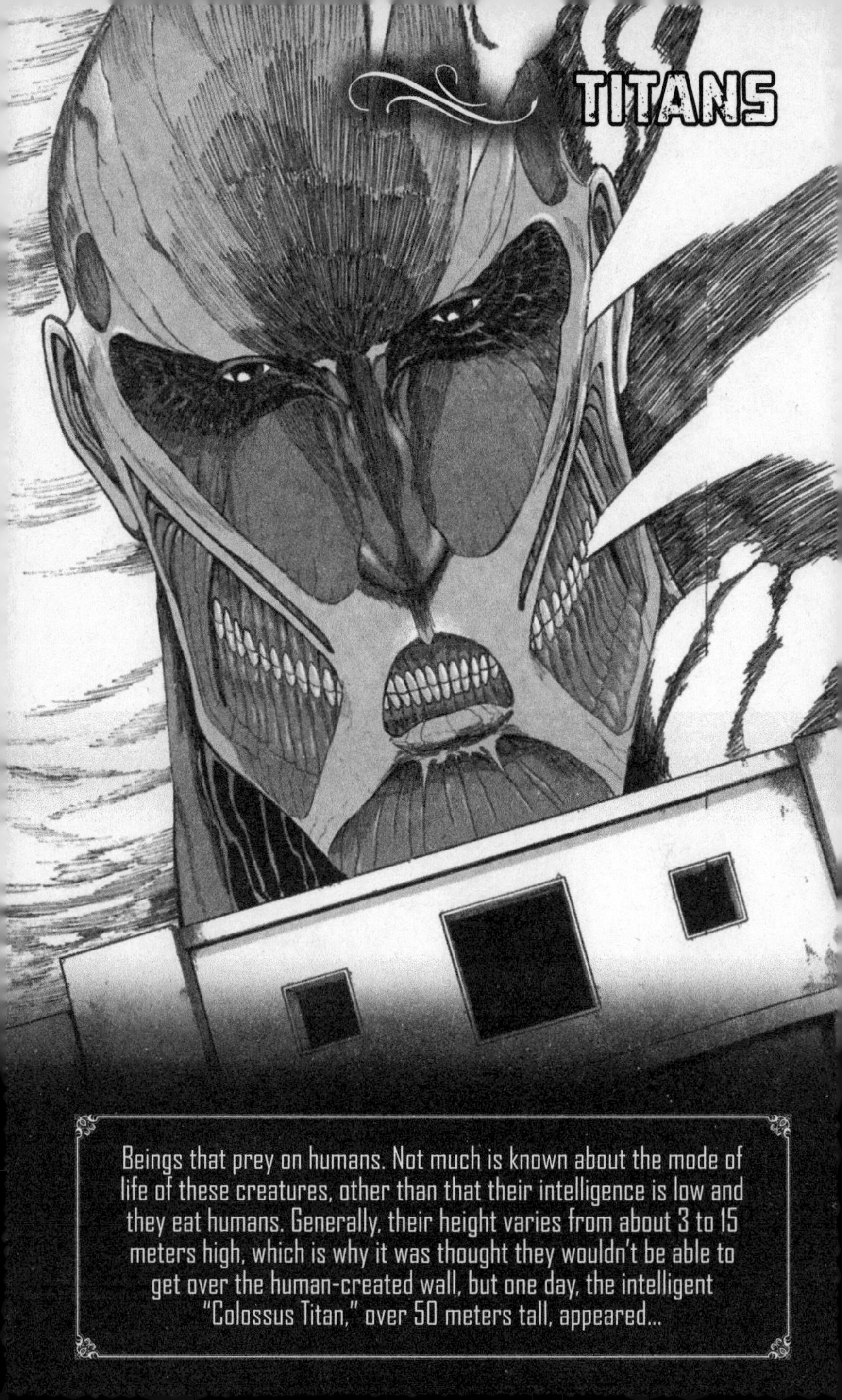

Beings that prey on humans. Not much is known about the mode of life of these creatures, other than that their intelligence is low and they eat humans. Generally, their height varies from about 3 to 15 meters high, which is why it was thought they wouldn't be able to get over the human-created wall, but one day, the intelligent "Colossus Titan," over 50 meters tall, appeared...

ATTACK on TITAN

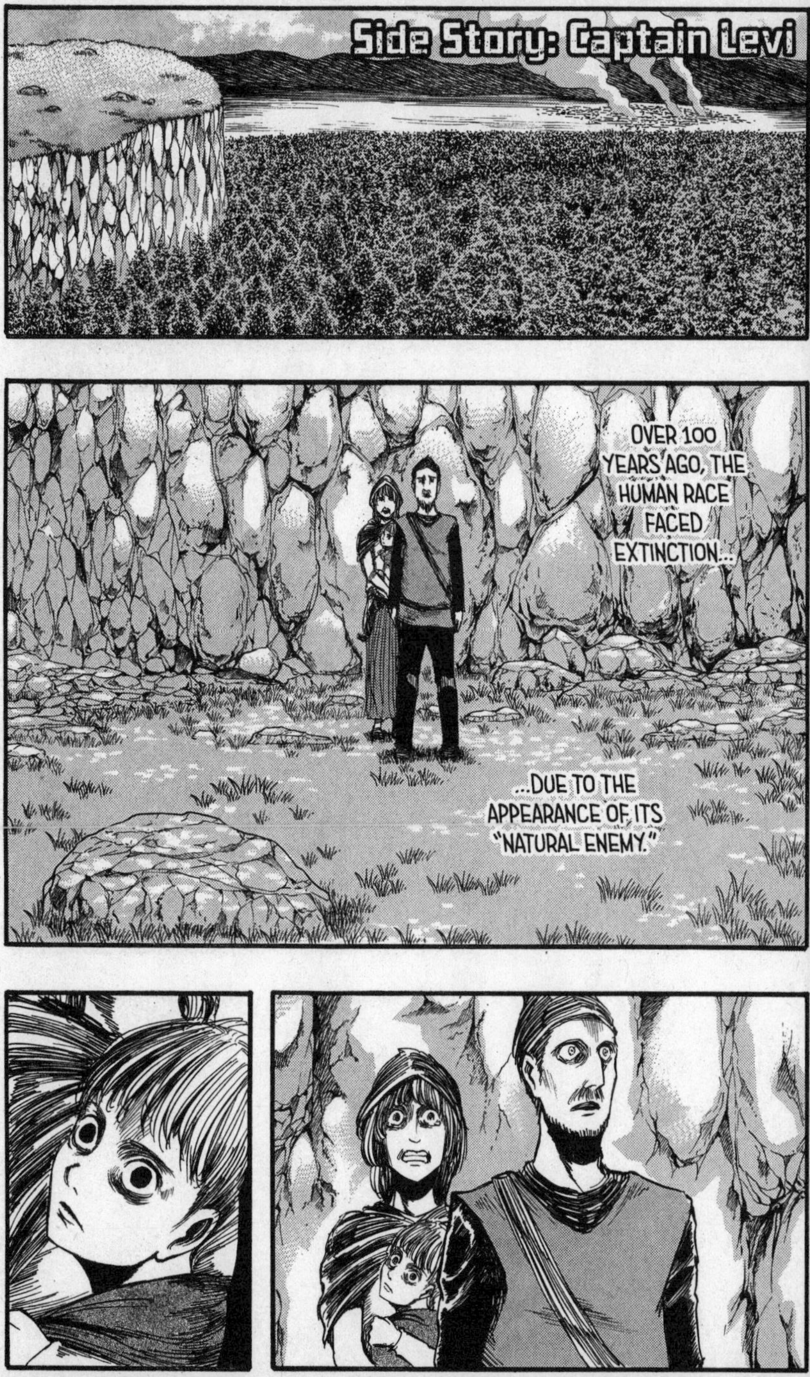
Side Story: Captain Levi
OVER 100 YEARS AGO, THE HUMAN RACE FACED EXTINCTION...
...DUE TO THE APPEARANCE OF ITS "NATURAL ENEMY."

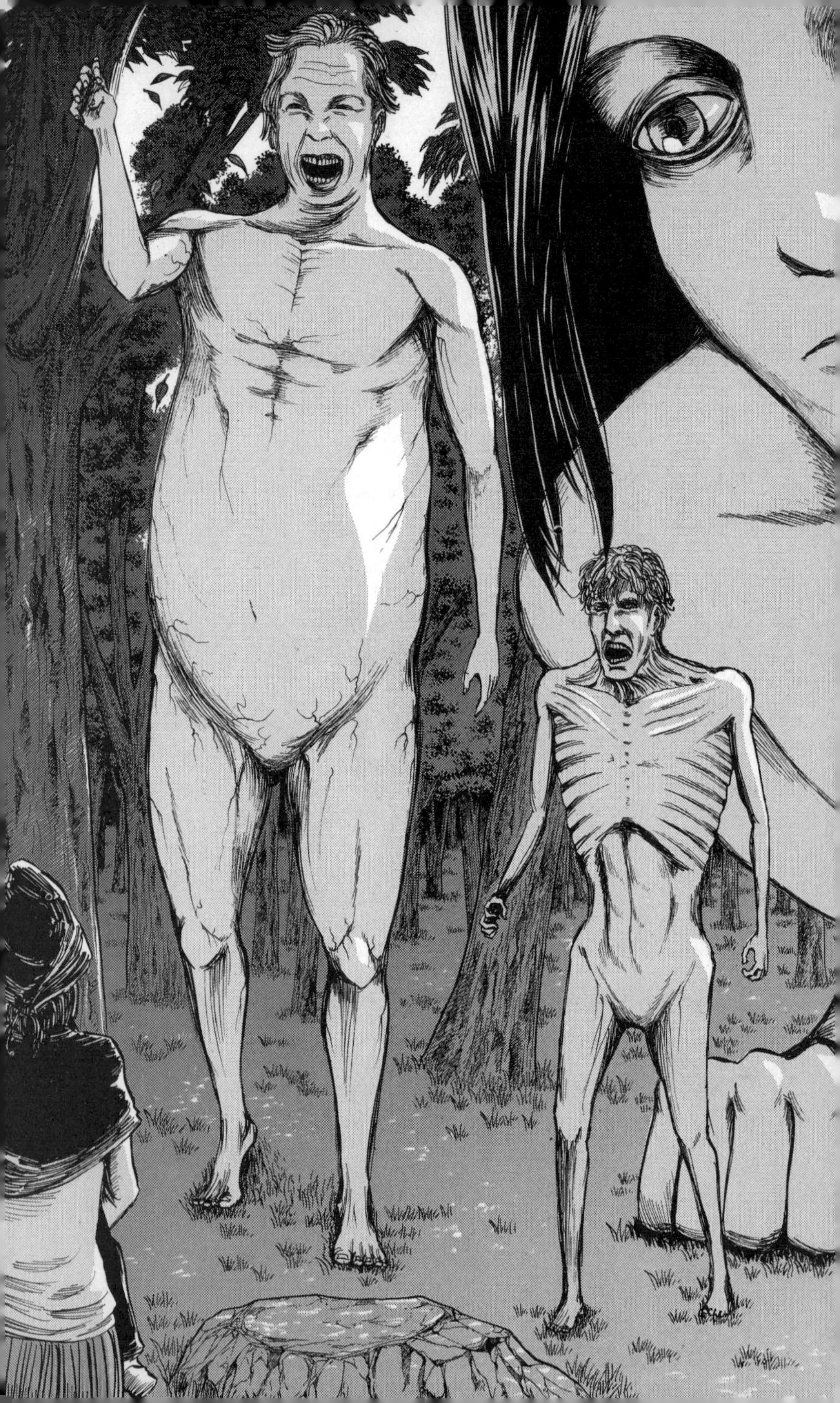

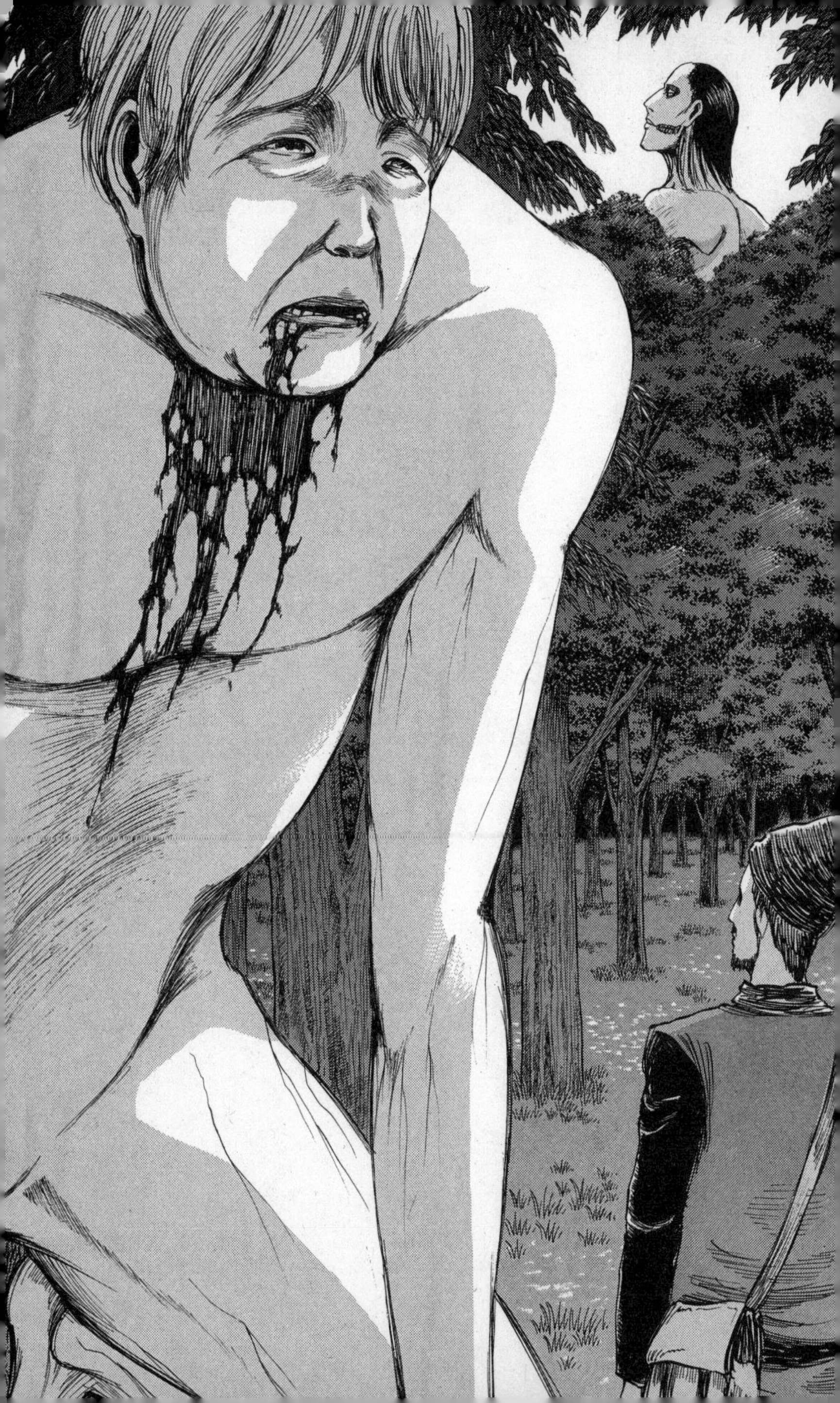

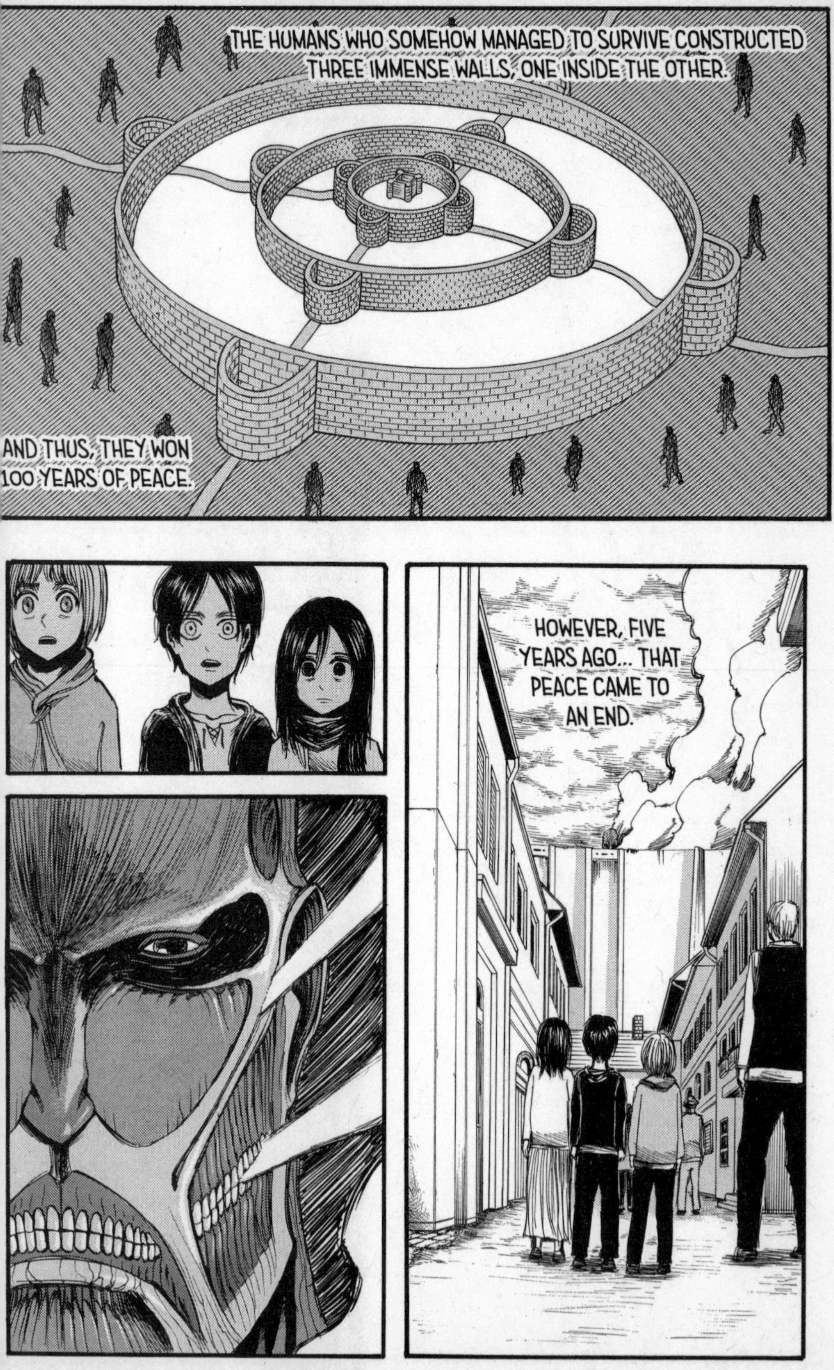
THE HUMANS WHO SOMEHOW MANAGED TO SURVIVE CONSTRUCTED THREE IMMENSE WALLS, ONE INSIDE THE OTHER.
AND THUS, THEY WON 100 YEARS OF PEACE.
HOWEVER, FIVE YEARS AGO... THAT PEACE CAME TO AN END.

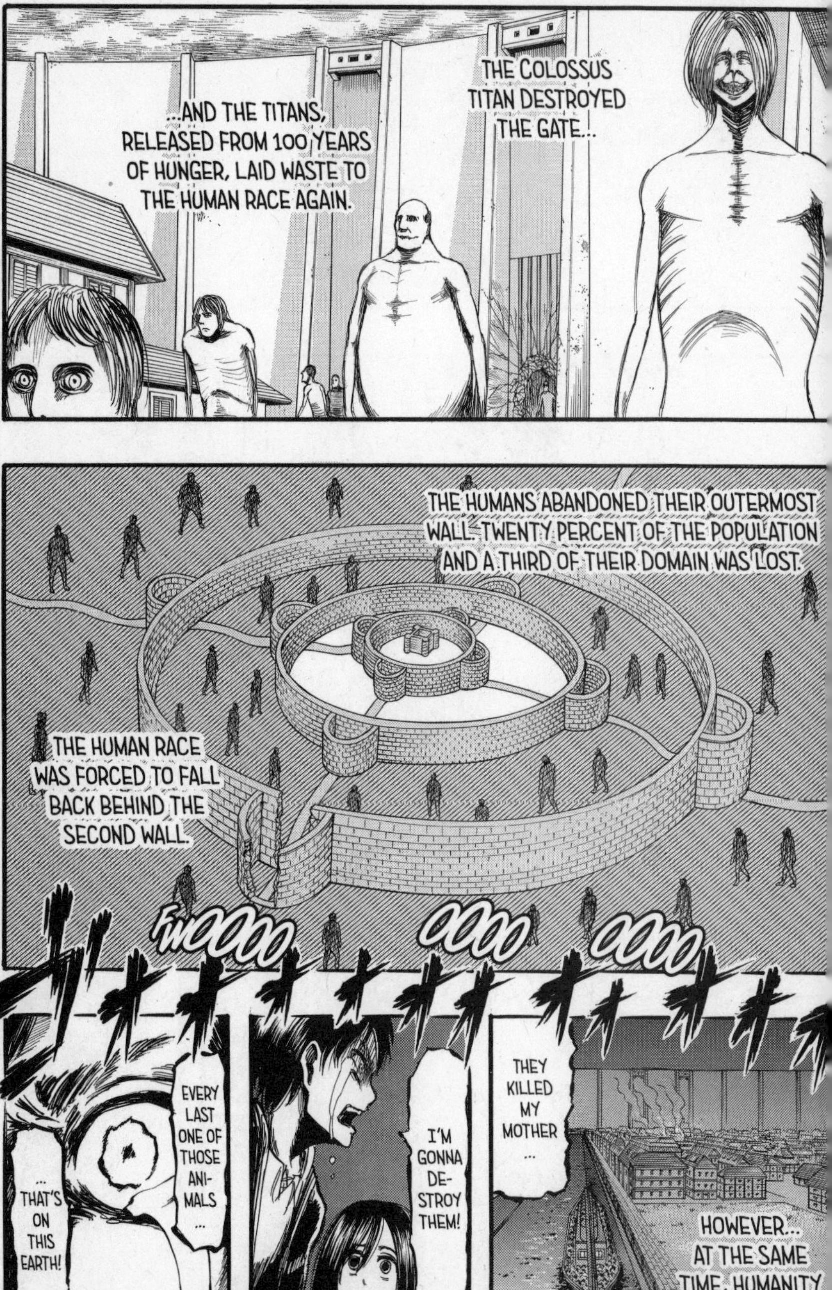
THE COLOSSUS TITAN DESTROYED THE GATE...
...AND THE TITANS, RELEASED FROM 100 YEARS OF HUNGER, LAID WASTE TO THE HUMAN RACE AGAIN.
THE HUMANS ABANDONED THEIR OUTERMOST WALL. TWENTY PERCENT OF THE POPULATION AND A THIRD OF THEIR DOMAIN WAS LOST.
THE HUMAN RACE WAS FORCED TO FALL BACK BEHIND THE SECOND WALL.
FWOOOO OOOO OOOO
THEY KILLED MY MOTHER ...
HOWEVER... AT THE SAME TIME, HUMANITY AWAKENED.
I'M GONNA DE-STROY THEM!
EVERY LAST ONE OF THOSE ANI-MALS ...
... THAT'S ON THIS EARTH!

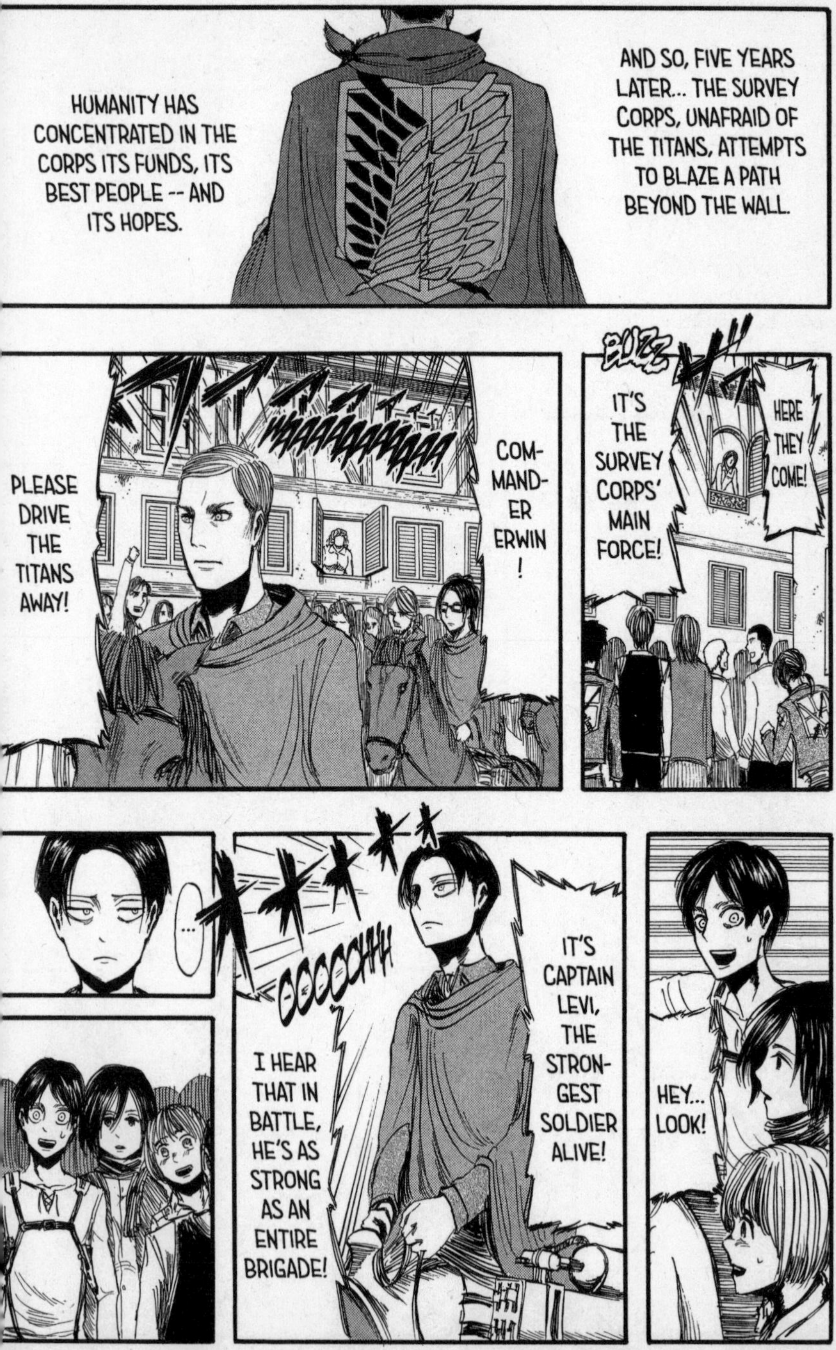
AND SO, FIVE YEARS LATER... THE SURVEY CORPS, UNAFRAID OF THE TITANS, ATTEMPTS TO BLAZE A PATH BEYOND THE WALL.
HUMANITY HAS CONCENTRATED IN THE CORPS ITS FUNDS, ITS BEST PEOPLE -- AND ITS HOPES.
BUZZ
HERE THEY COME!
IT'S THE SURVEY CORPS' MAIN FORCE!
WAAAAAAAAAAAA
COMMANDER ERWIN!
PLEASE DRIVE THE TITANS AWAY!
HEY... LOOK!
IT'S CAPTAIN LEVI, THE STRONGEST SOLDIER ALIVE!
I HEAR THAT IN BATTLE, HE'S AS STRONG AS AN ENTIRE BRIGADE!
OOOOOHHH
...

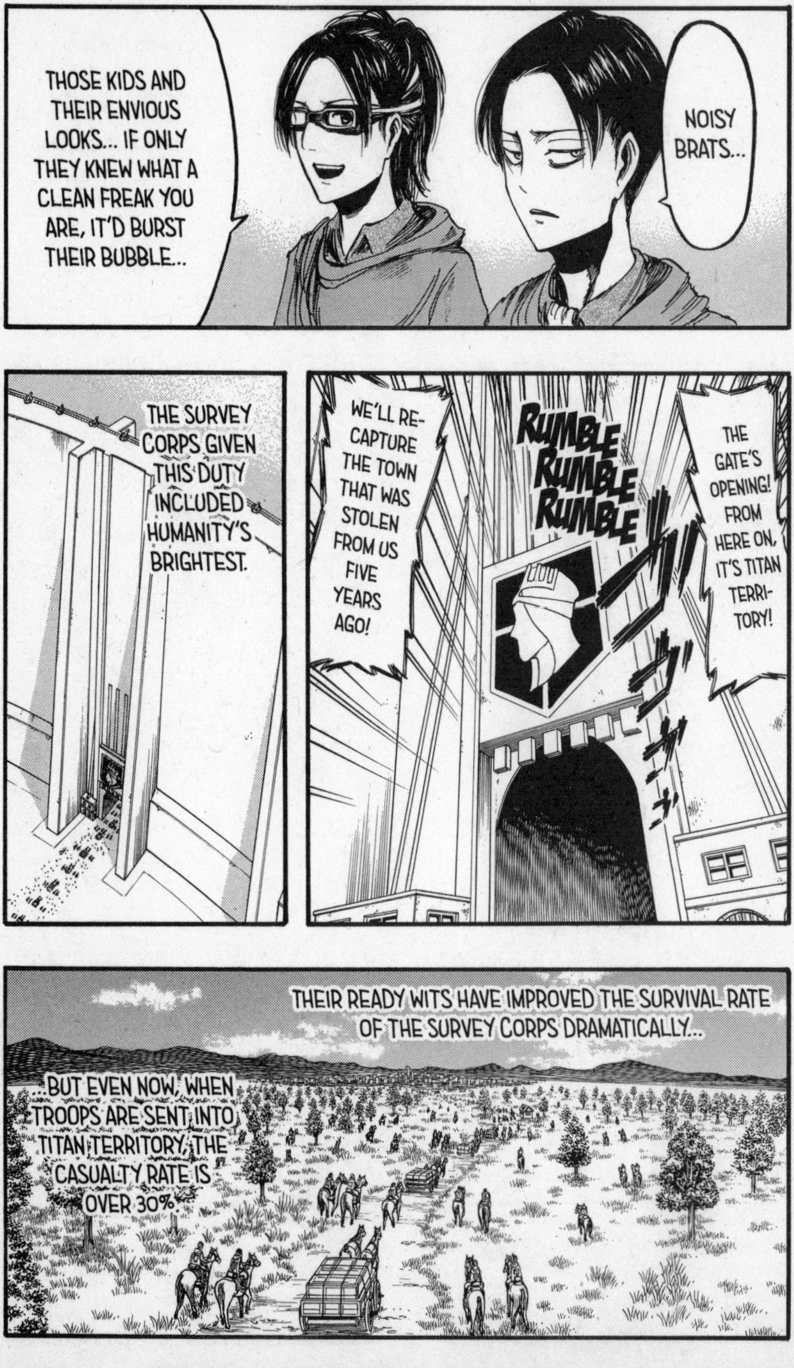
NOISY BRATS...
THOSE KIDS AND THEIR ENVIOUS LOOKS... IF ONLY THEY KNEW WHAT A CLEAN FREAK YOU ARE, IT'D BURST THEIR BUBBLE...
THE GATE'S OPENING! FROM HERE ON, IT'S TITAN TERRI-TORY!
RUMBLE RUMBLE RUMBLE
WE'LL RE-CAPTURE THE TOWN THAT WAS STOLEN FROM US FIVE YEARS AGO!
THE SURVEY CORPS GIVEN THIS DUTY INCLUDED HUMANITY'S BRIGHTEST.
THEIR READY WITS HAVE IMPROVED THE SURVIVAL RATE OF THE SURVEY CORPS DRAMATICALLY...
...BUT EVEN NOW, WHEN TROOPS ARE SENT INTO TITAN TERRITORY, THE CASUALTY RATE IS OVER 30%.

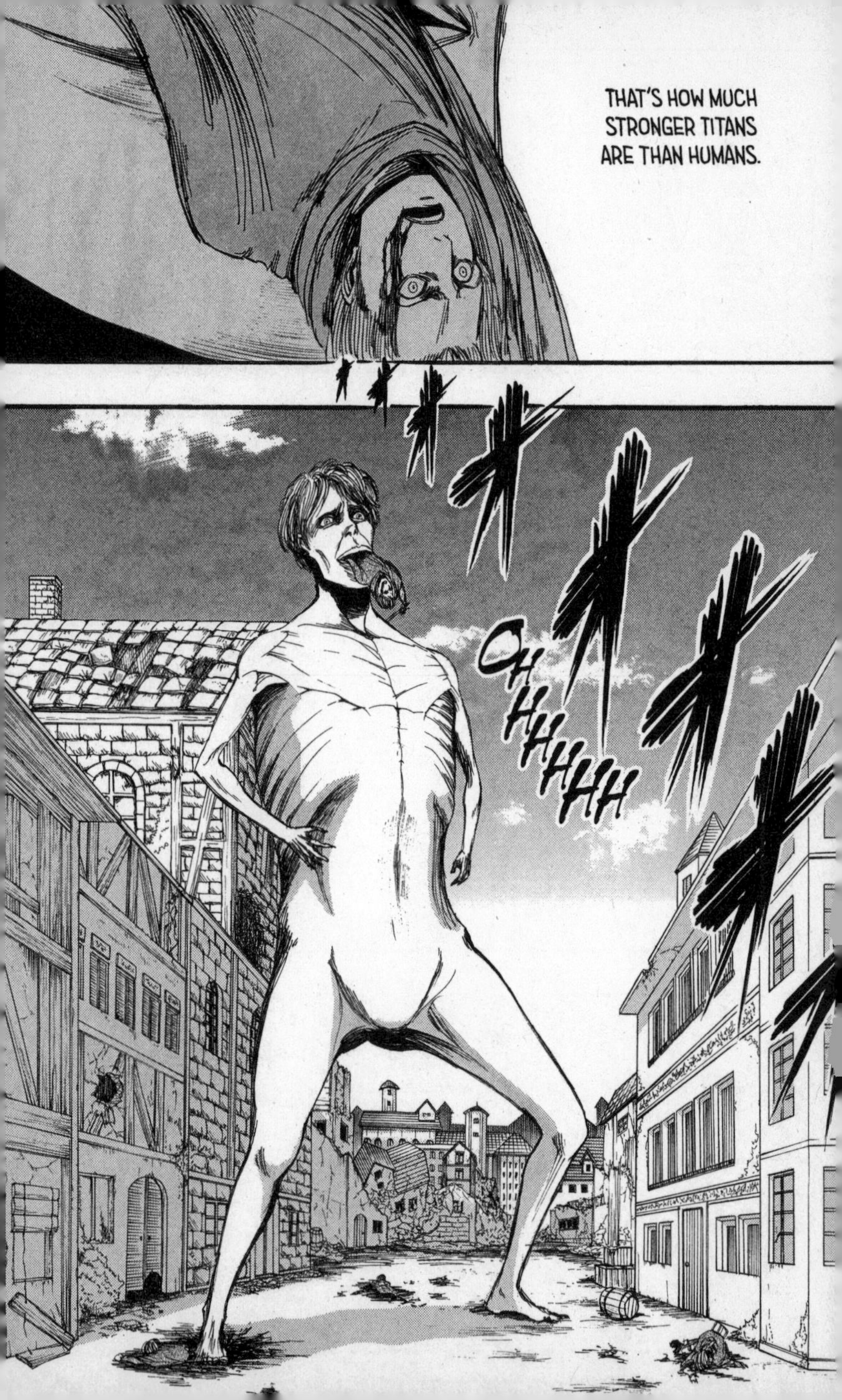
THAT'S HOW MUCH STRONGER TITANS ARE THAN HUMANS.
OHHHHHH

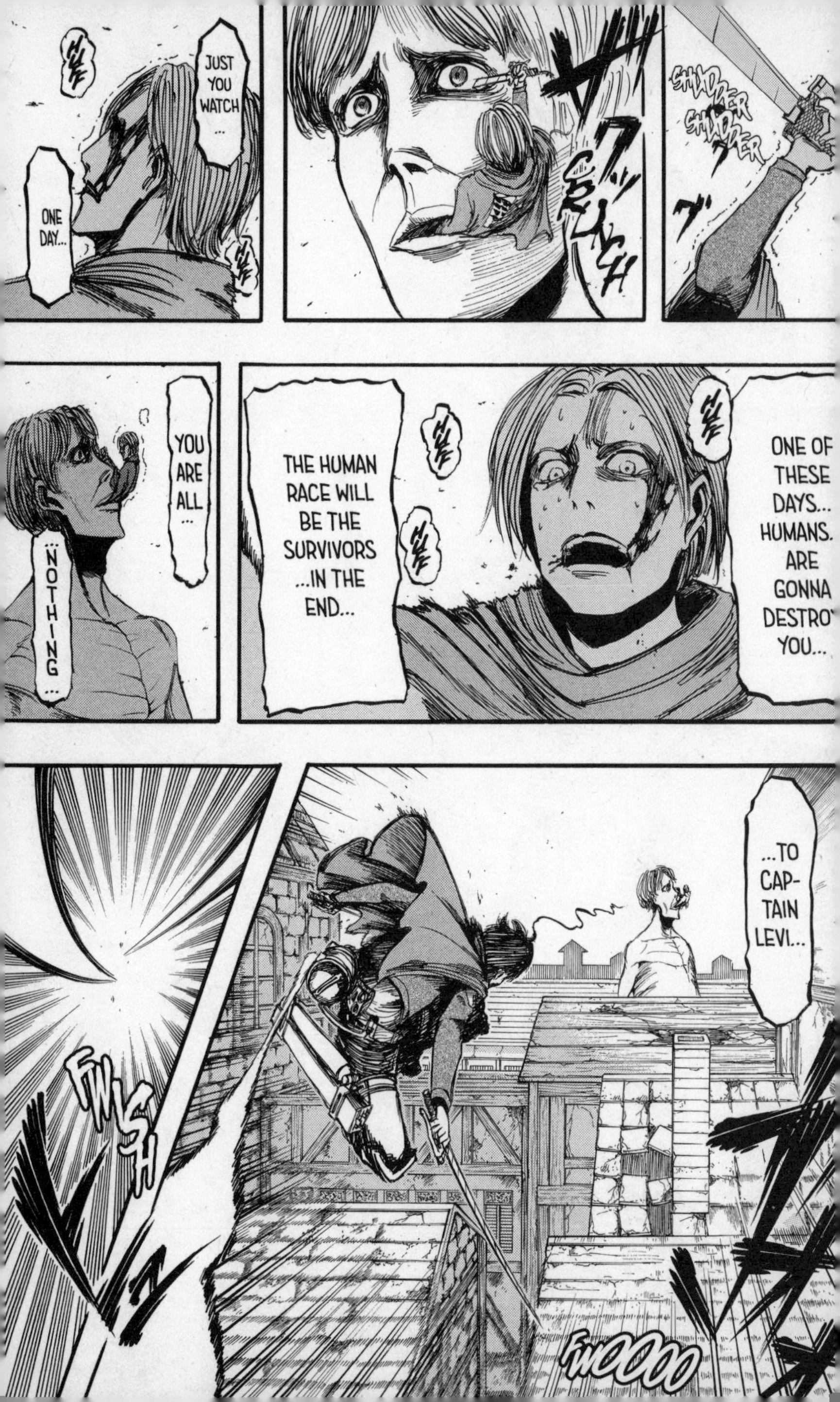
SHUDDER
SHUDDER
CRUNCH
JUST YOU WATCH ...
HUFF
HUFF
ONE DAY...
HUFF
ONE OF THESE DAYS... HUMANS. ARE GONNA DESTRO YOU...
HUFF
HUFF
THE HUMAN RACE WILL BE THE SURVIVORS ...IN THE END...
YOU ARE ALL ...
...NOTHING ...
...TO CAP- TAIN LEVI...
FWOOOOO
FWISH

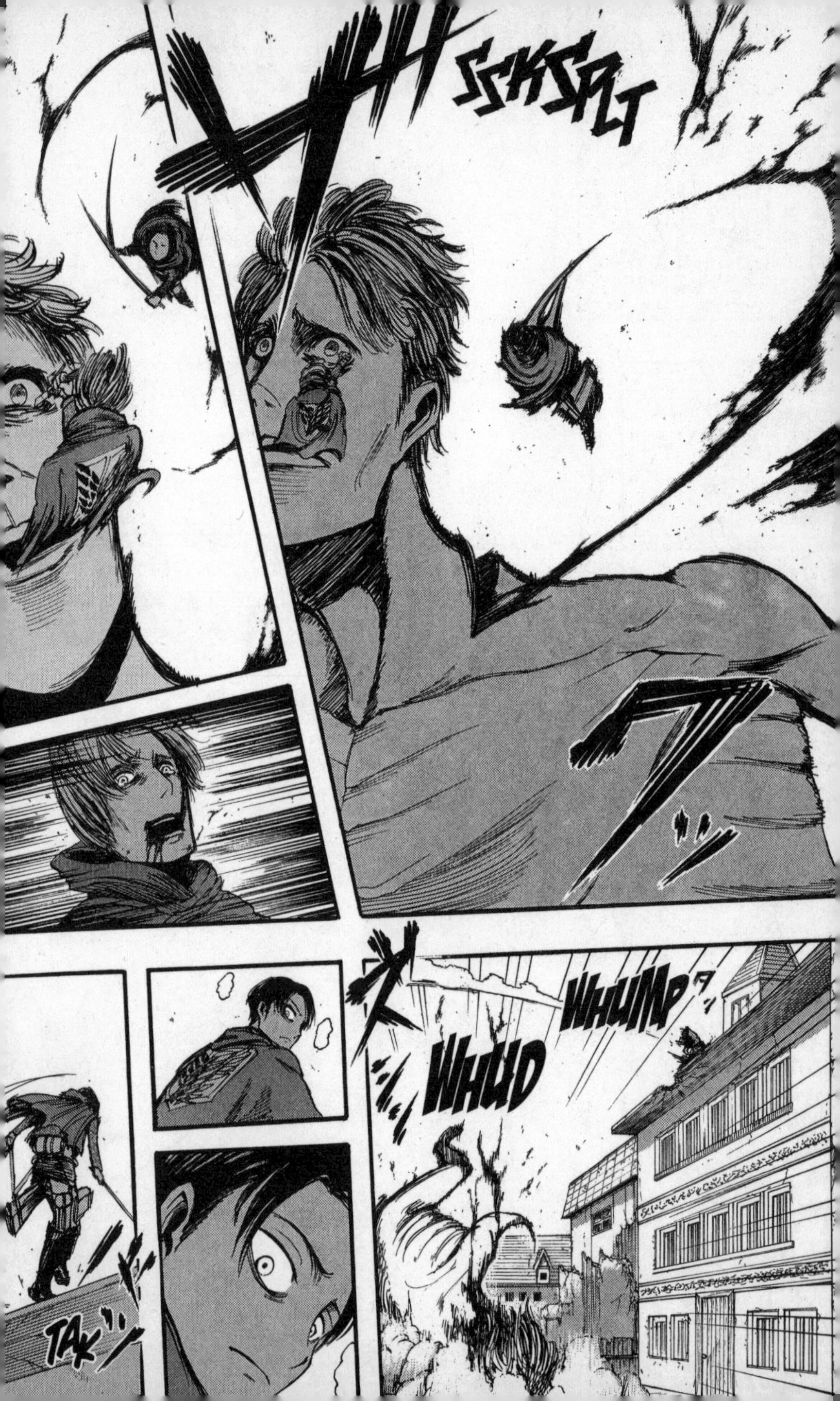
SSKSRLT
WHUMP
WHUD
TAK

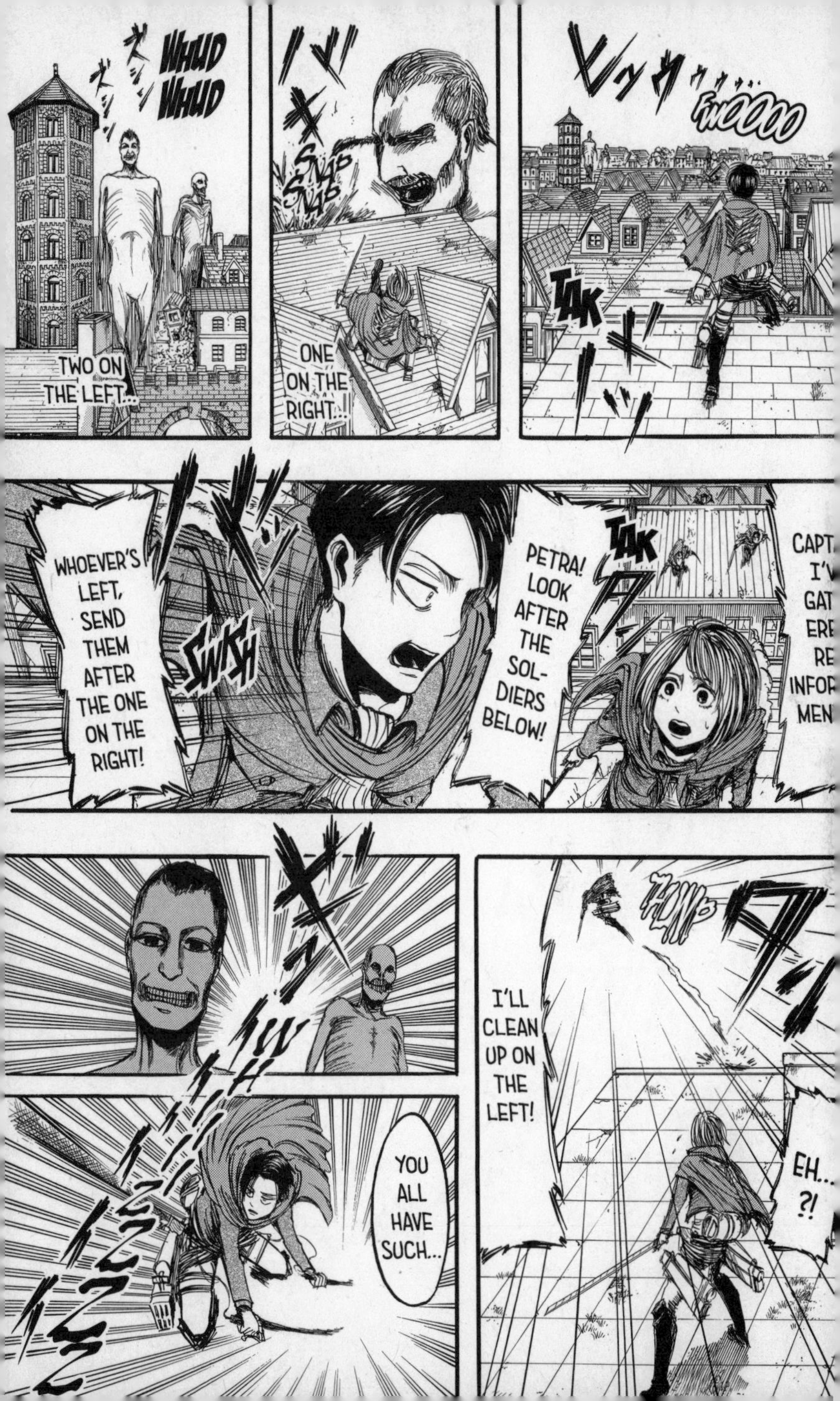
FWOOOO
TAK
SNAP SNAP
ONE ON THE RIGHT...
WHUD WHUD
TWO ON THE LEFT...
CAPT
I'V
GAT
ERE
RE
INFOR
MEN
TAK
PETRA! LOOK AFTER THE SOL-DIERS BELOW!
SWISH
WHOEVER'S LEFT, SEND THEM AFTER THE ONE ON THE RIGHT!
I'LL CLEAN UP ON THE LEFT!
EH... ?!
YOU ALL HAVE SUCH...

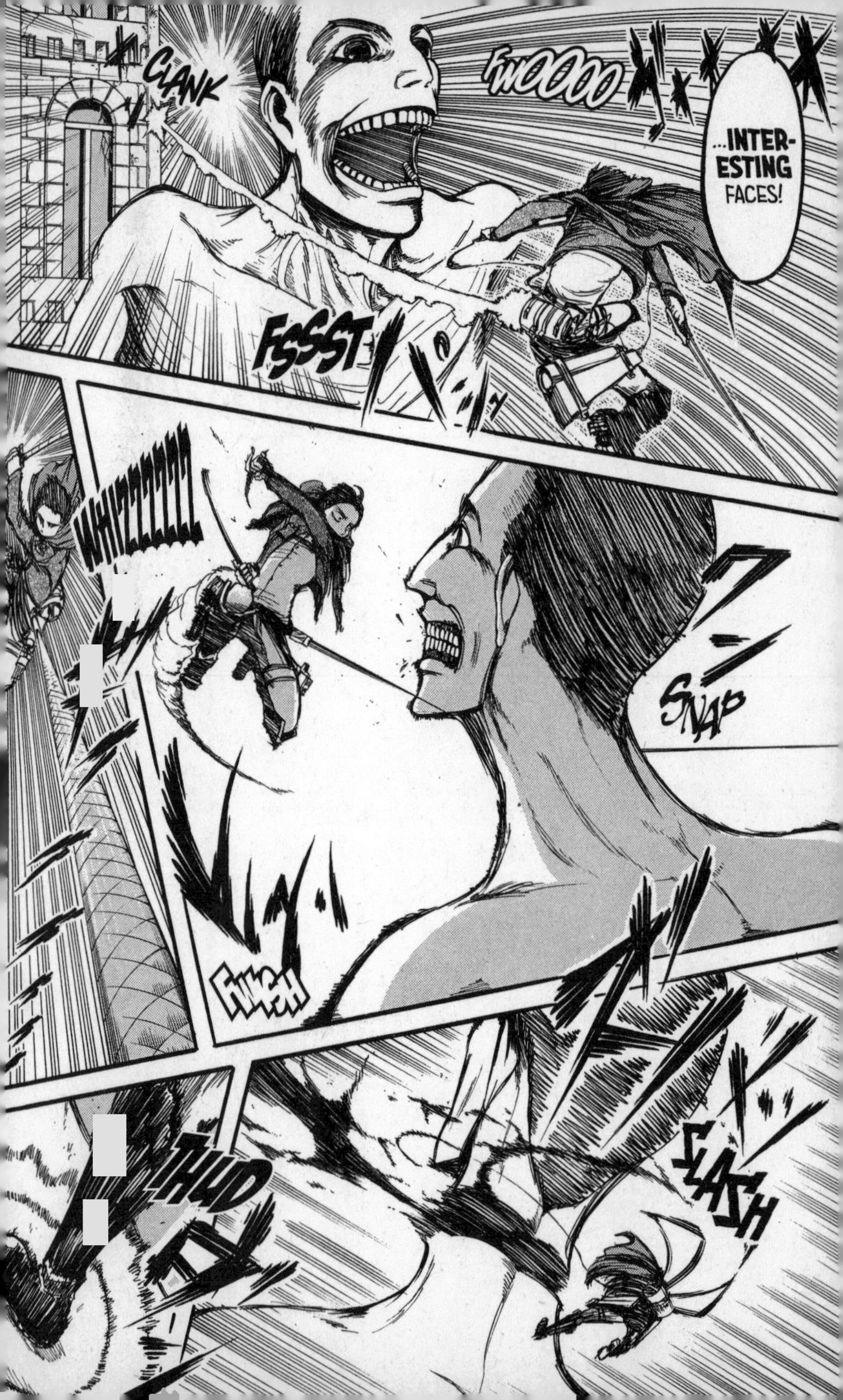
...INTERESTING FACES!
FWOOOO
CLANK
FSSST
SNAP
FWISH
WHIZZZZZ
SLASH
THUD

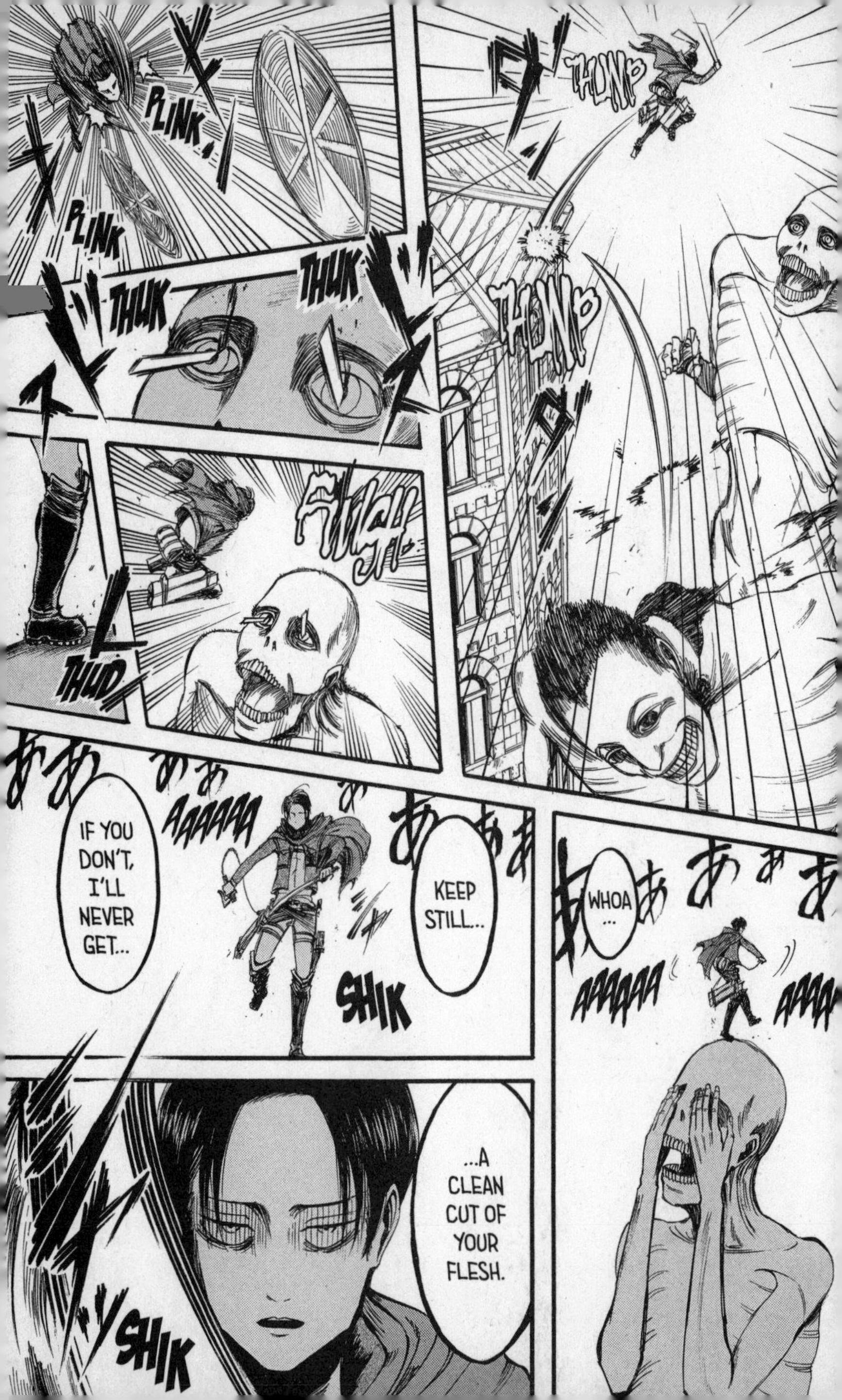

THUMP
THUMP
PLINK
PLINK
THUK
THUK
THUD
WHOA...
AAAAAA
AAAAA
KEEP STILL...
IF YOU DON'T, I'LL NEVER GET...
AAAAAA
SHIK
...A CLEAN CUT OF YOUR FLESH.
SHIK

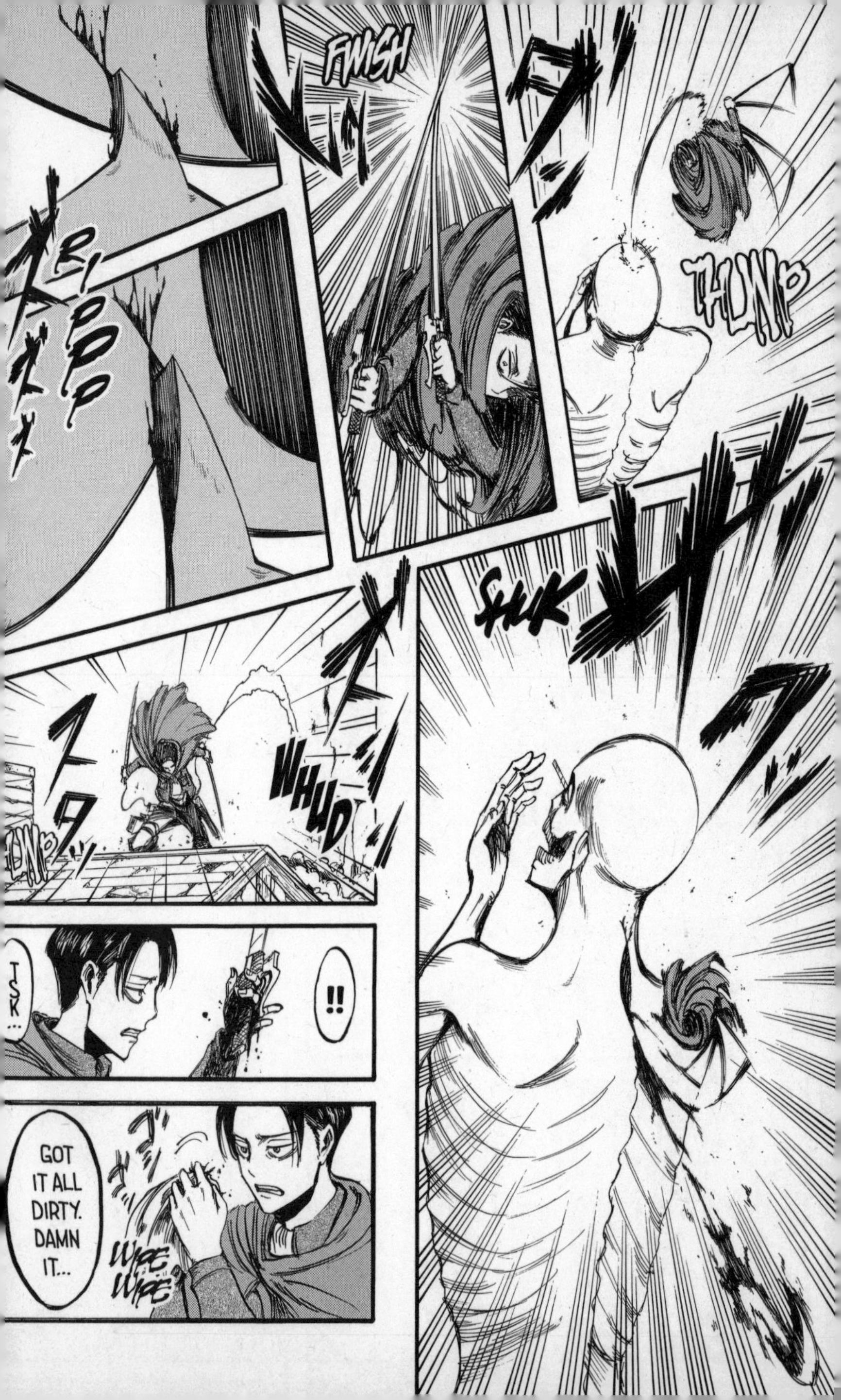
THUMP
FWISH
RIPPP
SHUK
WHUD
THUMP
!!
TSK...
GOT IT ALL DIRTY. DAMN IT...
WIPE WIPE

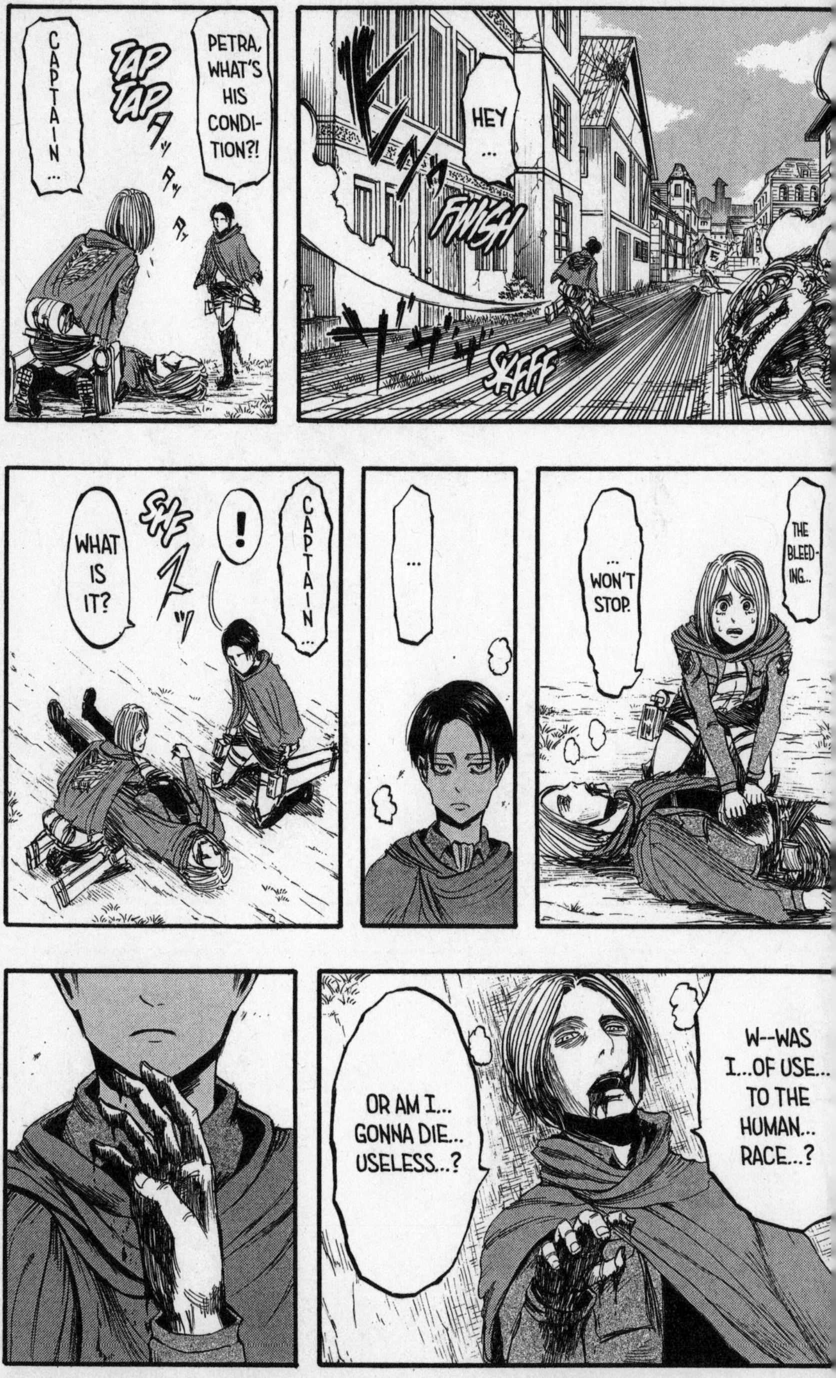
HEY...
FWISH
SKAFF
PETRA, WHAT'S HIS CONDITION?!
TAP TAP
CAPTAIN...
THE BLEEDING...
... WON'T STOP.
...
CAPTAIN...
!
SKE
WHAT IS IT?
W--WAS I...OF USE... TO THE HUMAN... RACE...?
OR AM I... GONNA DIE... USELESS...?

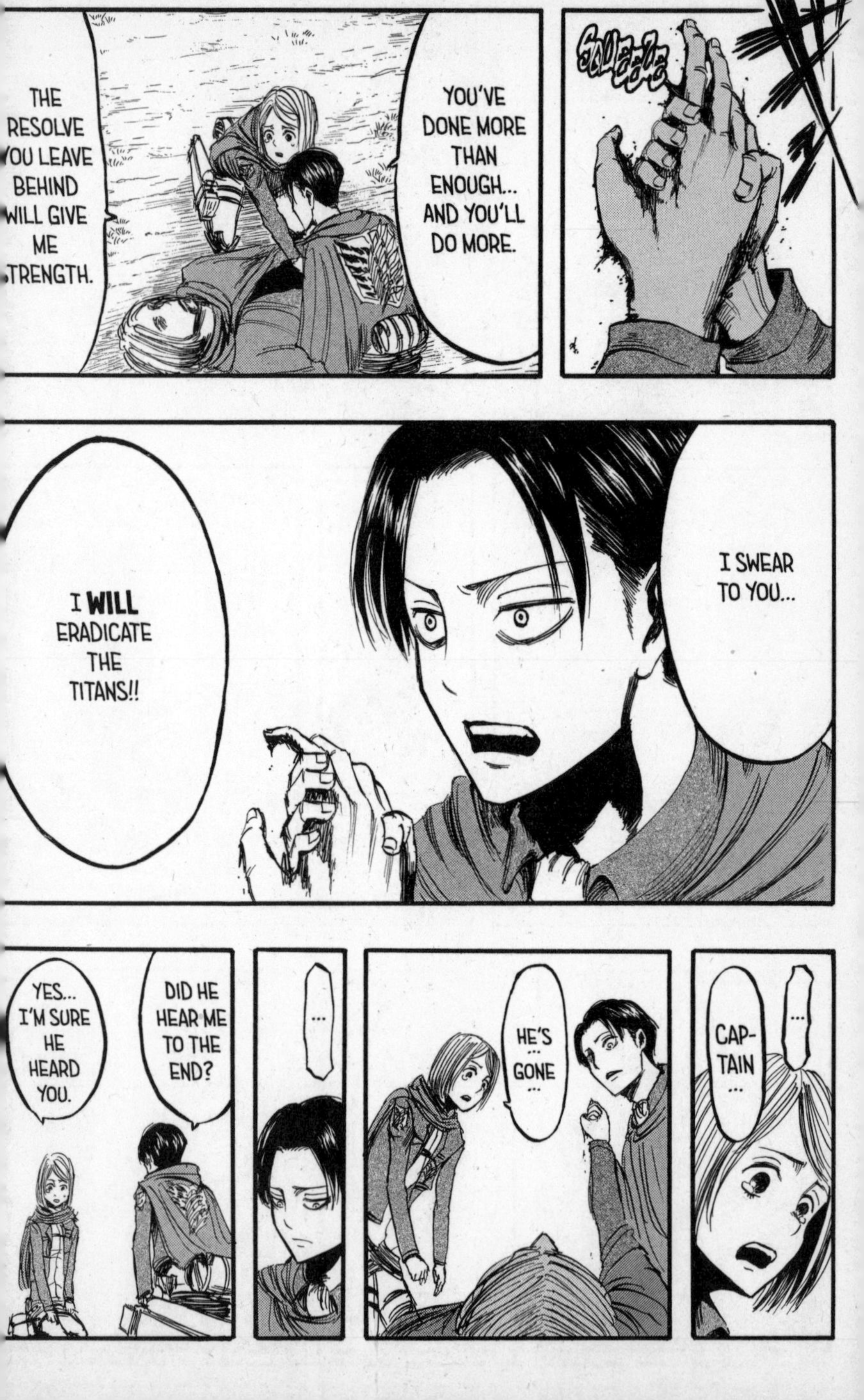
YOU'VE DONE MORE THAN ENOUGH... AND YOU'LL DO MORE.
THE RESOLVE YOU LEAVE BEHIND WILL GIVE ME STRENGTH.
I SWEAR TO YOU...
I **WILL** ERADICATE THE TITANS!!
...
CAP-TAIN ...
HE'S ... GONE ...
...
DID HE HEAR ME TO THE END?
YES... I'M SURE HE HEARD YOU.

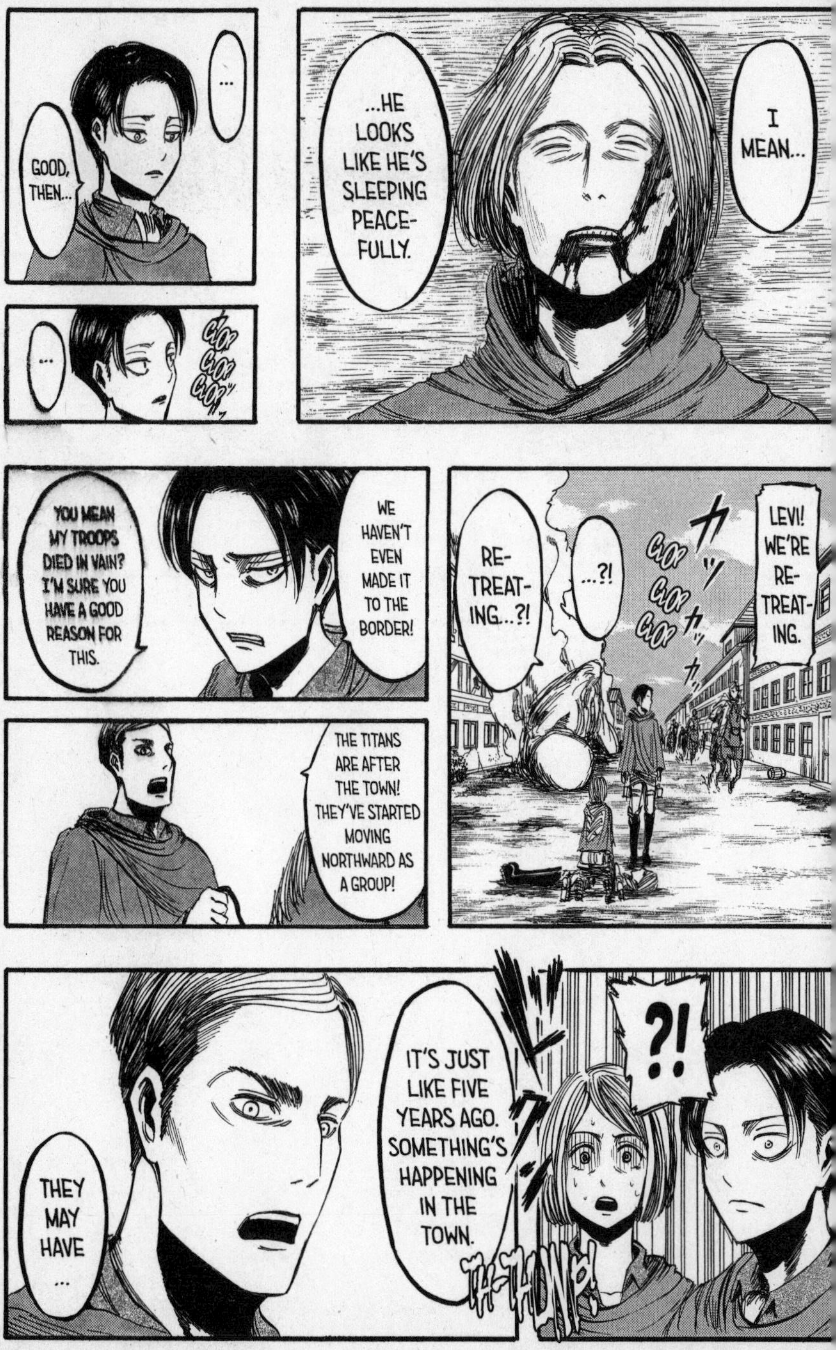

I MEAN...
...HE LOOKS LIKE HE'S SLEEPING PEACE-FULLY.
...
GOOD, THEN...
CLOP CLOP CLOP
...
LEVI! WE'RE RE-TREAT-ING.
カッ カッ カッ
CLOP CLOP CLOP
...?!
RE-TREAT-ING...?!
WE HAVEN'T EVEN MADE IT TO THE BORDER!
YOU MEAN MY TROOPS DIED IN VAIN? I'M SURE YOU HAVE A GOOD REASON FOR THIS.
THE TITANS ARE AFTER THE TOWN! THEY'VE STARTED MOVING NORTHWARD AS A GROUP!
?!
TH-THOMP!
IT'S JUST LIKE FIVE YEARS AGO. SOMETHING'S HAPPENING IN THE TOWN.
THEY MAY HAVE ...

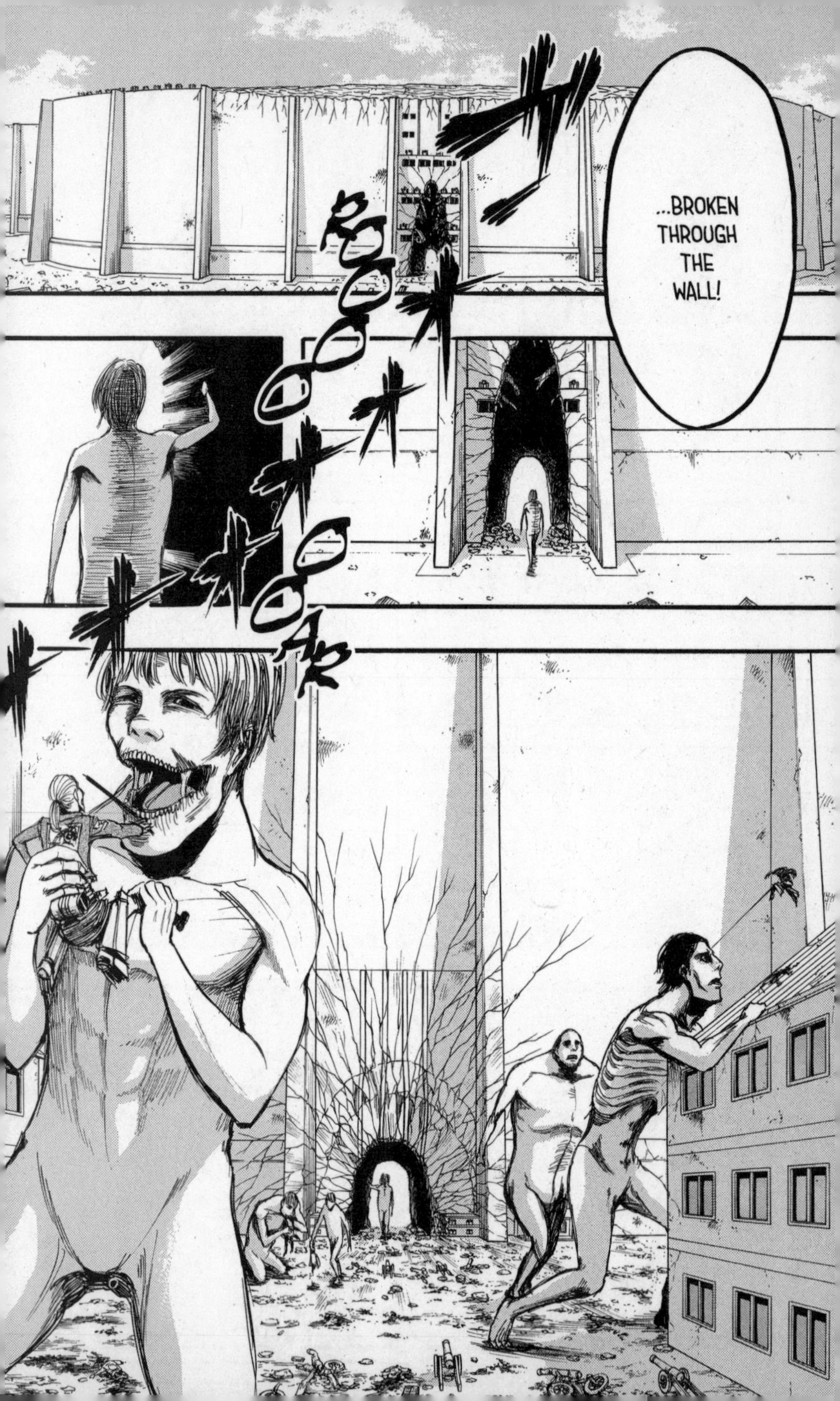
...BROKEN THROUGH THE WALL!
ROOOOOAR

Current Publicly Available Information

7. The Current State of the Survey Corp

THE CHIEF PURPOSE OF THE SURVEY CORPS WAS TO EXPLORE THE LAND OUTSIDE THE WALL, BUT THE ACTUAL ACTIVITIES OF THE CORPS CHANGED AFTER THE FALL OF WALL MARIA.

SINCE THE FALL, THE CORPS HAS BEEN LAYING THE GROUNDWORK FOR THE SECOND WALL MARIA RECAPTURE OPERATION. BRAVING SHIGANSHINA DISTRICT, WHERE THE WALL WAS DESTROYED, A LARGE FORCE HAS BEEN POSITIONING SUPPLIES IN THE ABANDONED TOWNS AND VILLAGES SCATTERED ALONG THEIR ROUTE, ESTABLISHING A SUPPLY LINE FOR THE CORPS.

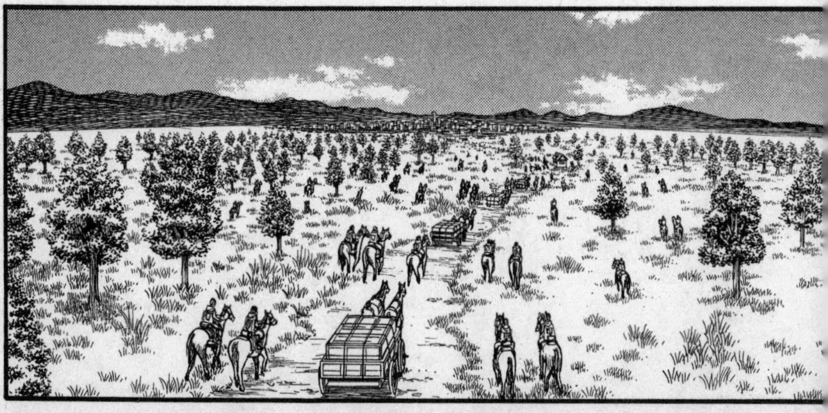

ATTACK on TITAN

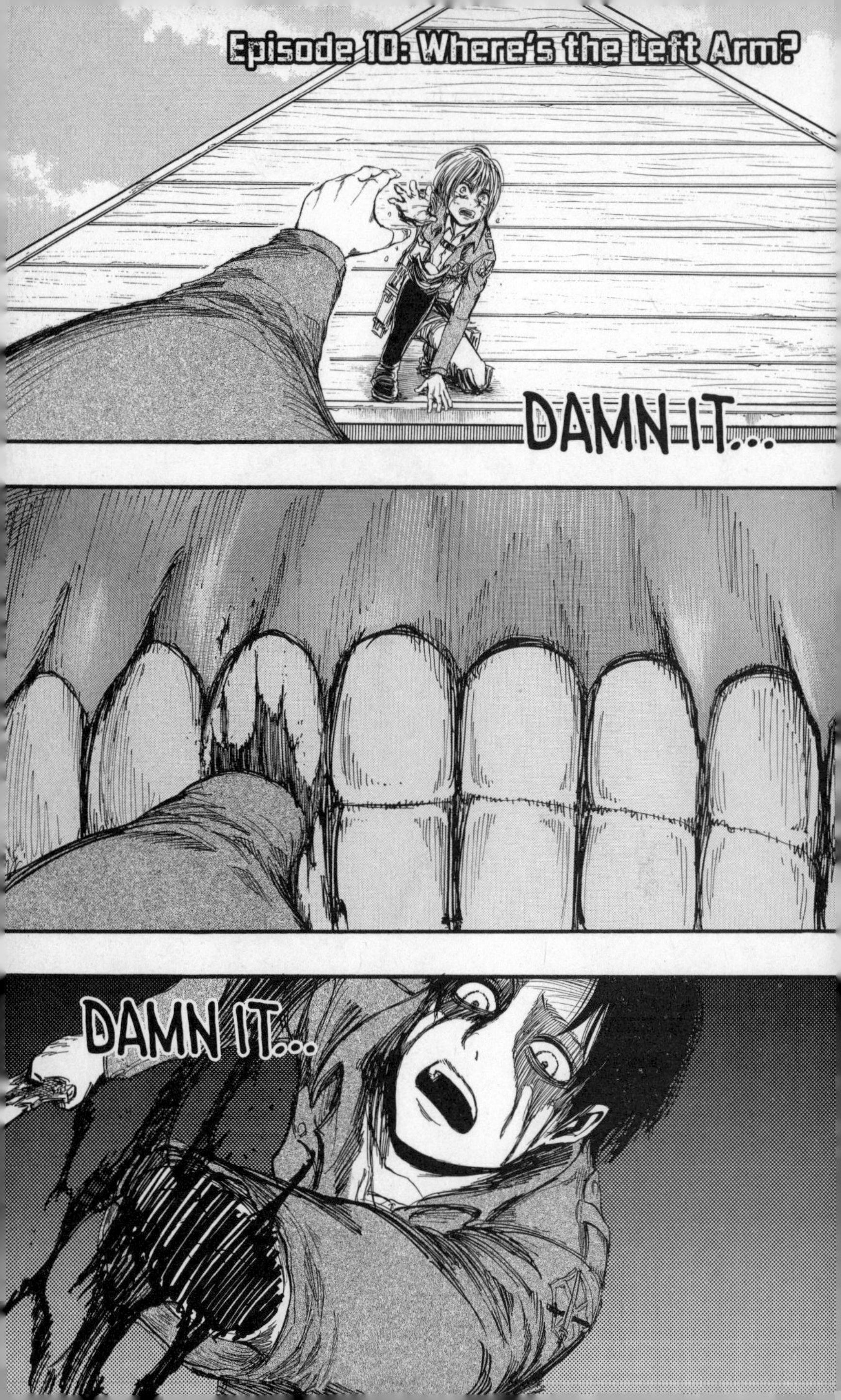
Episode 10: Where's the Left Arm?
DAMN IT...
DAMN IT...

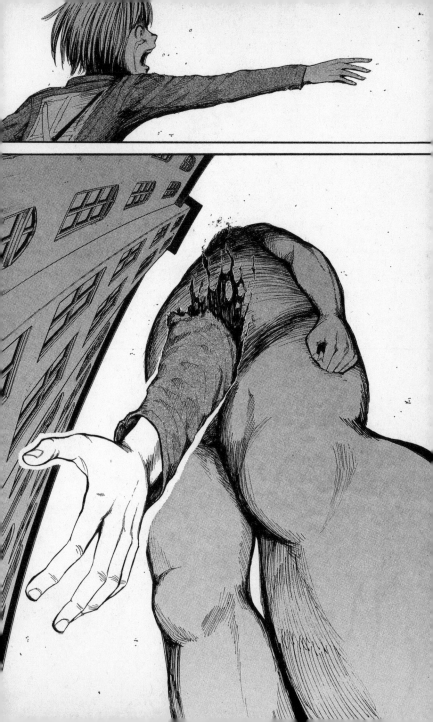

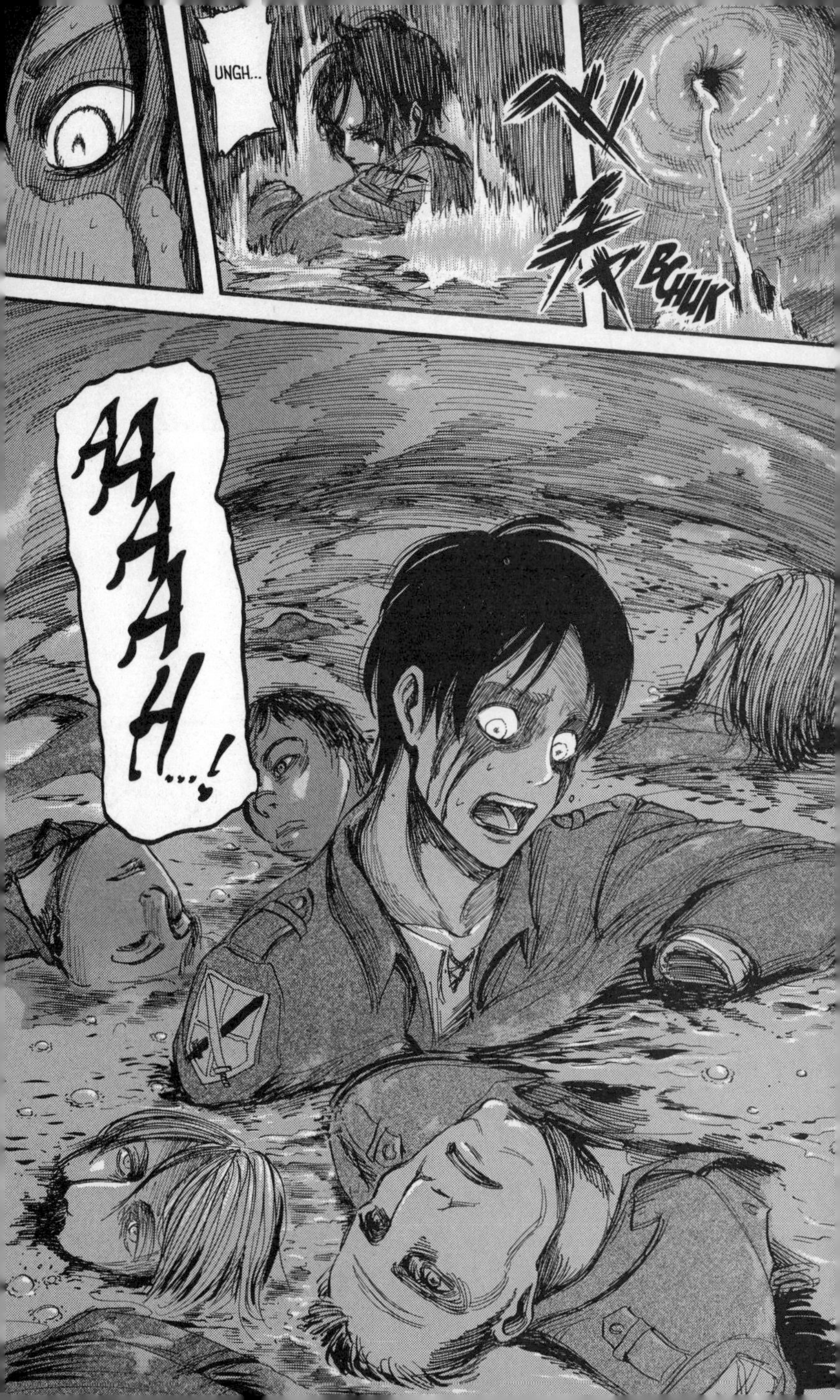
BCHUK
UNGH...
AAAAH...!

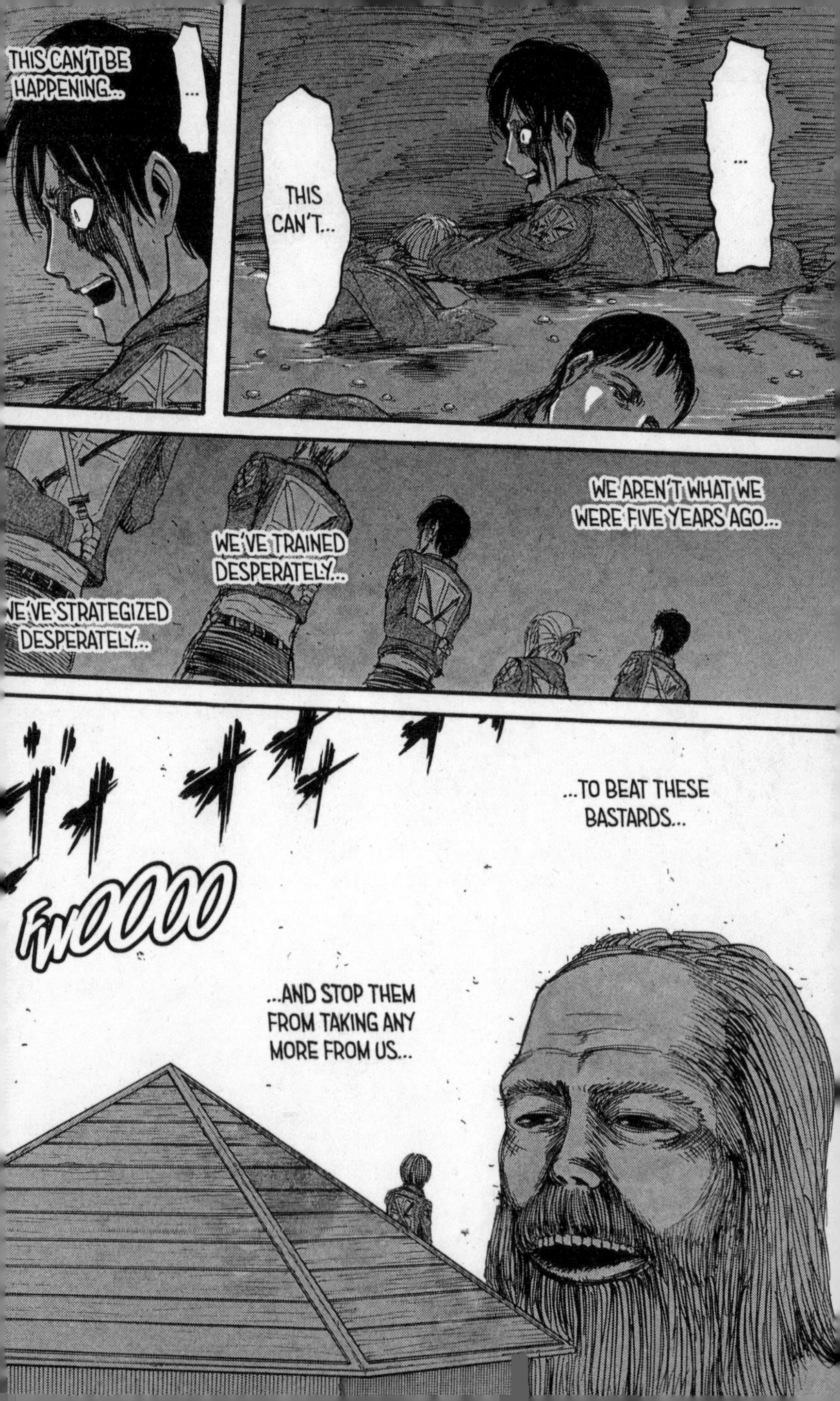

...
THIS CAN'T...
...
THIS CAN'T BE HAPPENING...
WE AREN'T WHAT WE WERE FIVE YEARS AGO...
WE'VE TRAINED DESPERATELY...
WE'VE STRATEGIZED DESPERATELY...
...TO BEAT THESE BASTARDS...
FWOOOO
...AND STOP THEM FROM TAKING ANY MORE FROM US...

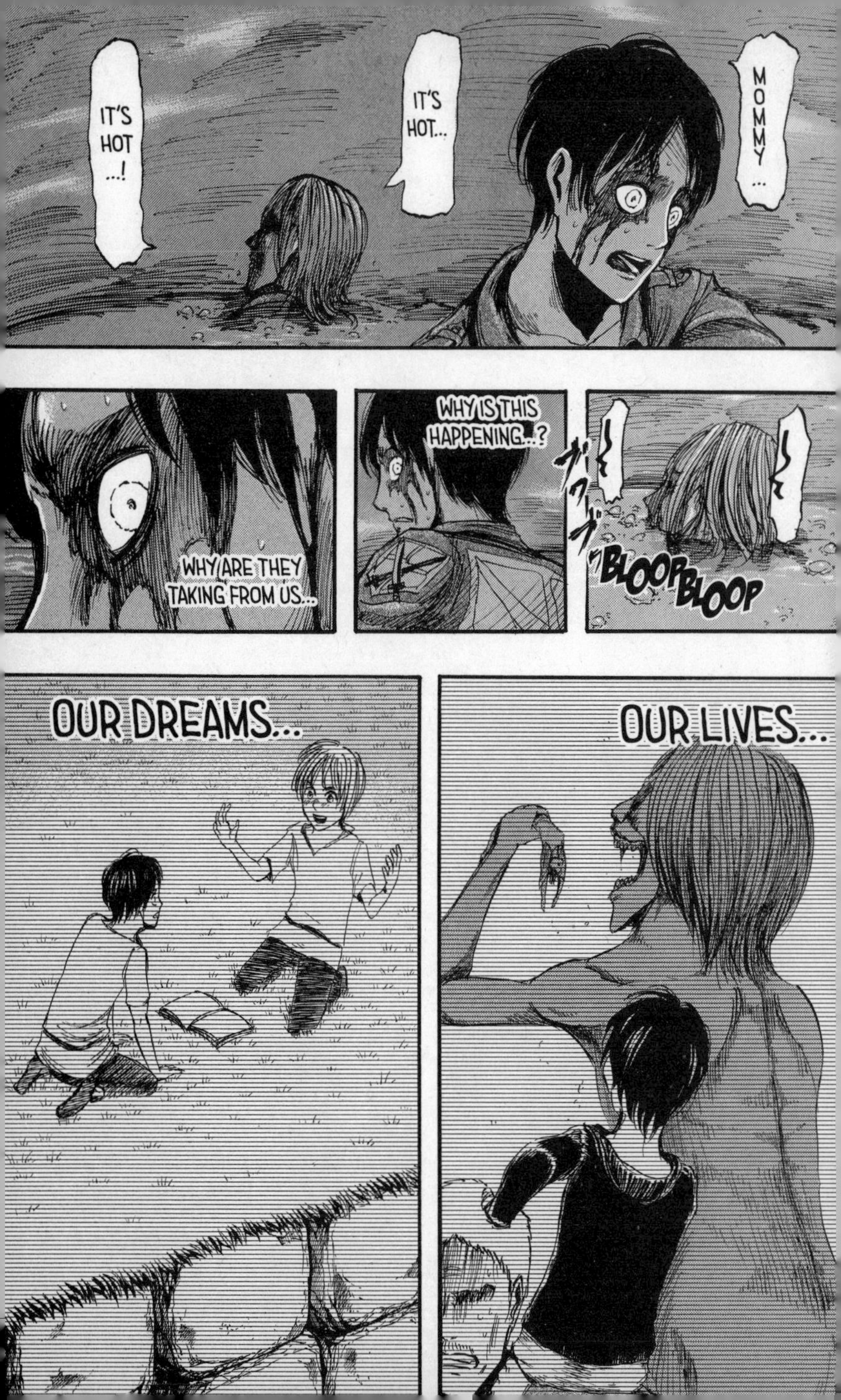
MOMMY...
IT'S HOT...
IT'S HOT ...!
BLOOP BLOOP
WHY IS THIS HAPPENING...?
WHY ARE THEY TAKING FROM US...
OUR LIVES...
OUR DREAMS...

UNGH...

AAHH...

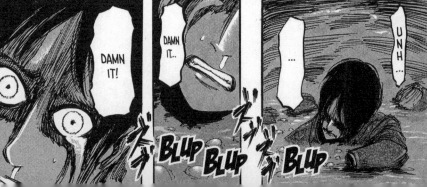

DAMN IT!

DAMN IT...

...

UNH...

BLUP BLUP BLUP

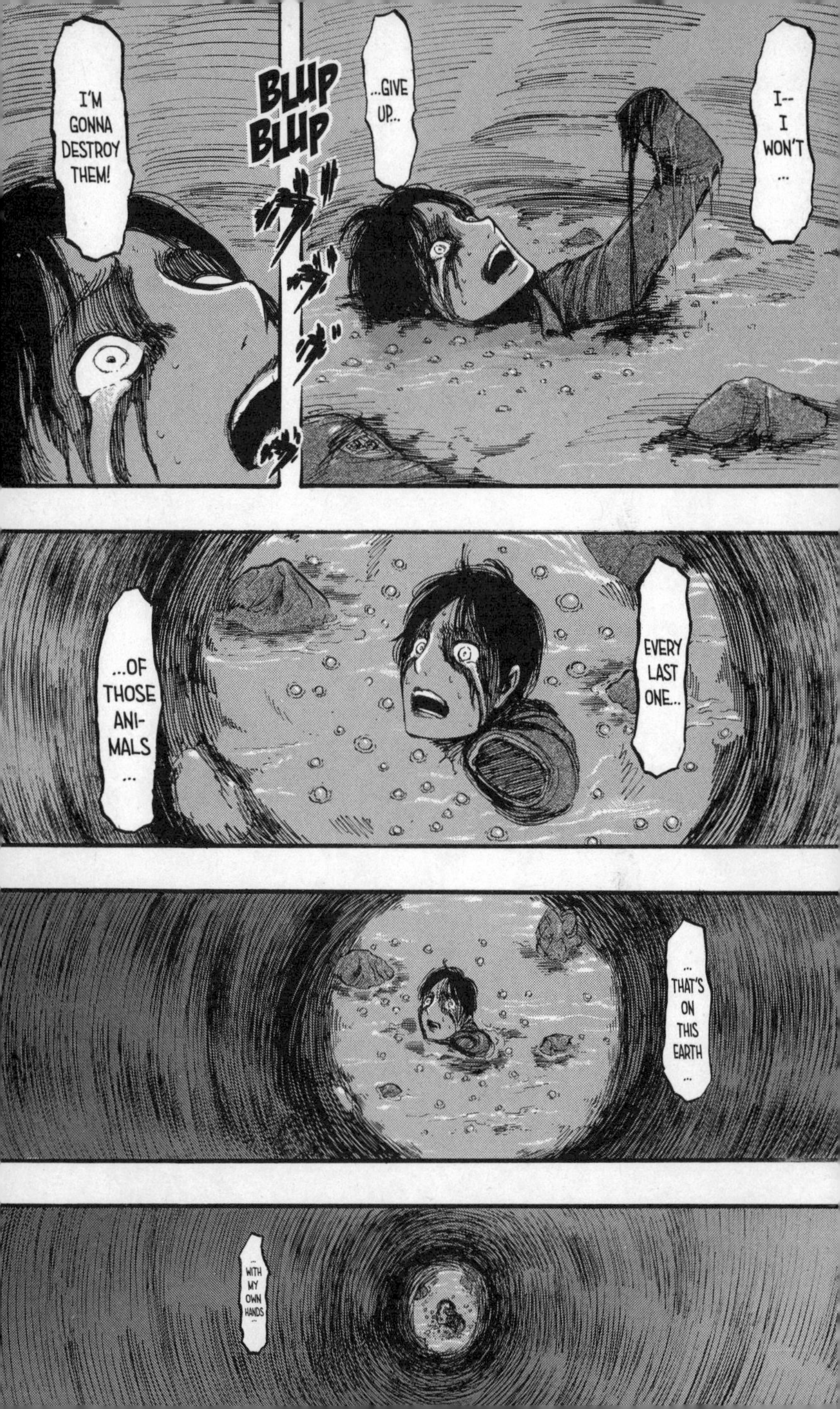
I-- I WON'T ...
...GIVE UP..
BLUP BLUP
I'M GONNA DESTROY THEM!
EVERY LAST ONE..
...OF THOSE ANI- MALS ...
... THAT'S ON THIS EARTH ...
... WITH MY OWN HANDS ...

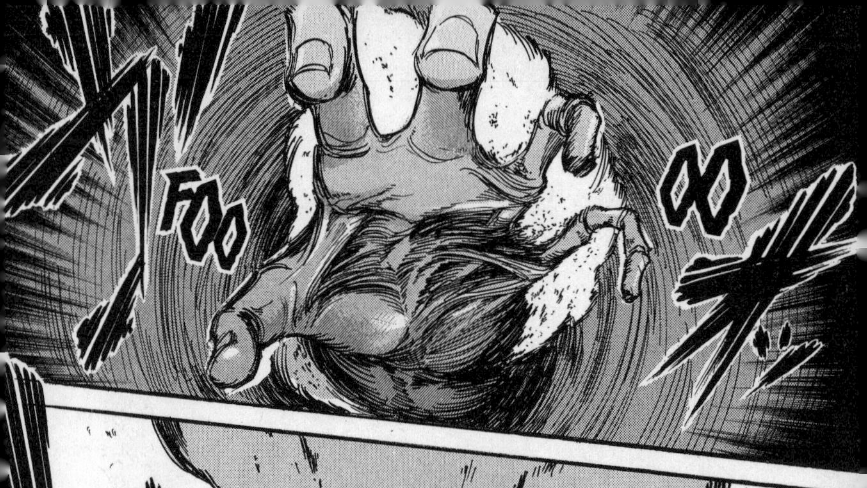
FOO
OO
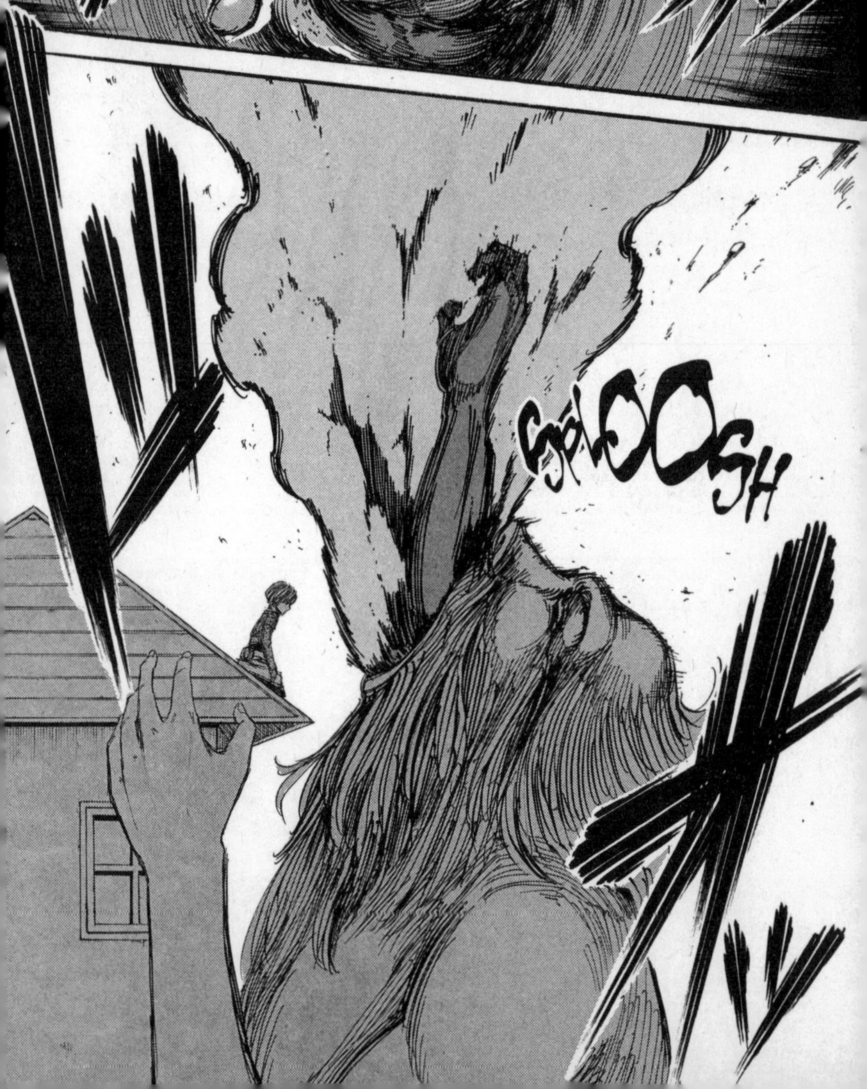
GSPLOOSH

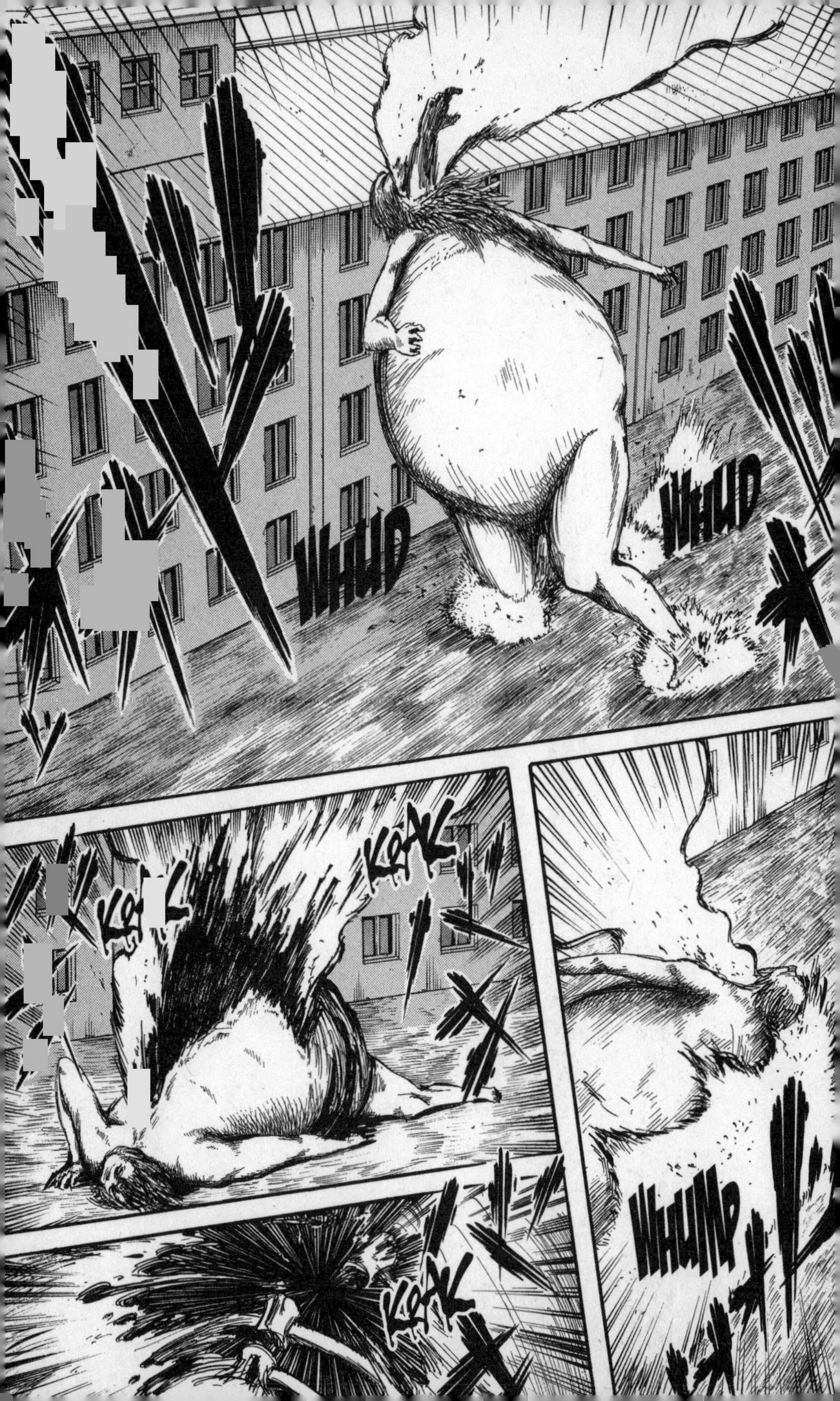
WHUD
WHUD
WHUMP
KRAK
KRAK
KRAK

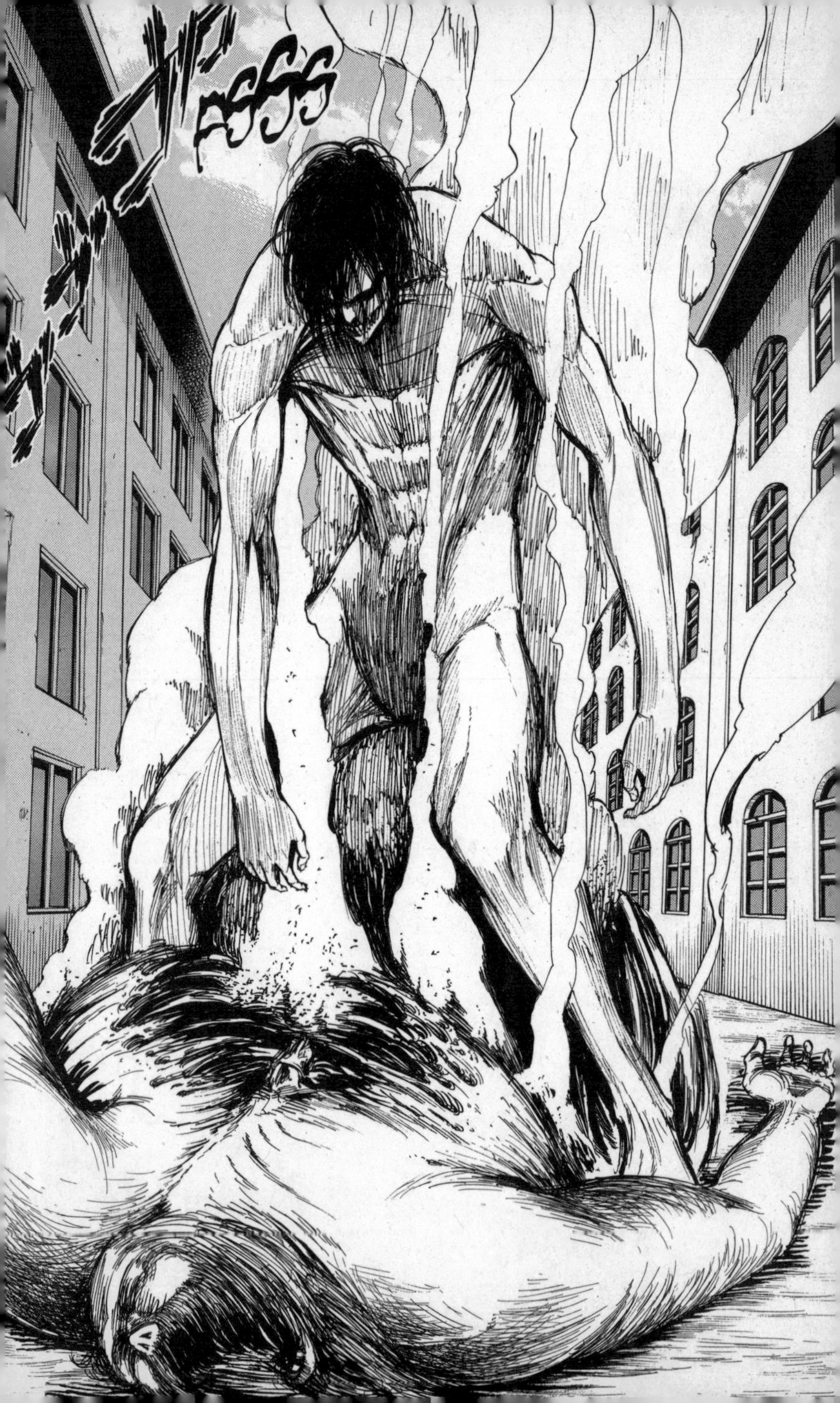
FSSS

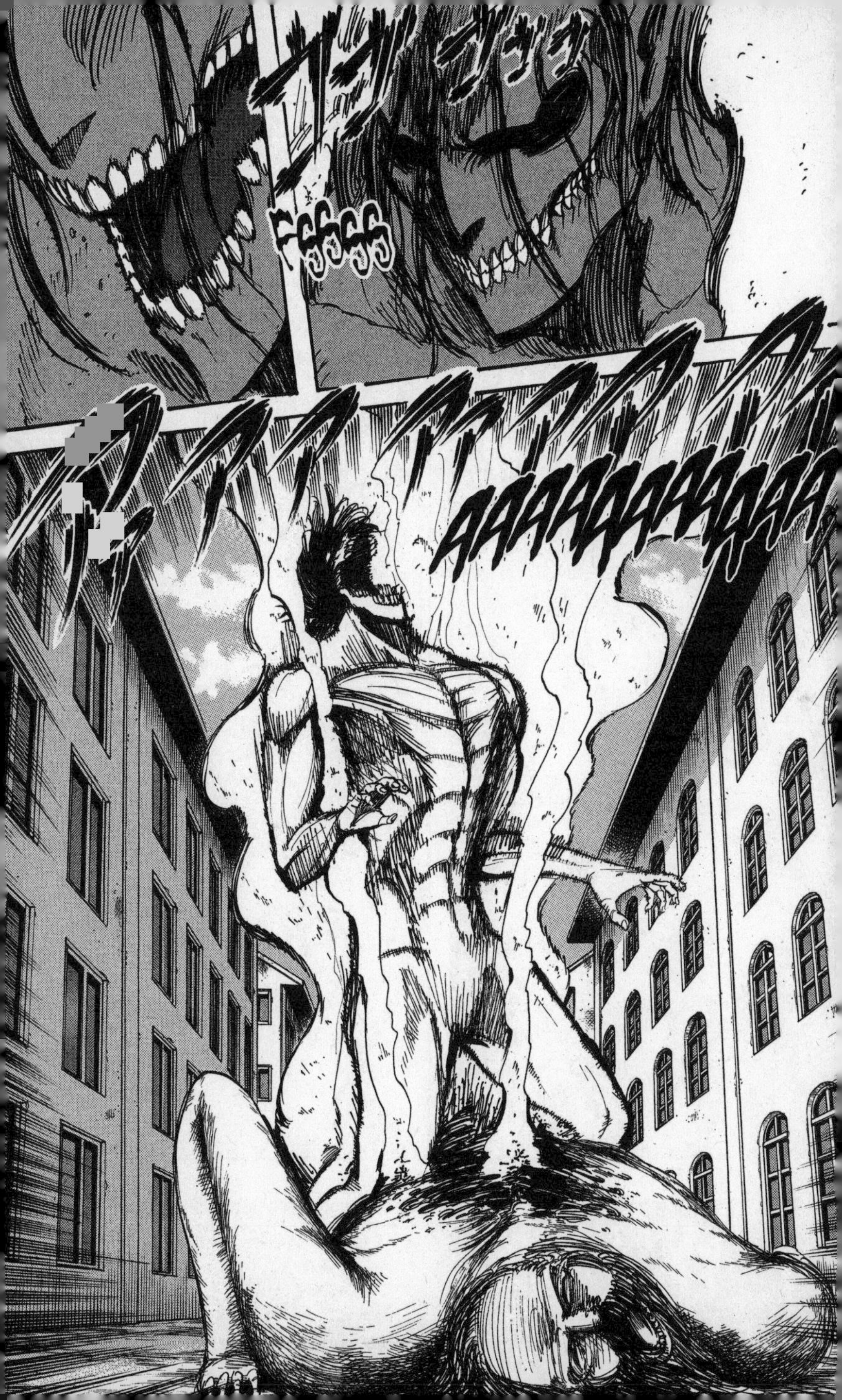
FSSSS
AAAAAAAAAAA

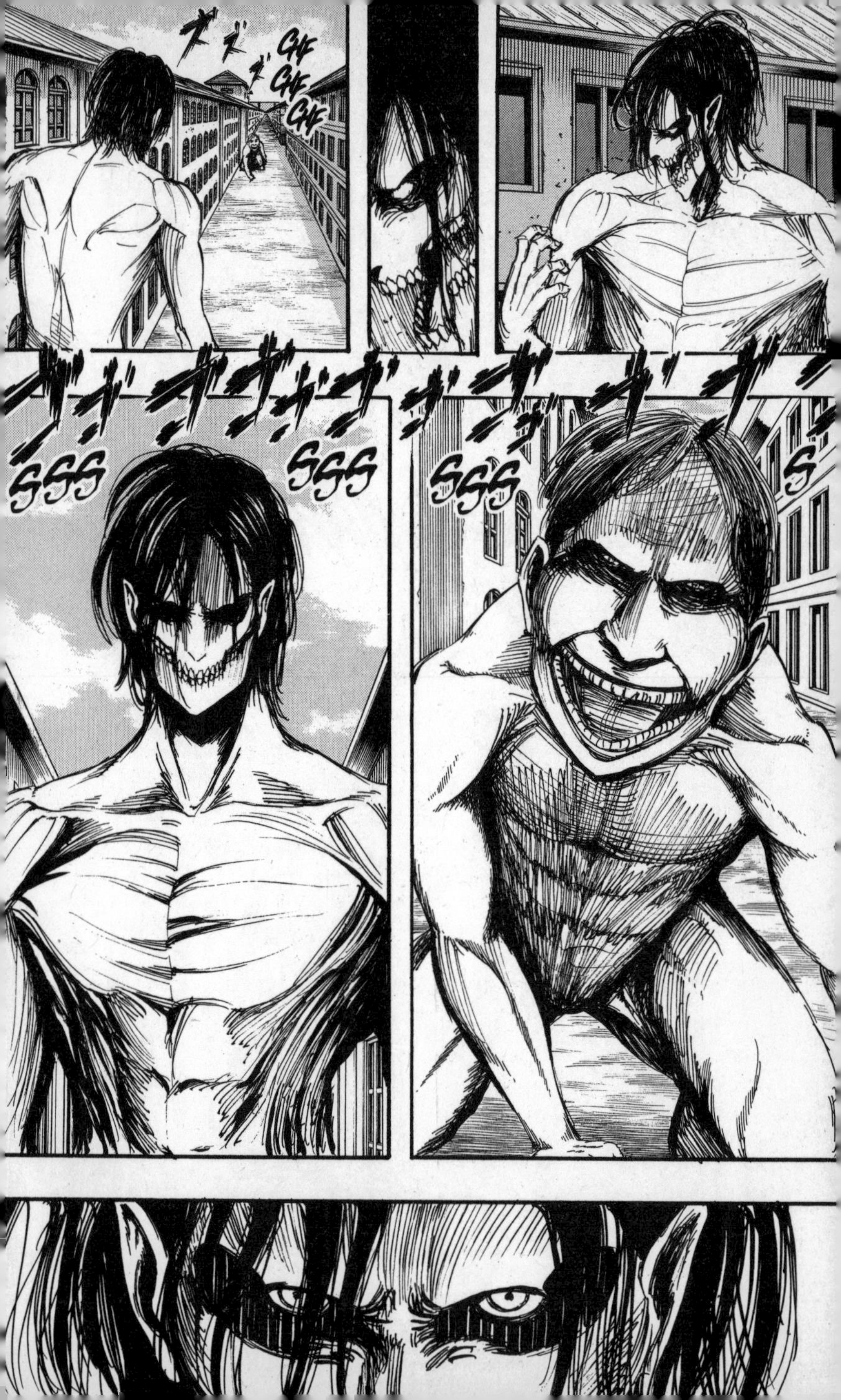
CHF
CHF
CHF
S
SSS
SSS
SSS

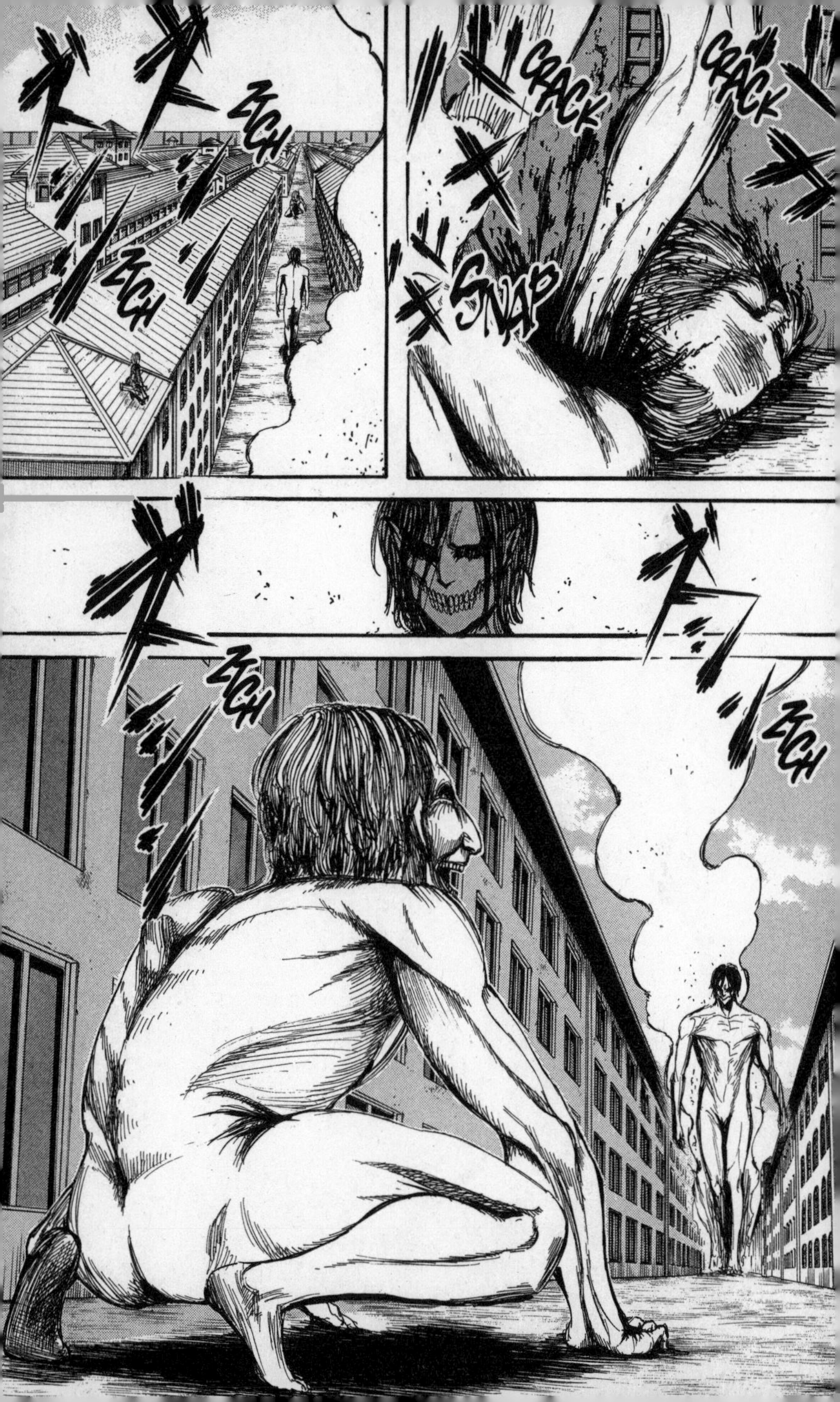
CRACK
CRACK
SNAP
ZCCH
ZCCH
ZCCH
ZCCH

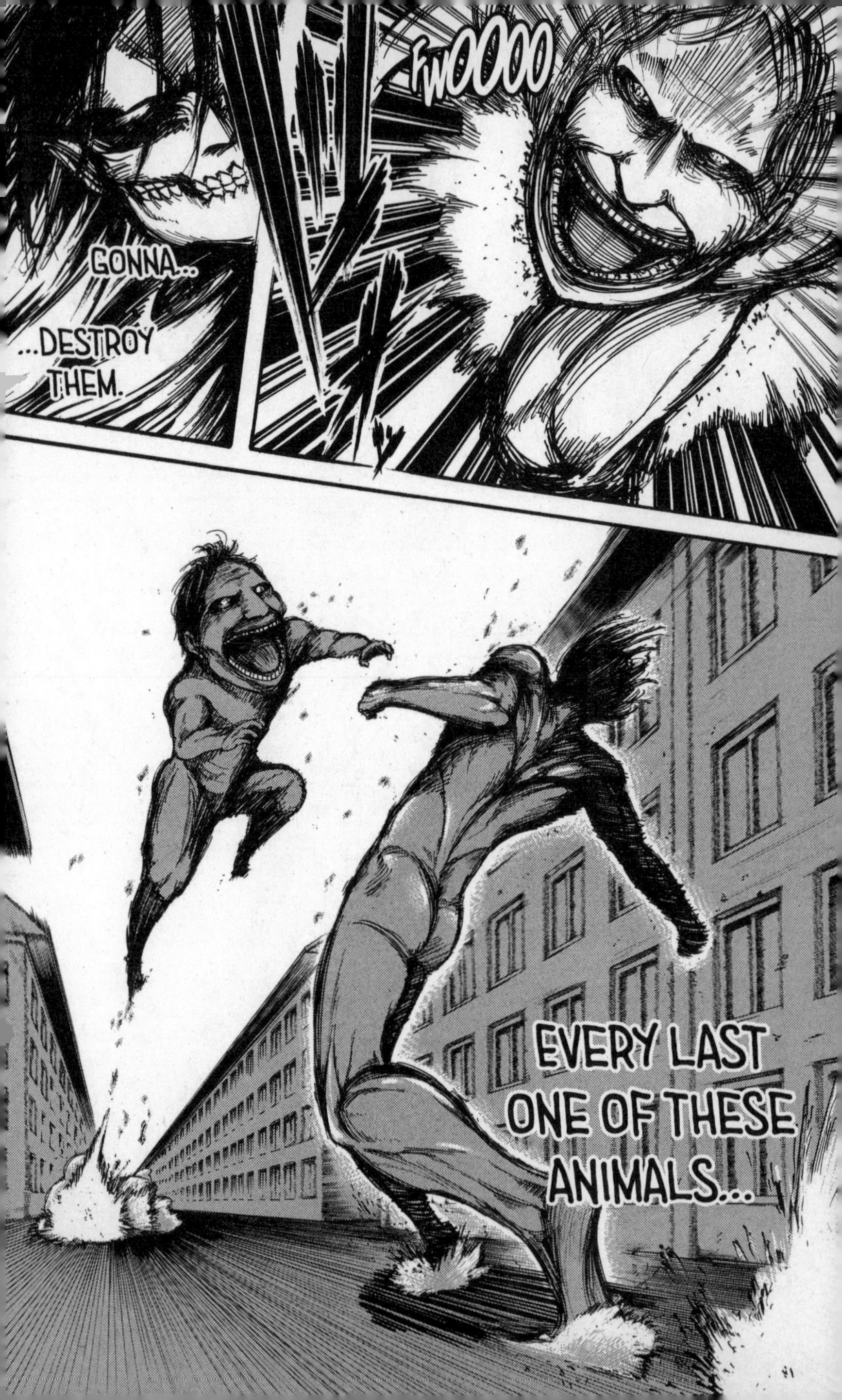
FWOOOO
GONNA...
...DESTROY THEM.
EVERY LAST ONE OF THESE ANIMALS...

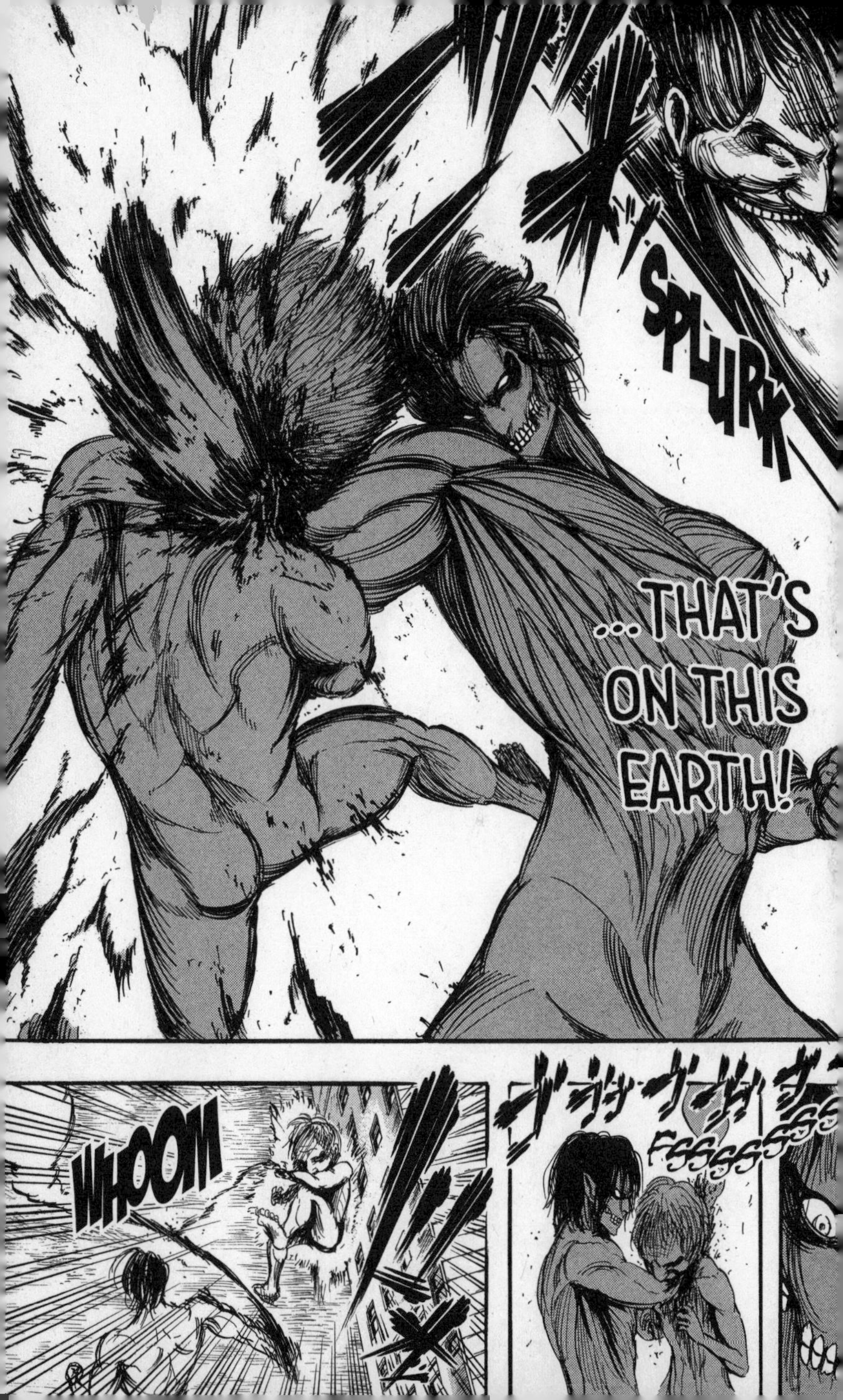
SPLURK
...THAT'S ON THIS EARTH!
FSSSSSSS
WHOOM

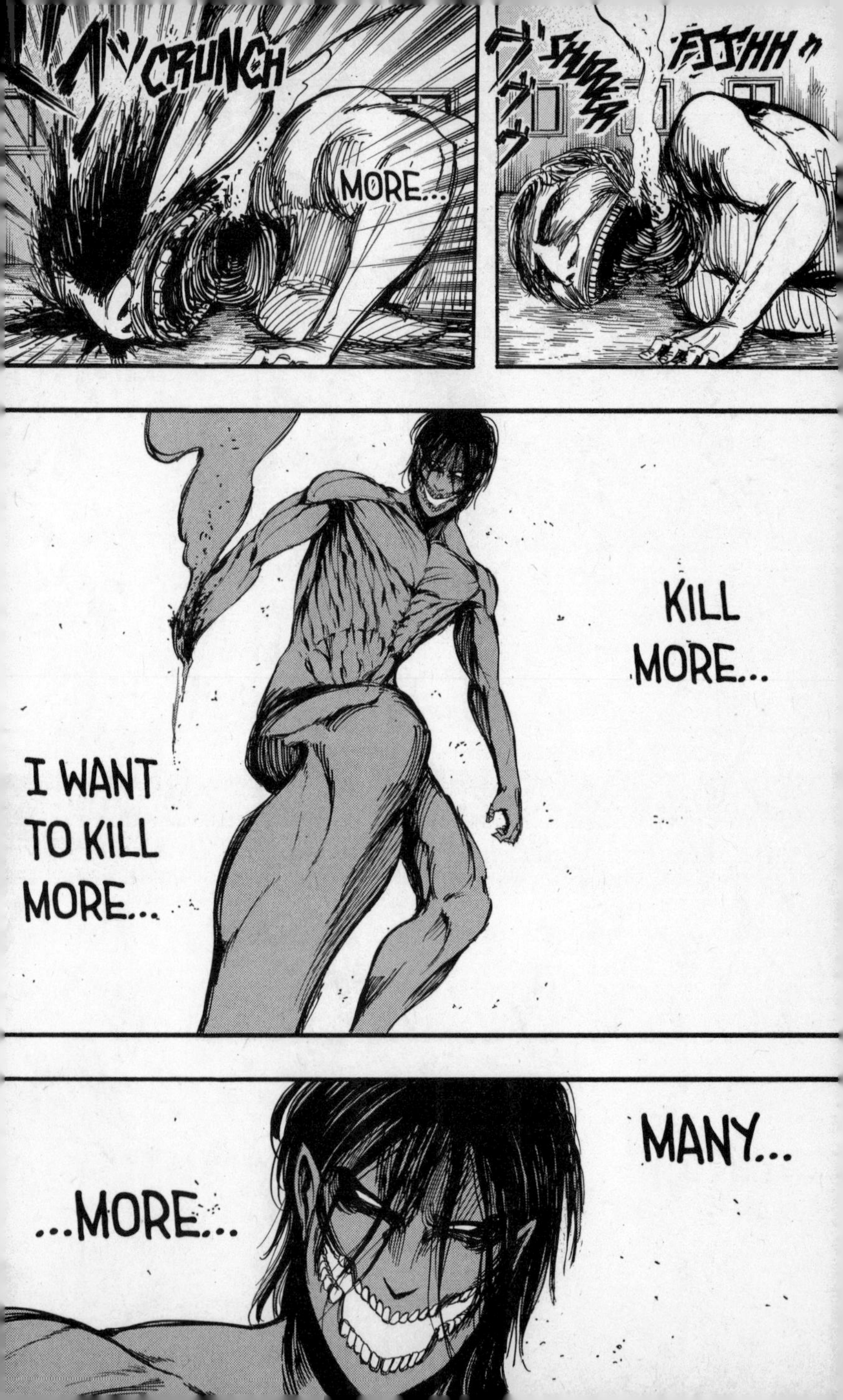
ヴヴヴ
FSSHH
CRUNCH
MORE...
KILL MORE...
I WANT TO KILL MORE...
MANY...
...MORE...

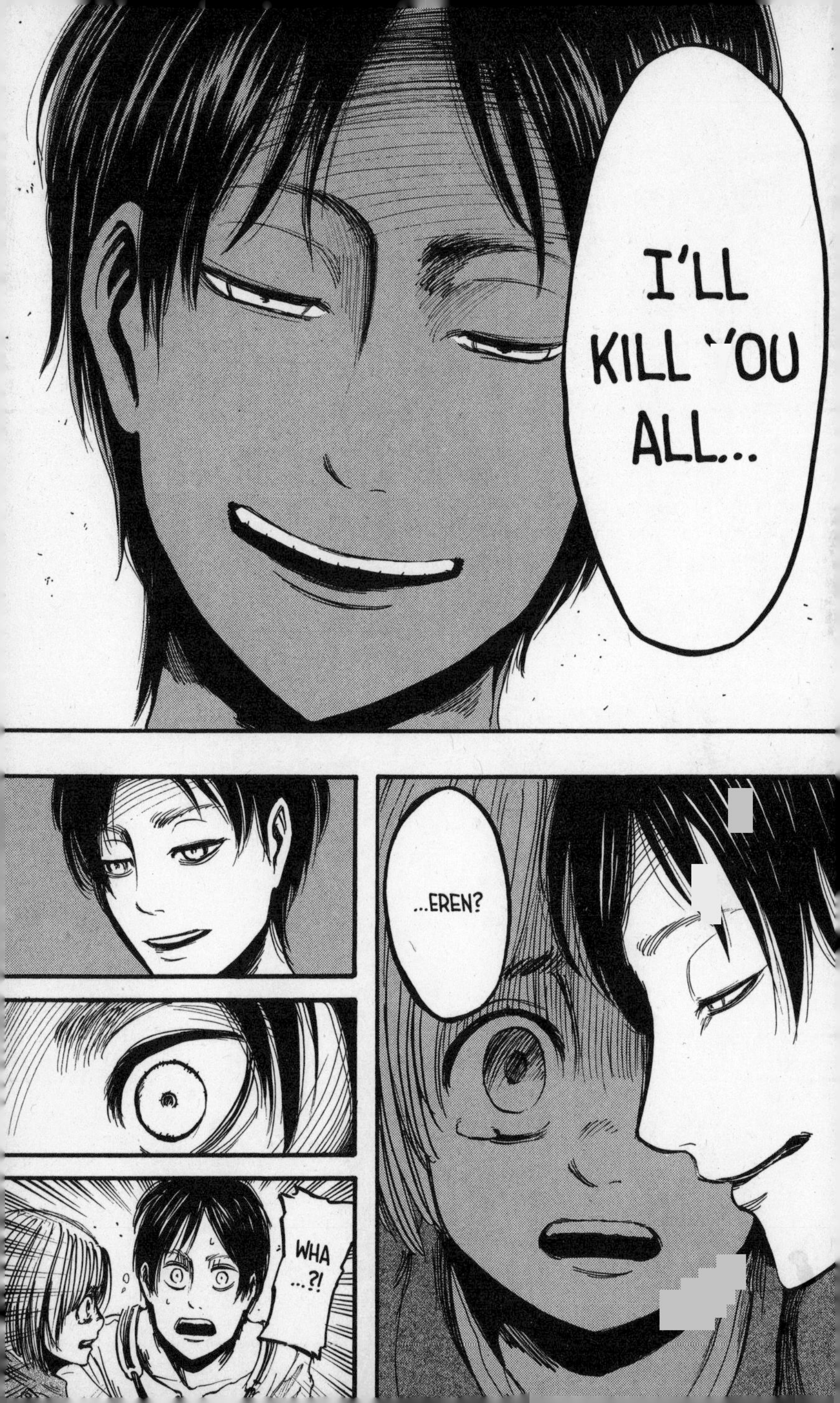
I'LL KILL YOU ALL...
...EREN?
WHA ...?!

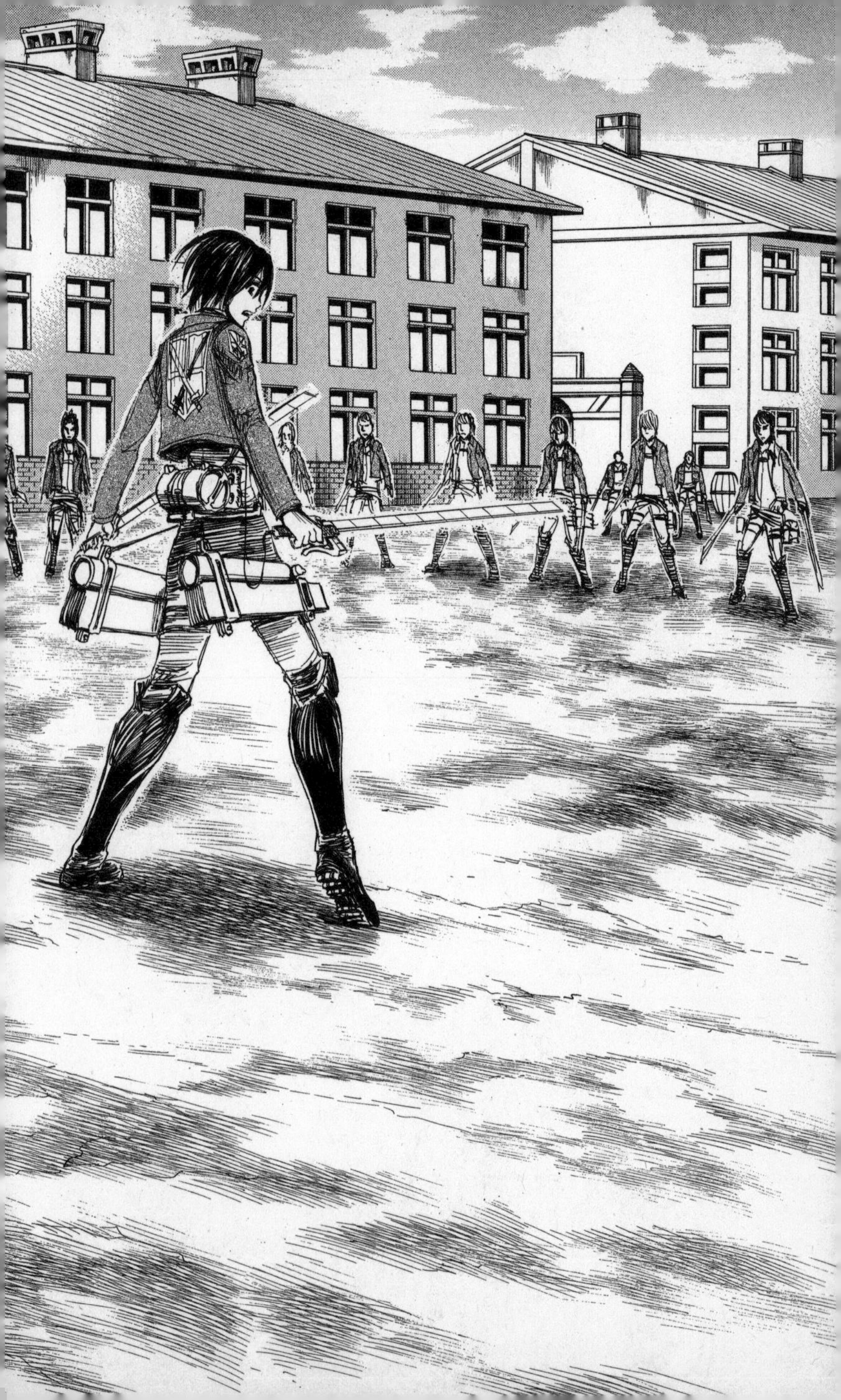

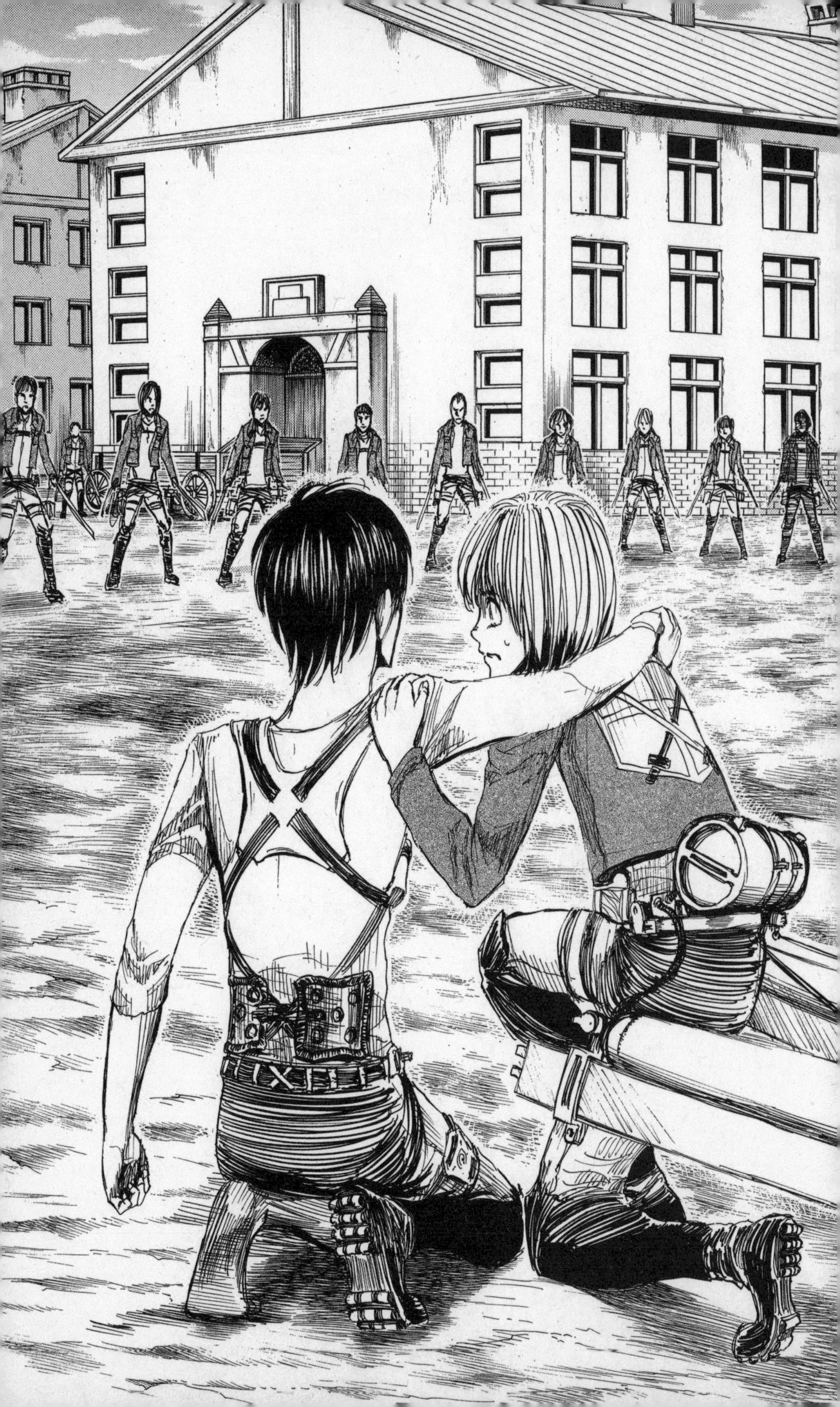

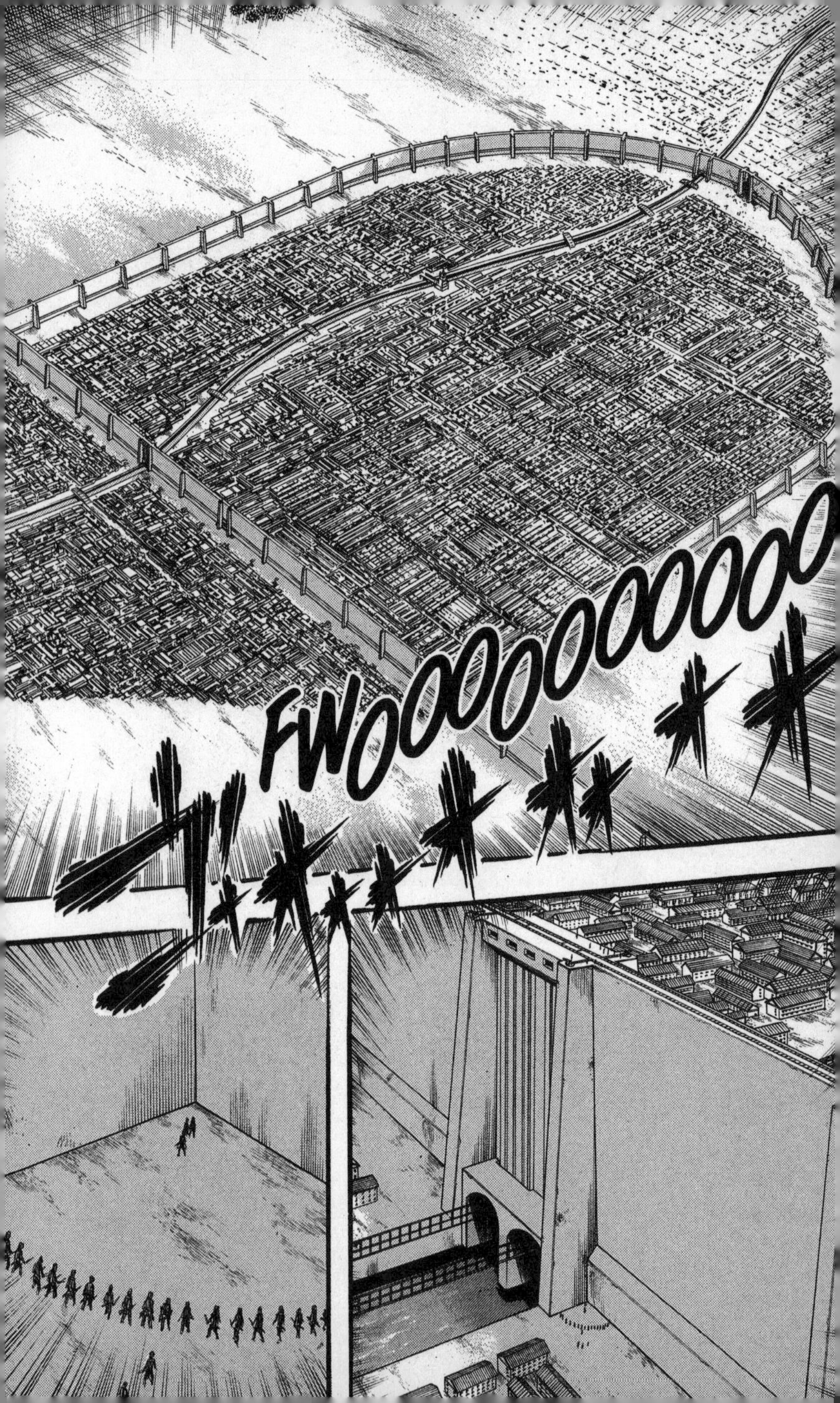
FWOOOOOOOOOO

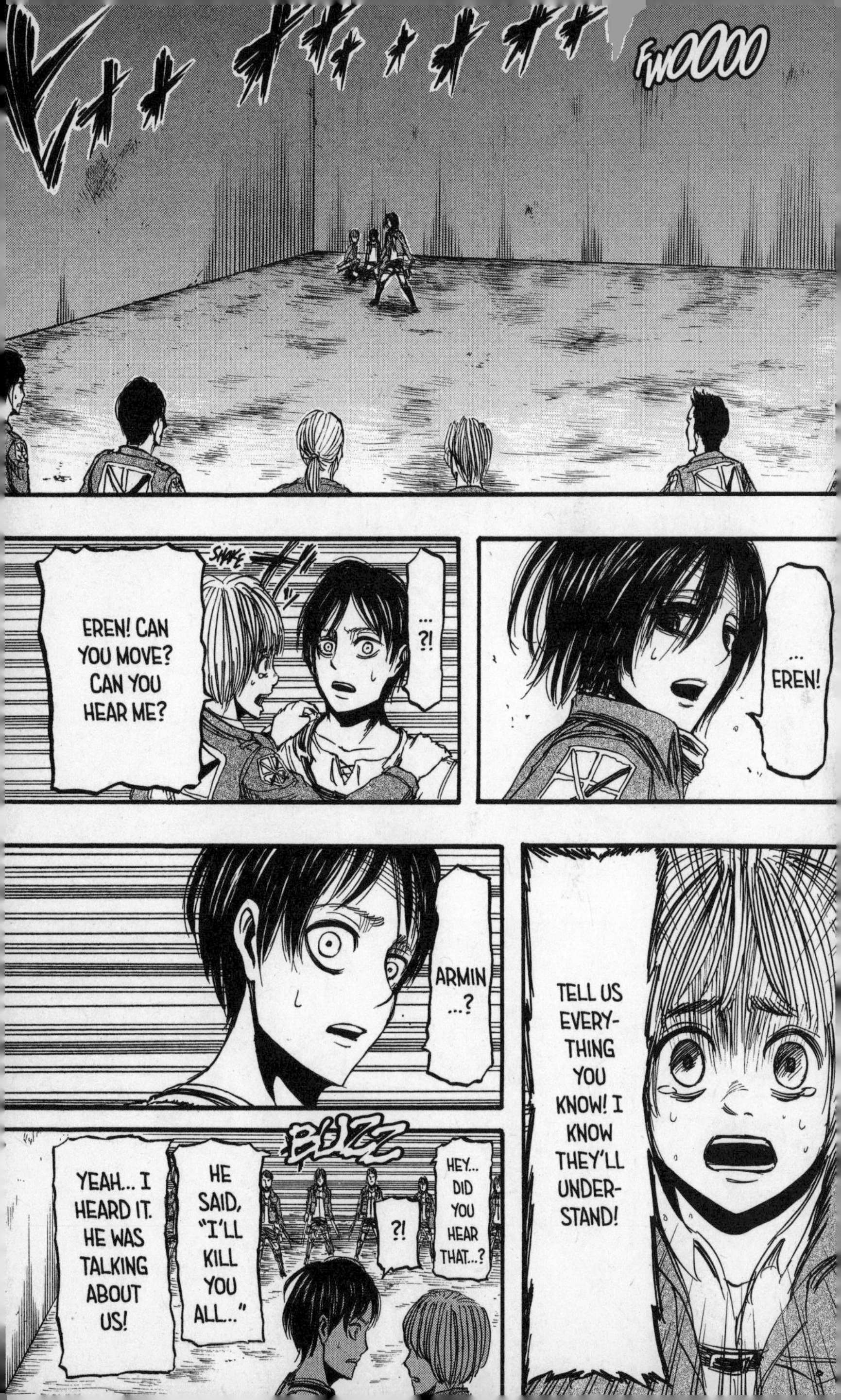
FWOOOO
... EREN!
SHAKE
...?!
EREN! CAN YOU MOVE? CAN YOU HEAR ME?
TELL US EVERY-THING YOU KNOW! I KNOW THEY'LL UNDER-STAND!
ARMIN ...?
BUZZ
HEY... DID YOU HEAR THAT...?
?!
HE SAID, "I'LL KILL YOU ALL..."
YEAH... I HEARD IT. HE WAS TALKING ABOUT US!

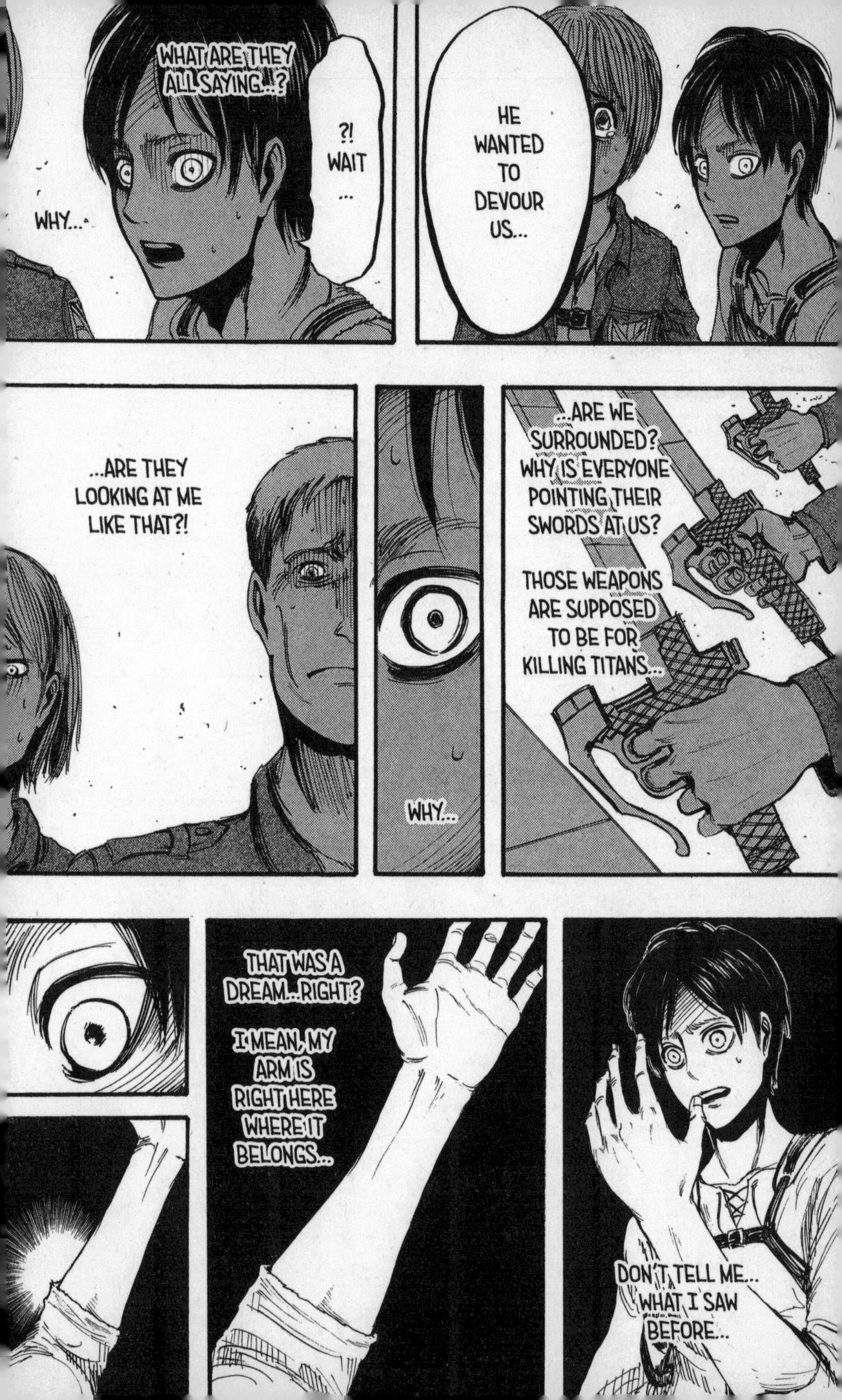
HE WANTED TO DEVOUR US...
?! WAIT ...
WHAT ARE THEY ALL SAYING...?
WHY...
...ARE WE SURROUNDED? WHY IS EVERYONE POINTING THEIR SWORDS AT US?
THOSE WEAPONS ARE SUPPOSED TO BE FOR KILLING TITANS...
WHY...
...ARE THEY LOOKING AT ME LIKE THAT?!
DON'T TELL ME... WHAT I SAW BEFORE...
THAT WAS A DREAM...RIGHT?
I MEAN, MY ARM IS RIGHT HERE WHERE IT BELONGS...

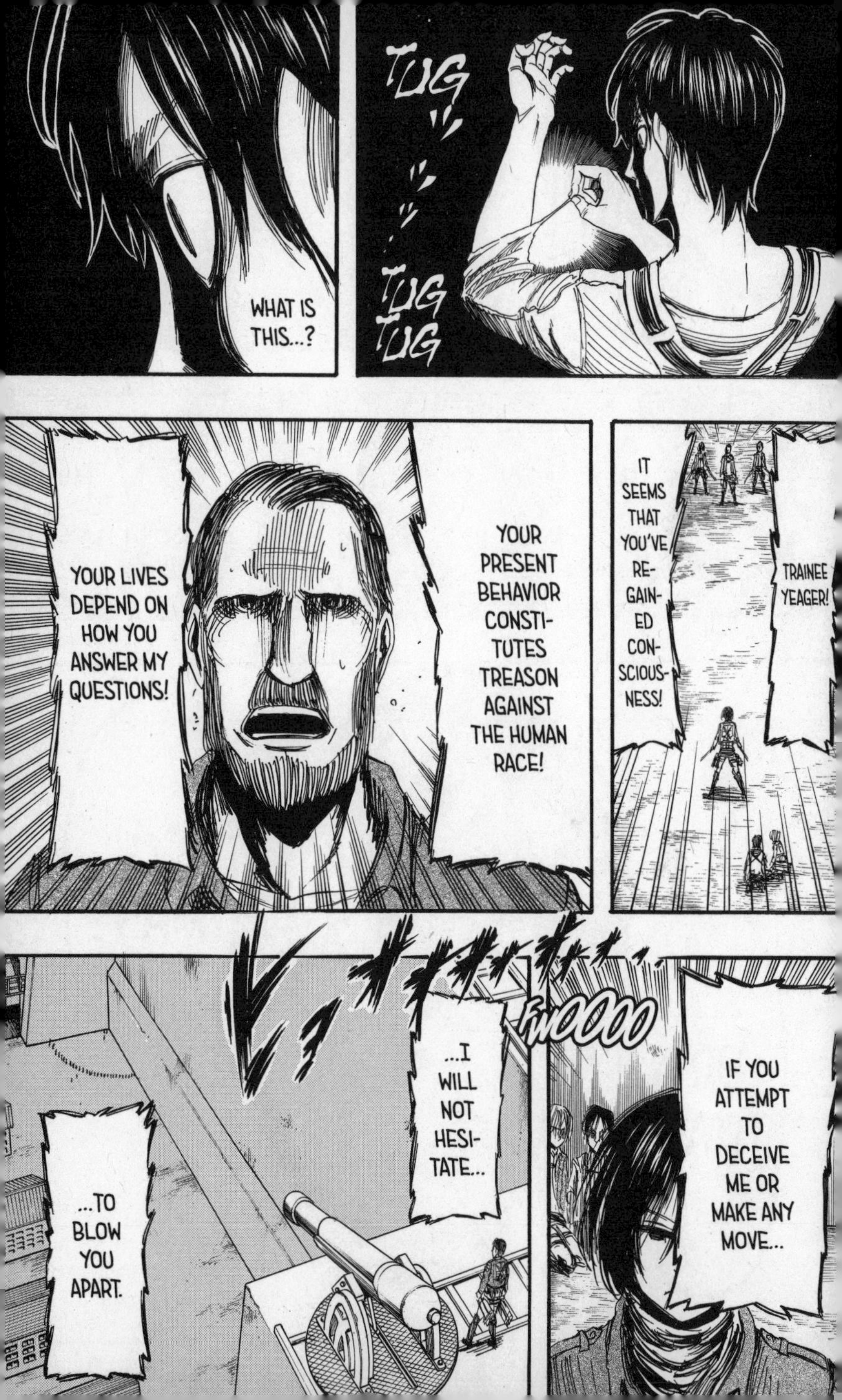
TUG
TUG TUG
WHAT IS THIS...?
TRAINEE YEAGER!
IT SEEMS THAT YOU'VE REGAINED CONSCIOUSNESS!
YOUR PRESENT BEHAVIOR CONSTITUTES TREASON AGAINST THE HUMAN RACE!
YOUR LIVES DEPEND ON HOW YOU ANSWER MY QUESTIONS!
FWOOOO
IF YOU ATTEMPT TO DECEIVE ME OR MAKE ANY MOVE...
...I WILL NOT HESITATE...
...TO BLOW YOU APART.

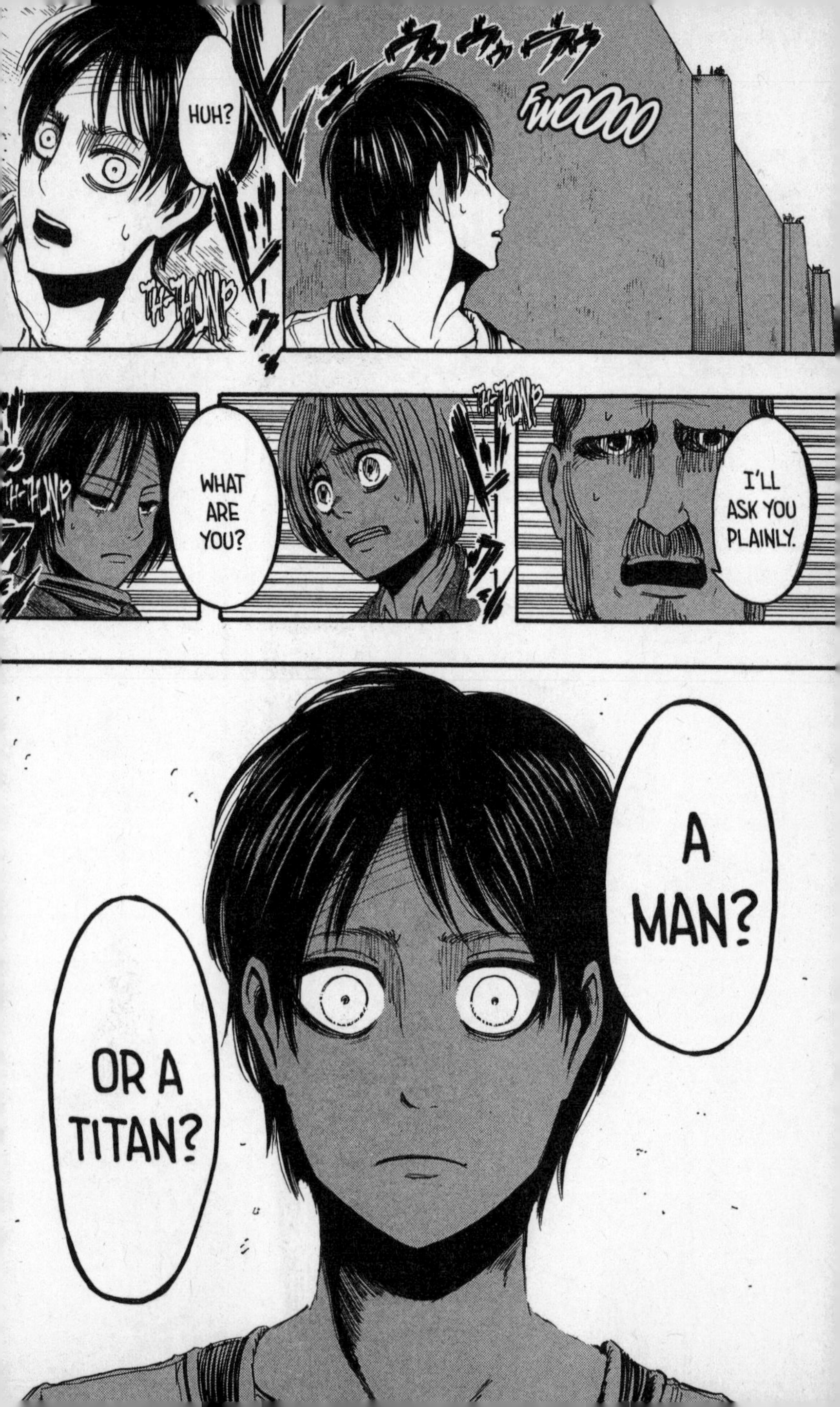
FWOOOO
HUH?
I'LL ASK YOU PLAINLY.
WHAT ARE YOU?
A MAN?
OR A TITAN?

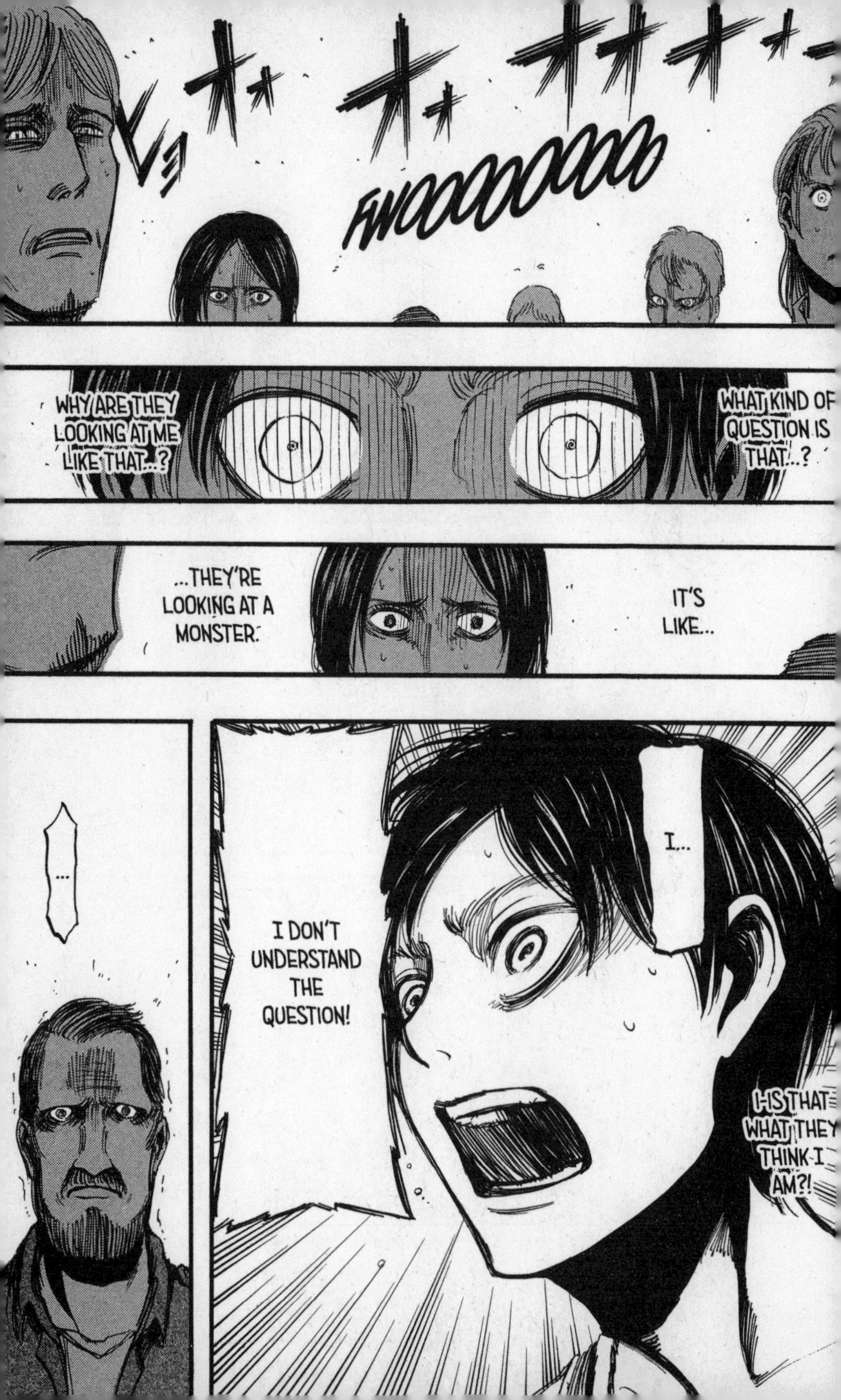
FWOOOOOOOO
WHAT KIND OF QUESTION IS THAT...?
WHY ARE THEY LOOKING AT ME LIKE THAT...?
IT'S LIKE...
...THEY'RE LOOKING AT A MONSTER.
I...
I-IS THAT WHAT THEY THINK I AM?!
I DON'T UNDERSTAND THE QUESTION!
...

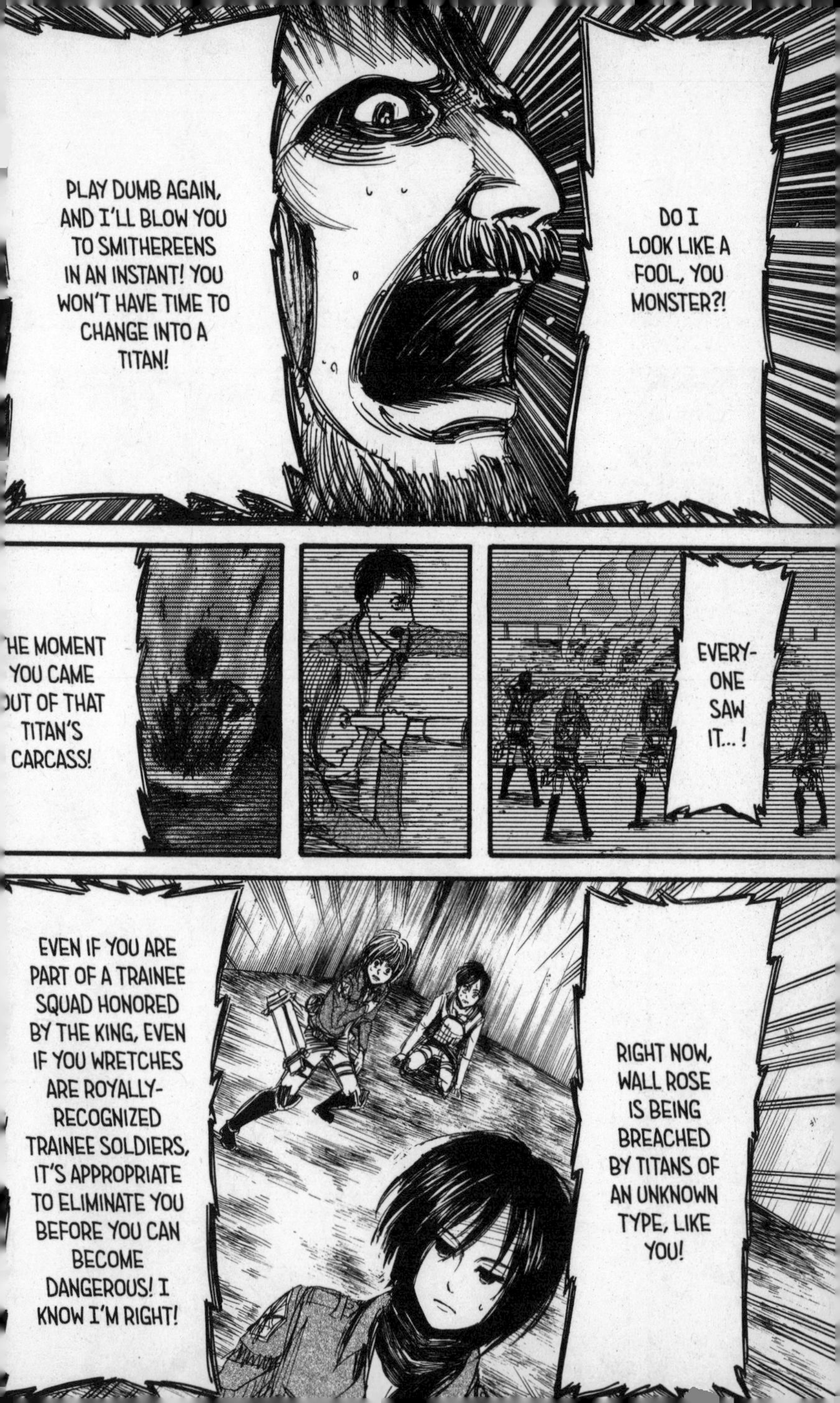
DO I LOOK LIKE A FOOL, YOU MONSTER?!
PLAY DUMB AGAIN, AND I'LL BLOW YOU TO SMITHEREENS IN AN INSTANT! YOU WON'T HAVE TIME TO CHANGE INTO A TITAN!
EVERY-ONE SAW IT... !
HE MOMENT YOU CAME UT OF THAT TITAN'S CARCASS!
RIGHT NOW, WALL ROSE IS BEING BREACHED BY TITANS OF AN UNKNOWN TYPE, LIKE YOU!
EVEN IF YOU ARE PART OF A TRAINEE SQUAD HONORED BY THE KING, EVEN IF YOU WRETCHES ARE ROYALLY-RECOGNIZED TRAINEE SOLDIERS, IT'S APPROPRIATE TO ELIMINATE YOU BEFORE YOU CAN BECOME DANGEROUS! I KNOW I'M RIGHT!

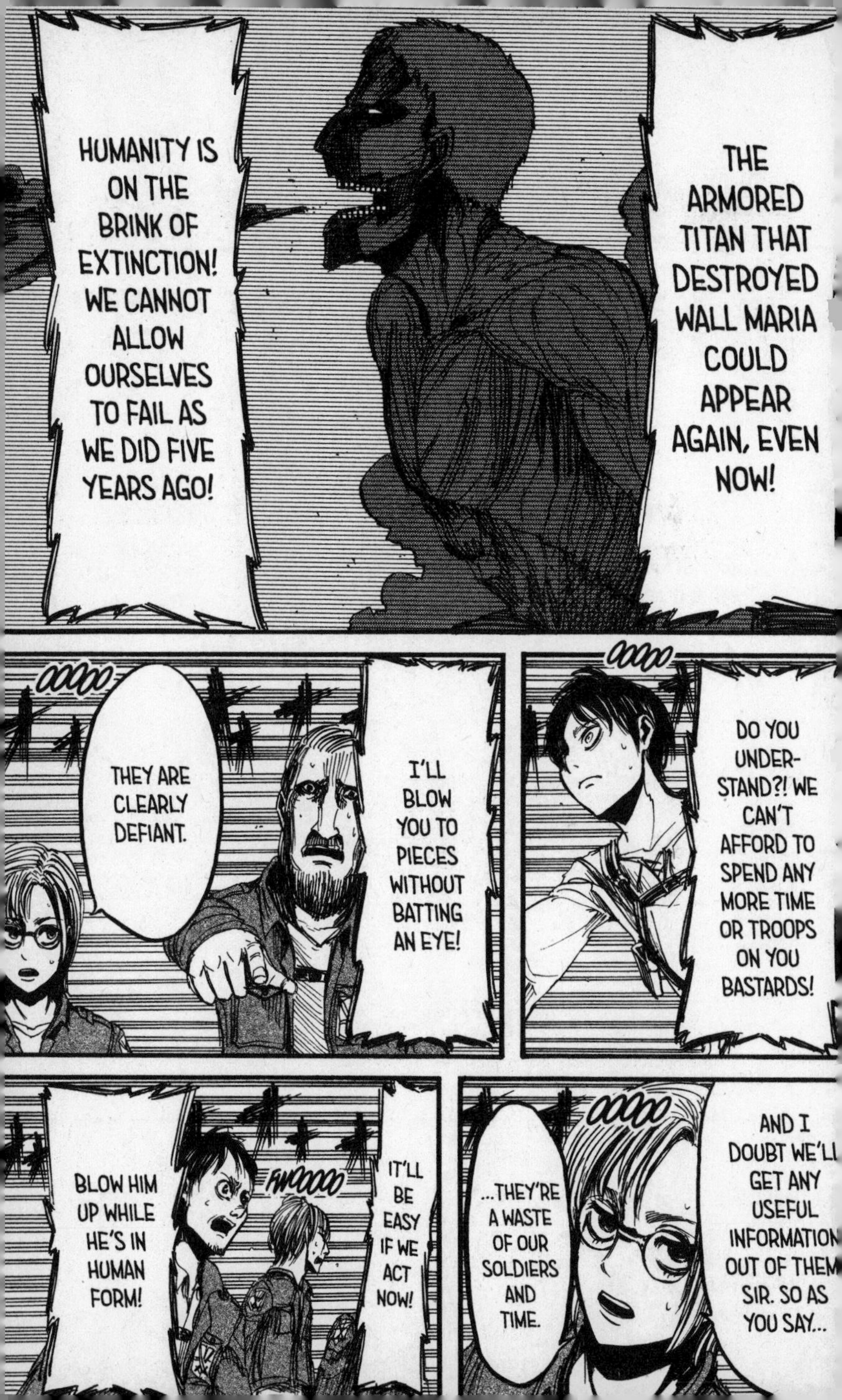

THE ARMORED TITAN THAT DESTROYED WALL MARIA COULD APPEAR AGAIN, EVEN NOW!
HUMANITY IS ON THE BRINK OF EXTINCTION! WE CANNOT ALLOW OURSELVES TO FAIL AS WE DID FIVE YEARS AGO!
OOOOO
DO YOU UNDER-STAND?! WE CAN'T AFFORD TO SPEND ANY MORE TIME OR TROOPS ON YOU BASTARDS!
I'LL BLOW YOU TO PIECES WITHOUT BATTING AN EYE!
OOOOO
THEY ARE CLEARLY DEFIANT.
OOOOO
AND I DOUBT WE'LL GET ANY USEFUL INFORMATION OUT OF THEM SIR. SO AS YOU SAY...
...THEY'RE A WASTE OF OUR SOLDIERS AND TIME.
IT'LL BE EASY IF WE ACT NOW!
FWOOOOO
BLOW HIM UP WHILE HE'S IN HUMAN FORM!

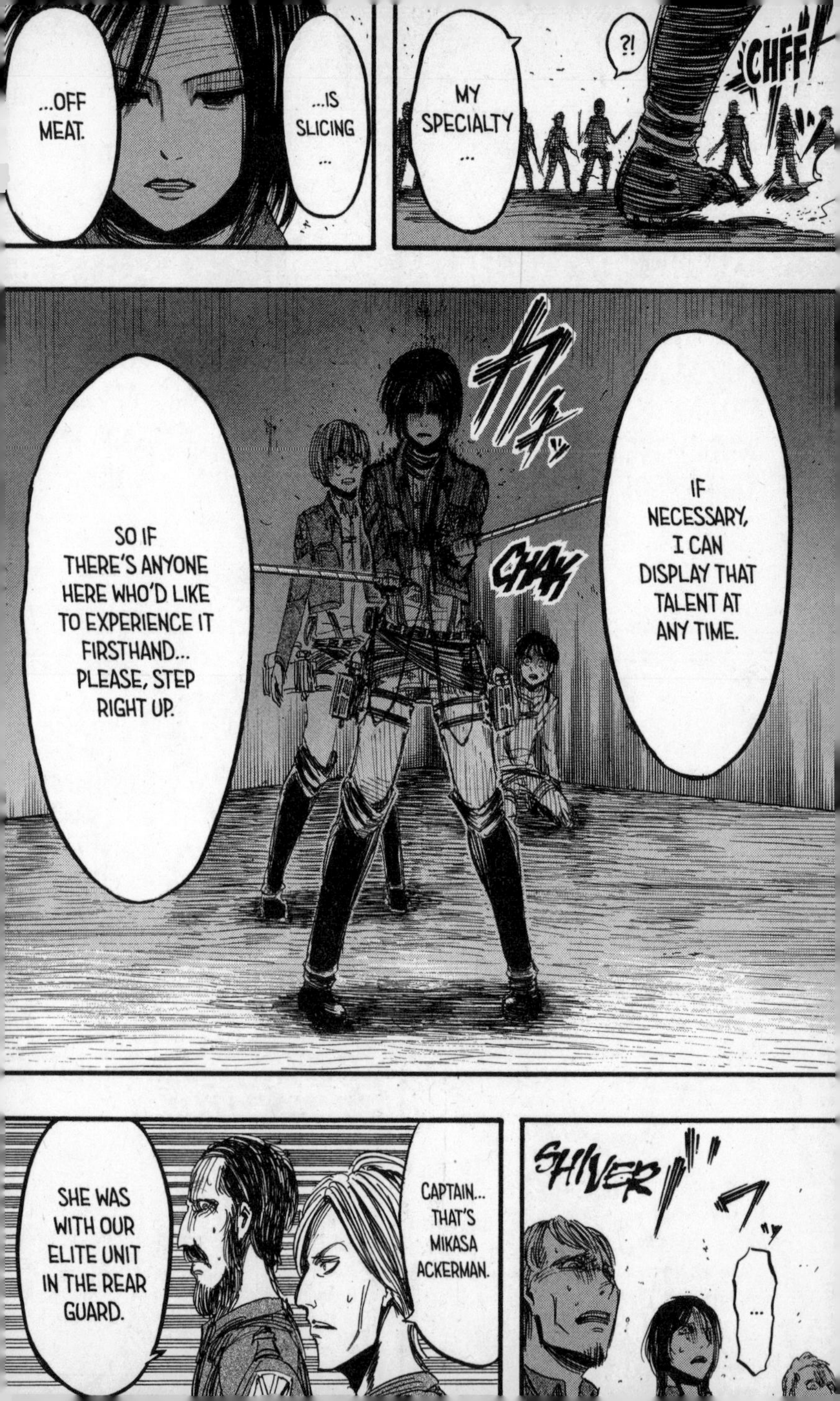
MY SPECIALTY ...
?!
CHFF
...IS SLICING ...
...OFF MEAT.
IF NECESSARY, I CAN DISPLAY THAT TALENT AT ANY TIME.
カチッ
CHAK
SO IF THERE'S ANYONE HERE WHO'D LIKE TO EXPERIENCE IT FIRSTHAND... PLEASE, STEP RIGHT UP.
SHIVER
...
CAPTAIN... THAT'S MIKASA ACKERMAN.
SHE WAS WITH OUR ELITE UNIT IN THE REAR GUARD.

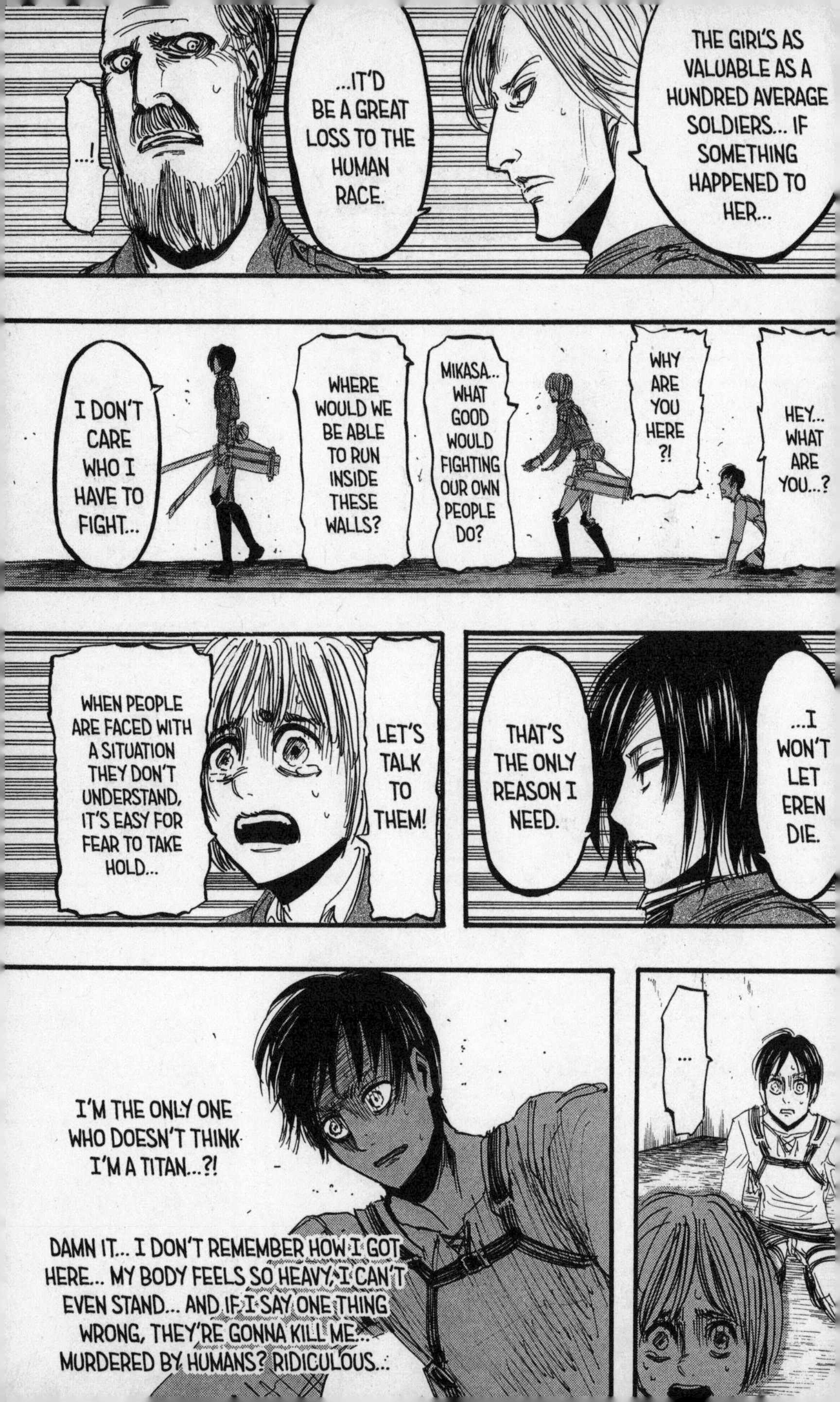
THE GIRL'S AS VALUABLE AS A HUNDRED AVERAGE SOLDIERS... IF SOMETHING HAPPENED TO HER...
...IT'D BE A GREAT LOSS TO THE HUMAN RACE.
...!
HEY... WHAT ARE YOU...?
WHY ARE YOU HERE?!
MIKASA... WHAT GOOD WOULD FIGHTING OUR OWN PEOPLE DO?
WHERE WOULD WE BE ABLE TO RUN INSIDE THESE WALLS?
I DON'T CARE WHO I HAVE TO FIGHT...
...I WON'T LET EREN DIE.
THAT'S THE ONLY REASON I NEED.
LET'S TALK TO THEM!
WHEN PEOPLE ARE FACED WITH A SITUATION THEY DON'T UNDERSTAND, IT'S EASY FOR FEAR TO TAKE HOLD...
...
I'M THE ONLY ONE WHO DOESN'T THINK I'M A TITAN...?!
DAMN IT... I DON'T REMEMBER HOW I GOT HERE... MY BODY FEELS SO HEAVY, I CAN'T EVEN STAND... AND IF I SAY ONE THING WRONG, THEY'RE GONNA KILL ME... MURDERED BY HUMANS? RIDICULOUS...

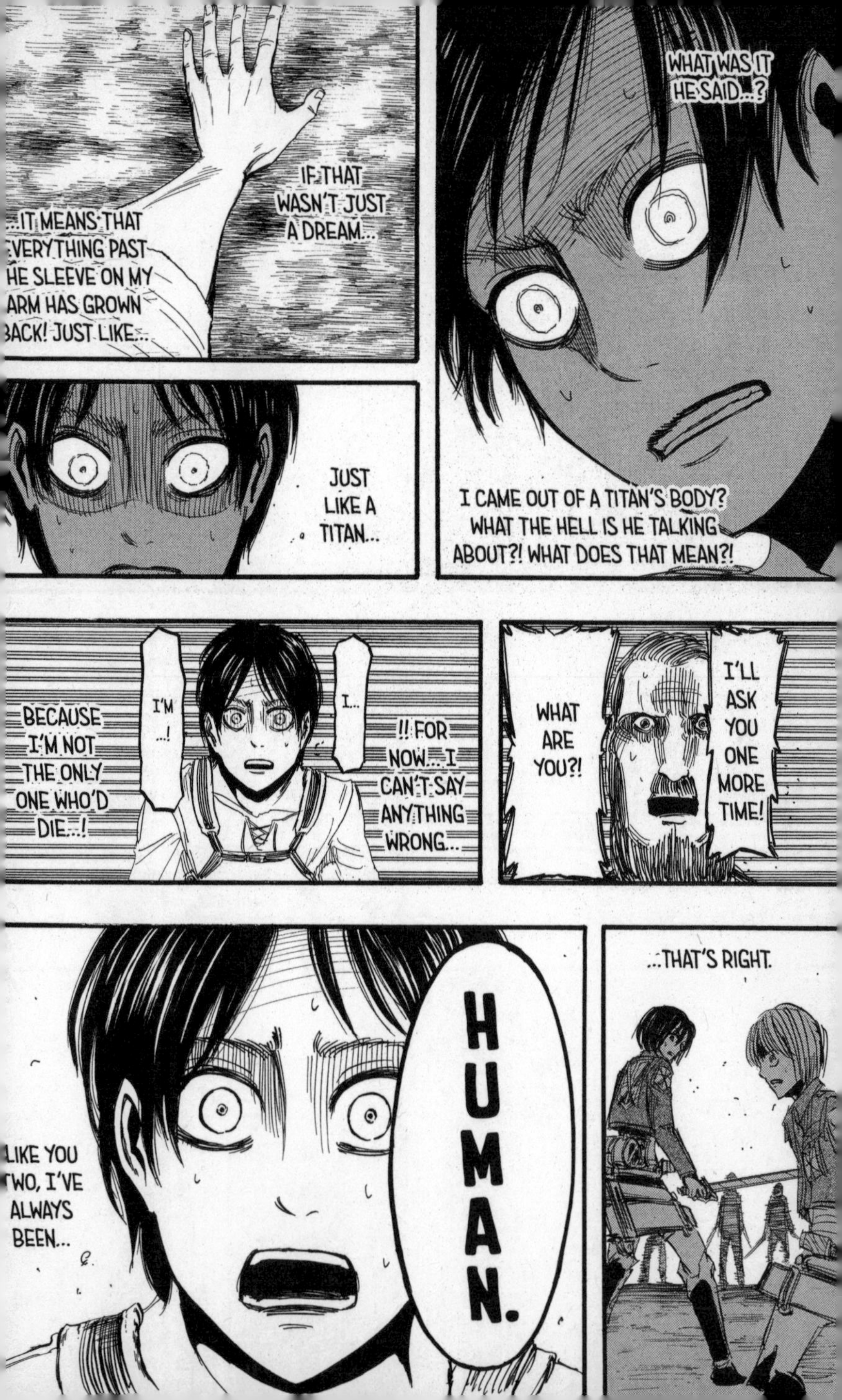

WHAT WAS IT HE SAID...?
I CAME OUT OF A TITAN'S BODY? WHAT THE HELL IS HE TALKING ABOUT?! WHAT DOES THAT MEAN?!
IF THAT WASN'T JUST A DREAM...
...IT MEANS THAT EVERYTHING PAST THE SLEEVE ON MY ARM HAS GROWN BACK! JUST LIKE...
JUST LIKE A TITAN...
I'LL ASK YOU ONE MORE TIME!
WHAT ARE YOU?!
I...
!! FOR NOW... I CAN'T SAY ANYTHING WRONG...
I'M ...!
BECAUSE I'M NOT THE ONLY ONE WHO'D DIE...!
...THAT'S RIGHT.
LIKE YOU TWO, I'VE ALWAYS BEEN...
HUMAN.

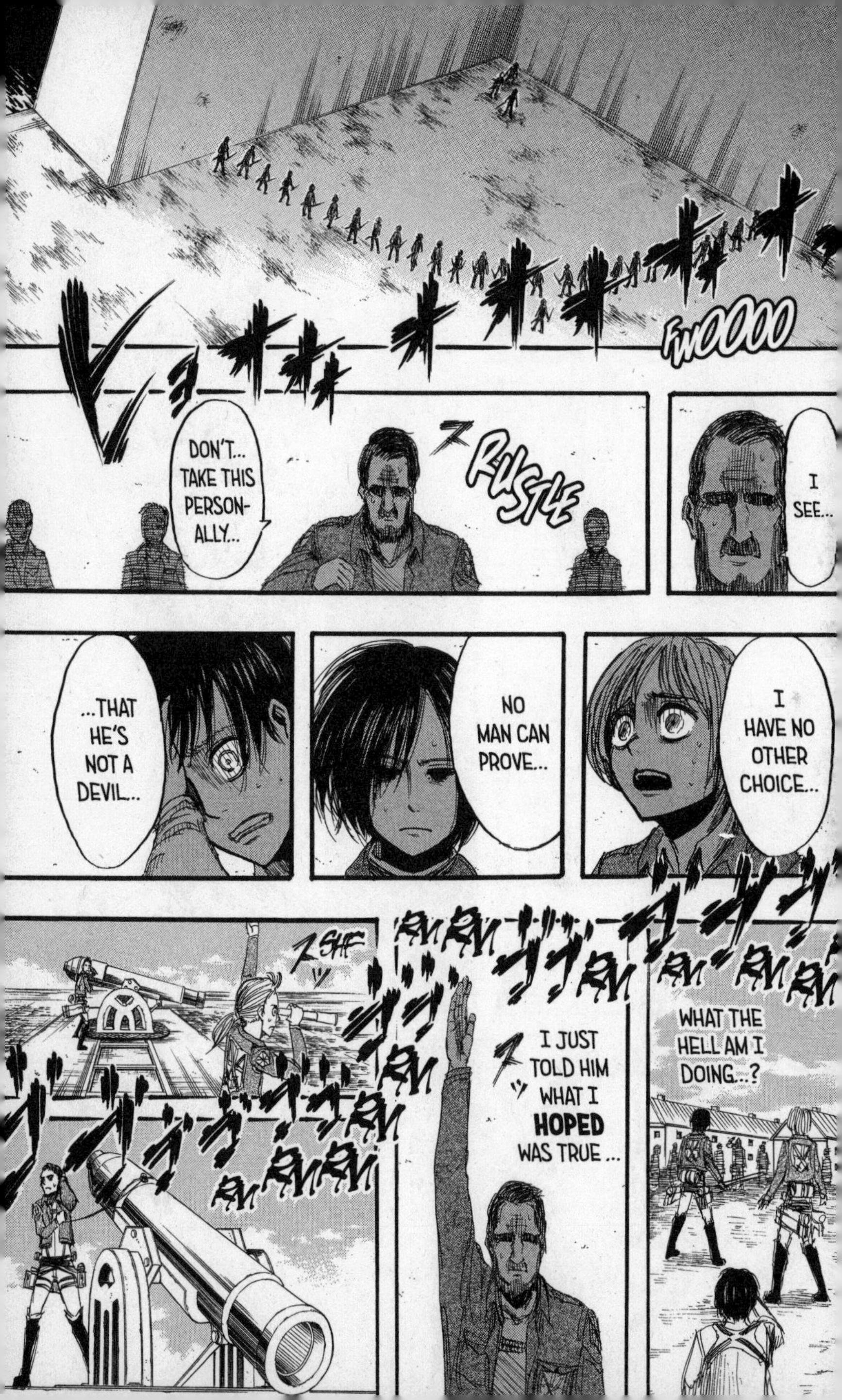
FWOOOO
I SEE...
DON'T... TAKE THIS PERSON-ALLY...
RUSTLE
I HAVE NO OTHER CHOICE...
NO MAN CAN PROVE...
...THAT HE'S NOT A DEVIL...
RM RM RM RM RM RM RM
WHAT THE HELL AM I DOING...?
I JUST TOLD HIM WHAT I HOPED WAS TRUE ...
SHF
RM RM RM RM RM

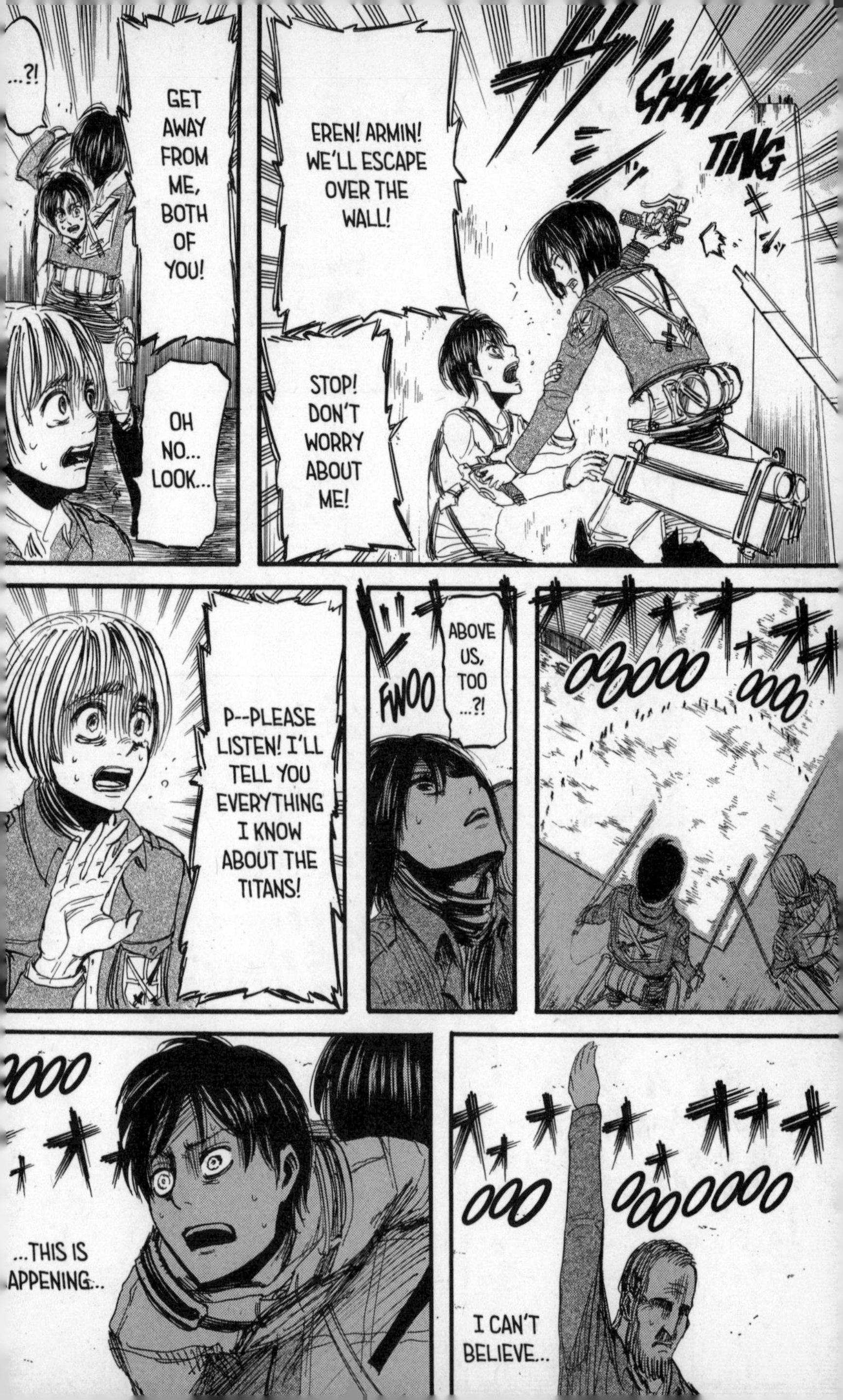
CHAK
TING
EREN! ARMIN! WE'LL ESCAPE OVER THE WALL!
STOP! DON'T WORRY ABOUT ME!
GET AWAY FROM ME, BOTH OF YOU!
...?!
OH NO... LOOK...
OOOOOO
OOOO
FWOO
ABOVE US, TOO ...?!
P--PLEASE LISTEN! I'LL TELL YOU EVERYTHING I KNOW ABOUT THE TITANS!
OOOOOOO
OOO
I CAN'T BELIEVE...
OOOO
...THIS IS
APPENING...

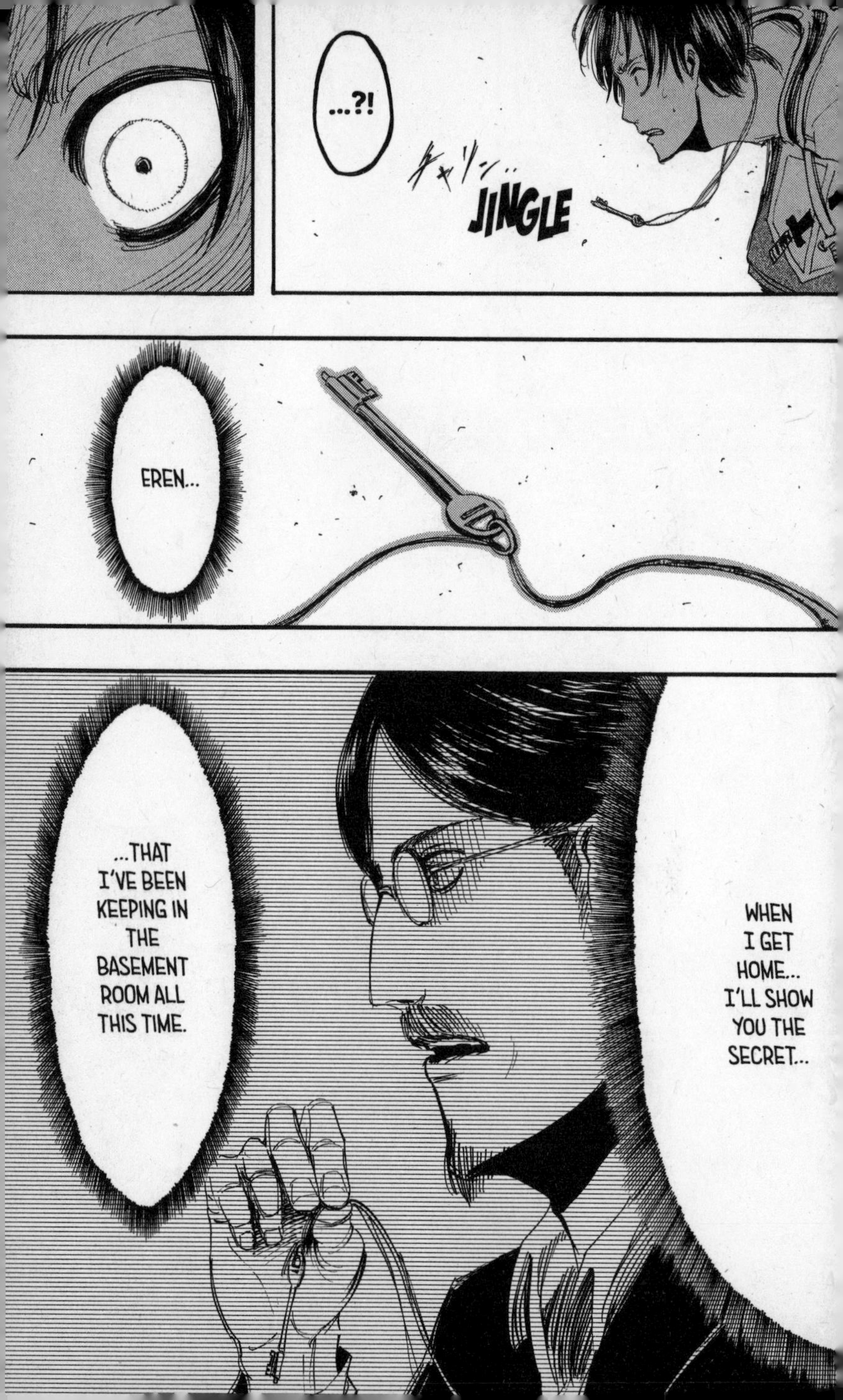
...?!
チャリン..
JINGLE
EREN...
WHEN I GET HOME... I'LL SHOW YOU THE SECRET...
...THAT I'VE BEEN KEEPING IN THE BASEMENT ROOM ALL THIS TIME.

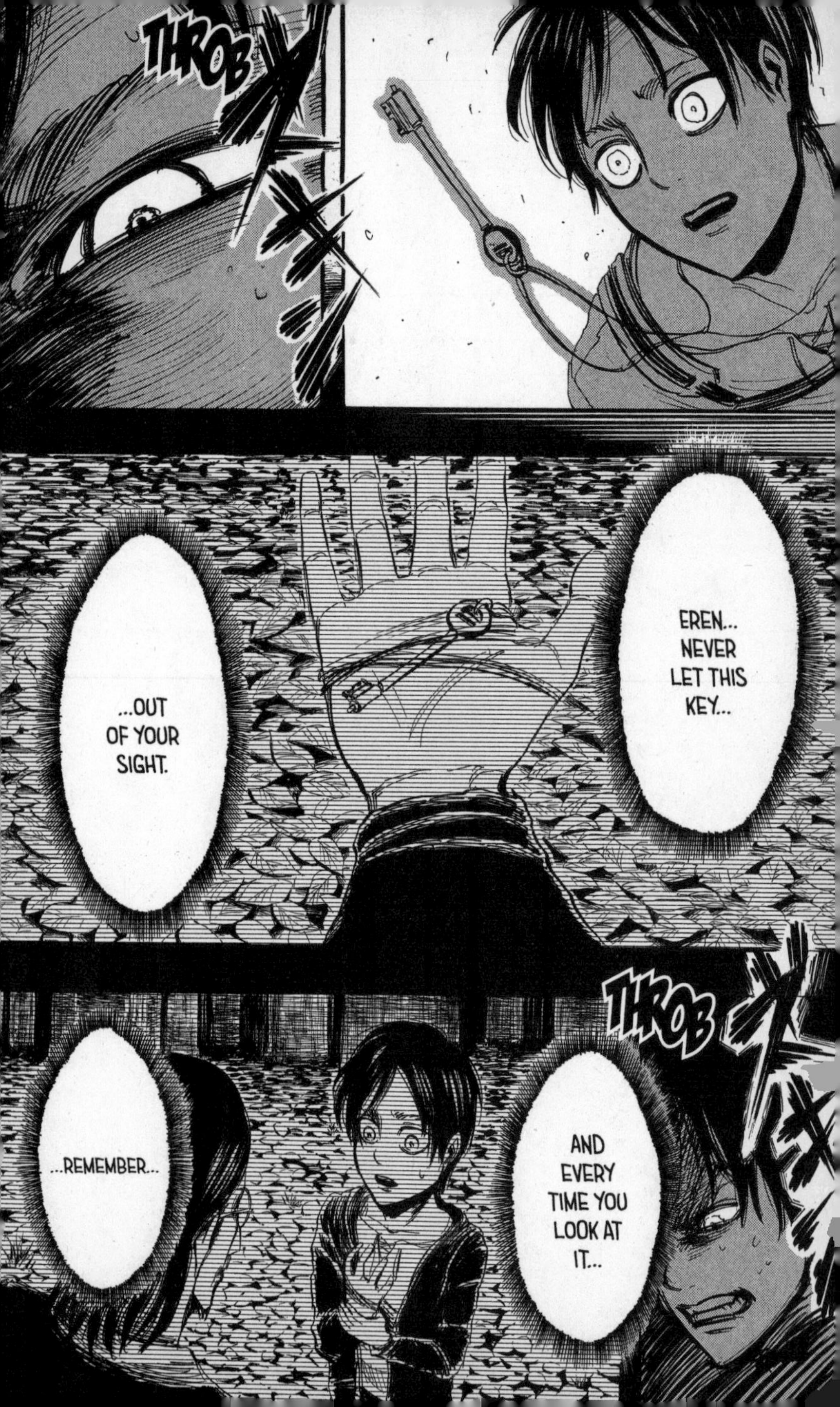
THROB
EREN... NEVER LET THIS KEY...
...OUT OF YOUR SIGHT.
THROB
AND EVERY TIME YOU LOOK AT IT...
...REMEMBER...

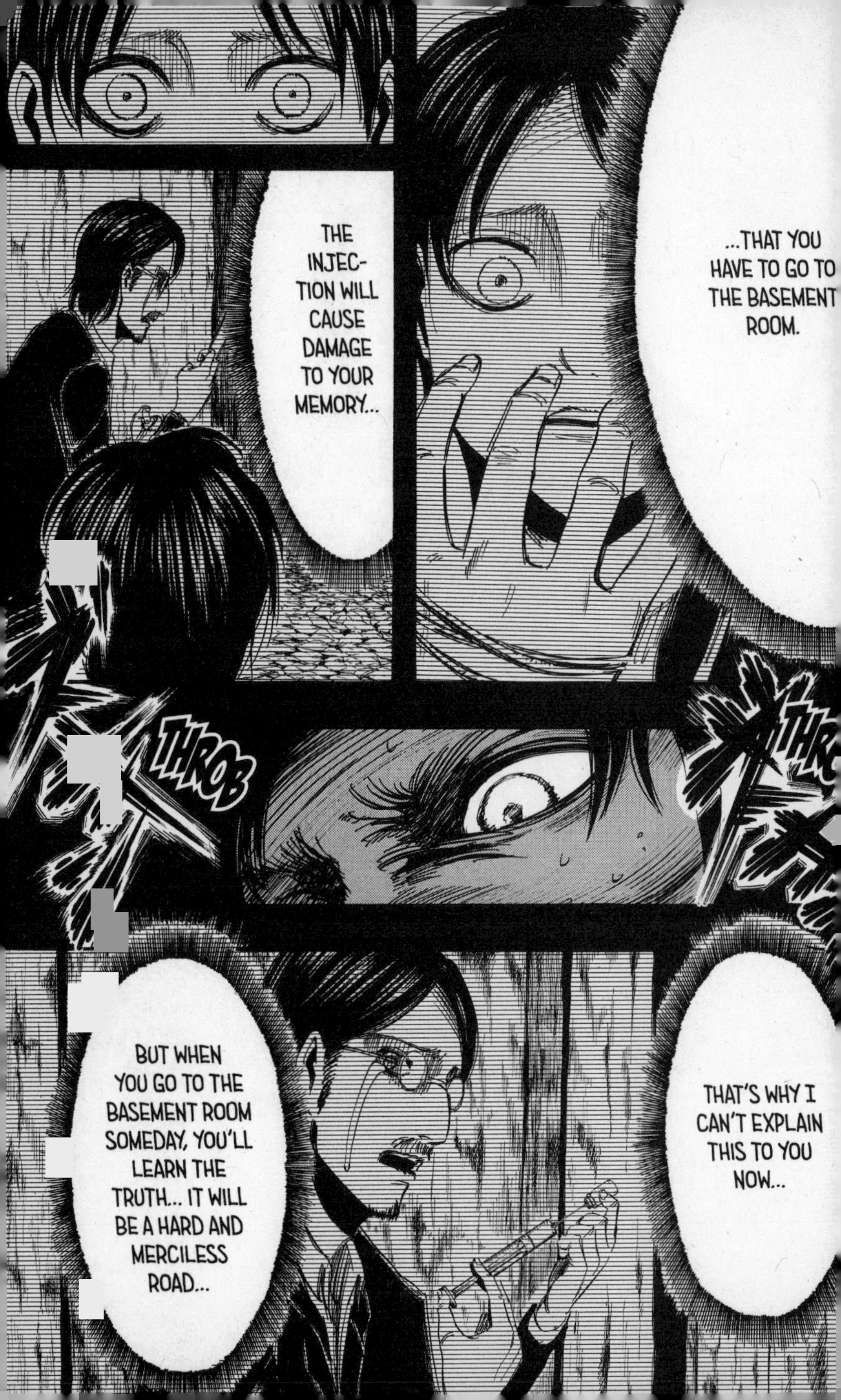
...THAT YOU HAVE TO GO TO THE BASEMENT ROOM.
THE INJECTION WILL CAUSE DAMAGE TO YOUR MEMORY...
THROB
THAT'S WHY I CAN'T EXPLAIN THIS TO YOU NOW...
BUT WHEN YOU GO TO THE BASEMENT ROOM SOMEDAY, YOU'LL LEARN THE TRUTH... IT WILL BE A HARD AND MERCILESS ROAD...

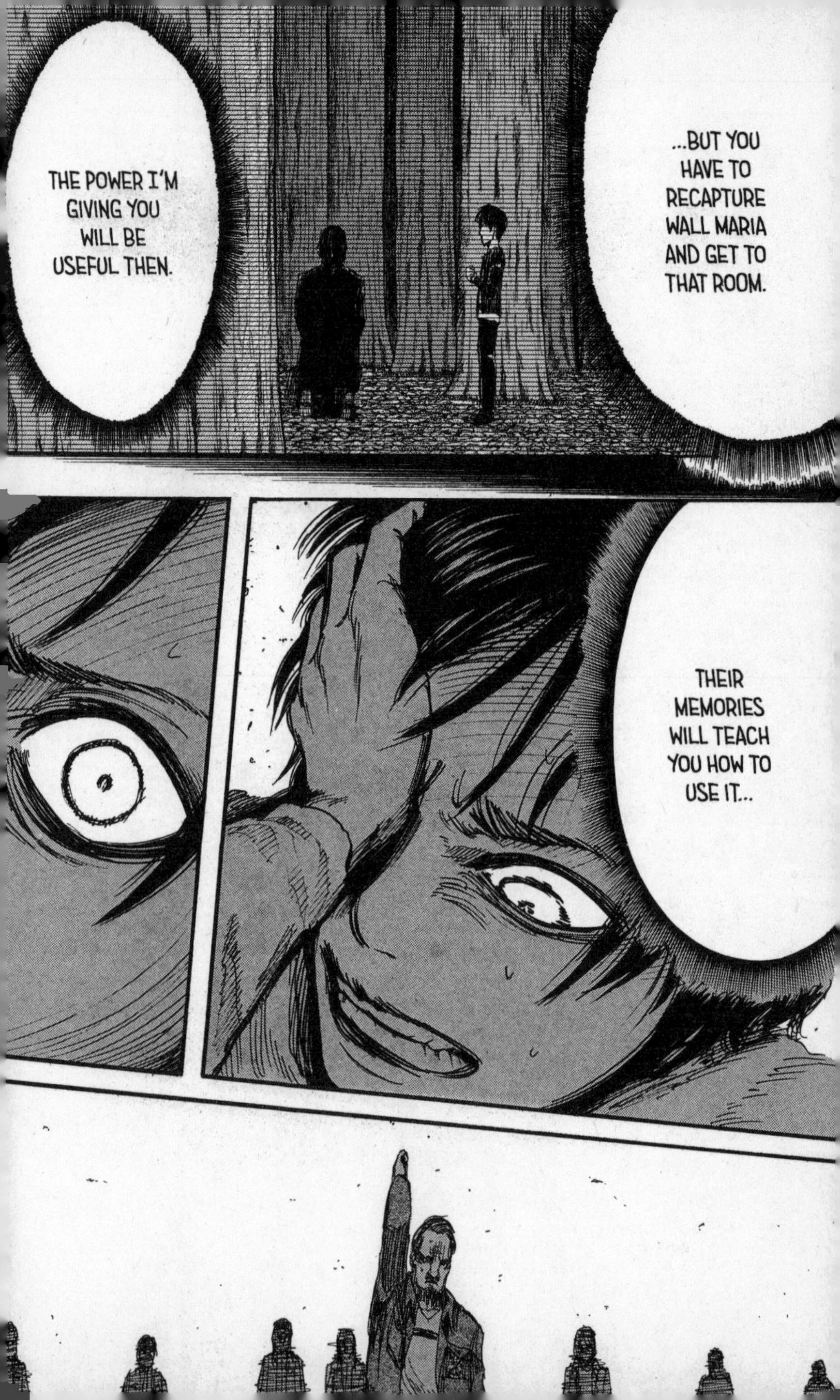
...BUT YOU HAVE TO RECAPTURE WALL MARIA AND GET TO THAT ROOM.
THE POWER I'M GIVING YOU WILL BE USEFUL THEN.
THEIR MEMORIES WILL TEACH YOU HOW TO USE IT...

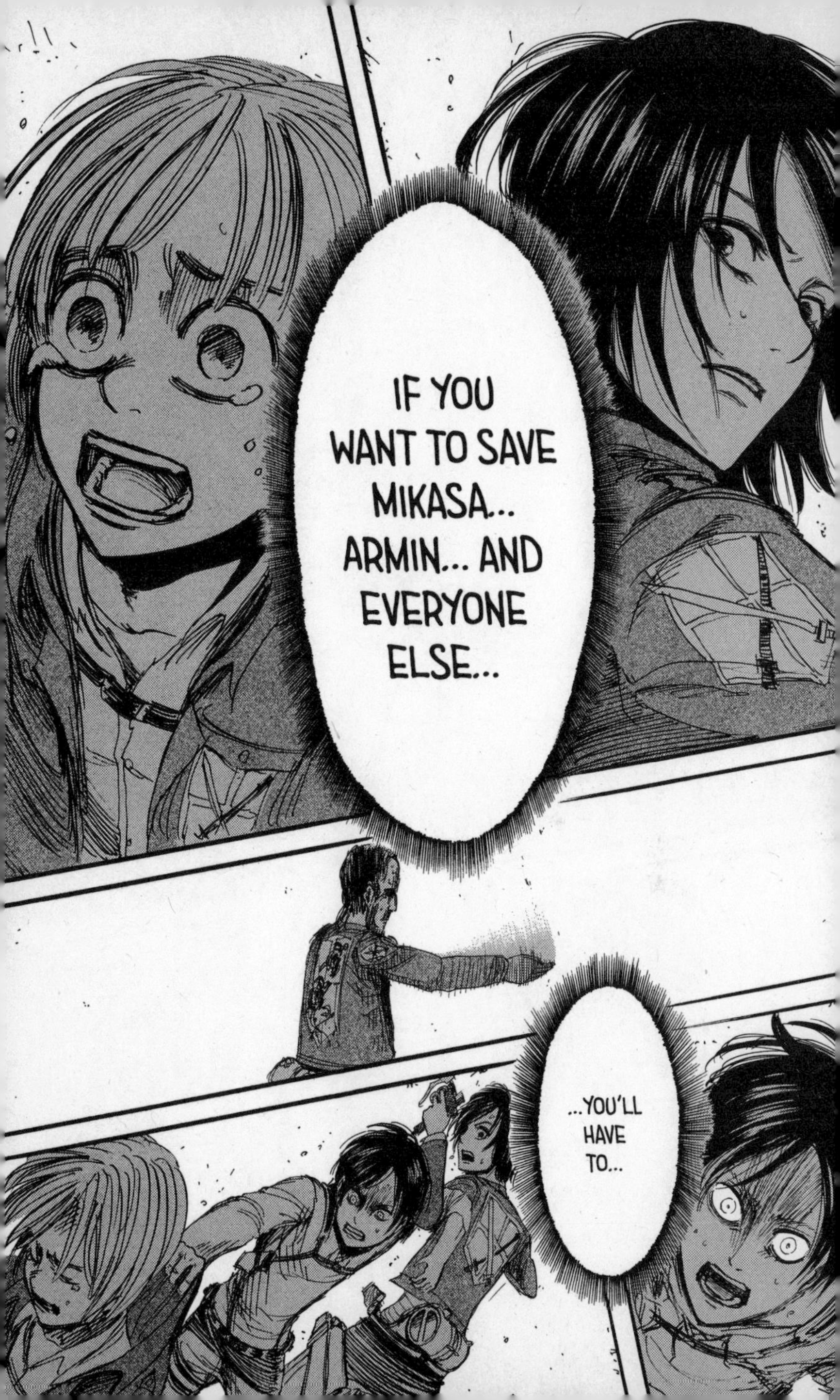
IF YOU WANT TO SAVE MIKASA... ARMIN... AND EVERYONE ELSE...
...YOU'LL HAVE TO...

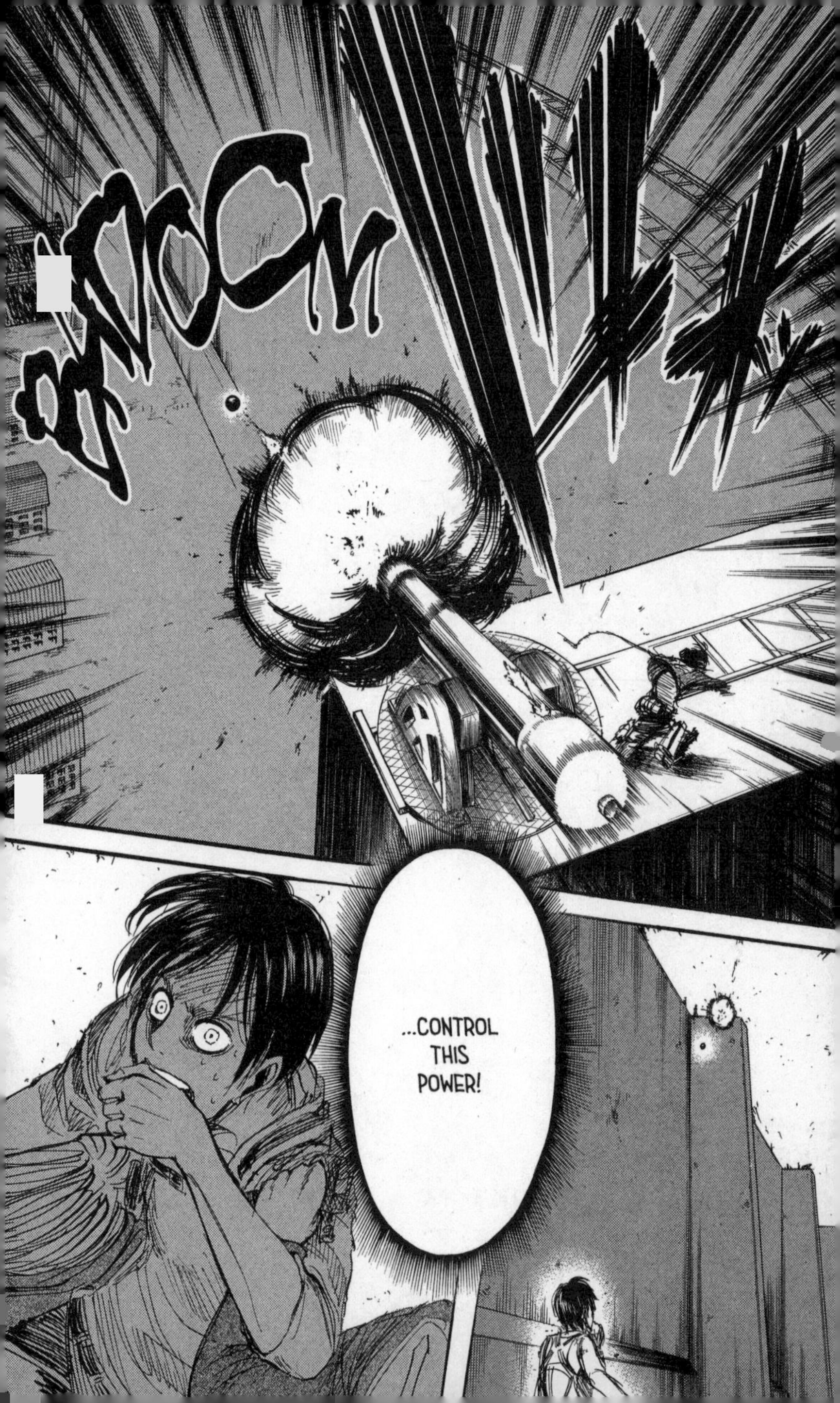
...CONTROL THIS POWER!

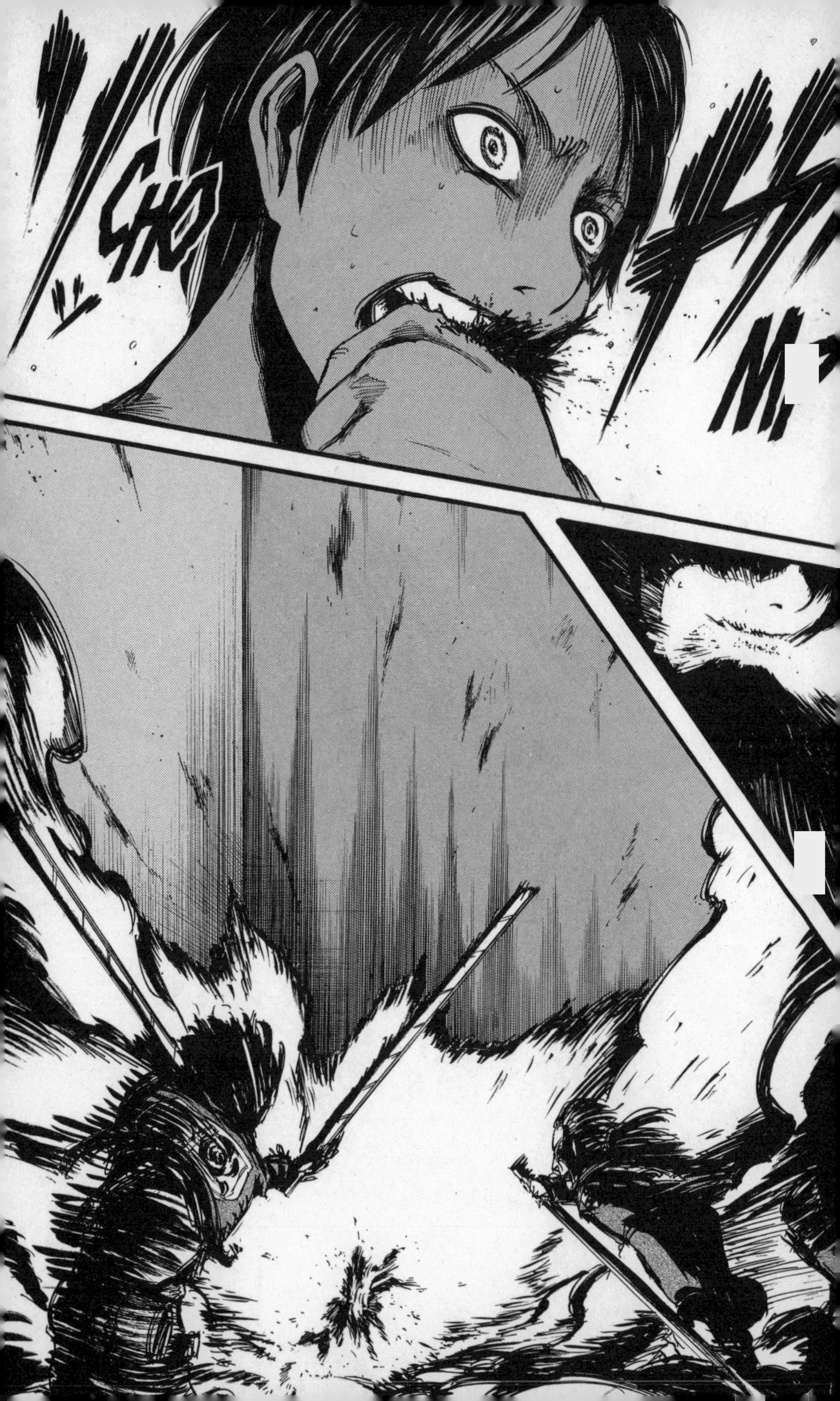
CHO

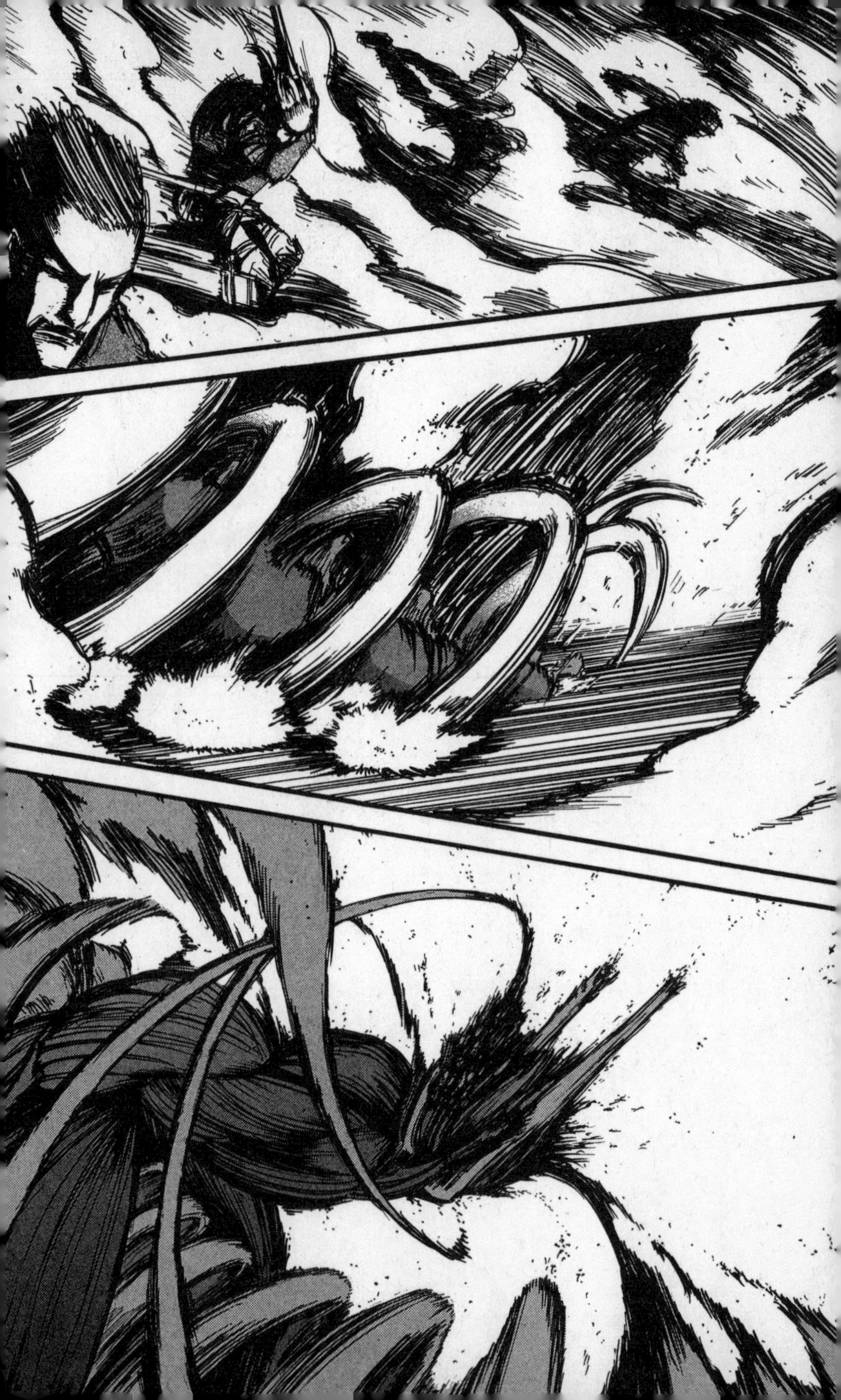

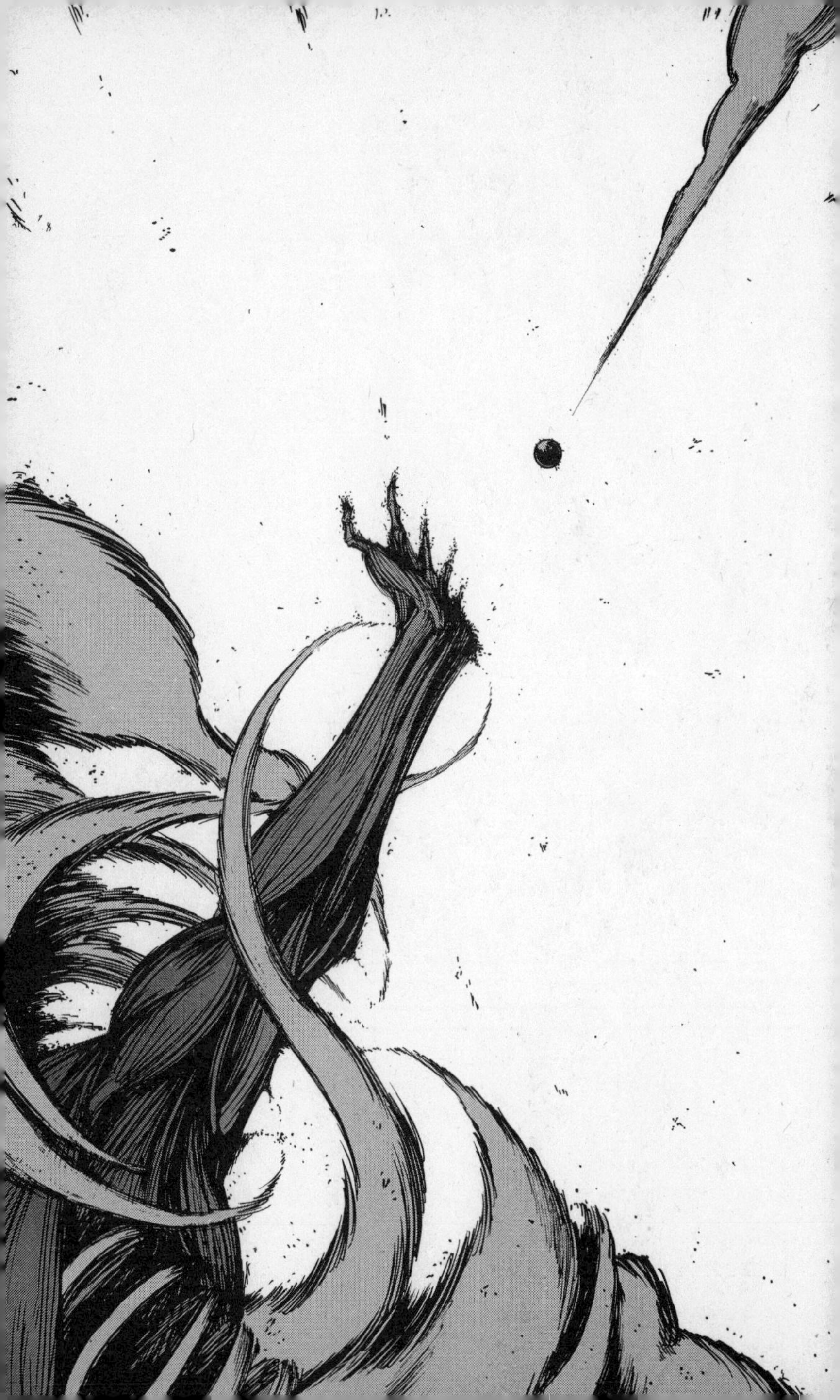

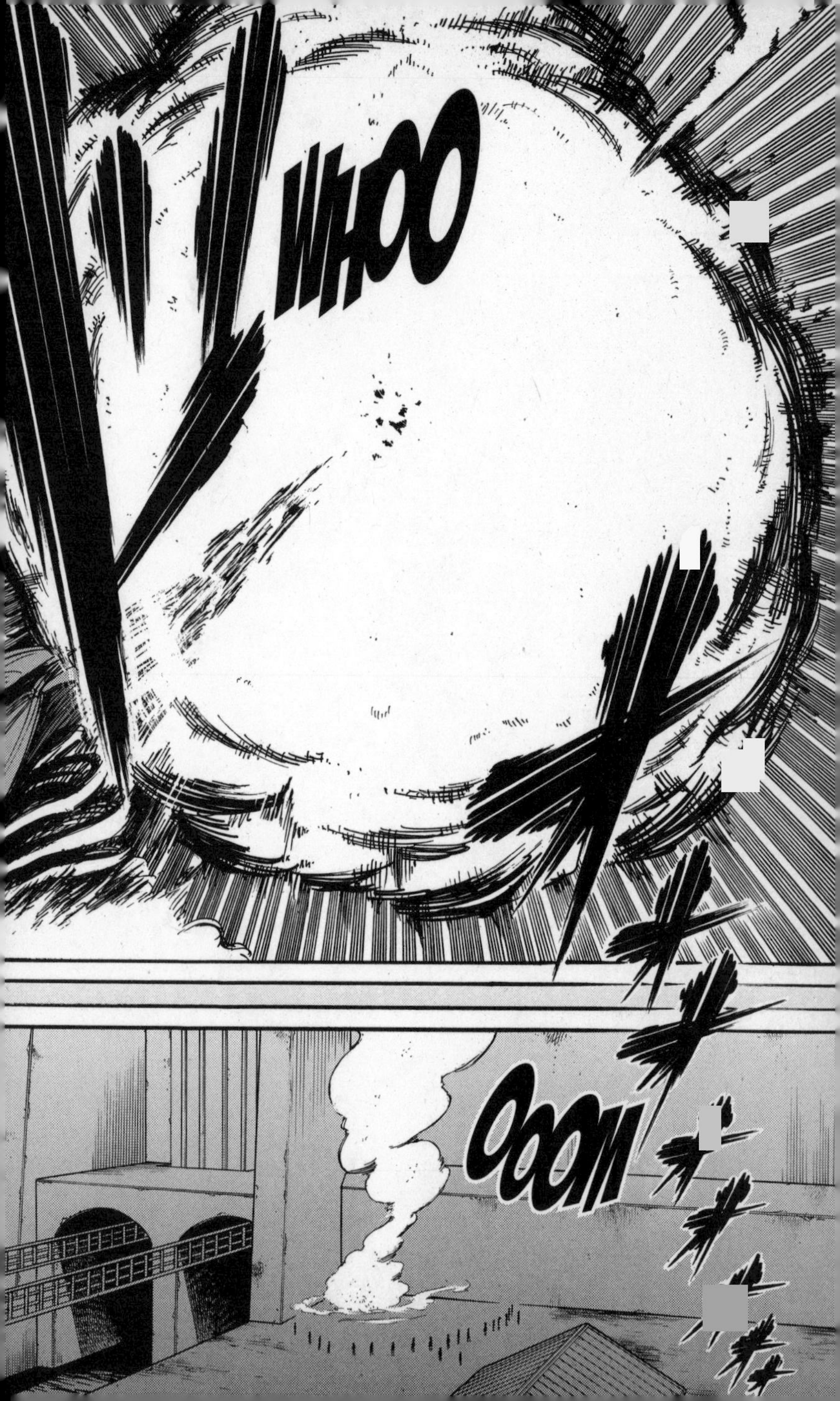
WHOO
OOOM

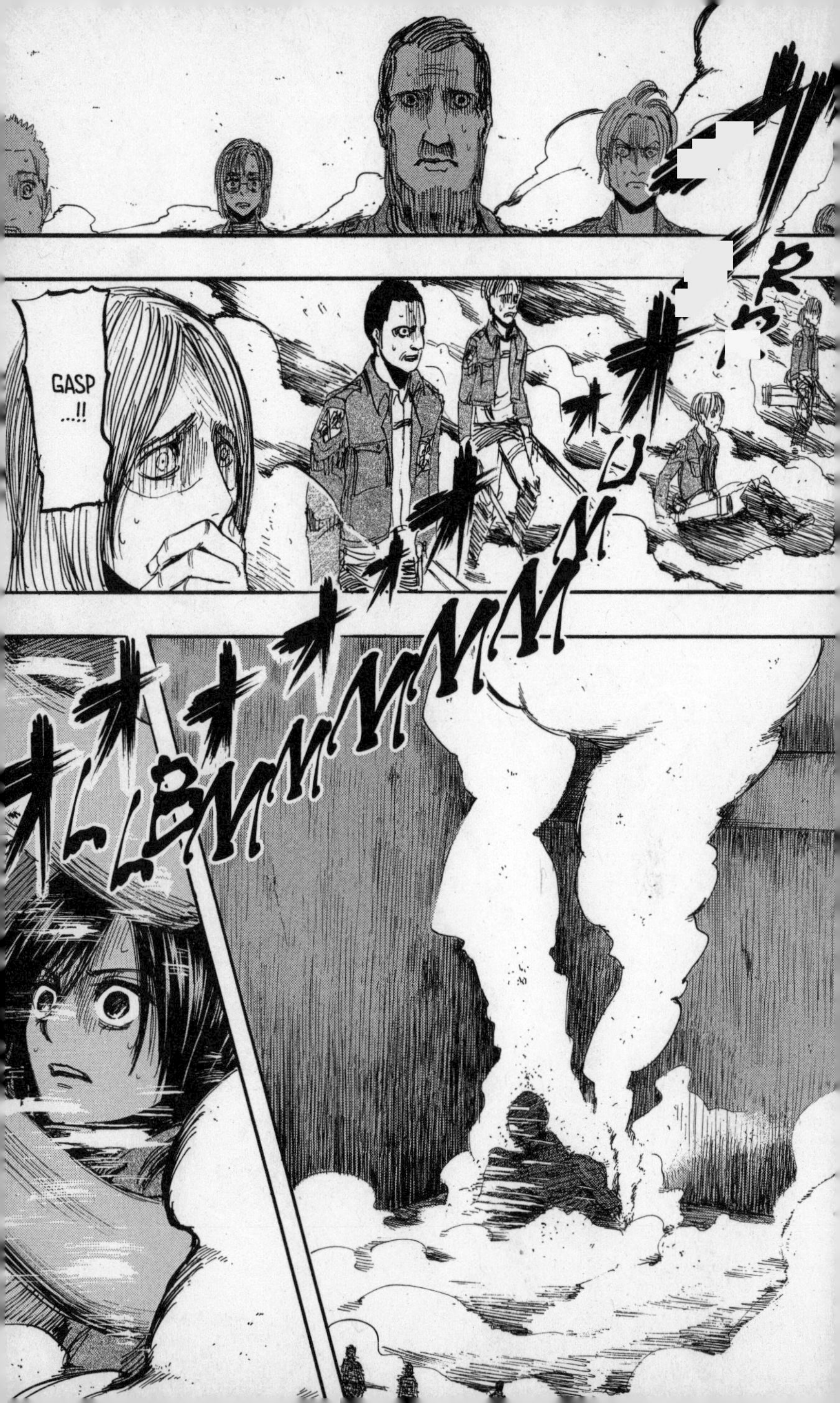
GASP
...!!

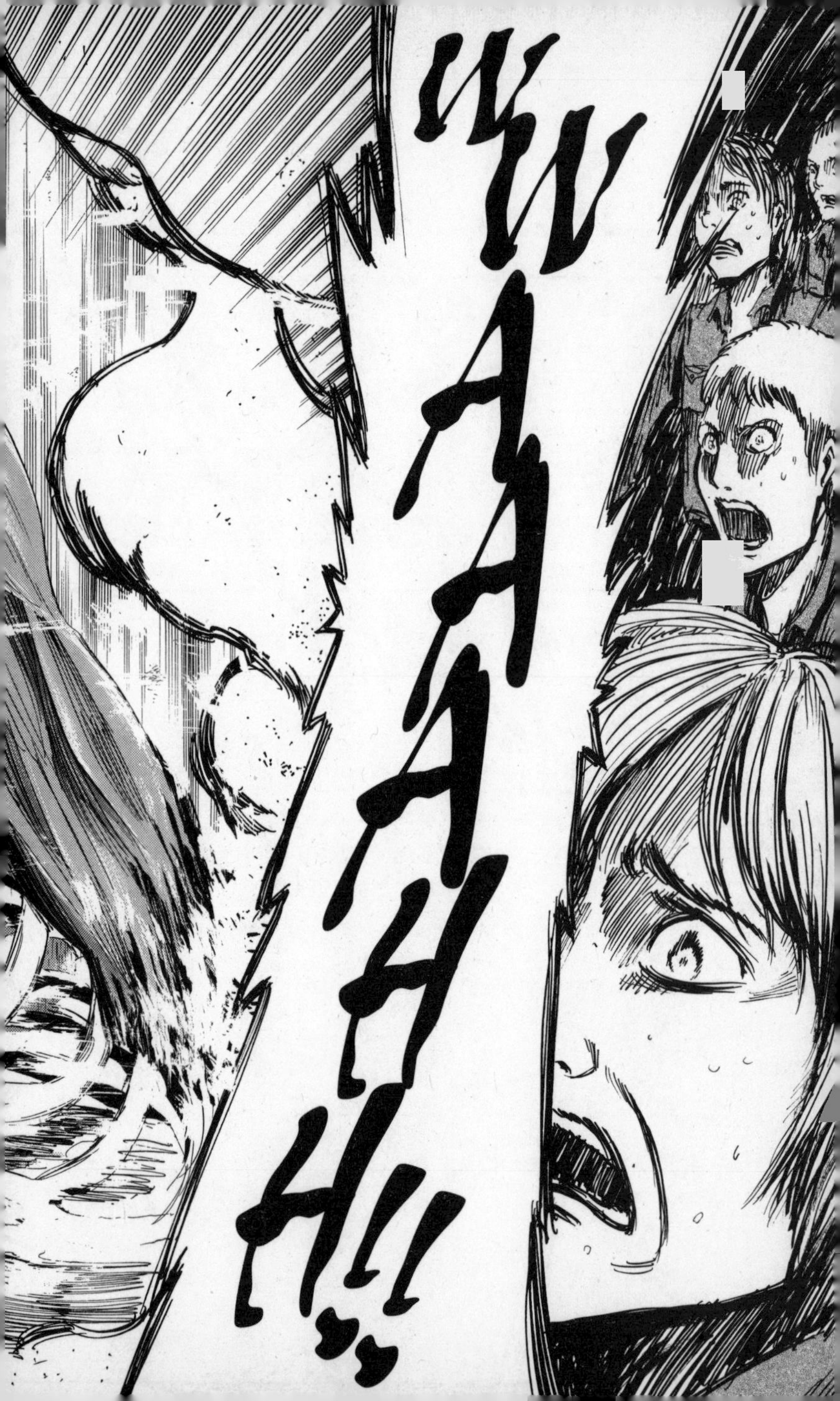
WWAAAHHH!!

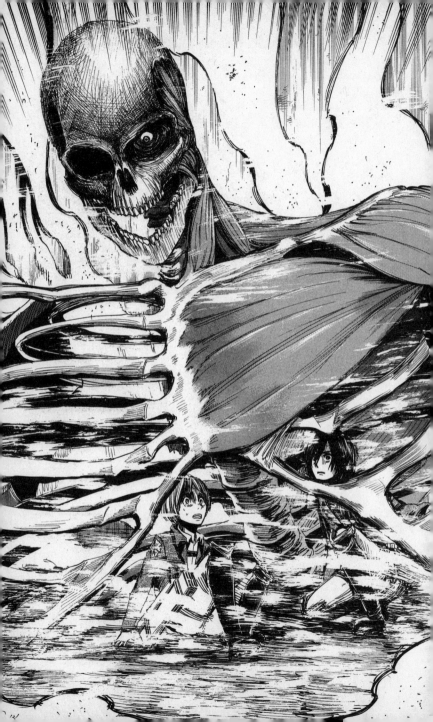

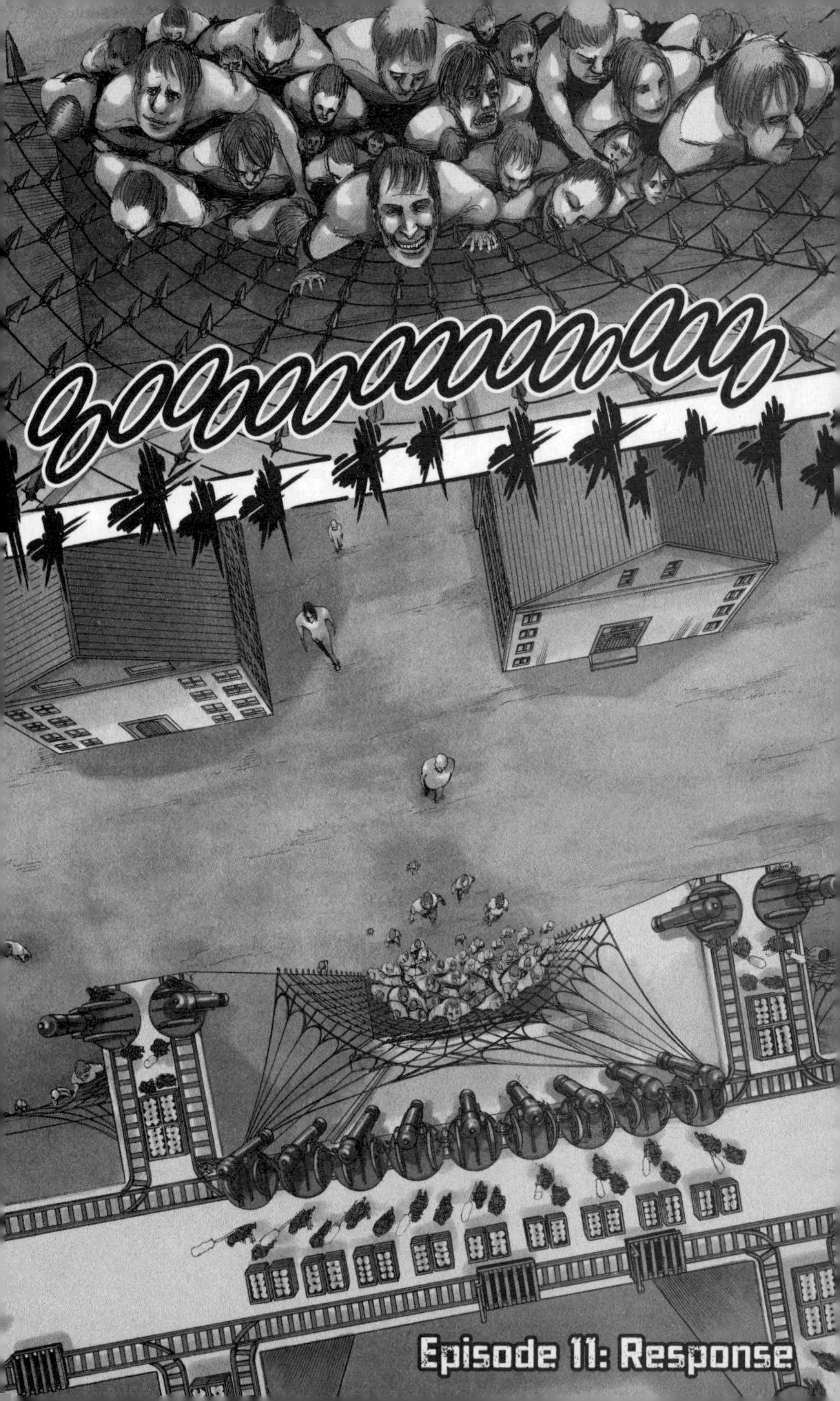
GOGOOOOOOOOOG
Episode 11: Response

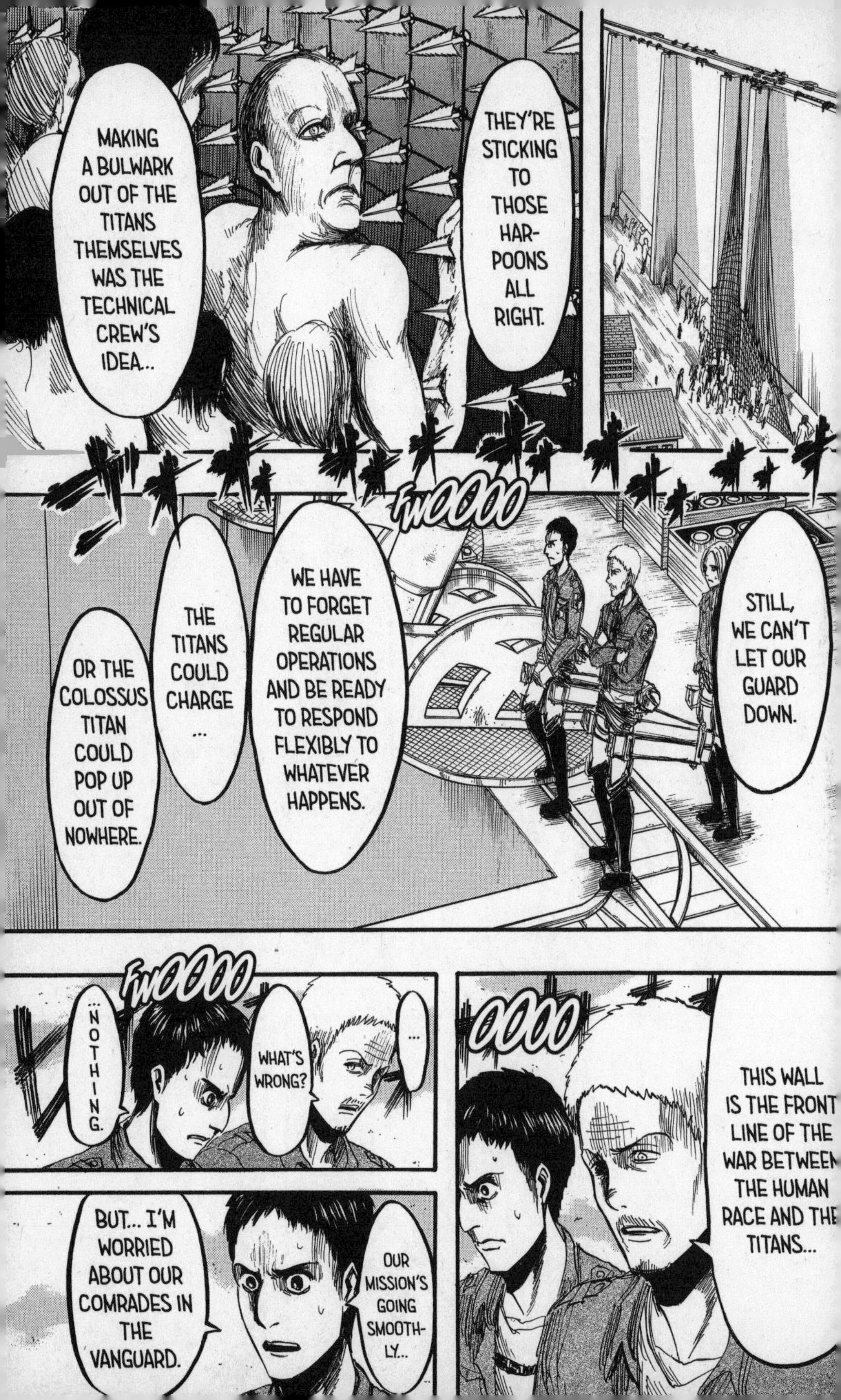

THEY'RE STICKING TO THOSE HAR-POONS ALL RIGHT.
MAKING A BULWARK OUT OF THE TITANS THEMSELVES WAS THE TECHNICAL CREW'S IDEA...
STILL, WE CAN'T LET OUR GUARD DOWN.
FWOOOO
WE HAVE TO FORGET REGULAR OPERATIONS AND BE READY TO RESPOND FLEXIBLY TO WHATEVER HAPPENS.
THE TITANS COULD CHARGE...
OR THE COLOSSUS TITAN COULD POP UP OUT OF NOWHERE.
OOOO
THIS WALL IS THE FRONT LINE OF THE WAR BETWEEN THE HUMAN RACE AND THE TITANS...
FWOOOO
...
WHAT'S WRONG?
...NOTHING.
OUR MISSION'S GOING SMOOTH-LY...
BUT... I'M WORRIED ABOUT OUR COMRADES IN THE VANGUARD.

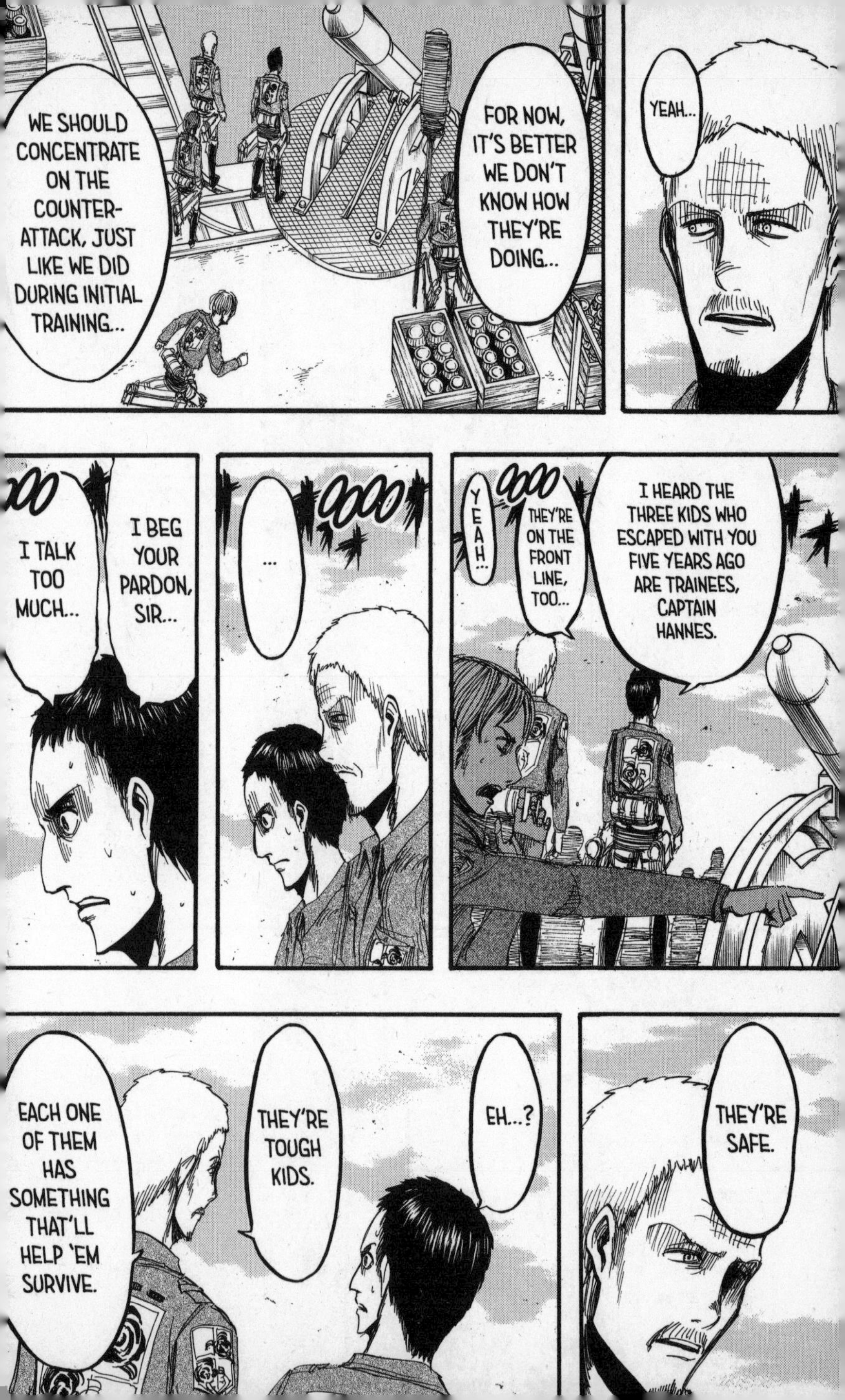
YEAH...
FOR NOW, IT'S BETTER WE DON'T KNOW HOW THEY'RE DOING...
WE SHOULD CONCENTRATE ON THE COUNTER-ATTACK, JUST LIKE WE DID DURING INITIAL TRAINING...
I HEARD THE THREE KIDS WHO ESCAPED WITH YOU FIVE YEARS AGO ARE TRAINEES, CAPTAIN HANNES.
THEY'RE ON THE FRONT LINE, TOO...
YEAH...
...
I BEG YOUR PARDON, SIR...
I TALK TOO MUCH...
THEY'RE SAFE.
EH...?
THEY'RE TOUGH KIDS.
EACH ONE OF THEM HAS SOMETHING THAT'LL HELP 'EM SURVIVE.

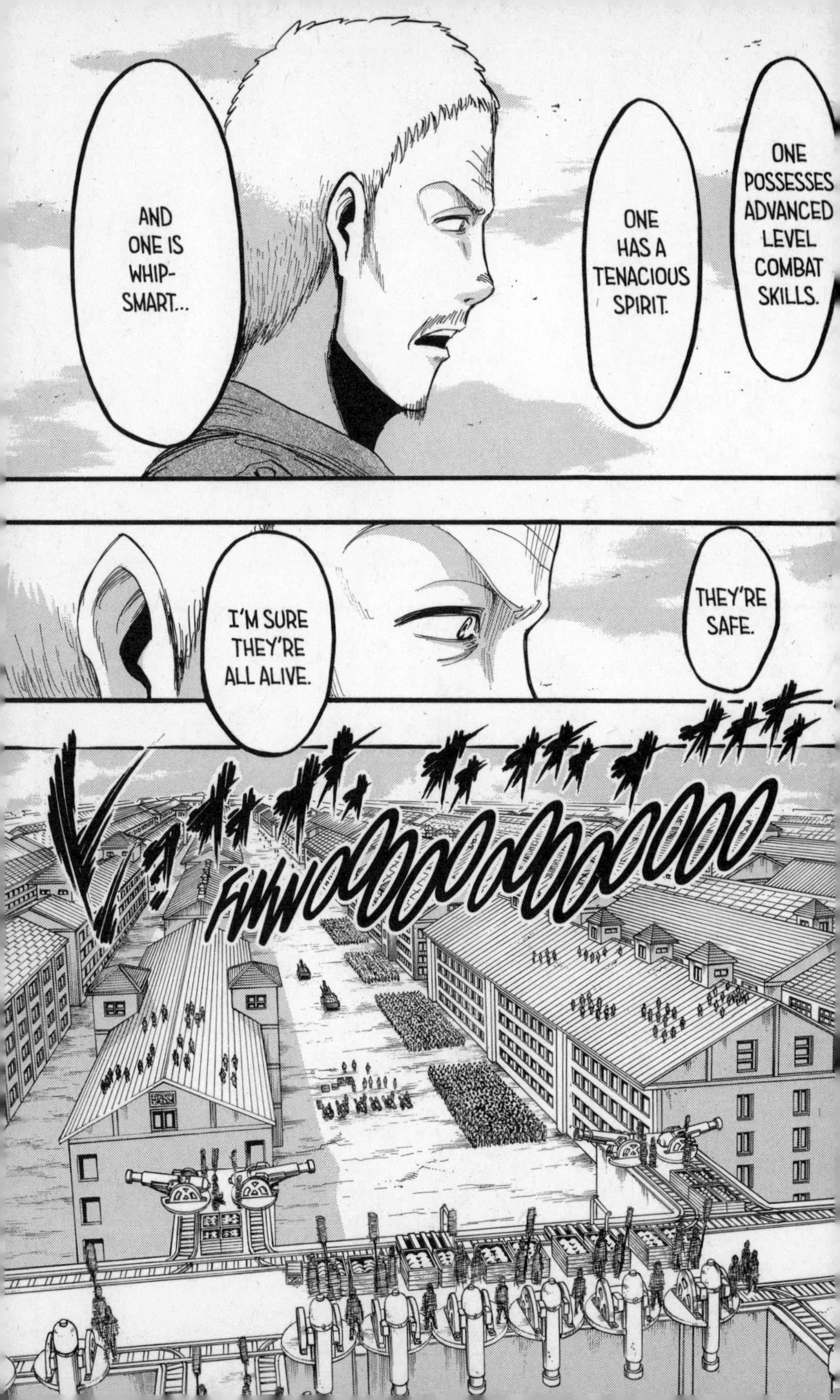
ONE POSSESSES ADVANCED LEVEL COMBAT SKILLS.
ONE HAS A TENACIOUS SPIRIT.
AND ONE IS WHIP-SMART...
THEY'RE SAFE.
I'M SURE THEY'RE ALL ALIVE.

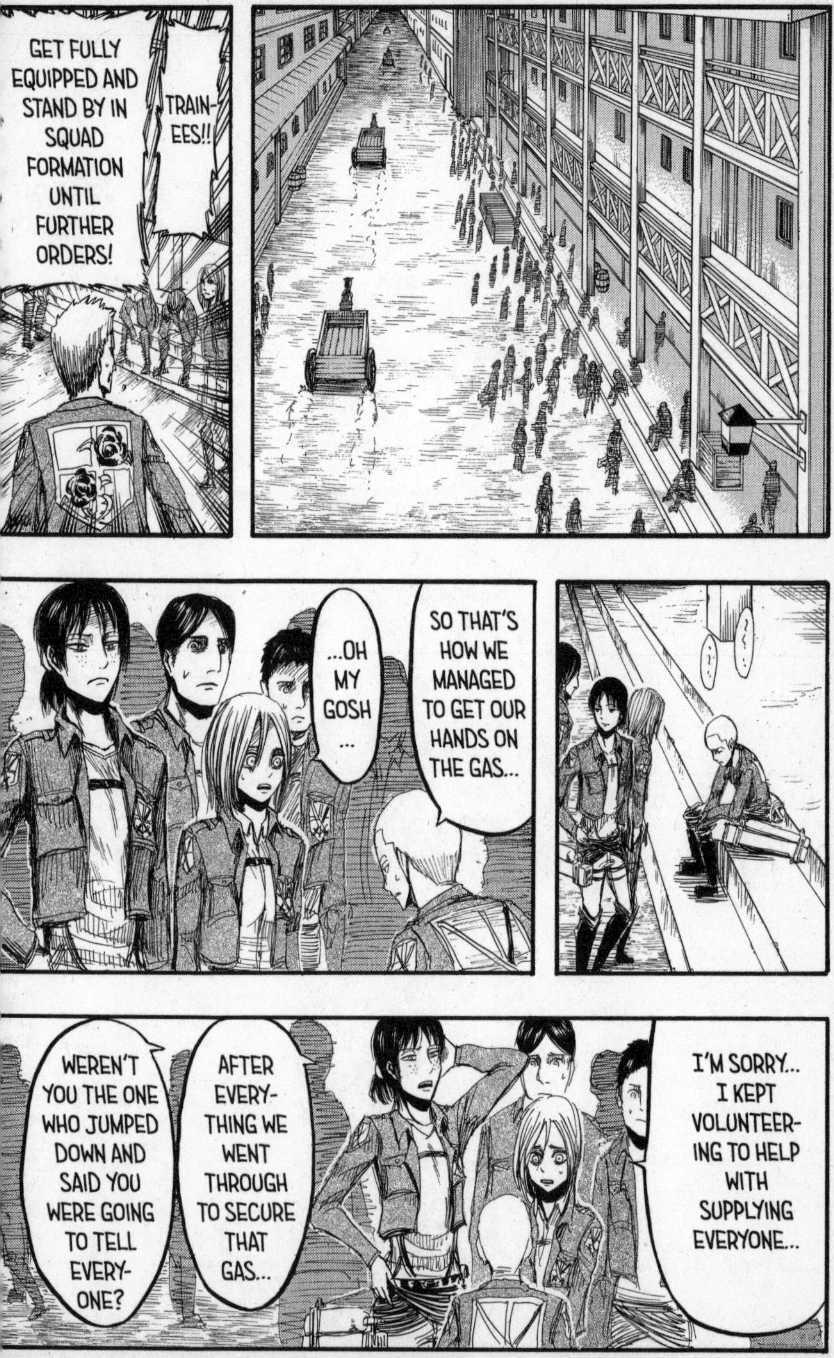

TRAIN-EES!!
GET FULLY EQUIPPED AND STAND BY IN SQUAD FORMATION UNTIL FURTHER ORDERS!
SO THAT'S HOW WE MANAGED TO GET OUR HANDS ON THE GAS...
...OH MY GOSH ...
I'M SORRY... I KEPT VOLUNTEER-ING TO HELP WITH SUPPLYING EVERYONE...
AFTER EVERY-THING WE WENT THROUGH TO SECURE THAT GAS...
WEREN'T YOU THE ONE WHO JUMPED DOWN AND SAID YOU WERE GOING TO TELL EVERY-ONE?

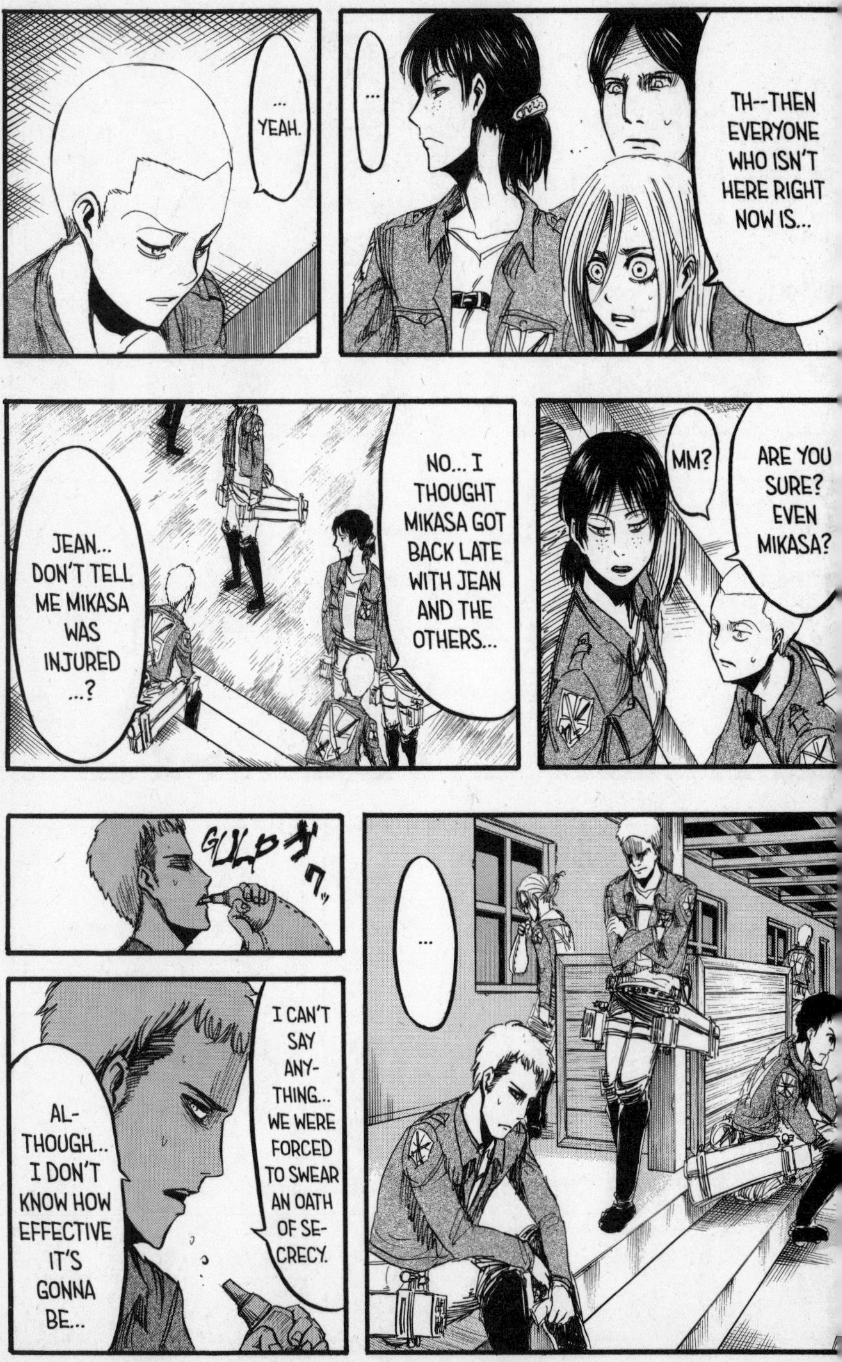

TH--THEN EVERYONE WHO ISN'T HERE RIGHT NOW IS...
...
... YEAH.
ARE YOU SURE? EVEN MIKASA?
MM?
NO... I THOUGHT MIKASA GOT BACK LATE WITH JEAN AND THE OTHERS...
JEAN... DON'T TELL ME MIKASA WAS INJURED ...?
...
GULP
I CAN'T SAY ANYTHING... WE WERE FORCED TO SWEAR AN OATH OF SECRECY.
AL-THOUGH... I DON'T KNOW HOW EFFECTIVE IT'S GONNA BE...

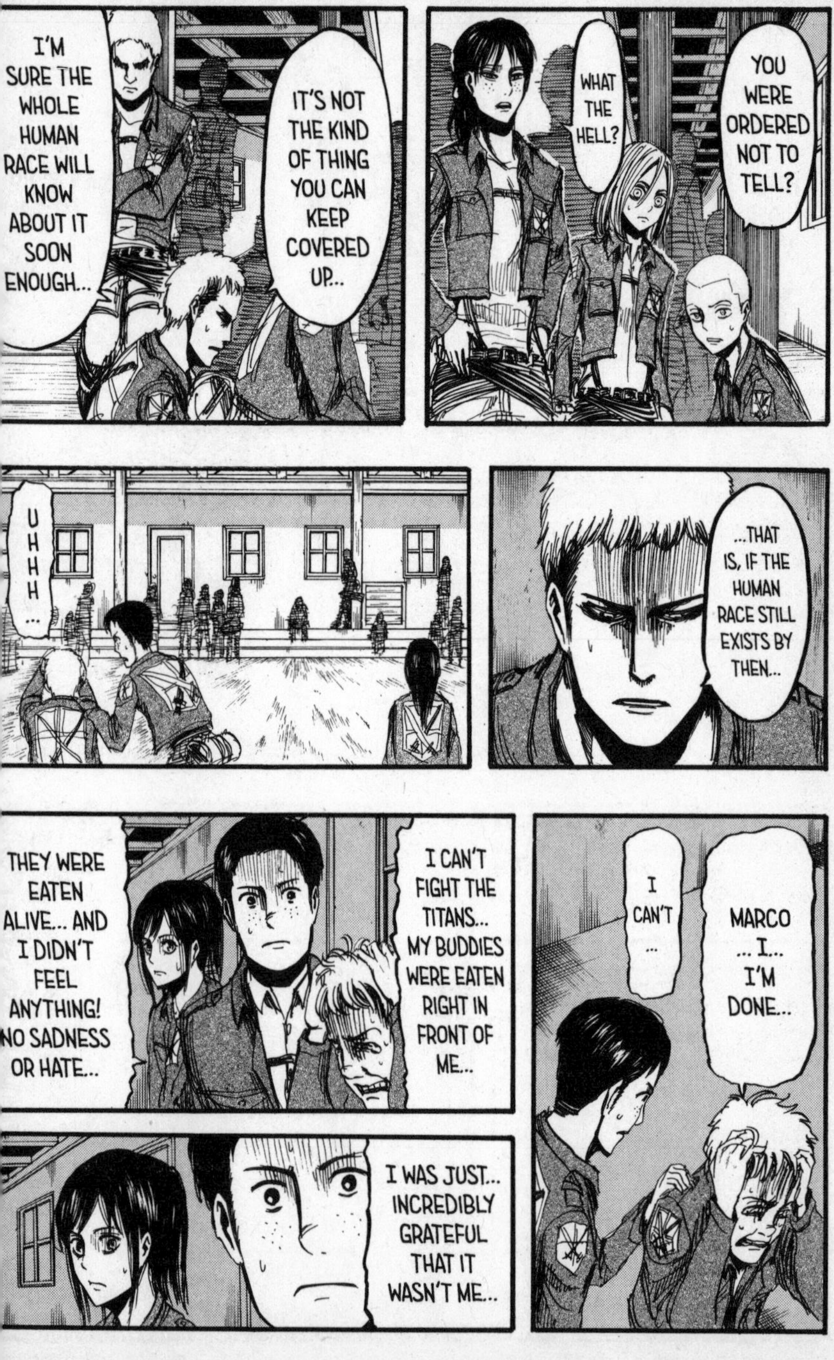
YOU WERE ORDERED NOT TO TELL?
WHAT THE HELL?
IT'S NOT THE KIND OF THING YOU CAN KEEP COVERED UP...
I'M SURE THE WHOLE HUMAN RACE WILL KNOW ABOUT IT SOON ENOUGH...
...THAT IS, IF THE HUMAN RACE STILL EXISTS BY THEN...
UHHH...
MARCO ... I... I'M DONE...
I CAN'T ...
I CAN'T FIGHT THE TITANS... MY BUDDIES WERE EATEN RIGHT IN FRONT OF ME...
THEY WERE EATEN ALIVE... AND I DIDN'T FEEL ANYTHING! NO SADNESS OR HATE...
I WAS JUST... INCREDIBLY GRATEFUL THAT IT WASN'T ME...

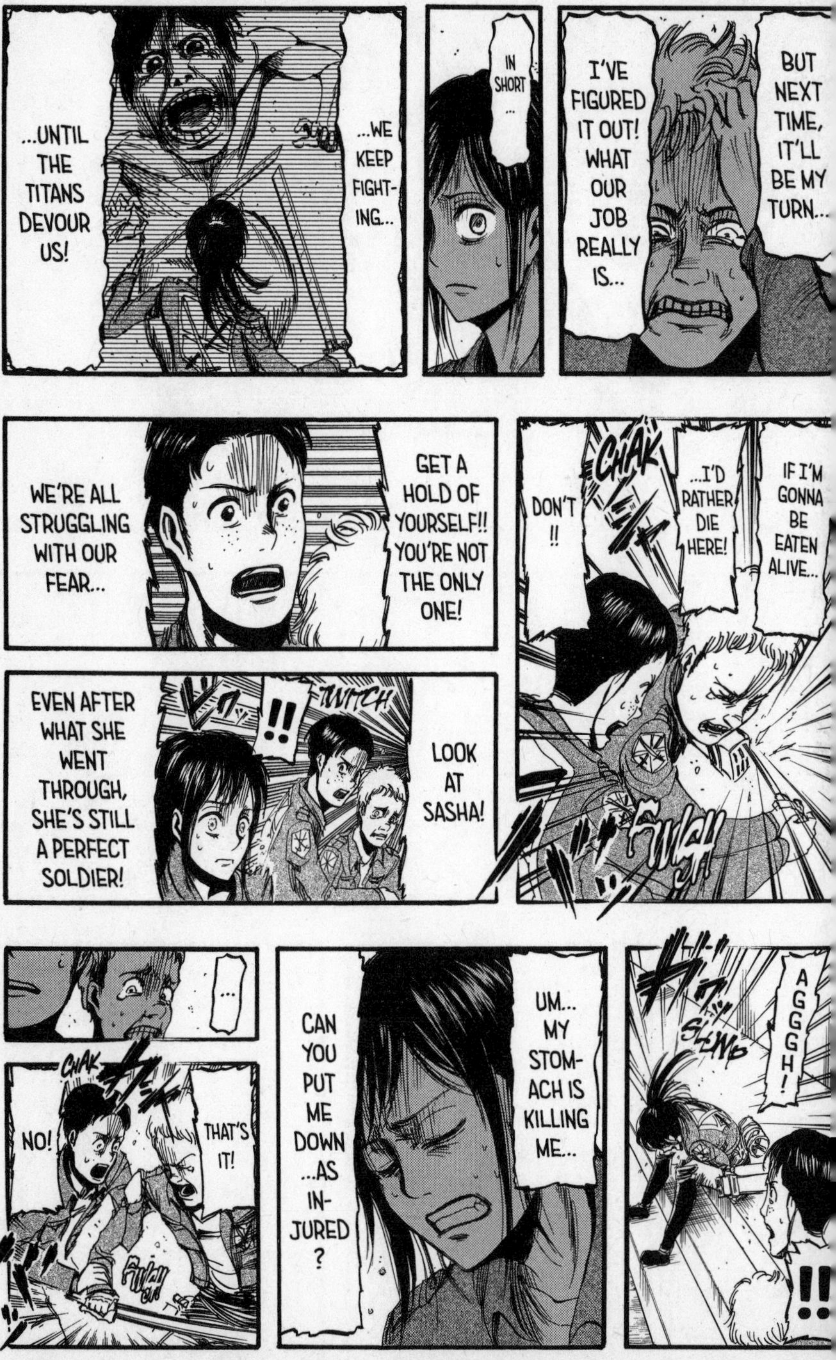
BUT NEXT TIME, IT'LL BE MY TURN...
I'VE FIGURED IT OUT! WHAT OUR JOB REALLY IS...
IN SHORT...
...WE KEEP FIGHTING...
...UNTIL THE TITANS DEVOUR US!
IF I'M GONNA BE EATEN ALIVE...
...I'D RATHER DIE HERE!
CHAK
DON'T !!
FWISH
GET A HOLD OF YOURSELF!! YOU'RE NOT THE ONLY ONE!
WE'RE ALL STRUGGLING WITH OUR FEAR...
LOOK AT SASHA!
TWITCH
!!
EVEN AFTER WHAT SHE WENT THROUGH, SHE'S STILL A PERFECT SOLDIER!
AGGGH!
SLUMP
!!
UM... MY STOMACH IS KILLING ME...
CAN YOU PUT ME DOWN ...AS INJURED?
...
THAT'S IT!
CHAK
NO!
FWISH

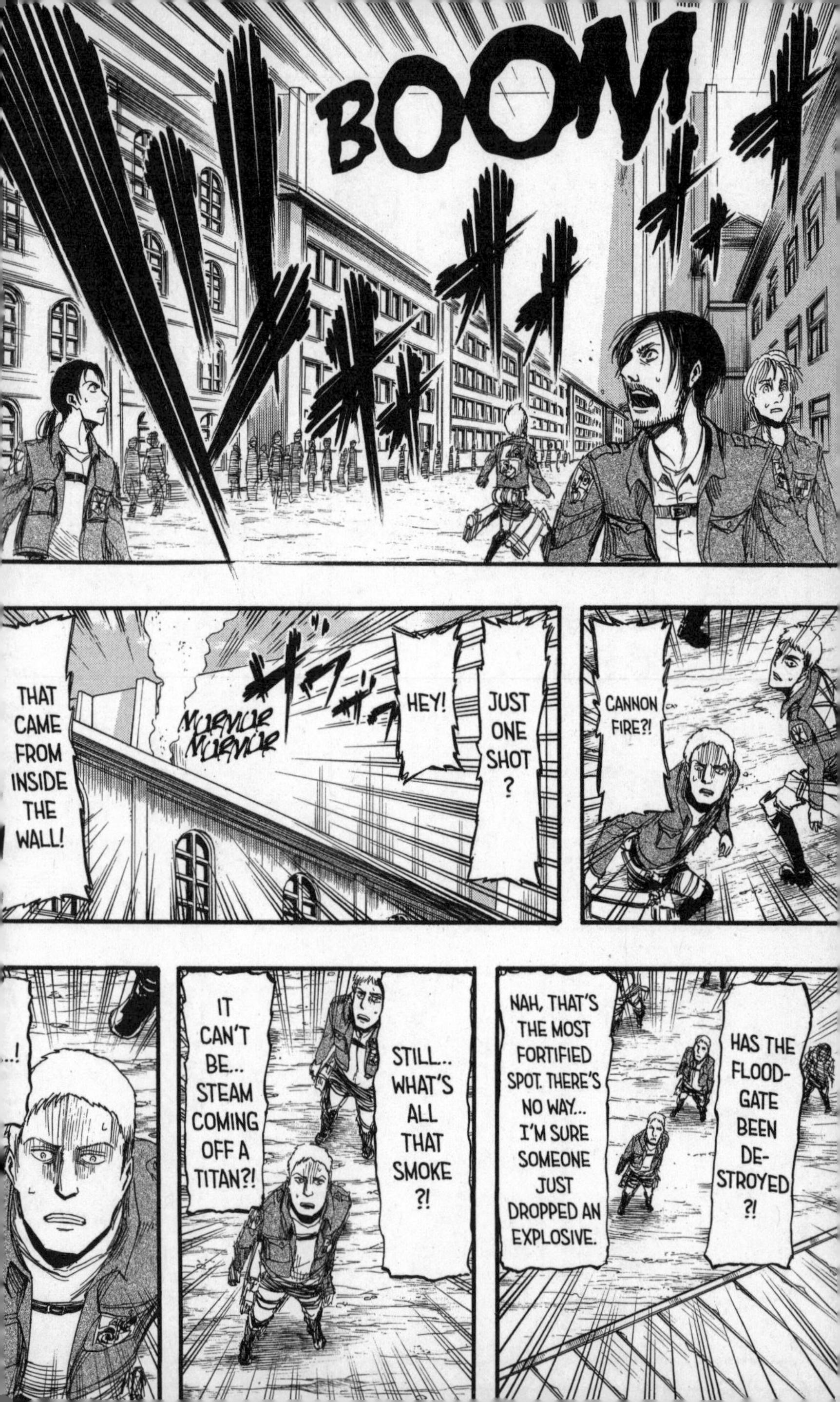
BOOM
CANNON FIRE?!
JUST ONE SHOT?
HEY!
MURMUR MURMUR
THAT CAME FROM INSIDE THE WALL!
HAS THE FLOODGATE BEEN DESTROYED?!
NAH, THAT'S THE MOST FORTIFIED SPOT. THERE'S NO WAY... I'M SURE SOMEONE JUST DROPPED AN EXPLOSIVE.
STILL... WHAT'S ALL THAT SMOKE?!
IT CAN'T BE... STEAM COMING OFF A TITAN?!
...!

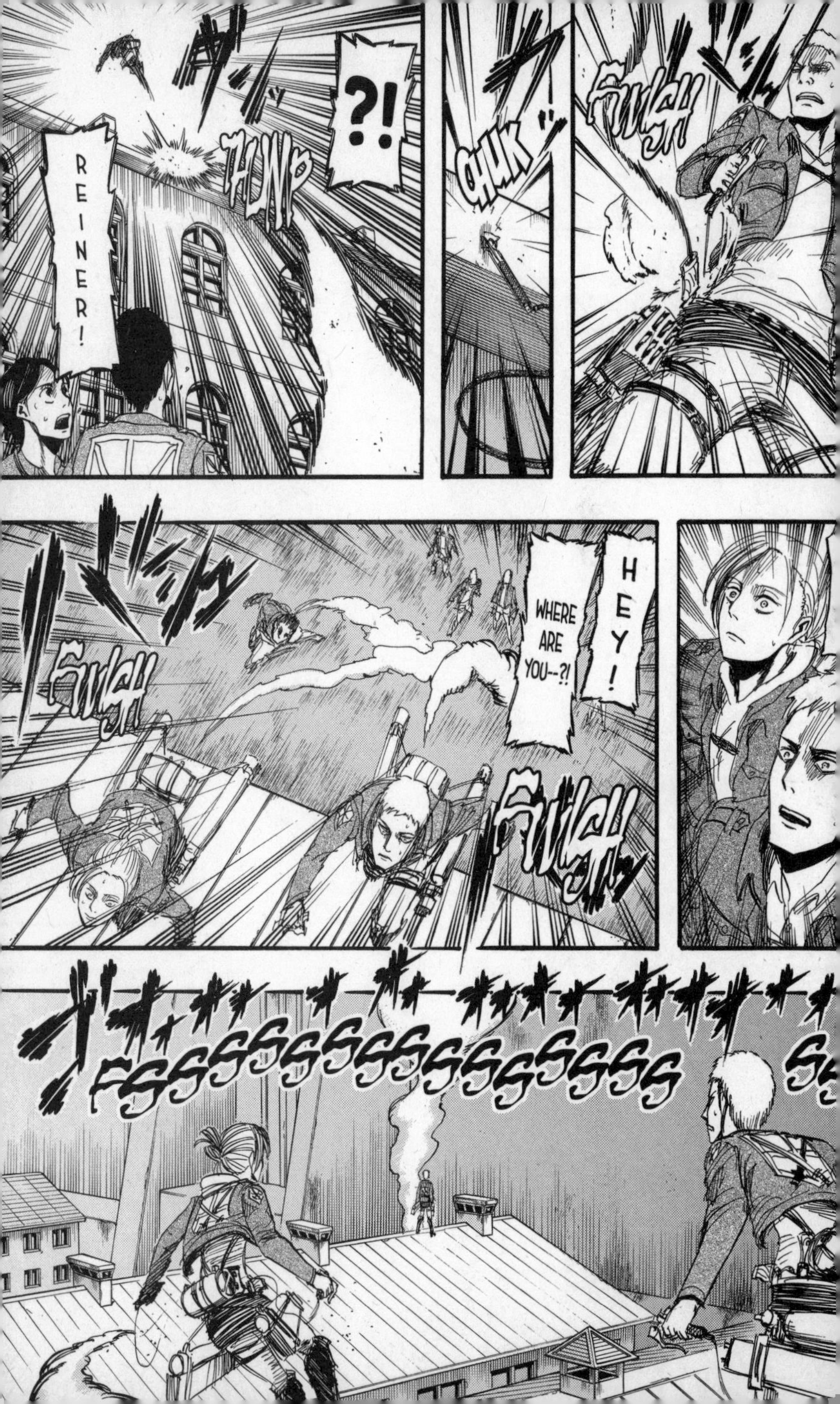

FWUSH
CHUK
?!
THWP
REINER!
HEY!
WHERE ARE YOU--?!
FWUSH
FWUSH
SS
FSSSSSSSSSSSSSSS

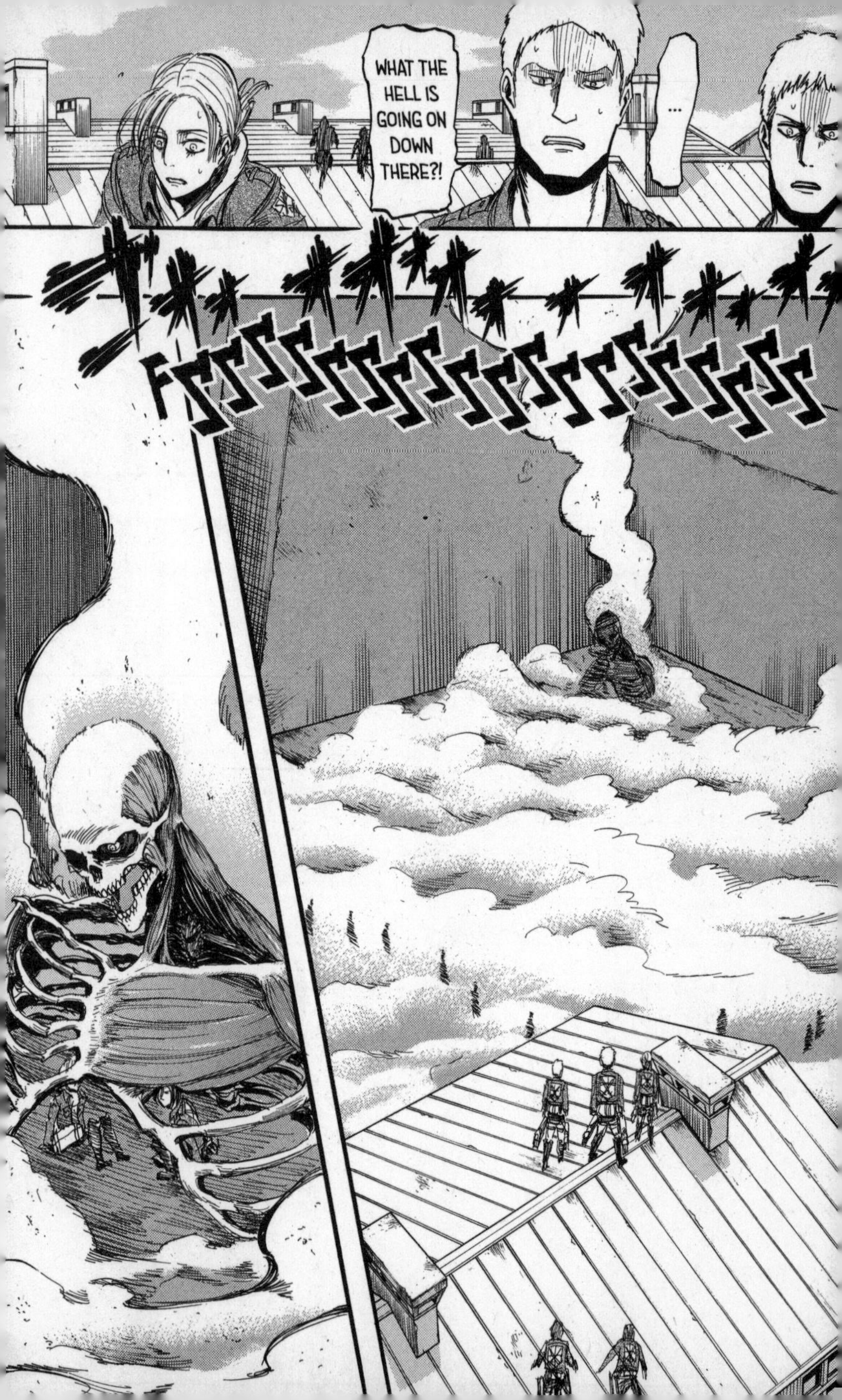
...
WHAT THE HELL IS GOING ON DOWN THERE?!
FSSSSSSSSSSSSSSSSSSS

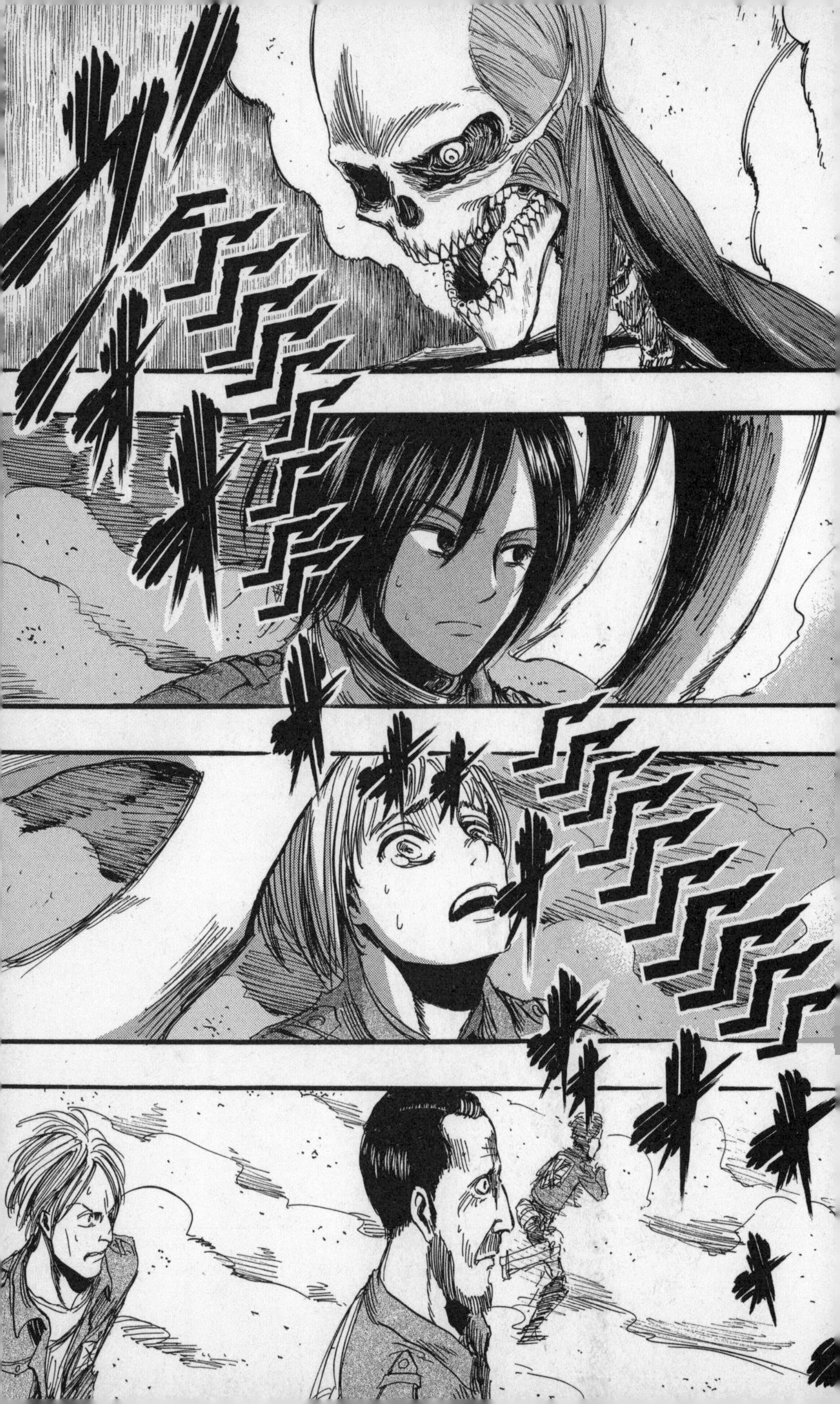

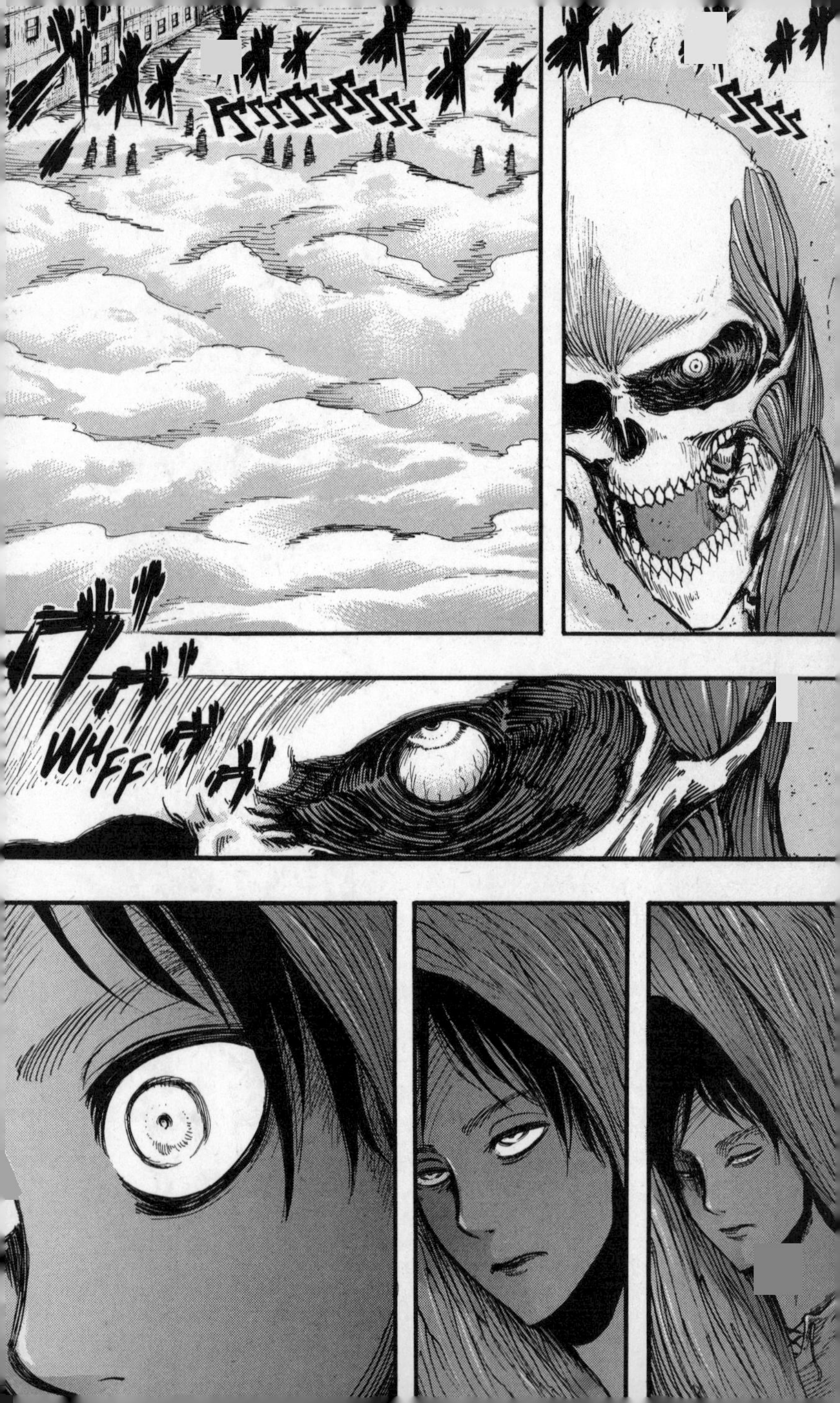
SSSSS
FSSSSSSSSS
WHFF

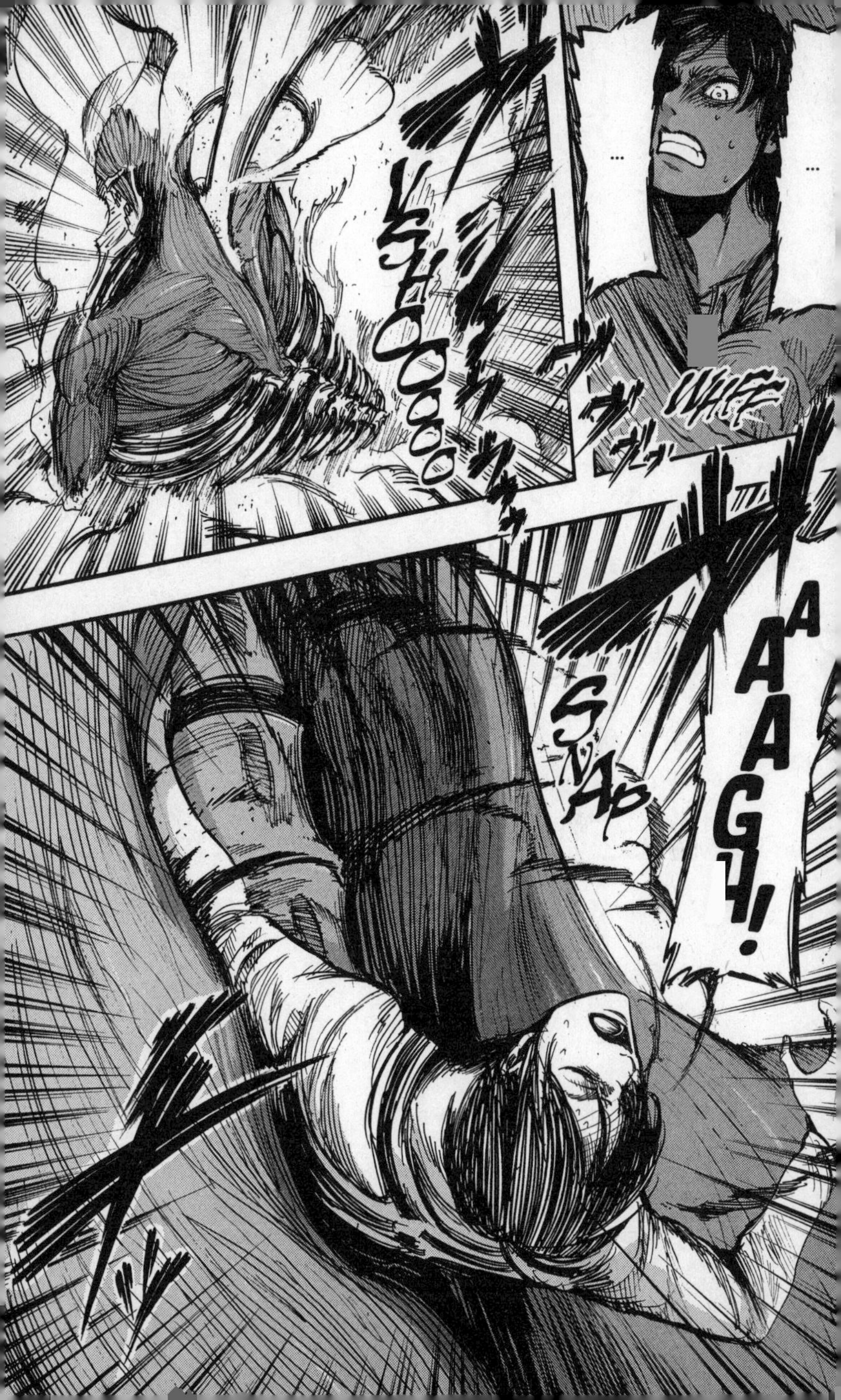
...
...
WAFF
VSHOOOOOOO
AAAGH!
SNAP

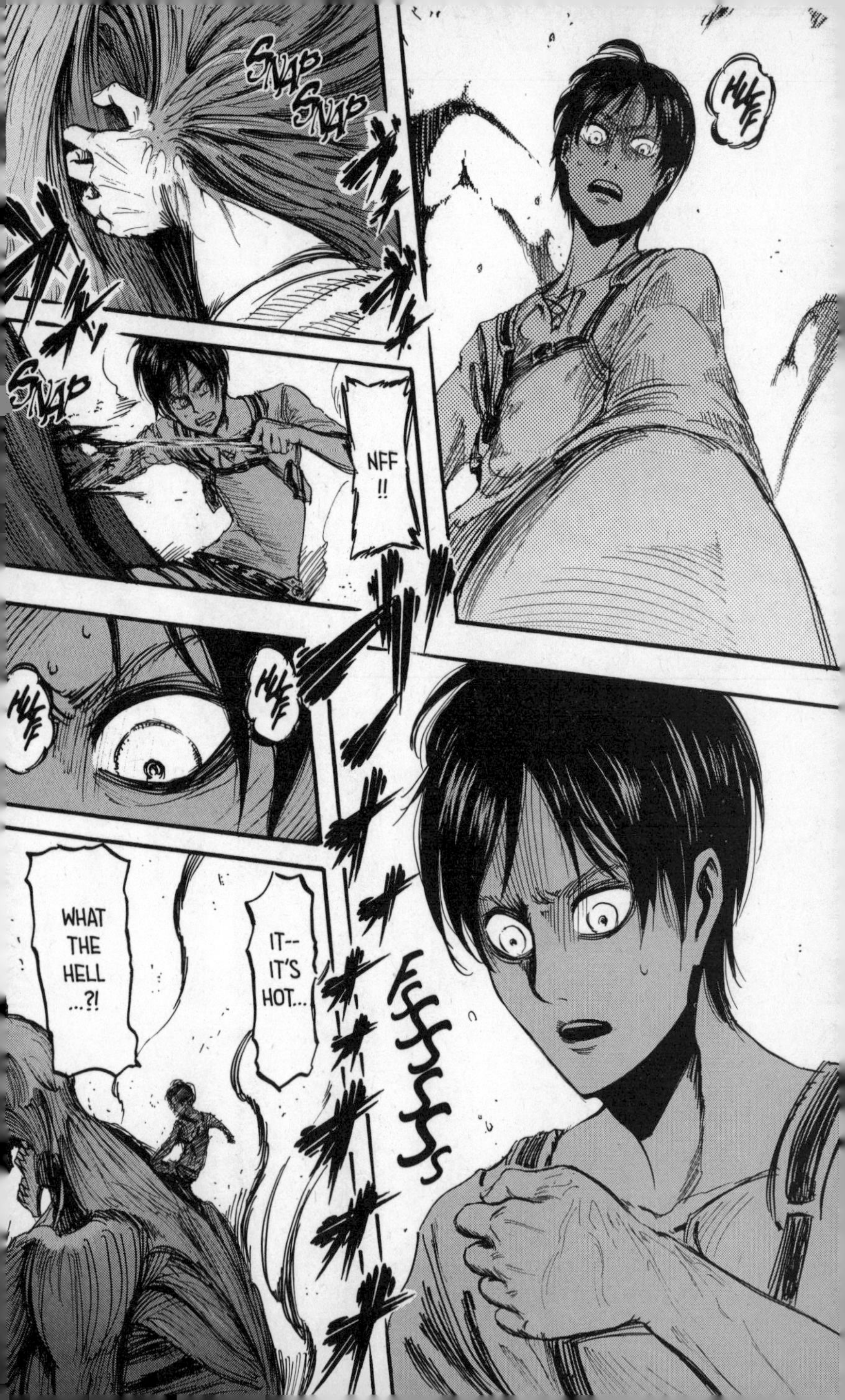
HUFF
SNAP SNAP
SNAP
NFF!!
HUFF
HUFF
FSSSSS
IT-- IT'S HOT...
WHAT THE HELL...?!

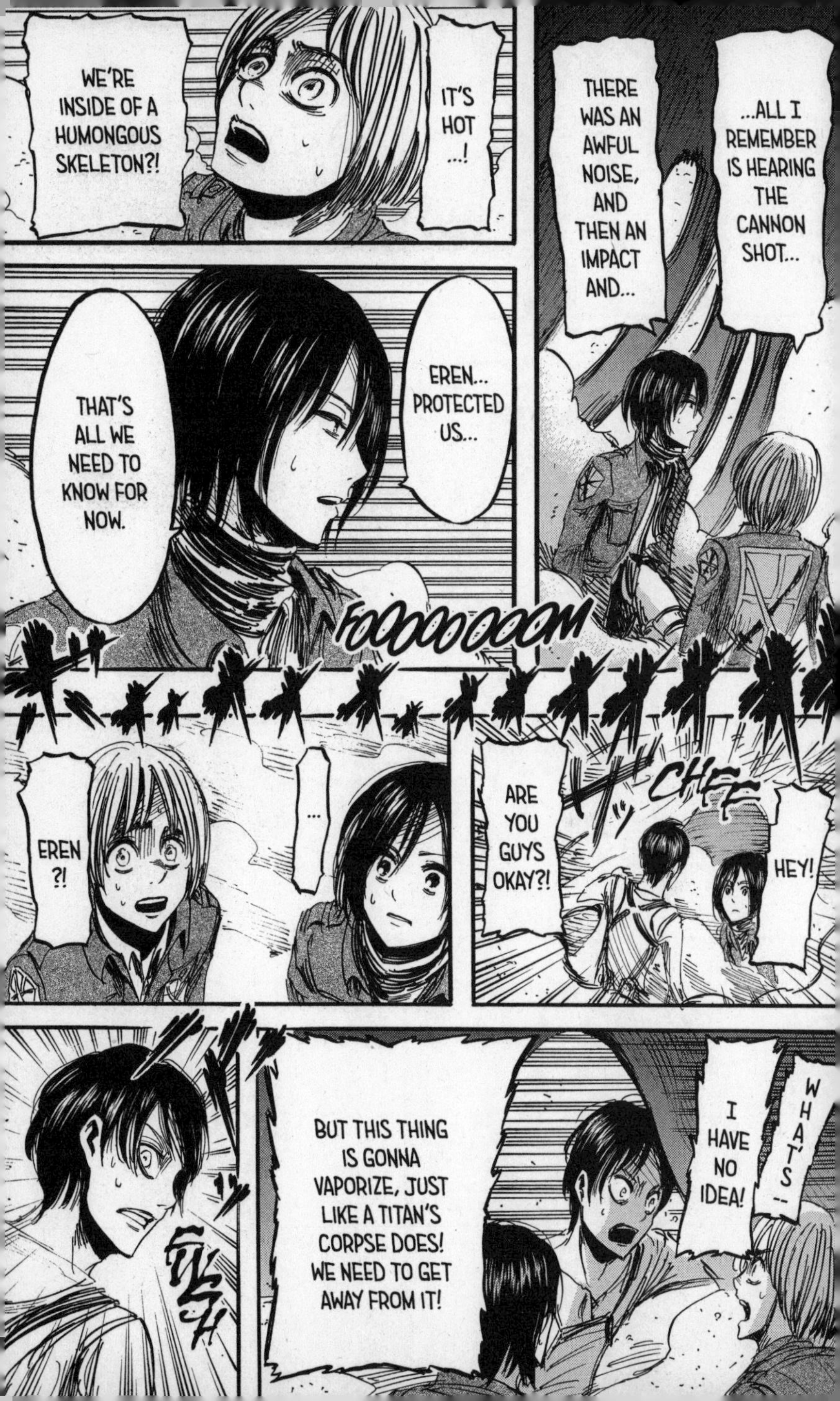
...ALL I REMEMBER IS HEARING THE CANNON SHOT...
THERE WAS AN AWFUL NOISE, AND THEN AN IMPACT AND...
IT'S HOT ...!
WE'RE INSIDE OF A HUMONGOUS SKELETON?!
EREN... PROTECTED US...
THAT'S ALL WE NEED TO KNOW FOR NOW.
FOOOOOOOM
HEY!
CHFF
ARE YOU GUYS OKAY?!
...
EREN ?!
WHAT'S--
I HAVE NO IDEA!
BUT THIS THING IS GONNA VAPORIZE, JUST LIKE A TITAN'S CORPSE DOES! WE NEED TO GET AWAY FROM IT!
FWSH!

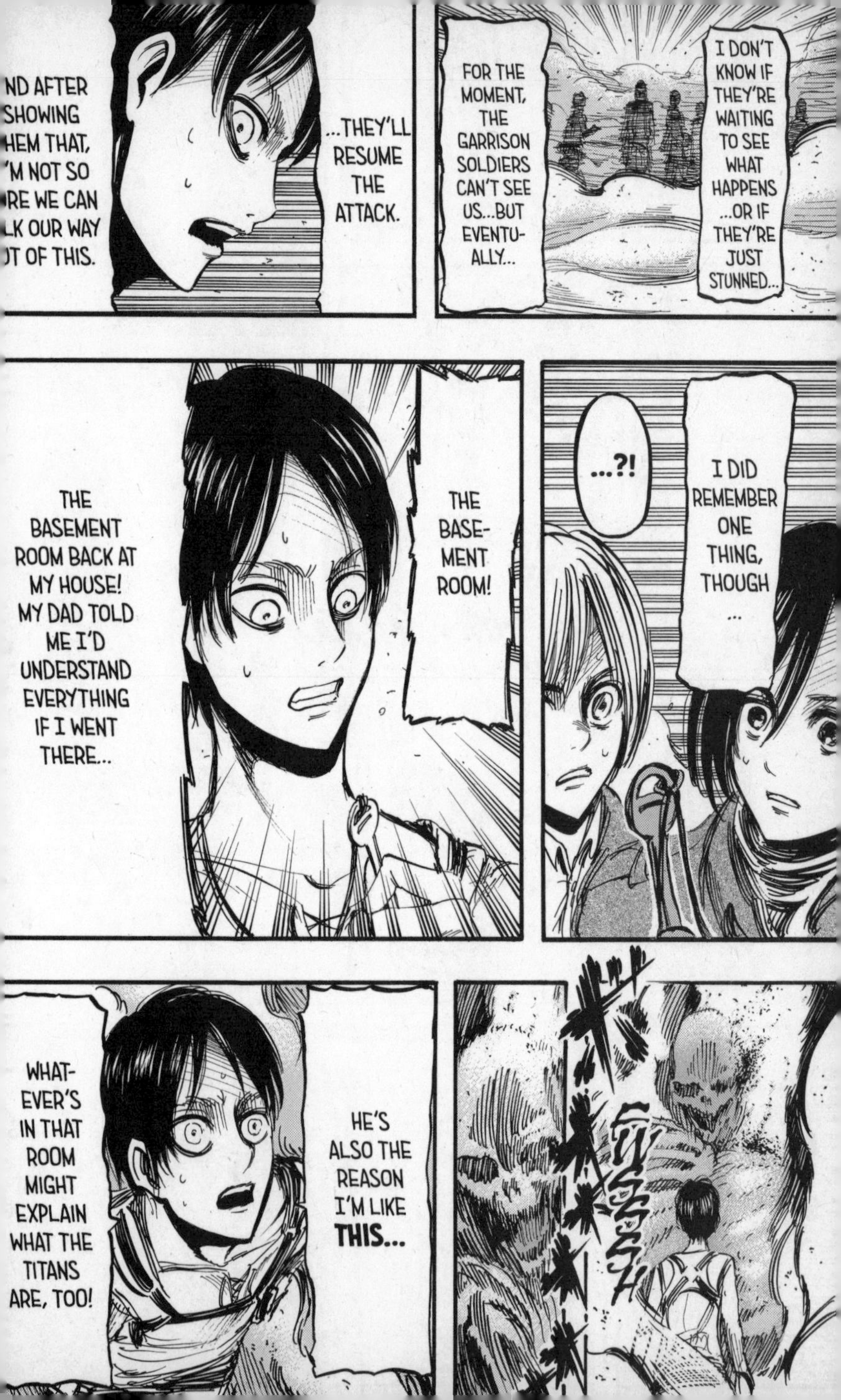
I DON'T KNOW IF THEY'RE WAITING TO SEE WHAT HAPPENS ...OR IF THEY'RE JUST STUNNED...
FOR THE MOMENT, THE GARRISON SOLDIERS CAN'T SEE US...BUT EVENTU-ALLY...
...THEY'LL RESUME THE ATTACK.
ND AFTER SHOWING HEM THAT, 'M NOT SO RE WE CAN LK OUR WAY UT OF THIS.
I DID REMEMBER ONE THING, THOUGH ...
...?!
THE BASE-MENT ROOM!
THE BASEMENT ROOM BACK AT MY HOUSE! MY DAD TOLD ME I'D UNDERSTAND EVERYTHING IF I WENT THERE...
HE'S ALSO THE REASON I'M LIKE **THIS...**
WHAT-EVER'S IN THAT ROOM MIGHT EXPLAIN WHAT THE TITANS ARE, TOO!

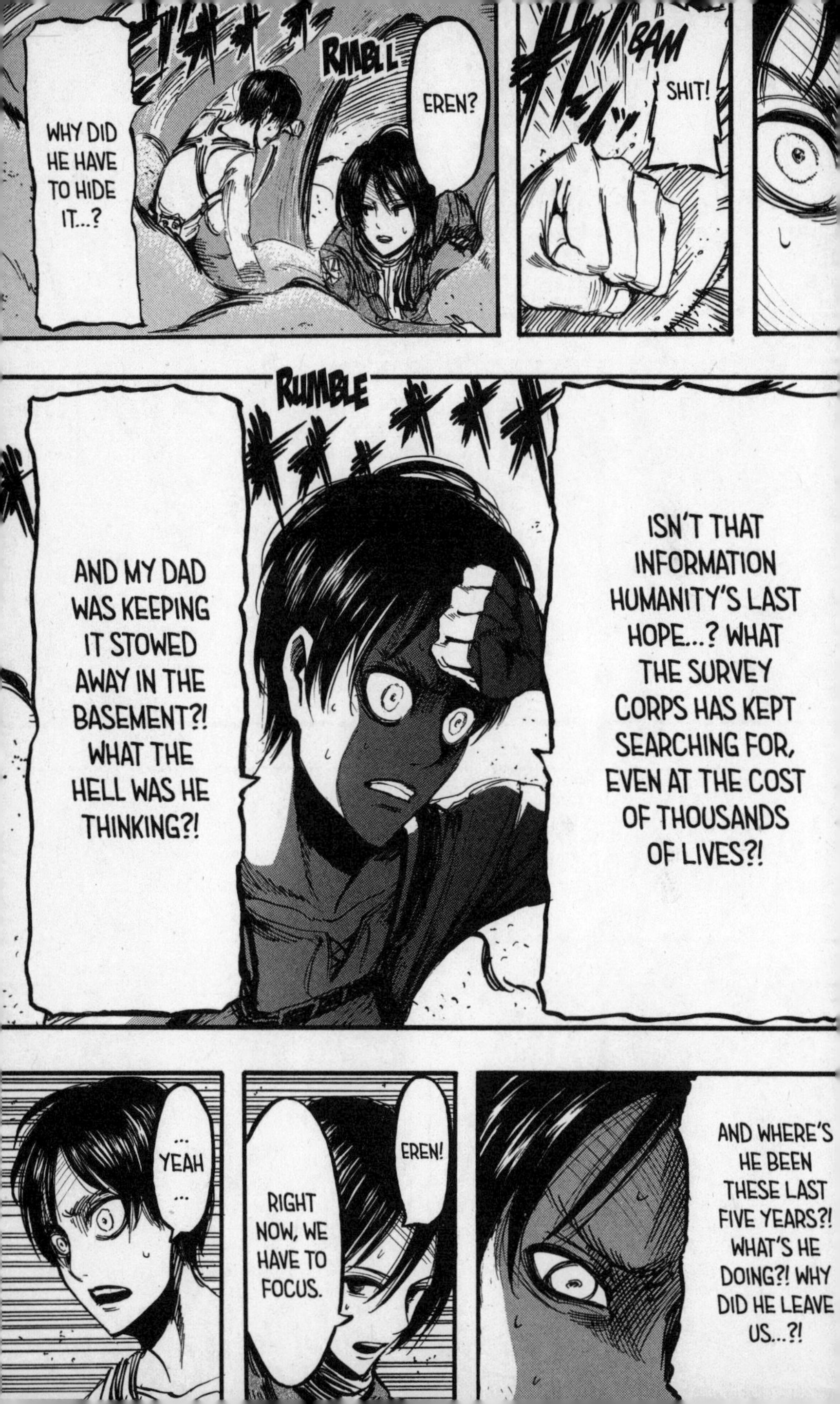
BAM
SHIT!
EREN?
RMBLL
WHY DID HE HAVE TO HIDE IT...?
RUMBLE
ISN'T THAT INFORMATION HUMANITY'S LAST HOPE...? WHAT THE SURVEY CORPS HAS KEPT SEARCHING FOR, EVEN AT THE COST OF THOUSANDS OF LIVES?!
AND MY DAD WAS KEEPING IT STOWED AWAY IN THE BASEMENT?! WHAT THE HELL WAS HE THINKING?!
AND WHERE'S HE BEEN THESE LAST FIVE YEARS?! WHAT'S HE DOING?! WHY DID HE LEAVE US...?!
EREN!
RIGHT NOW, WE HAVE TO FOCUS.
... YEAH ...

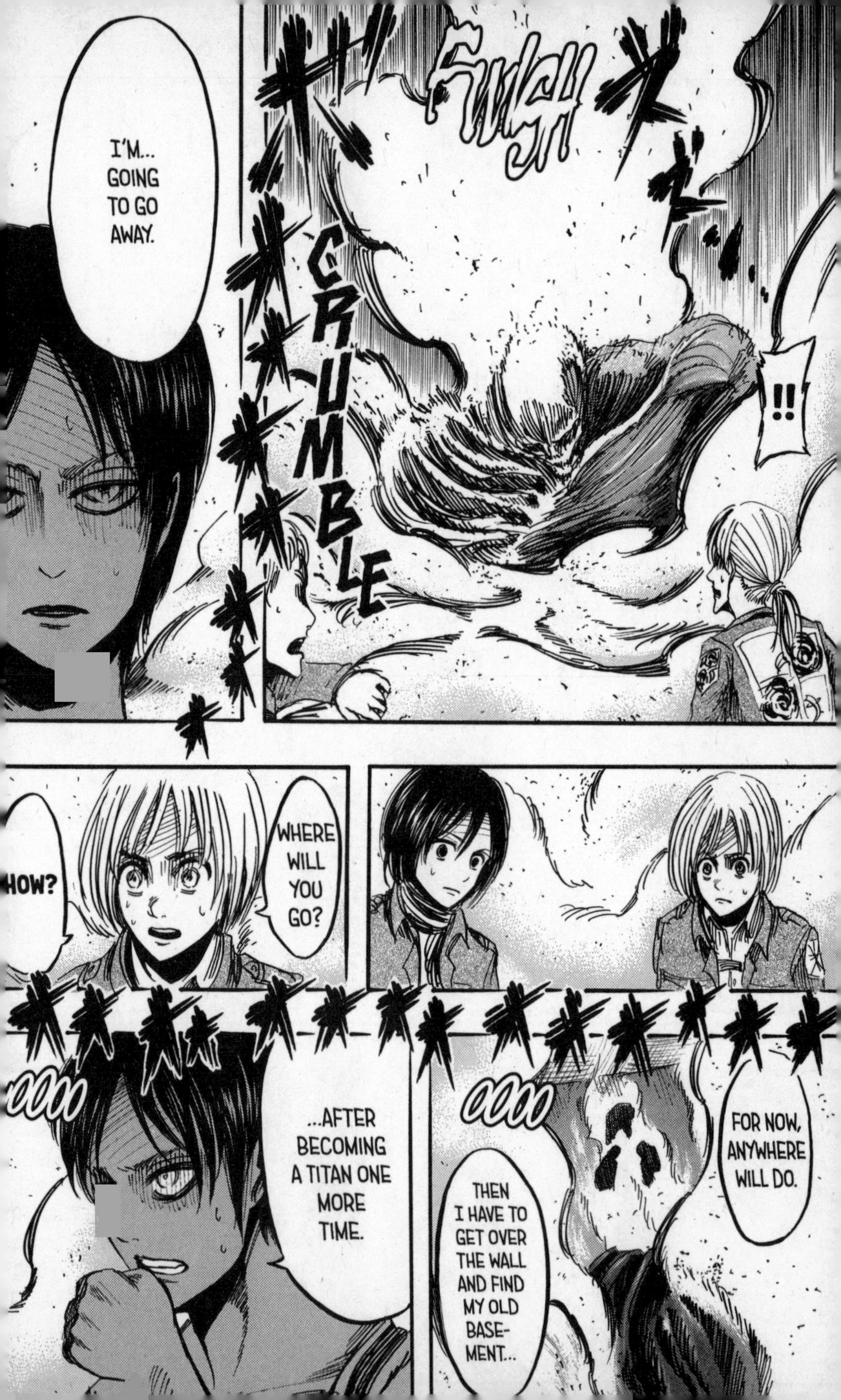
CRUMBLE
!!
I'M... GOING TO GO AWAY.
WHERE WILL YOU GO?
HOW?
FOR NOW, ANYWHERE WILL DO.
THEN I HAVE TO GET OVER THE WALL AND FIND MY OLD BASE-MENT...
...AFTER BECOMING A TITAN ONE MORE TIME.

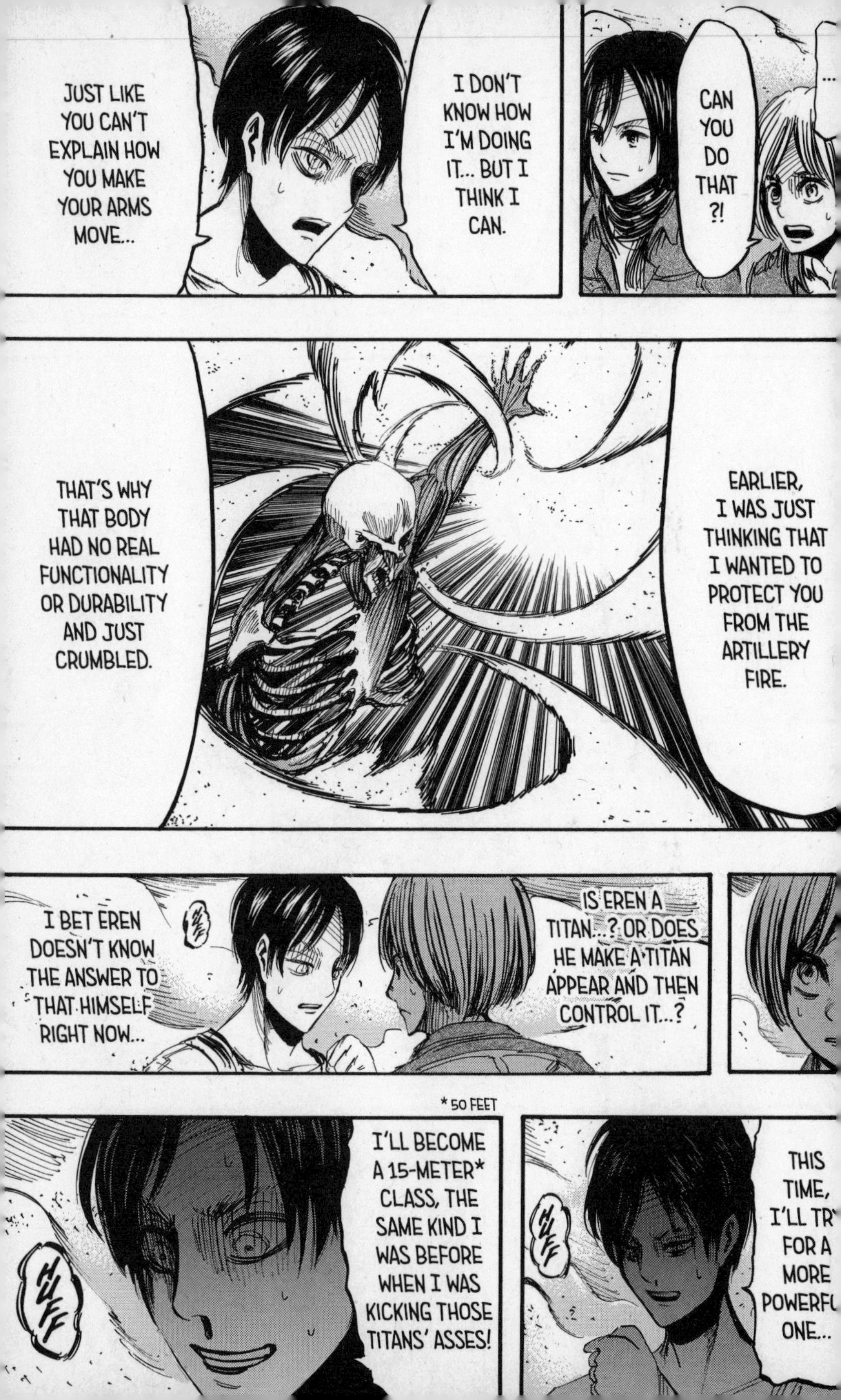
...
CAN YOU DO THAT?!
I DON'T KNOW HOW I'M DOING IT... BUT I THINK I CAN.
JUST LIKE YOU CAN'T EXPLAIN HOW YOU MAKE YOUR ARMS MOVE...
EARLIER, I WAS JUST THINKING THAT I WANTED TO PROTECT YOU FROM THE ARTILLERY FIRE.
THAT'S WHY THAT BODY HAD NO REAL FUNCTIONALITY OR DURABILITY AND JUST CRUMBLED.
IS EREN A TITAN...? OR DOES HE MAKE A TITAN APPEAR AND THEN CONTROL IT...?
I BET EREN DOESN'T KNOW THE ANSWER TO THAT HIMSELF RIGHT NOW...
HUFF
THIS TIME, I'LL TR
FOR A MORE POWERF
ONE...
I'LL BECOME A 15-METER* CLASS, THE SAME KIND I WAS BEFORE WHEN I WAS KICKING THOSE TITANS' ASSES!
HUFF
* 50 FEET

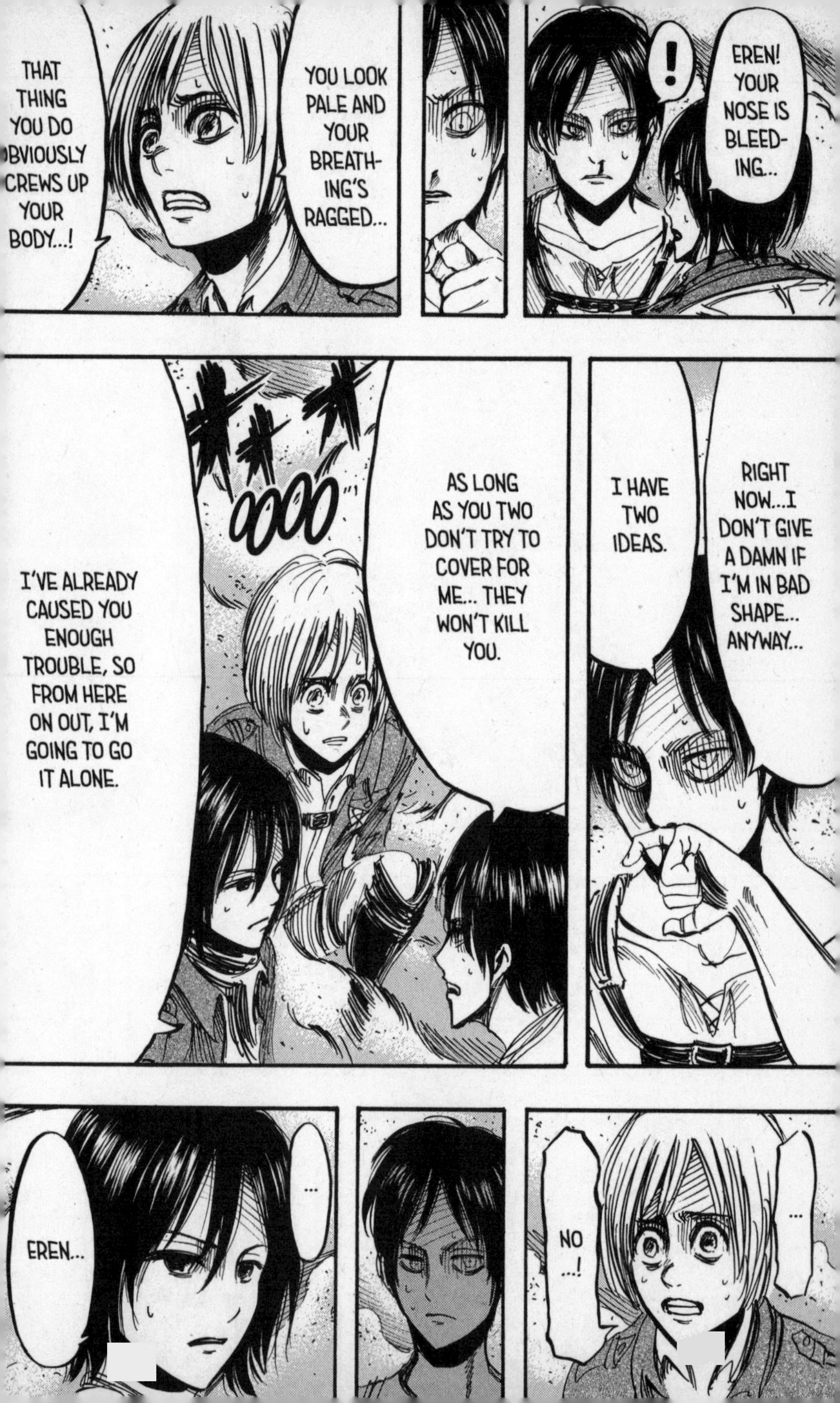
!
EREN! YOUR NOSE IS BLEED-ING...
YOU LOOK PALE AND YOUR BREATH-ING'S RAGGED...
THAT THING YOU DO BVIOUSLY CREWS UP YOUR BODY...!
RIGHT NOW...I DON'T GIVE A DAMN IF I'M IN BAD SHAPE... ANYWAY...
I HAVE TWO IDEAS.
OOOO
AS LONG AS YOU TWO DON'T TRY TO COVER FOR ME... THEY WON'T KILL YOU.
I'VE ALREADY CAUSED YOU ENOUGH TROUBLE, SO FROM HERE ON OUT, I'M GOING TO GO IT ALONE.
...
NO ...!
...
EREN...

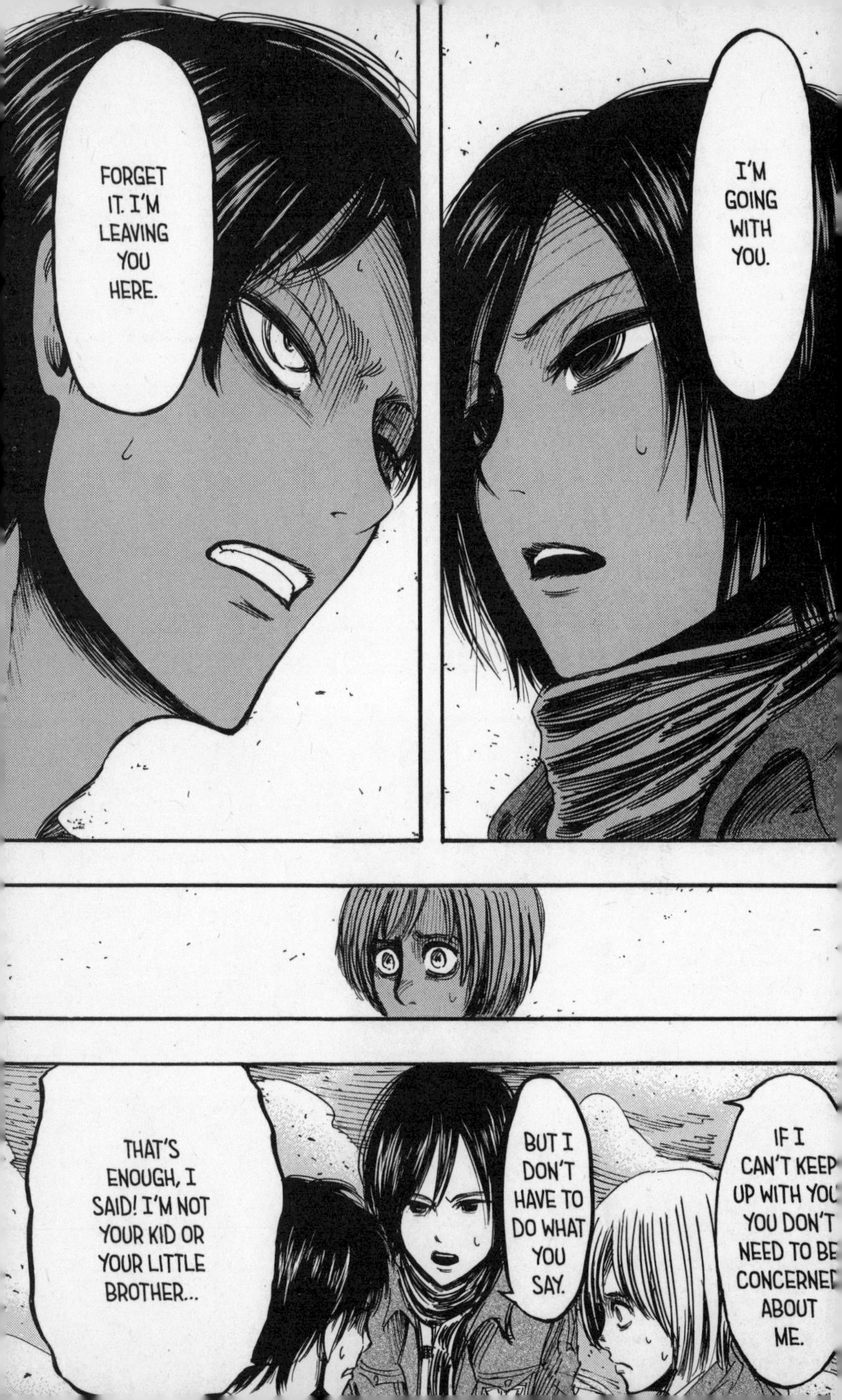
I'M GOING WITH YOU.
FORGET IT. I'M LEAVING YOU HERE.
IF I CAN'T KEEP UP WITH YOU YOU DON'T NEED TO BE CONCERNED ABOUT ME.
BUT I DON'T HAVE TO DO WHAT YOU SAY.
THAT'S ENOUGH, I SAID! I'M NOT YOUR KID OR YOUR LITTLE BROTHER...

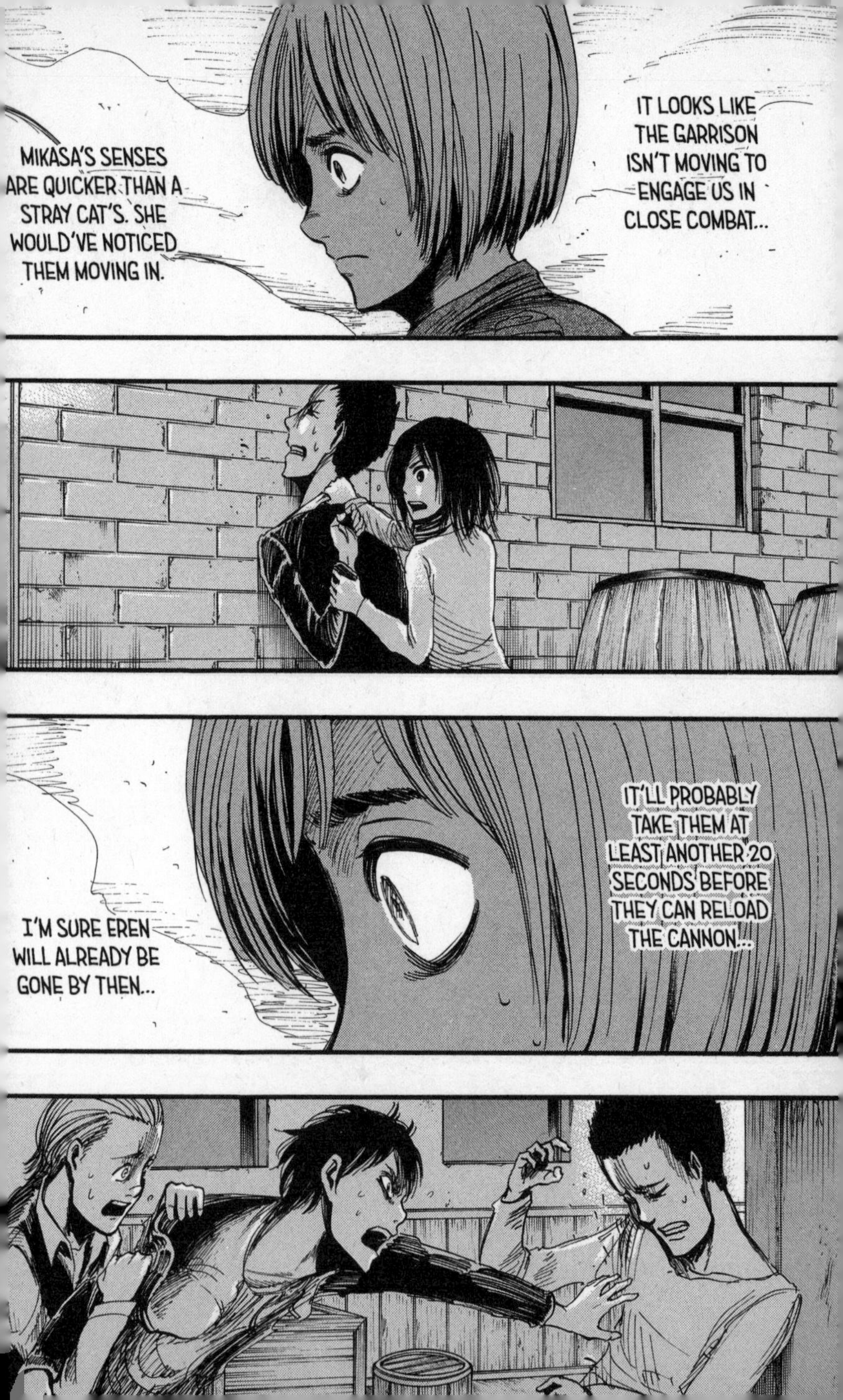
IT LOOKS LIKE THE GARRISON ISN'T MOVING TO ENGAGE US IN CLOSE COMBAT...
MIKASA'S SENSES ARE QUICKER THAN A STRAY CAT'S. SHE WOULD'VE NOTICED THEM MOVING IN.
IT'LL PROBABLY TAKE THEM AT LEAST ANOTHER 20 SECONDS BEFORE THEY CAN RELOAD THE CANNON...
I'M SURE EREN WILL ALREADY BE GONE BY THEN...

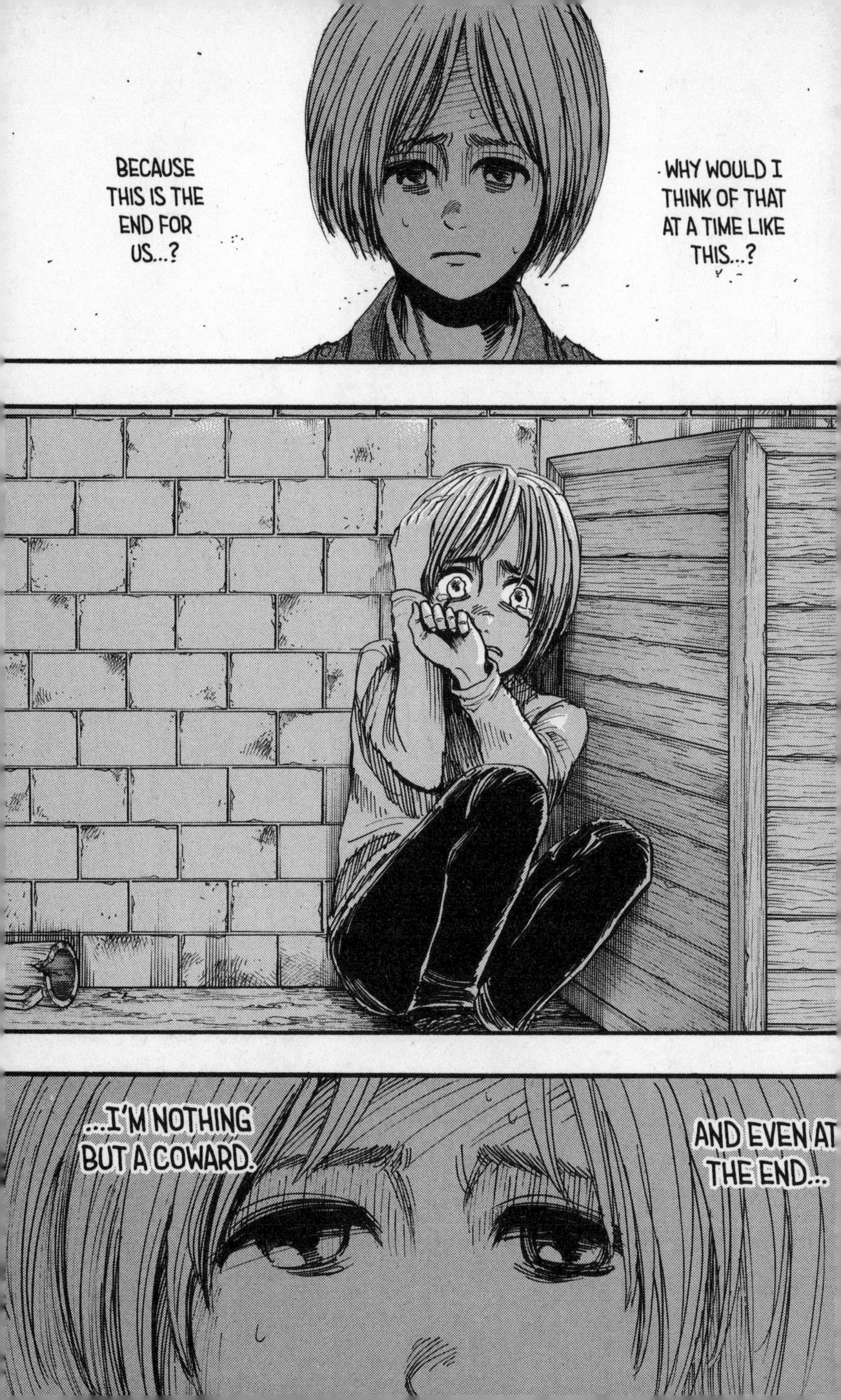
WHY WOULD I THINK OF THAT AT A TIME LIKE THIS...?
BECAUSE THIS IS THE END FOR US...?
AND EVEN AT THE END...
...I'M NOTHING BUT A COWARD.

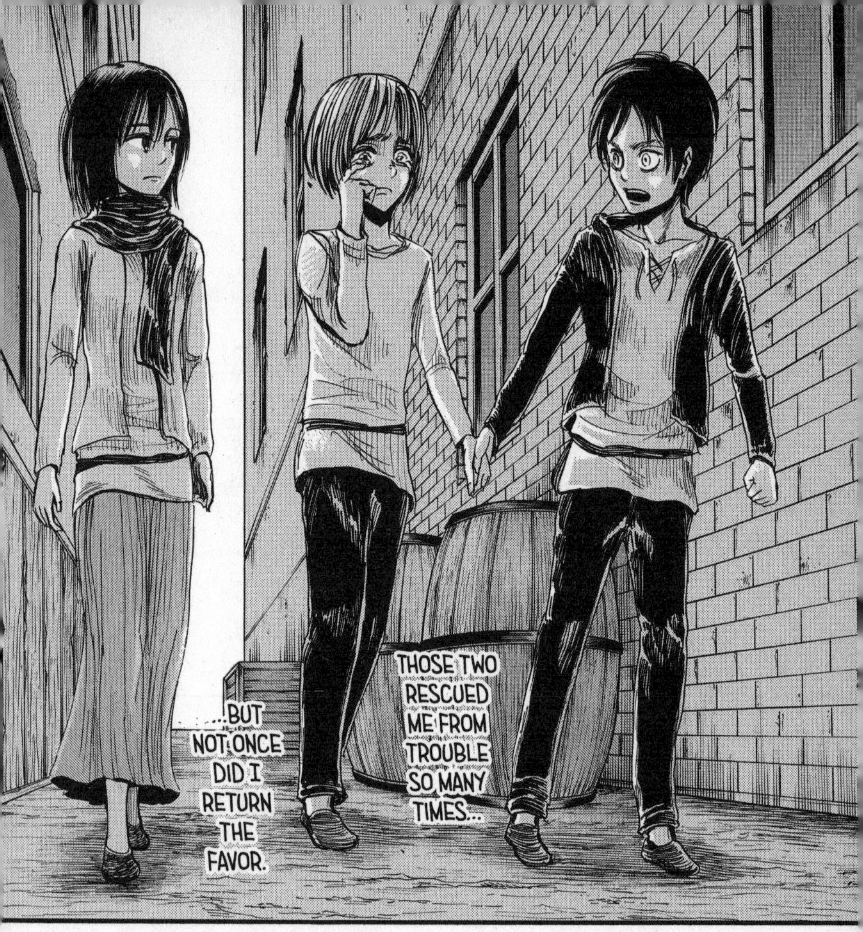
THOSE TWO RESCUED ME FROM TROUBLE SO MANY TIMES...
...BUT NOT ONCE DID I RETURN THE FAVOR.

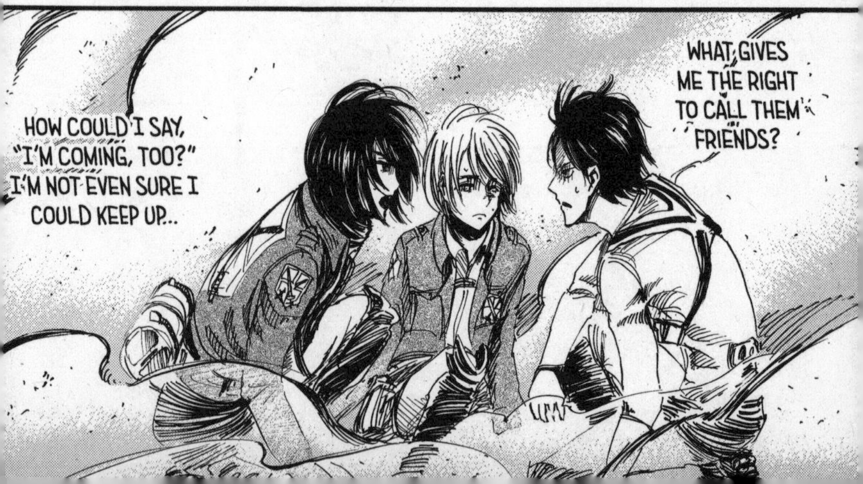
WHAT GIVES ME THE RIGHT TO CALL THEM FRIENDS?
HOW COULD I SAY, "I'M COMING, TOO?" I'M NOT EVEN SURE I COULD KEEP UP...

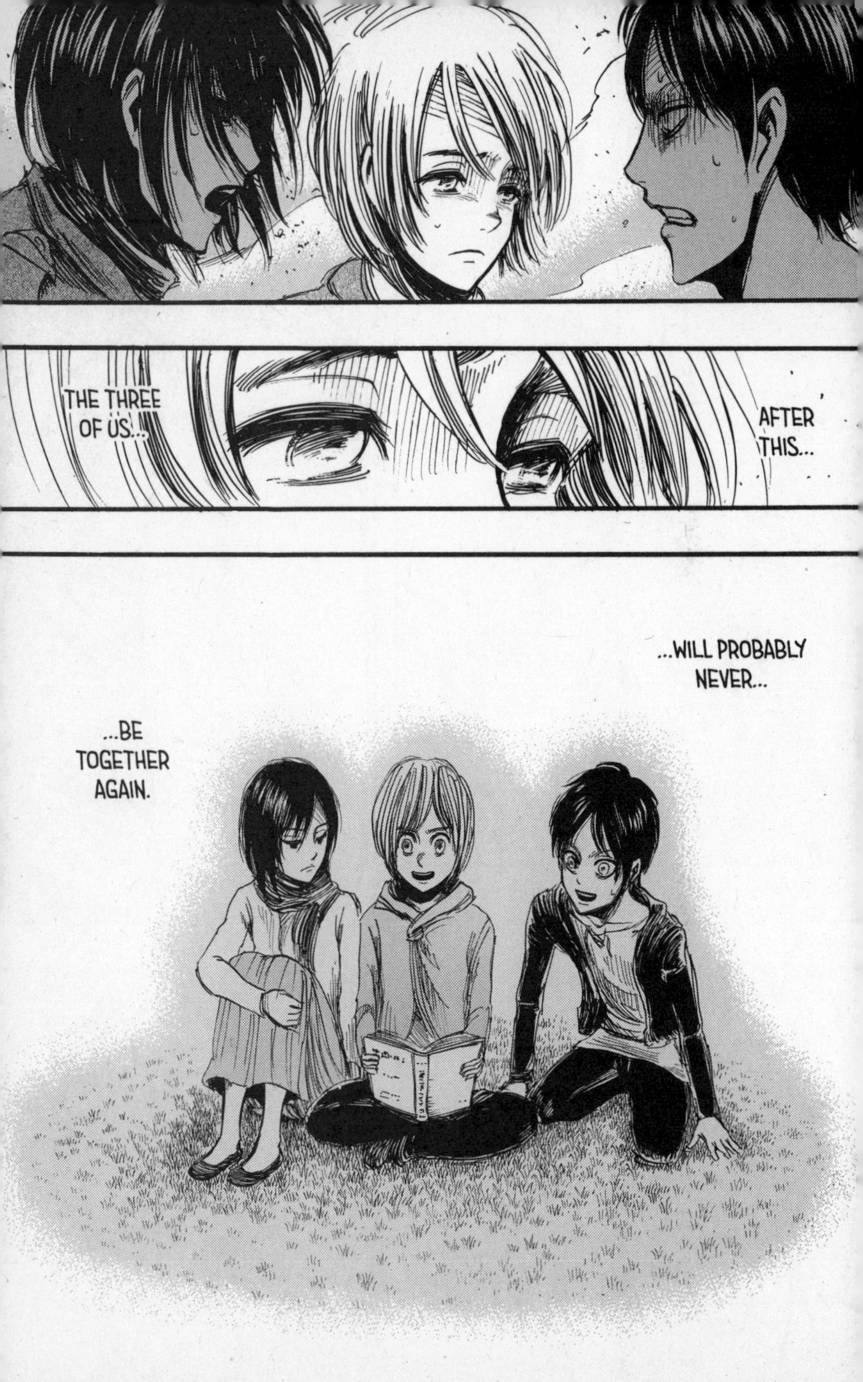
AFTER THIS...
THE THREE OF US...
...WILL PROBABLY NEVER...
...BE TOGETHER AGAIN.

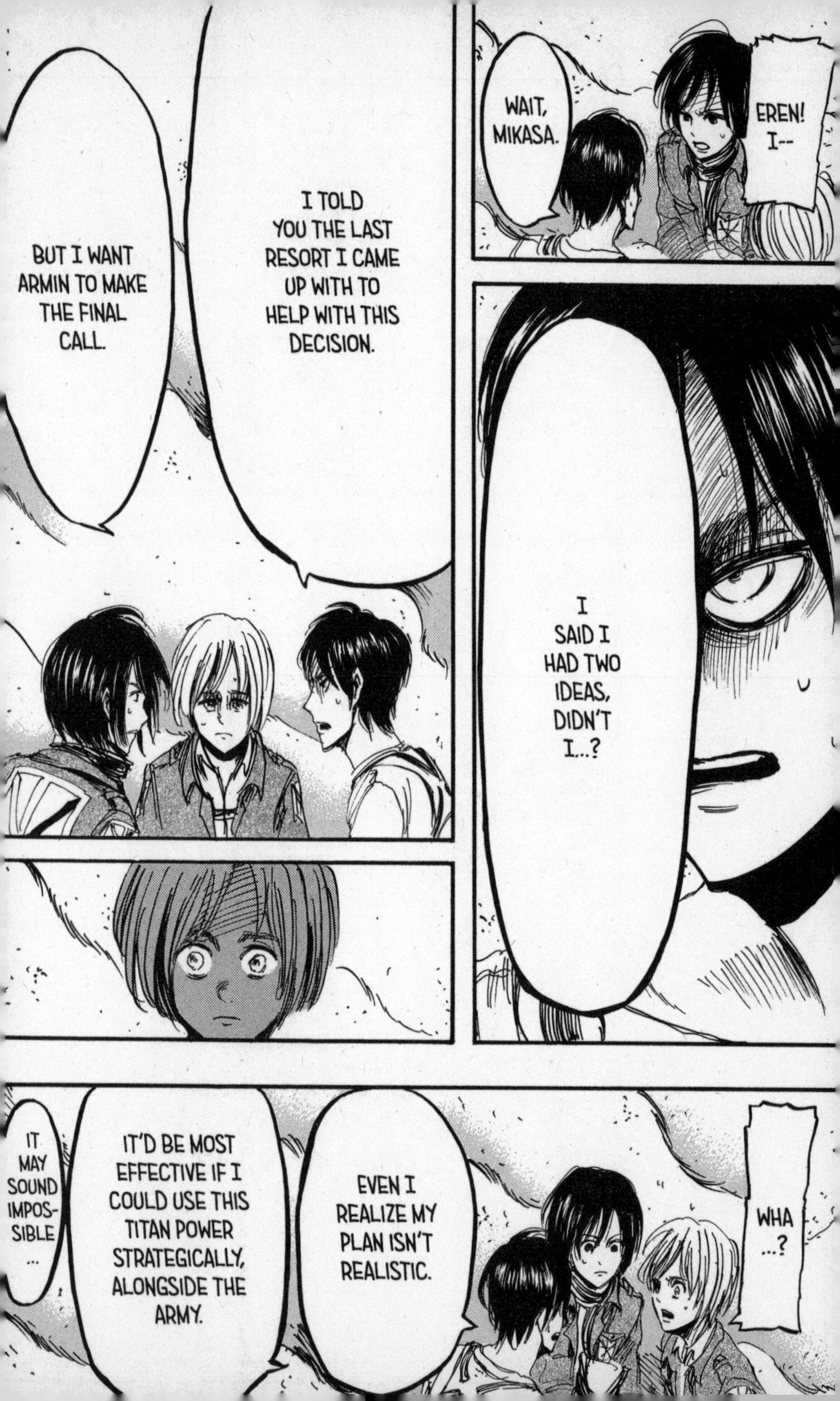
EREN! I--
WAIT, MIKASA.
I SAID I HAD TWO IDEAS, DIDN'T I...?
I TOLD YOU THE LAST RESORT I CAME UP WITH TO HELP WITH THIS DECISION.
BUT I WANT ARMIN TO MAKE THE FINAL CALL.
WHA ...?
EVEN I REALIZE MY PLAN ISN'T REALISTIC.
IT'D BE MOST EFFECTIVE IF I COULD USE THIS TITAN POWER STRATEGICALLY, ALONGSIDE THE ARMY.
IT MAY SOUND IMPOS-SIBLE ...

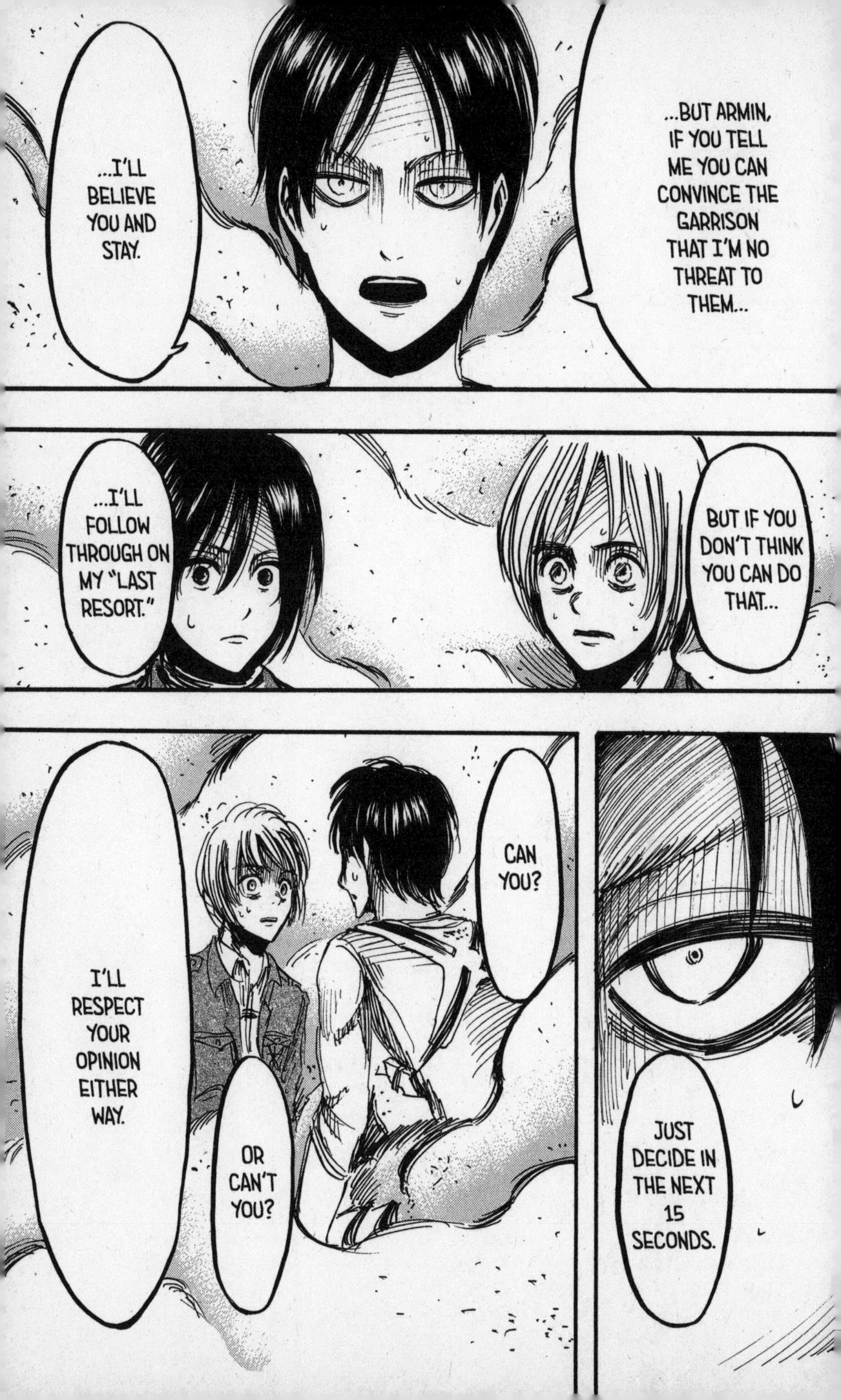
...BUT ARMIN, IF YOU TELL ME YOU CAN CONVINCE THE GARRISON THAT I'M NO THREAT TO THEM...
...I'LL BELIEVE YOU AND STAY.
BUT IF YOU DON'T THINK YOU CAN DO THAT...
...I'LL FOLLOW THROUGH ON MY "LAST RESORT."
JUST DECIDE IN THE NEXT 15 SECONDS.
CAN YOU?
OR CAN'T YOU?
I'LL RESPECT YOUR OPINION EITHER WAY.

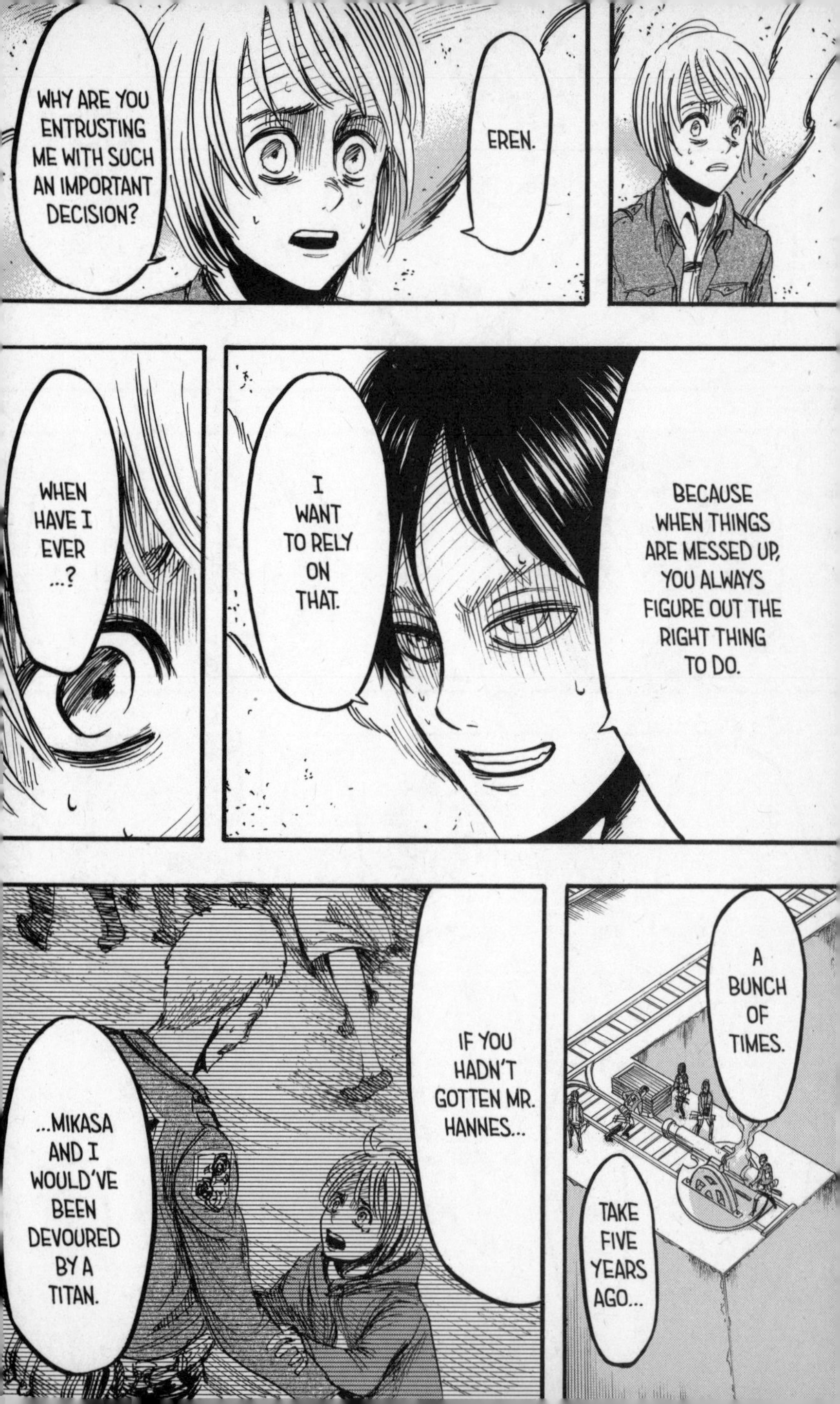
EREN.
WHY ARE YOU ENTRUSTING ME WITH SUCH AN IMPORTANT DECISION?
BECAUSE WHEN THINGS ARE MESSED UP, YOU ALWAYS FIGURE OUT THE RIGHT THING TO DO.
I WANT TO RELY ON THAT.
WHEN HAVE I EVER ...?
A BUNCH OF TIMES.
TAKE FIVE YEARS AGO...
IF YOU HADN'T GOTTEN MR. HANNES...
...MIKASA AND I WOULD'VE BEEN DEVOURED BY A TITAN.

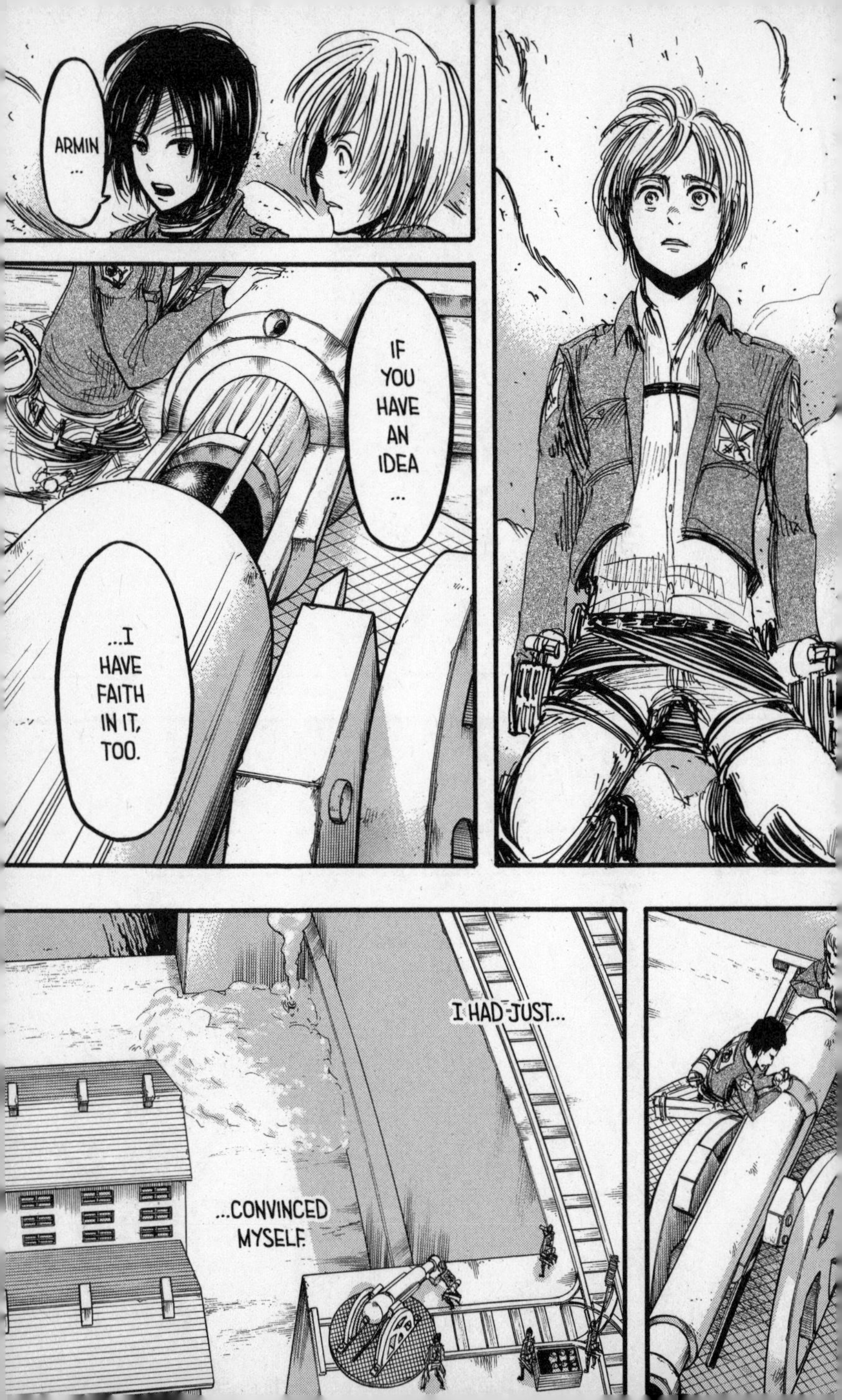
ARMIN ...
IF YOU HAVE AN IDEA ...
...I HAVE FAITH IN IT, TOO.
I HAD JUST...
...CONVINCED MYSELF.

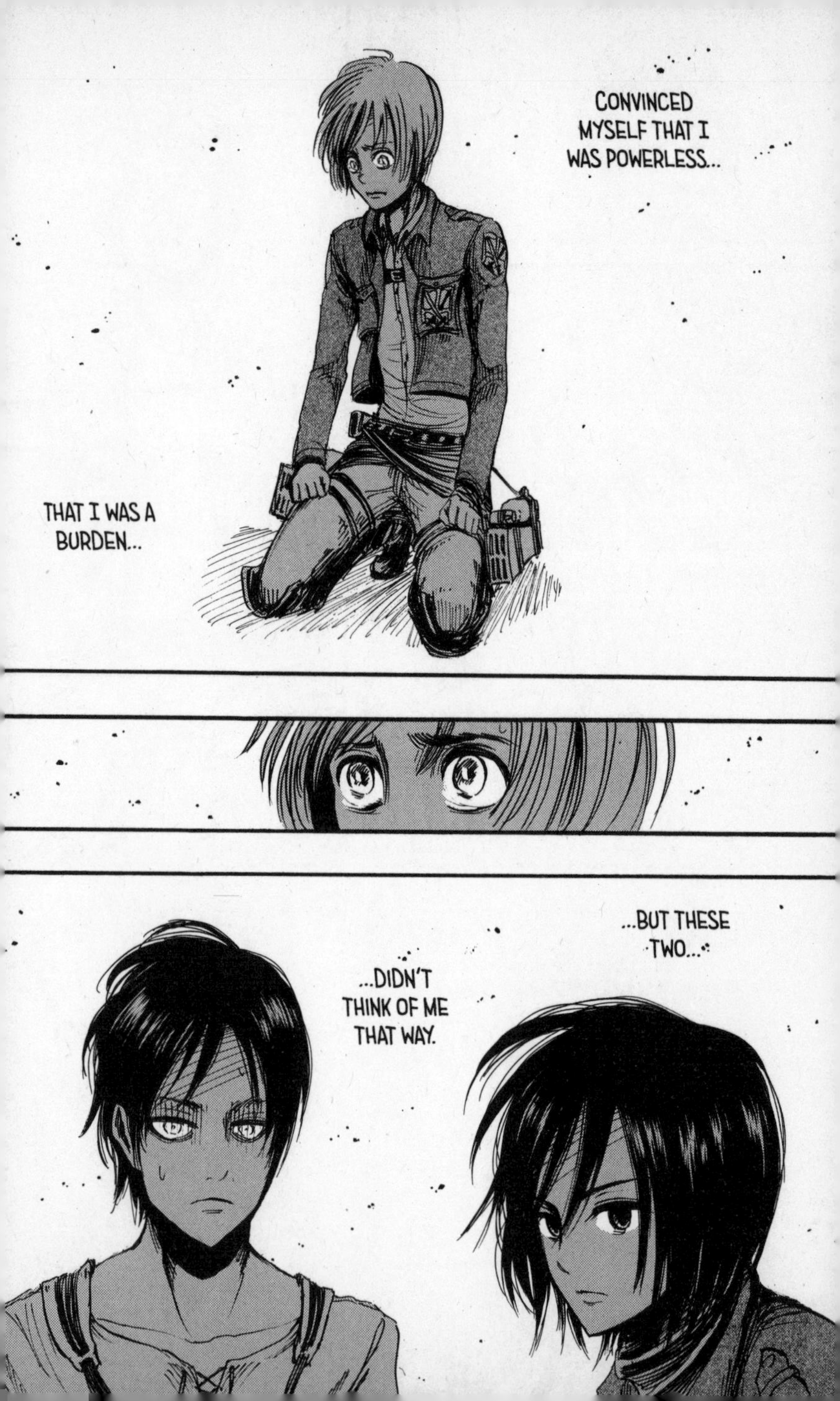
CONVINCED MYSELF THAT I WAS POWERLESS...
THAT I WAS A BURDEN...
...BUT THESE TWO...
...DIDN'T THINK OF ME THAT WAY.

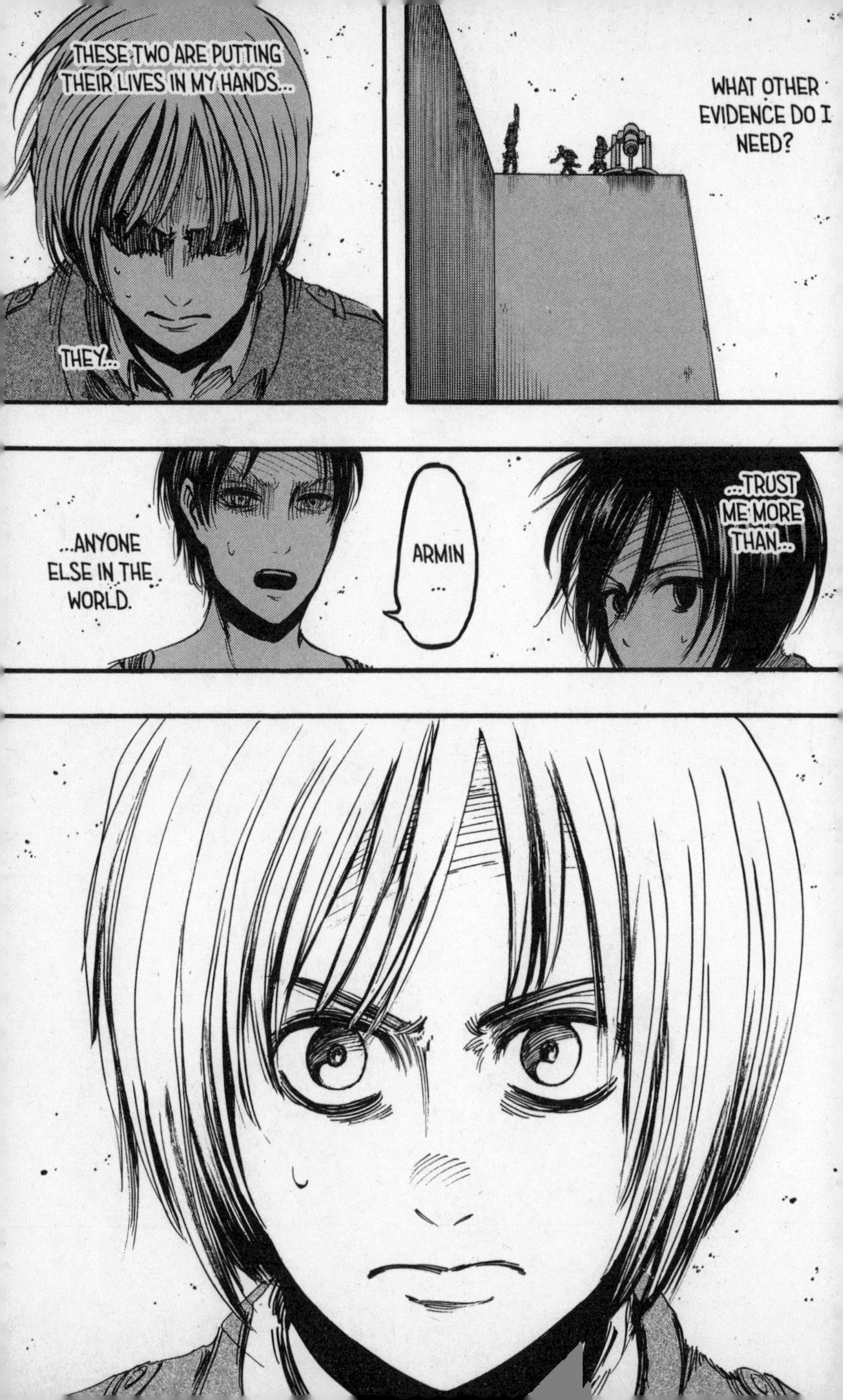
WHAT OTHER EVIDENCE DO I NEED?
THESE TWO ARE PUTTING THEIR LIVES IN MY HANDS...
THEY...
...TRUST ME MORE THAN...
ARMIN ...
...ANYONE ELSE IN THE WORLD.

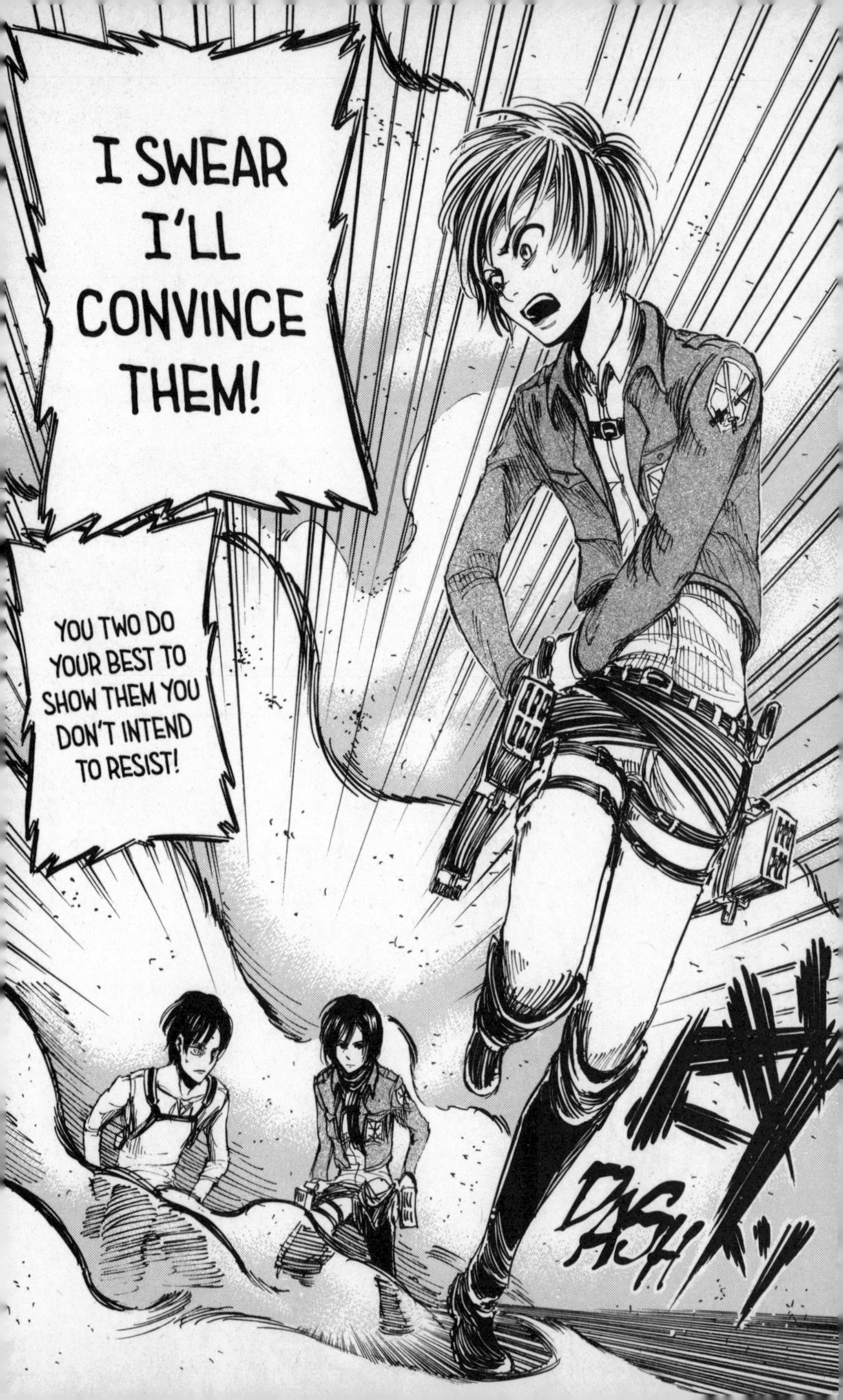
I SWEAR I'LL CONVINCE THEM!
YOU TWO DO YOUR BEST TO SHOW THEM YOU DON'T INTEND TO RESIST!
DASH

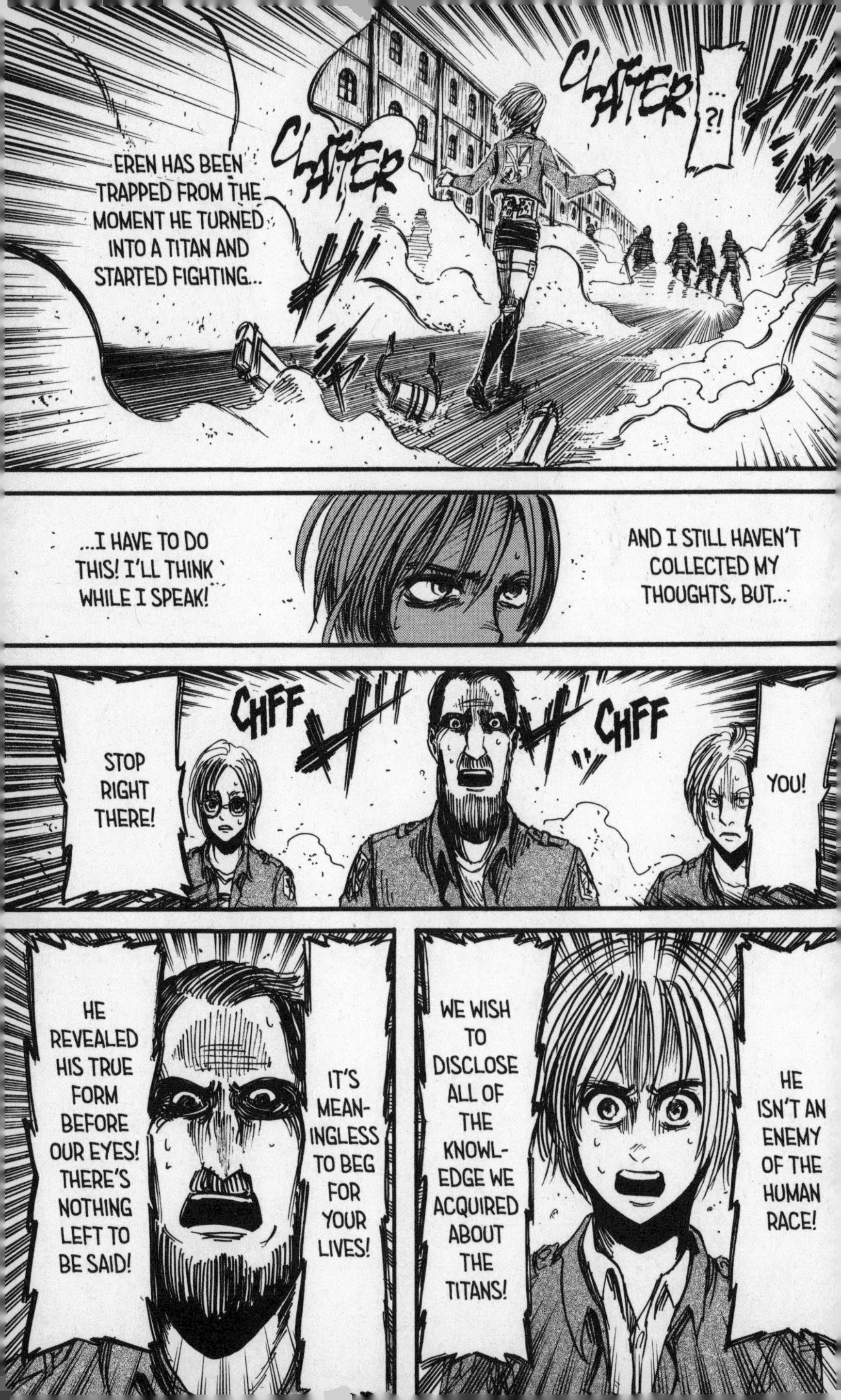

...?!
CLATTER
CLATTER
EREN HAS BEEN TRAPPED FROM THE MOMENT HE TURNED INTO A TITAN AND STARTED FIGHTING...
AND I STILL HAVEN'T COLLECTED MY THOUGHTS, BUT...
...I HAVE TO DO THIS! I'LL THINK WHILE I SPEAK!
YOU!
CHFF
CHFF
STOP RIGHT THERE!
HE ISN'T AN ENEMY OF THE HUMAN RACE!
WE WISH TO DISCLOSE ALL OF THE KNOWLEDGE WE ACQUIRED ABOUT THE TITANS!
IT'S MEANINGLESS TO BEG FOR YOUR LIVES!
HE REVEALED HIS TRUE FORM BEFORE OUR EYES! THERE'S NOTHING LEFT TO BE SAID!

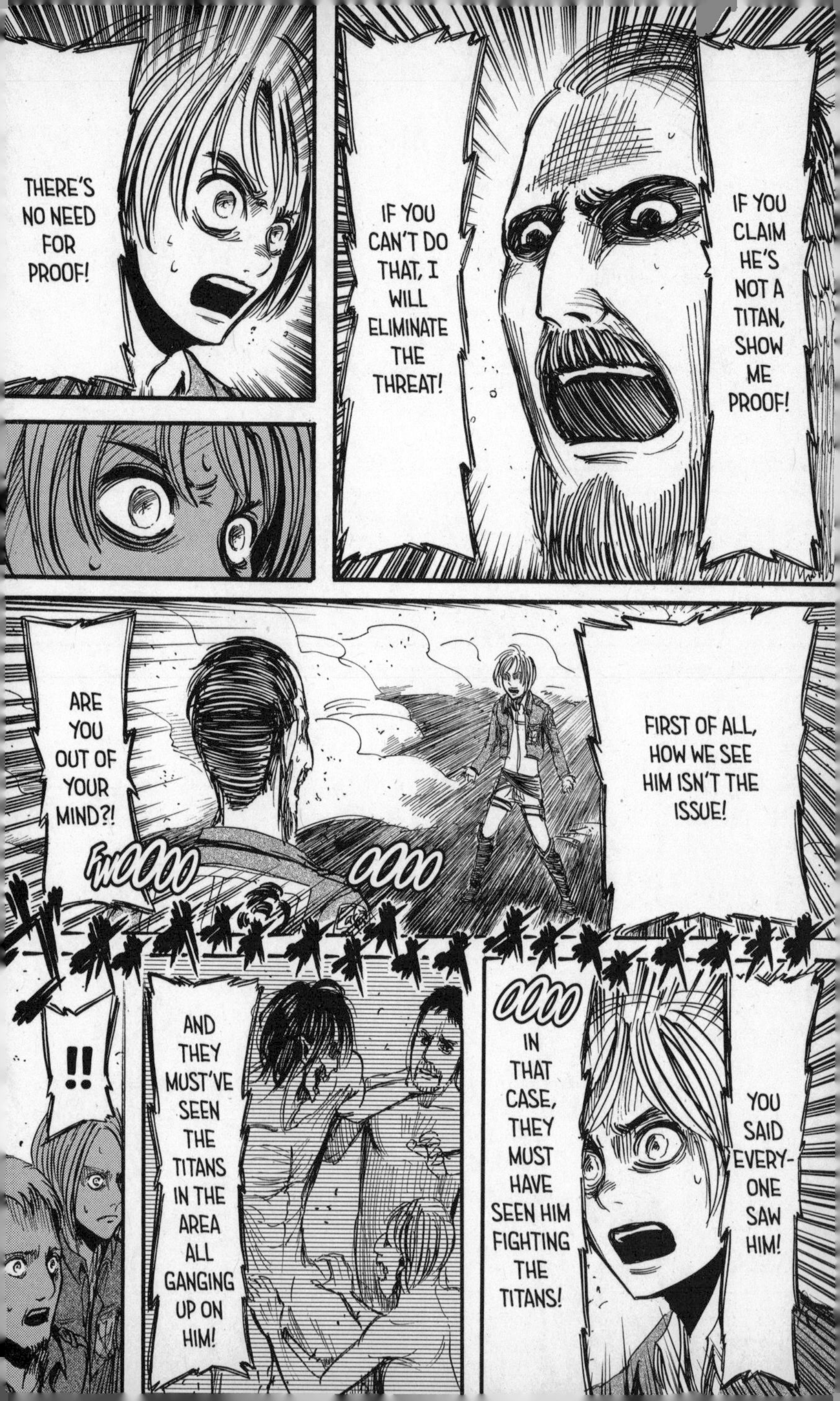
IF YOU CLAIM HE'S NOT A TITAN, SHOW ME PROOF!
IF YOU CAN'T DO THAT, I WILL ELIMINATE THE THREAT!
THERE'S NO NEED FOR PROOF!
FIRST OF ALL, HOW WE SEE HIM ISN'T THE ISSUE!
ARE YOU OUT OF YOUR MIND?!
FWOOOO
OOOO
YOU SAID EVERY-ONE SAW HIM!
OOOO
IN THAT CASE, THEY MUST HAVE SEEN HIM FIGHTING THE TITANS!
AND THEY MUST'VE SEEN THE TITANS IN THE AREA ALL GANGING UP ON HIM!
!!

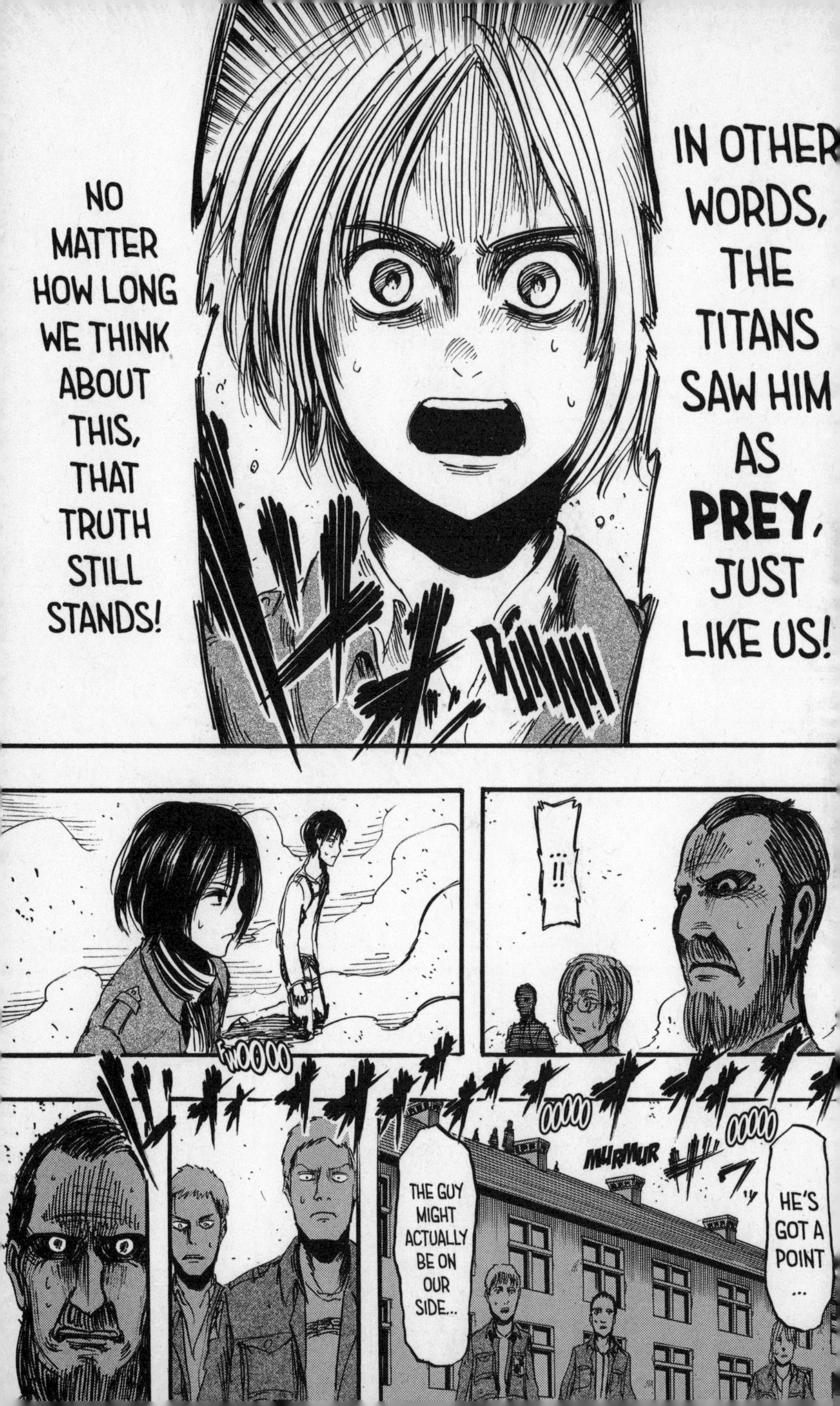
IN OTHER WORDS, THE TITANS SAW HIM AS **PREY**, JUST LIKE US!
NO MATTER HOW LONG WE THINK ABOUT THIS, THAT TRUTH STILL STANDS!
BUNNN
...!!
FWOOOO
OOOOO
HE'S GOT A POINT ...
MURMUR
OOOOO
THE GUY MIGHT ACTUALLY BE ON OUR SIDE...

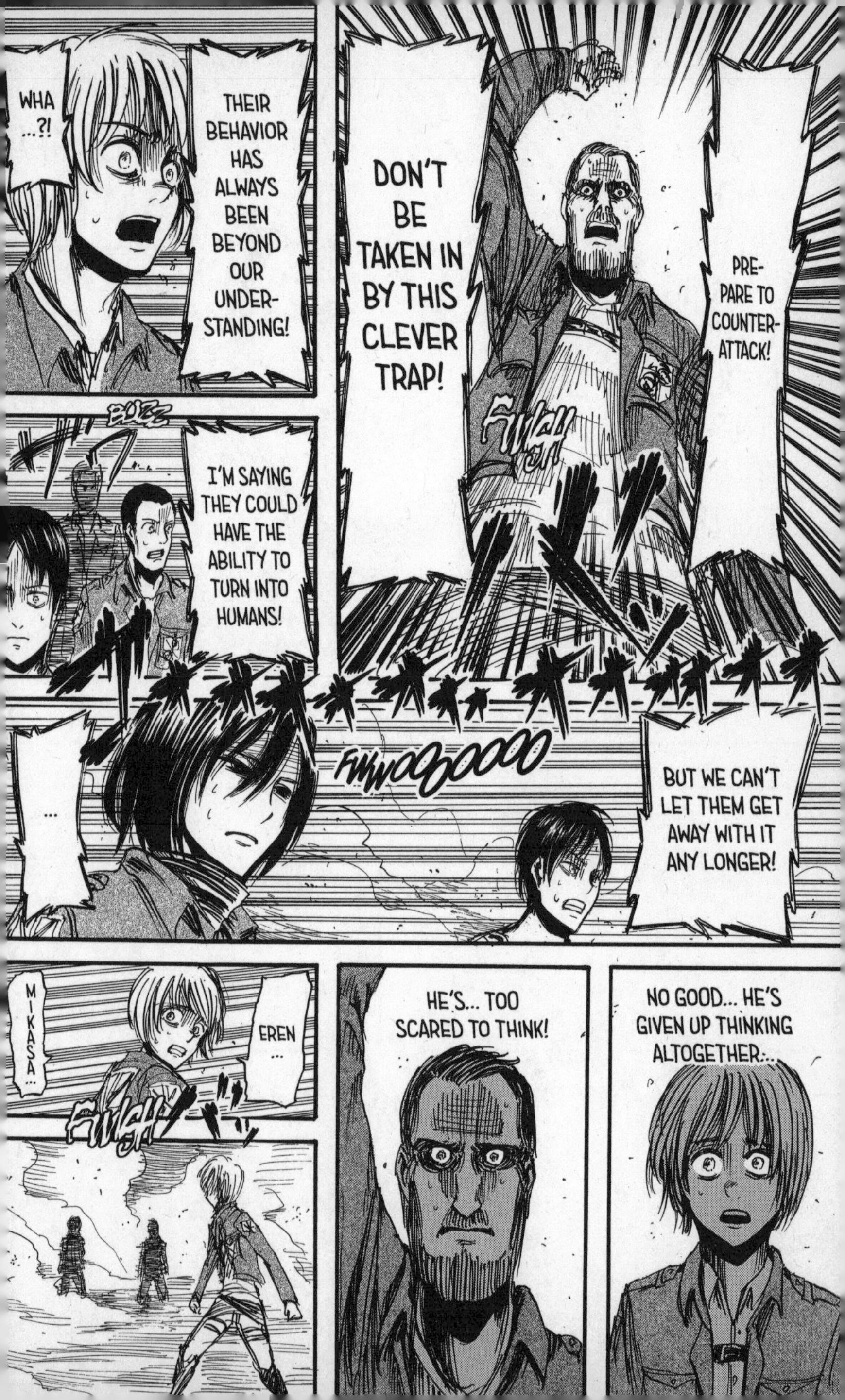
DON'T BE TAKEN IN BY THIS CLEVER TRAP!
PRE-PARE TO COUNTER-ATTACK!
FWISH
THEIR BEHAVIOR HAS ALWAYS BEEN BEYOND OUR UNDER-STANDING!
WHA ...?!
BUZZ
I'M SAYING THEY COULD HAVE THE ABILITY TO TURN INTO HUMANS!
BUT WE CAN'T LET THEM GET AWAY WITH IT ANY LONGER!
...
NO GOOD... HE'S GIVEN UP THINKING ALTOGETHER...
HE'S... TOO SCARED TO THINK!
EREN ...
MIKASA...
FWISH

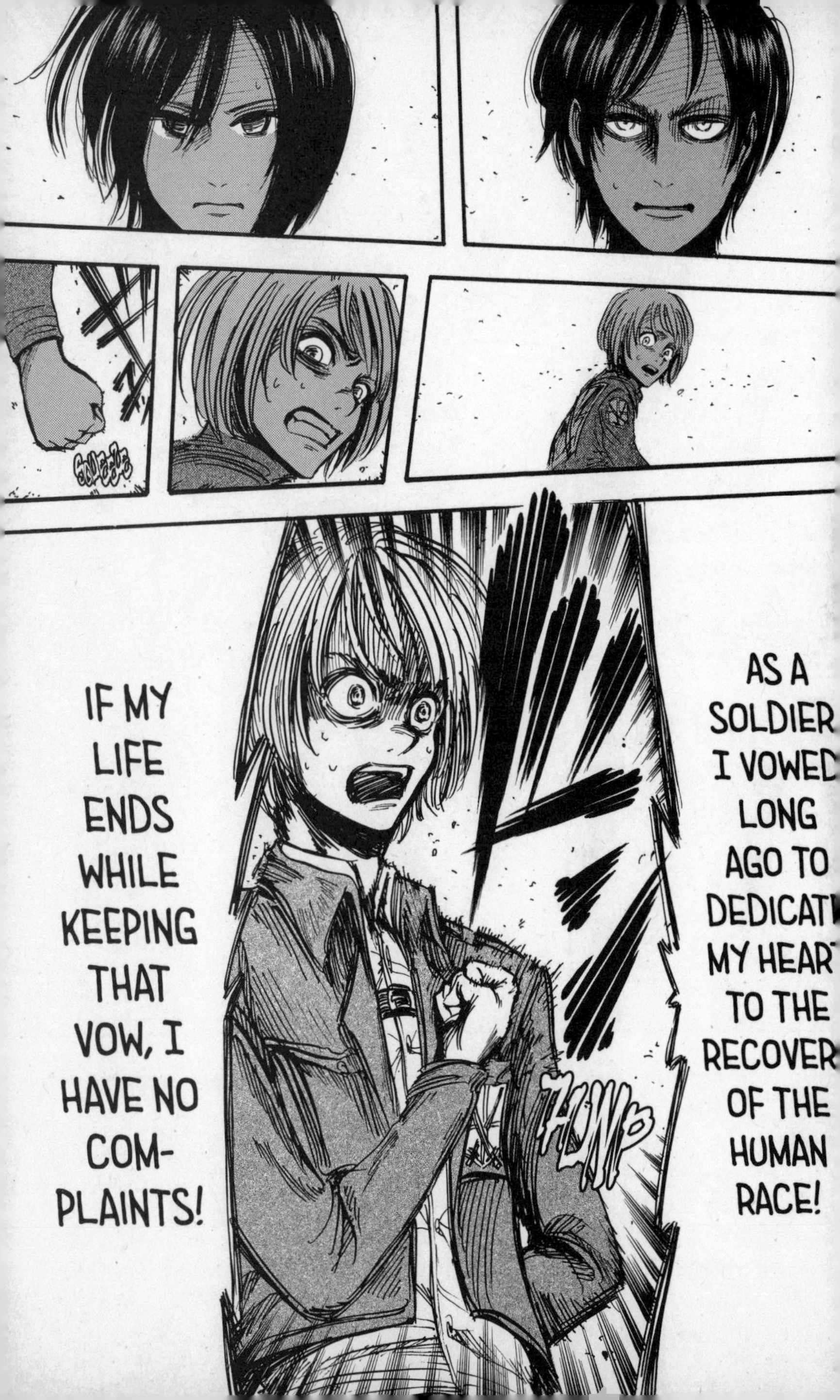
AS A SOLDIER I VOWED LONG AGO TO DEDICAT MY HEAR TO THE RECOVER OF THE HUMAN RACE!
IF MY LIFE ENDS WHILE KEEPING THAT VOW, I HAVE NO COM-PLAINTS!

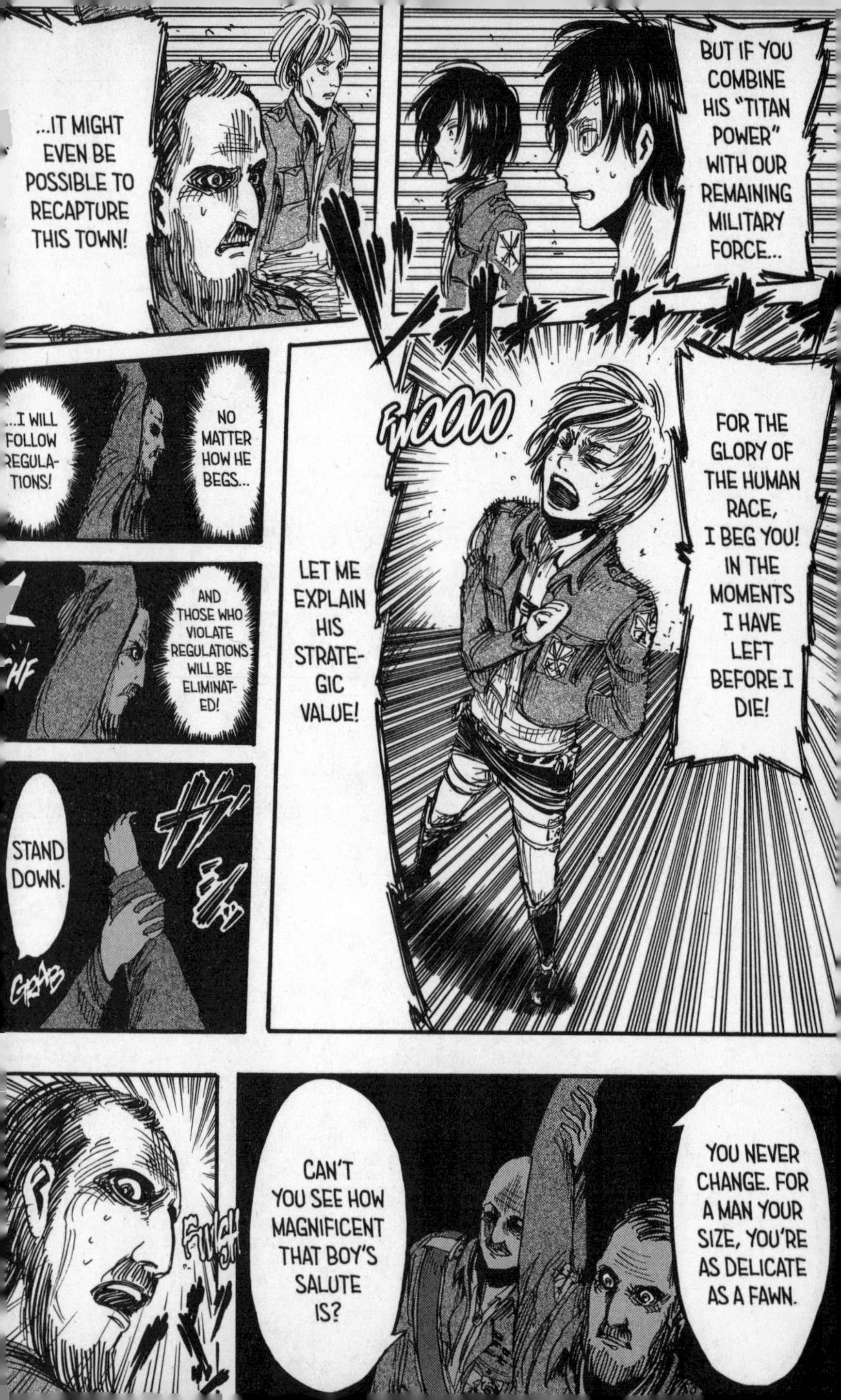
BUT IF YOU COMBINE HIS "TITAN POWER" WITH OUR REMAINING MILITARY FORCE...
...IT MIGHT EVEN BE POSSIBLE TO RECAPTURE THIS TOWN!
FWOOOO
FOR THE GLORY OF THE HUMAN RACE, I BEG YOU! IN THE MOMENTS I HAVE LEFT BEFORE I DIE!
LET ME EXPLAIN HIS STRATEGIC VALUE!
NO MATTER HOW HE BEGS...
...I WILL FOLLOW REGULATIONS!
AND THOSE WHO VIOLATE REGULATIONS WILL BE ELIMINATED!
STAND DOWN.
GRAB
YOU NEVER CHANGE. FOR A MAN YOUR SIZE, YOU'RE AS DELICATE AS A FAWN.
CAN'T YOU SEE HOW MAGNIFICENT THAT BOY'S SALUTE IS?

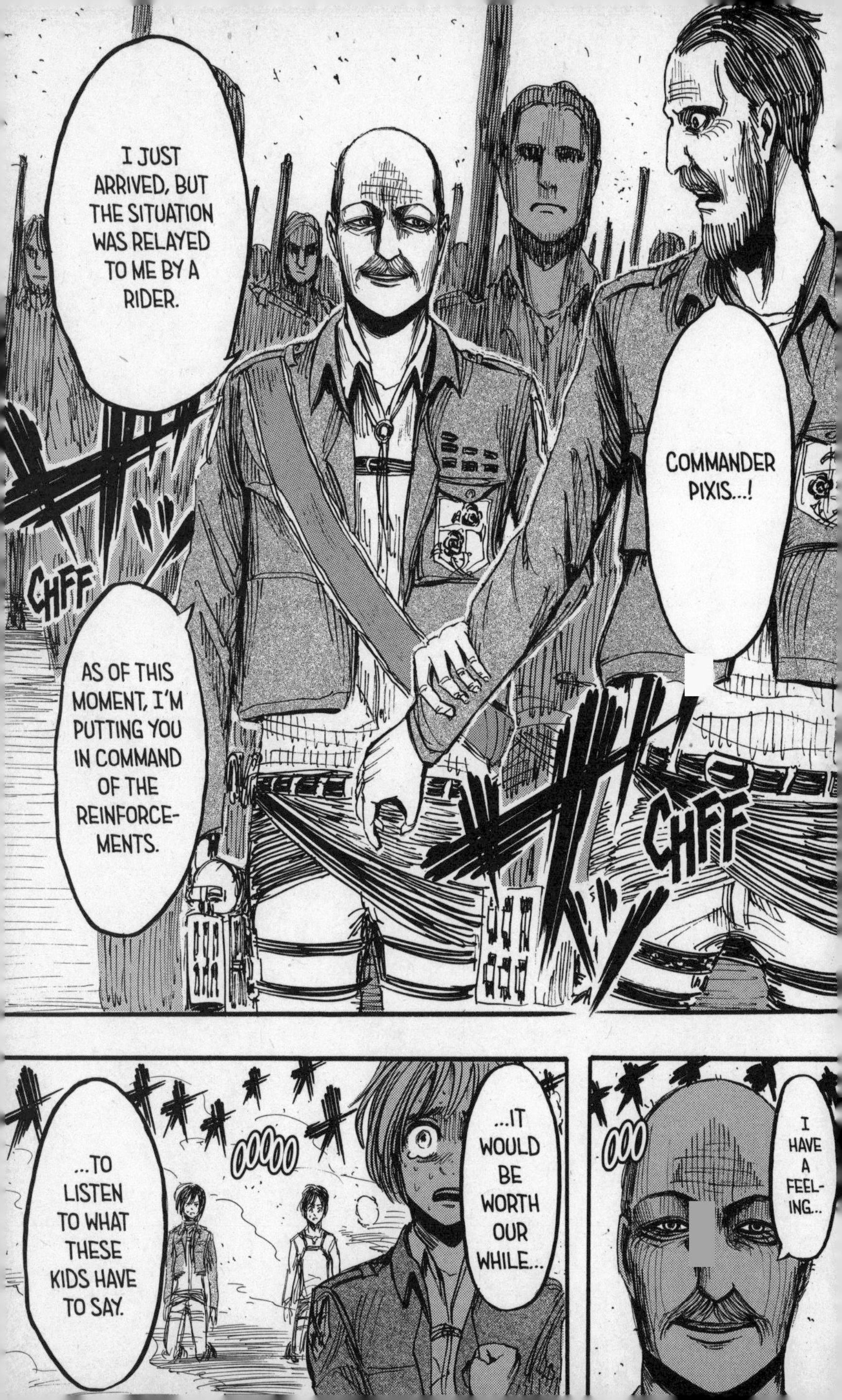
COMMANDER PIXIS...!
I JUST ARRIVED, BUT THE SITUATION WAS RELAYED TO ME BY A RIDER.
CHFF
AS OF THIS MOMENT, I'M PUTTING YOU IN COMMAND OF THE REINFORCE-MENTS.
CHFF
OOO
I HAVE A FEEL-ING...
...IT WOULD BE WORTH OUR WHILE...
OOOOO
...TO LISTEN TO WHAT THESE KIDS HAVE TO SAY.

ATTACK on TITAN

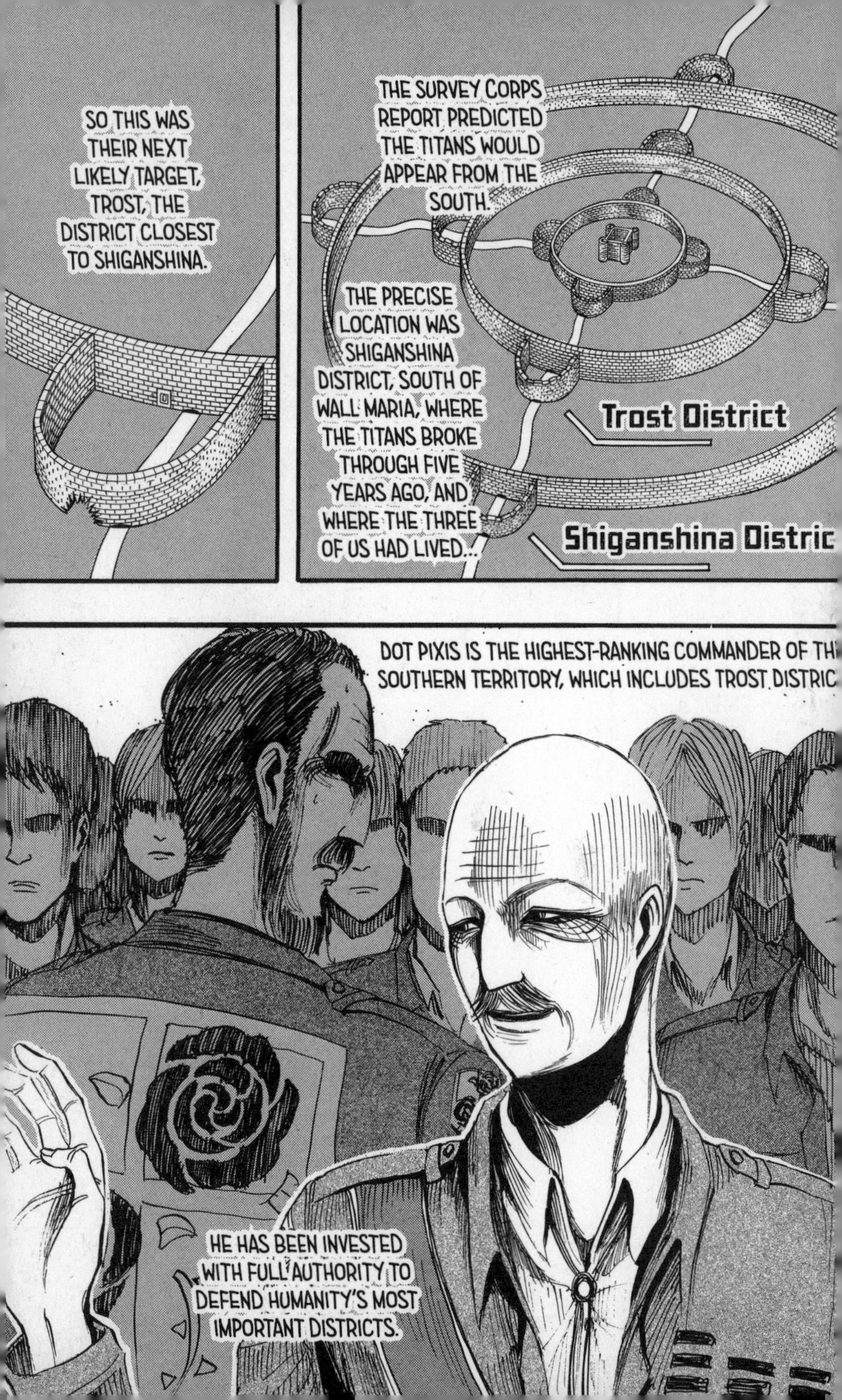
THE SURVEY CORPS REPORT PREDICTED THE TITANS WOULD APPEAR FROM THE SOUTH.
THE PRECISE LOCATION WAS SHIGANSHINA DISTRICT, SOUTH OF WALL MARIA, WHERE THE TITANS BROKE THROUGH FIVE YEARS AGO, AND WHERE THE THREE OF US HAD LIVED...
Trost District
Shiganshina Distric
SO THIS WAS THEIR NEXT LIKELY TARGET, TROST, THE DISTRICT CLOSEST TO SHIGANSHINA.
DOT PIXIS IS THE HIGHEST-RANKING COMMANDER OF TH
SOUTHERN TERRITORY, WHICH INCLUDES TROST DISTRIC
HE HAS BEEN INVESTED WITH FULL AUTHORITY TO DEFEND HUMANITY'S MOST IMPORTANT DISTRICTS.

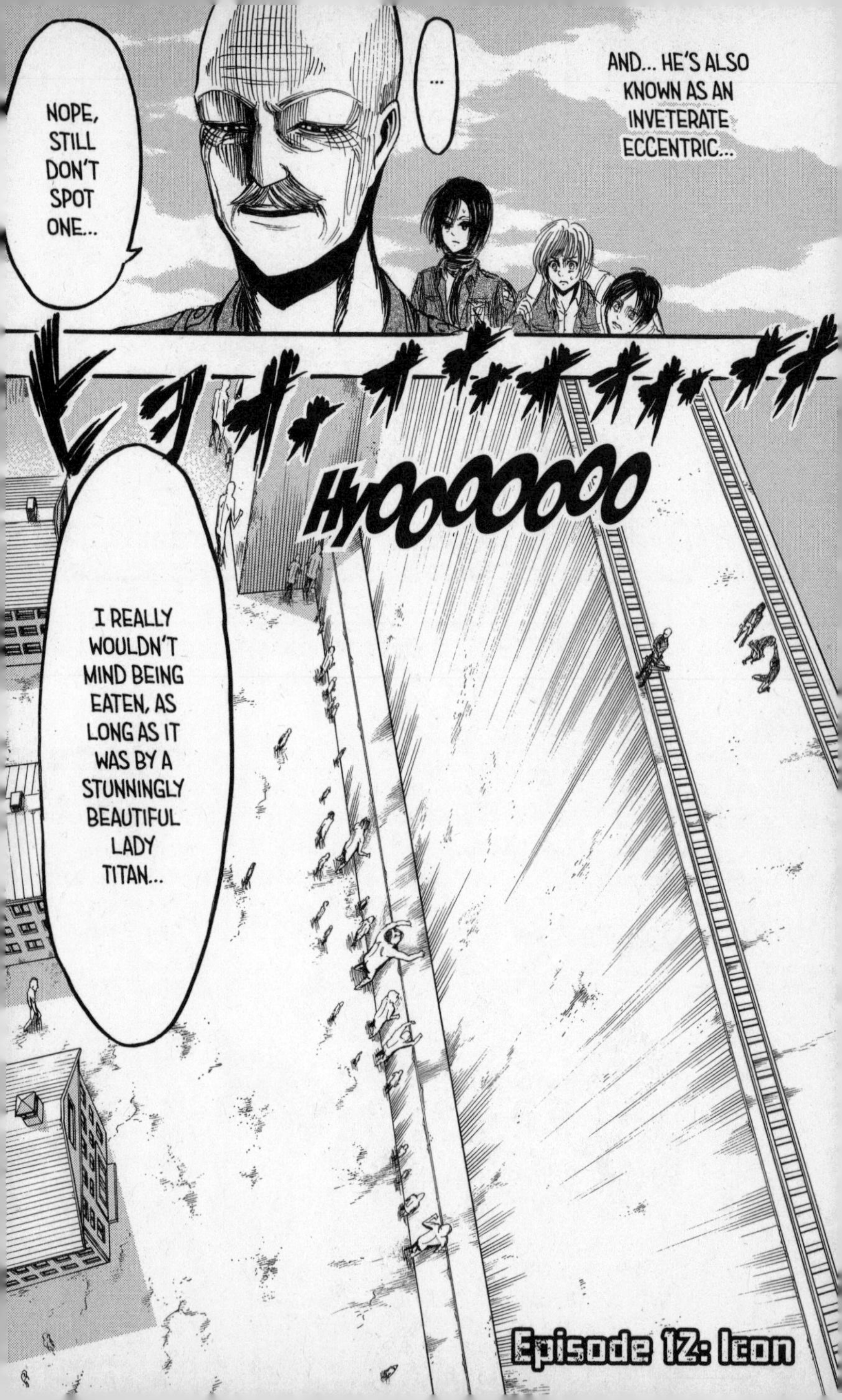
AND... HE'S ALSO KNOWN AS AN INVETERATE ECCENTRIC...
...
NOPE, STILL DON'T SPOT ONE...
HYOOOOOOO
I REALLY WOULDN'T MIND BEING EATEN, AS LONG AS IT WAS BY A STUNNINGLY BEAUTIFUL LADY TITAN...
Episode 12: Icon

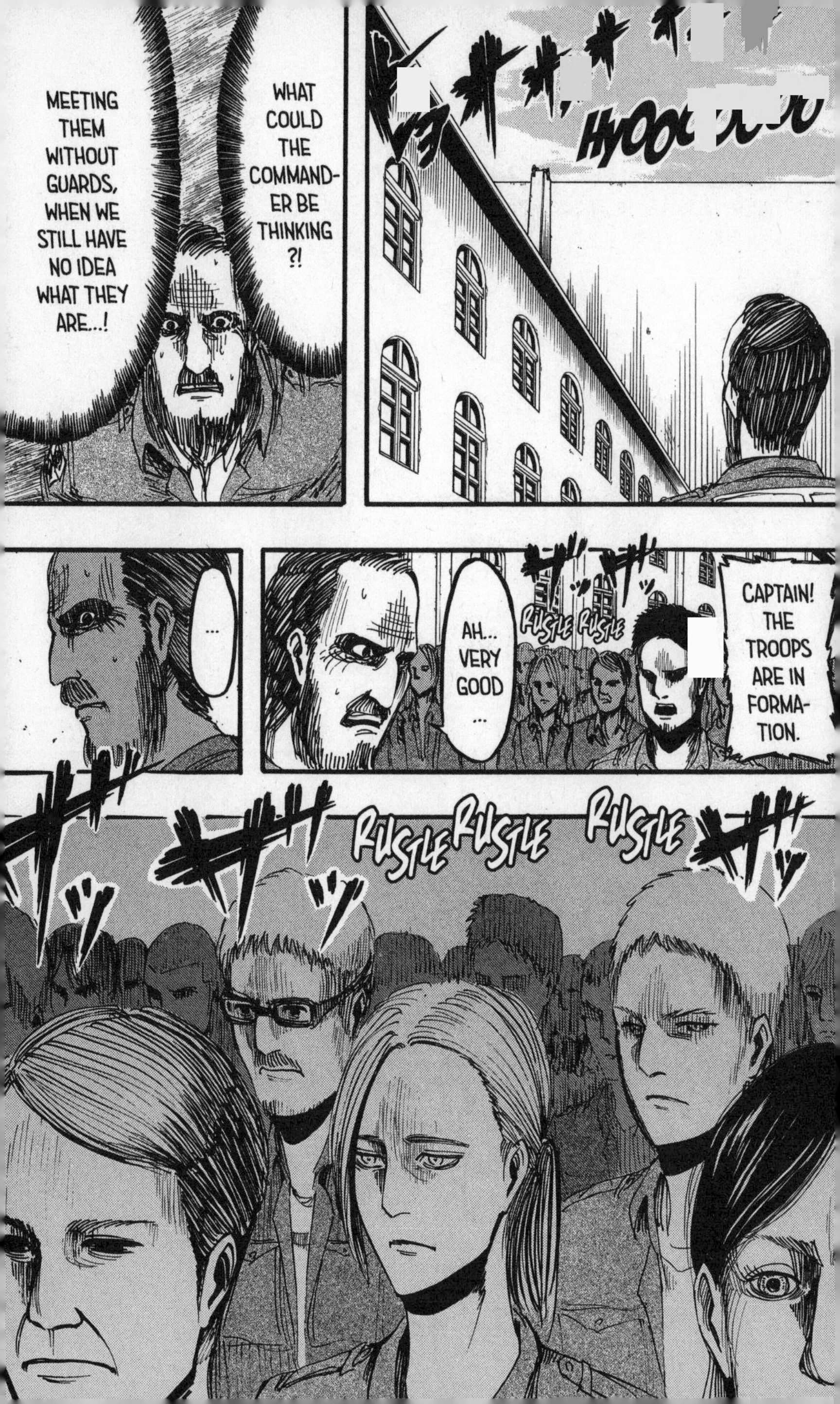
HYOO
WHAT COULD THE COMMANDER BE THINKING?!
MEETING THEM WITHOUT GUARDS, WHEN WE STILL HAVE NO IDEA WHAT THEY ARE...!
CAPTAIN! THE TROOPS ARE IN FORMATION.
RUSTLE RUSTLE
AH... VERY GOOD...
...
RUSTLE
RUSTLE RUSTLE

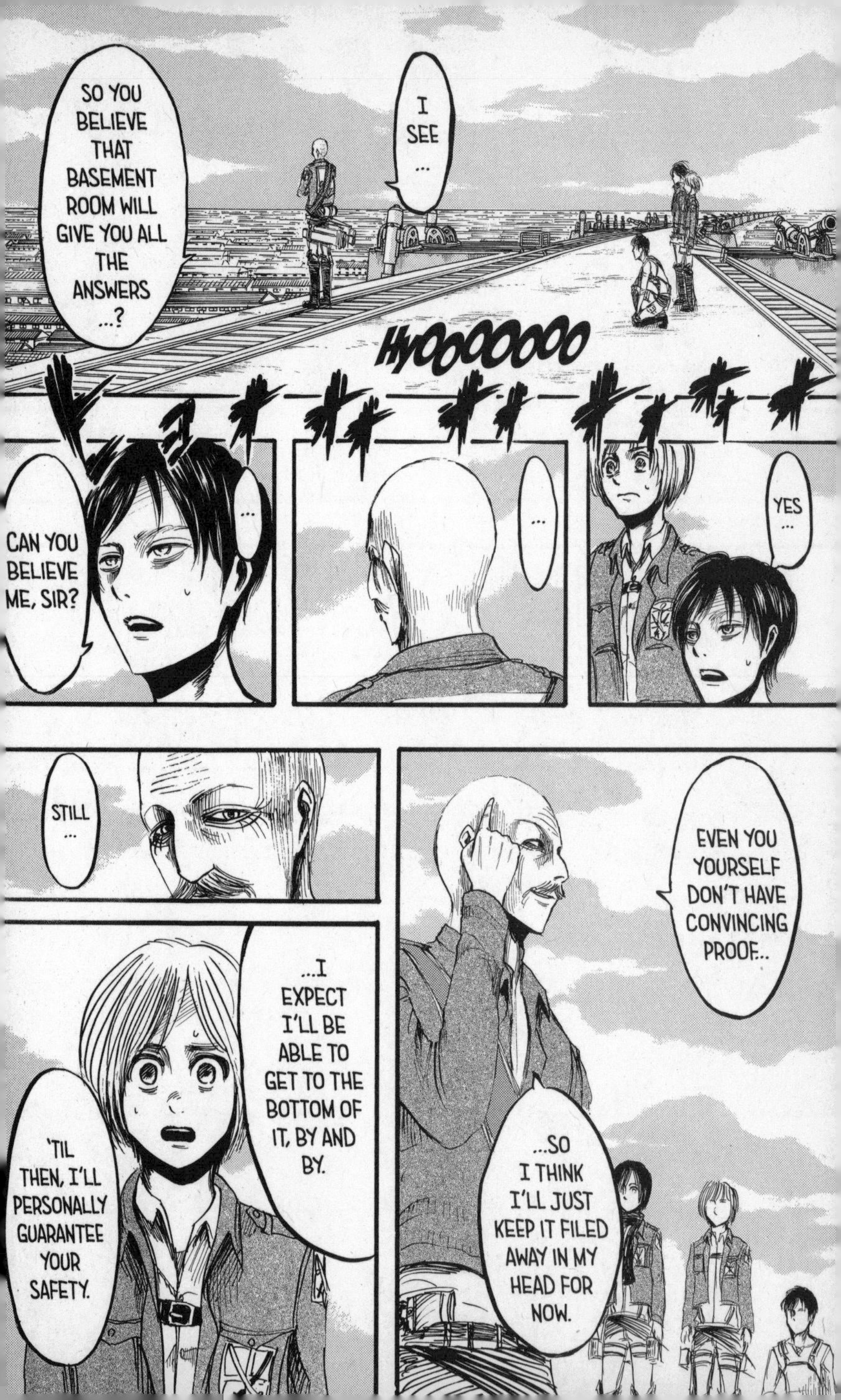

I SEE ...
SO YOU BELIEVE THAT BASEMENT ROOM WILL GIVE YOU ALL THE ANSWERS ...?
HYOOOOOOO
YES ...
...
...
CAN YOU BELIEVE ME, SIR?
EVEN YOU YOURSELF DON'T HAVE CONVINCING PROOF...
...SO I THINK I'LL JUST KEEP IT FILED AWAY IN MY HEAD FOR NOW.
STILL ...
...I EXPECT I'LL BE ABLE TO GET TO THE BOTTOM OF IT, BY AND BY.
'TIL THEN, I'LL PERSONALLY GUARANTEE YOUR SAFETY.

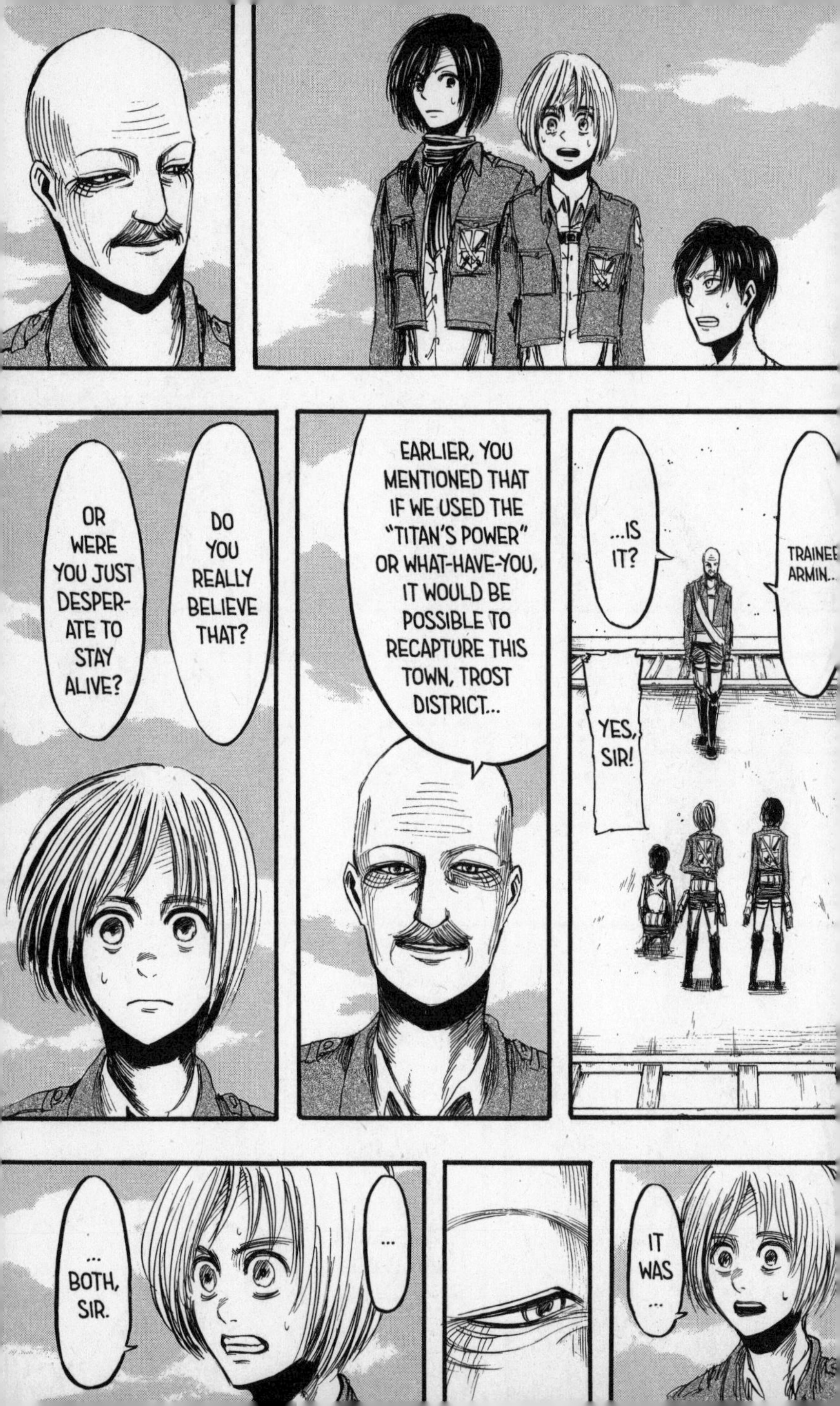

TRAINEE ARMIN...
...IS IT?
YES, SIR!
EARLIER, YOU MENTIONED THAT IF WE USED THE "TITAN'S POWER" OR WHAT-HAVE-YOU, IT WOULD BE POSSIBLE TO RECAPTURE THIS TOWN, TROST DISTRICT...
DO YOU REALLY BELIEVE THAT?
OR WERE YOU JUST DESPER-ATE TO STAY ALIVE?
IT WAS ...
...
... BOTH, SIR.

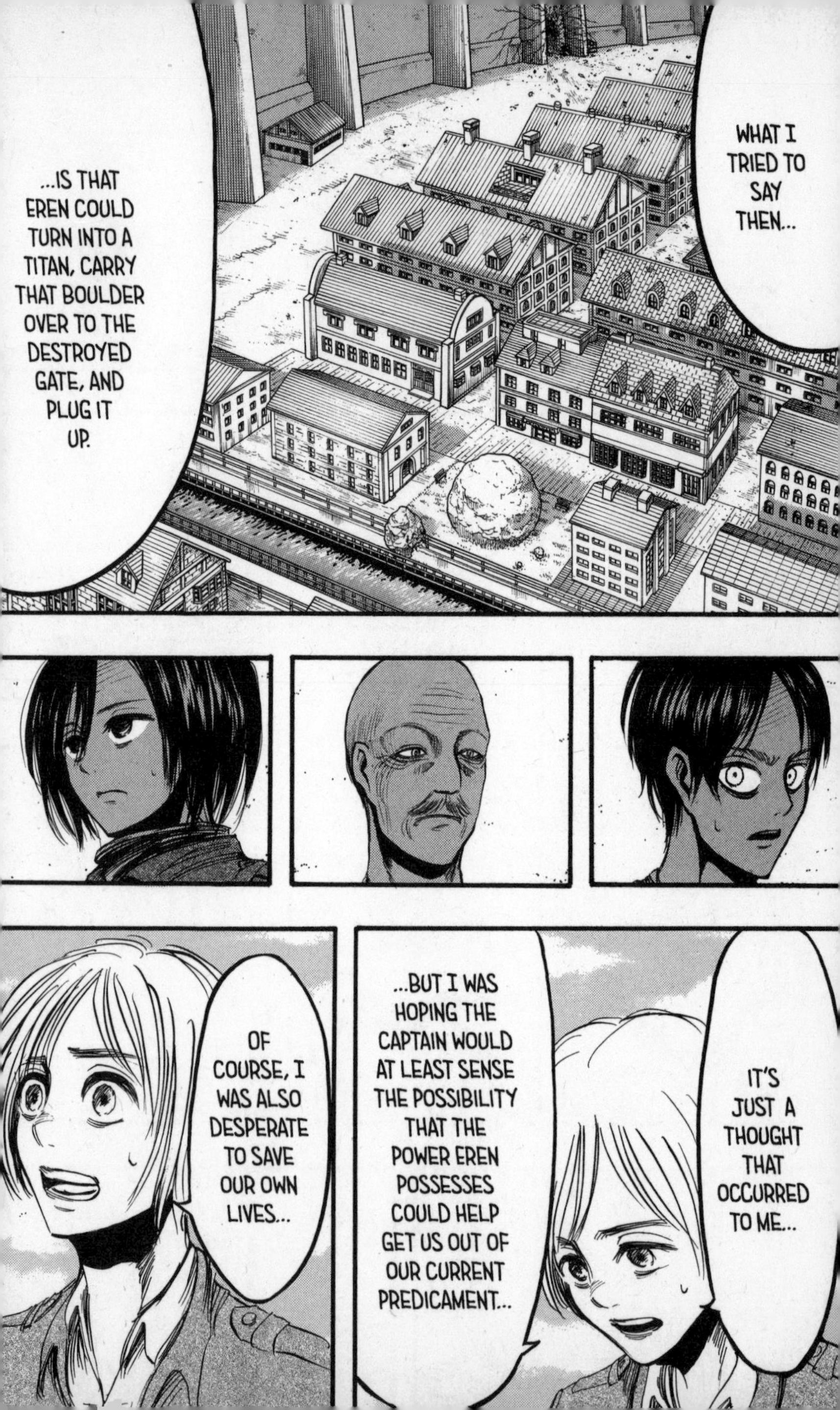
WHAT I TRIED TO SAY THEN...
...IS THAT EREN COULD TURN INTO A TITAN, CARRY THAT BOULDER OVER TO THE DESTROYED GATE, AND PLUG IT UP.
IT'S JUST A THOUGHT THAT OCCURRED TO ME...
...BUT I WAS HOPING THE CAPTAIN WOULD AT LEAST SENSE THE POSSIBILITY THAT THE POWER EREN POSSESSES COULD HELP GET US OUT OF OUR CURRENT PREDICAMENT...
OF COURSE, I WAS ALSO DESPERATE TO SAVE OUR OWN LIVES...

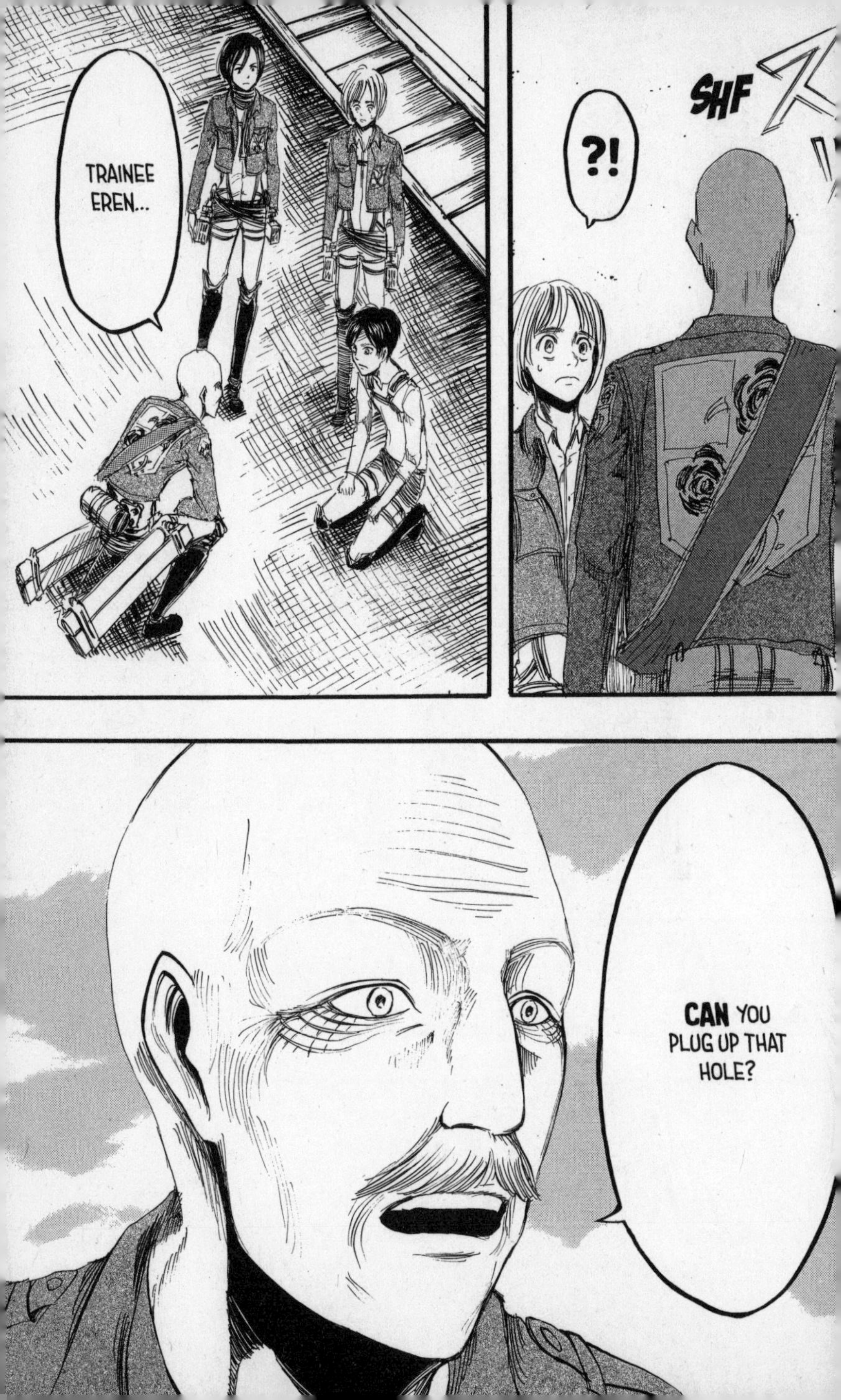

SHF
?!
TRAINEE EREN...
CAN YOU PLUG UP THAT HOLE?

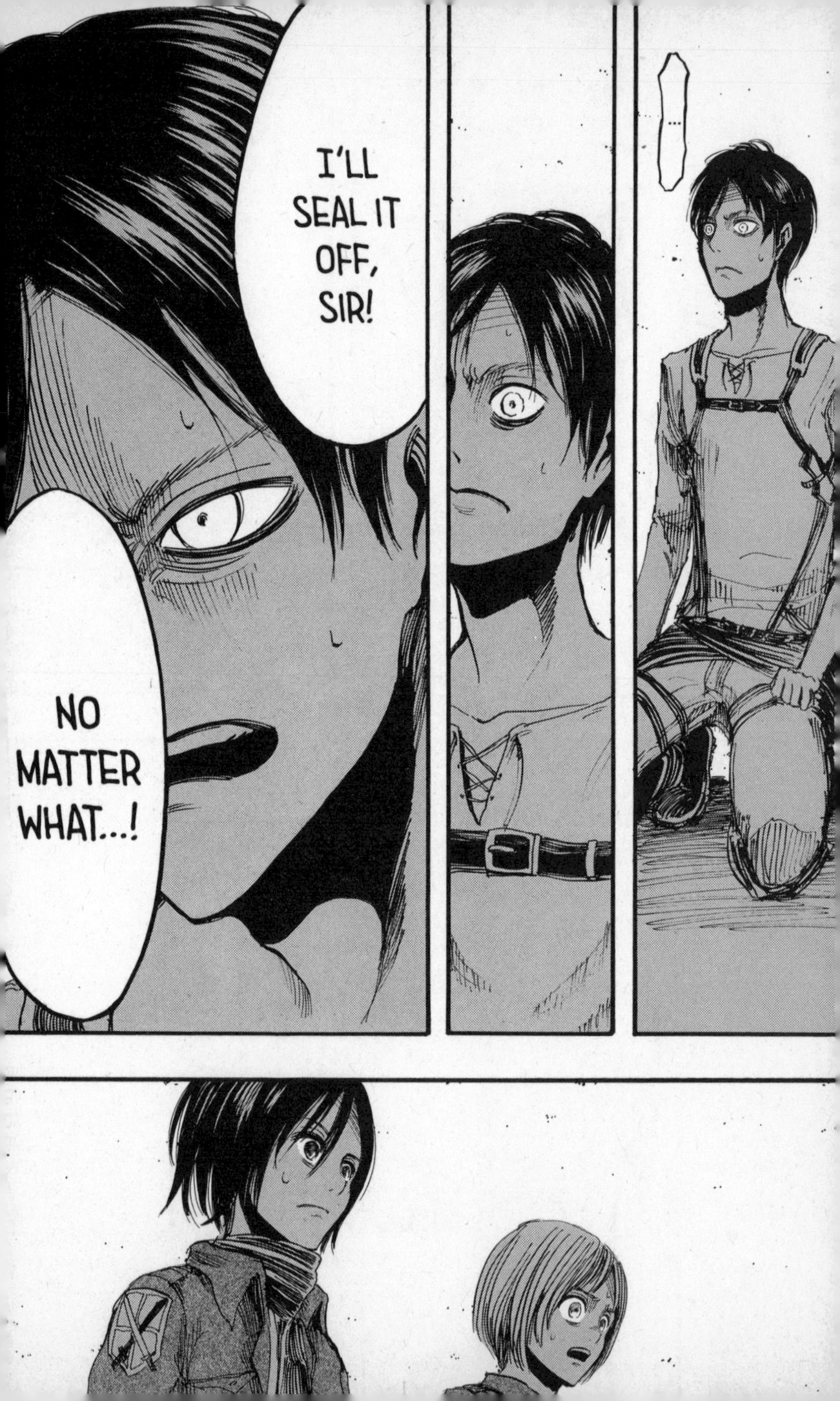
…
I'LL SEAL IT OFF, SIR!
NO MATTER WHAT…!

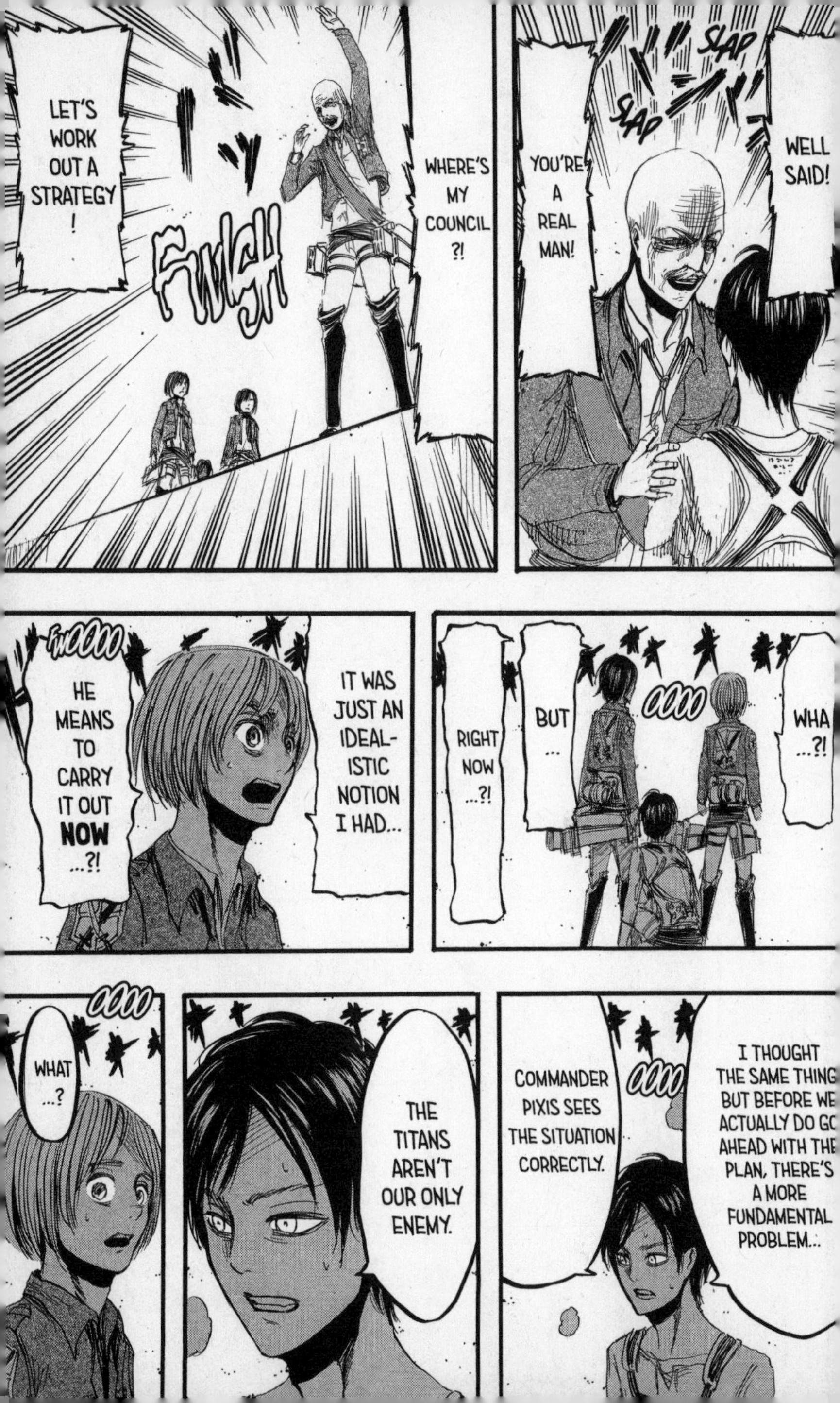
SLAP
SLAP
WELL SAID!
YOU'RE A REAL MAN!
WHERE'S MY COUNCIL ?!
LET'S WORK OUT A STRATEGY !
WHA ...?!
OOOO
BUT ...
RIGHT NOW ...?!
IT WAS JUST AN IDEAL-ISTIC NOTION I HAD...
FWOOOO
HE MEANS TO CARRY IT OUT NOW ...?!
I THOUGHT THE SAME THING BUT BEFORE WE ACTUALLY DO GO AHEAD WITH THE PLAN, THERE'S A MORE FUNDAMENTAL PROBLEM...
OOOO
COMMANDER PIXIS SEES THE SITUATION CORRECTLY.
THE TITANS AREN'T OUR ONLY ENEMY.
OOOO
WHAT ...?

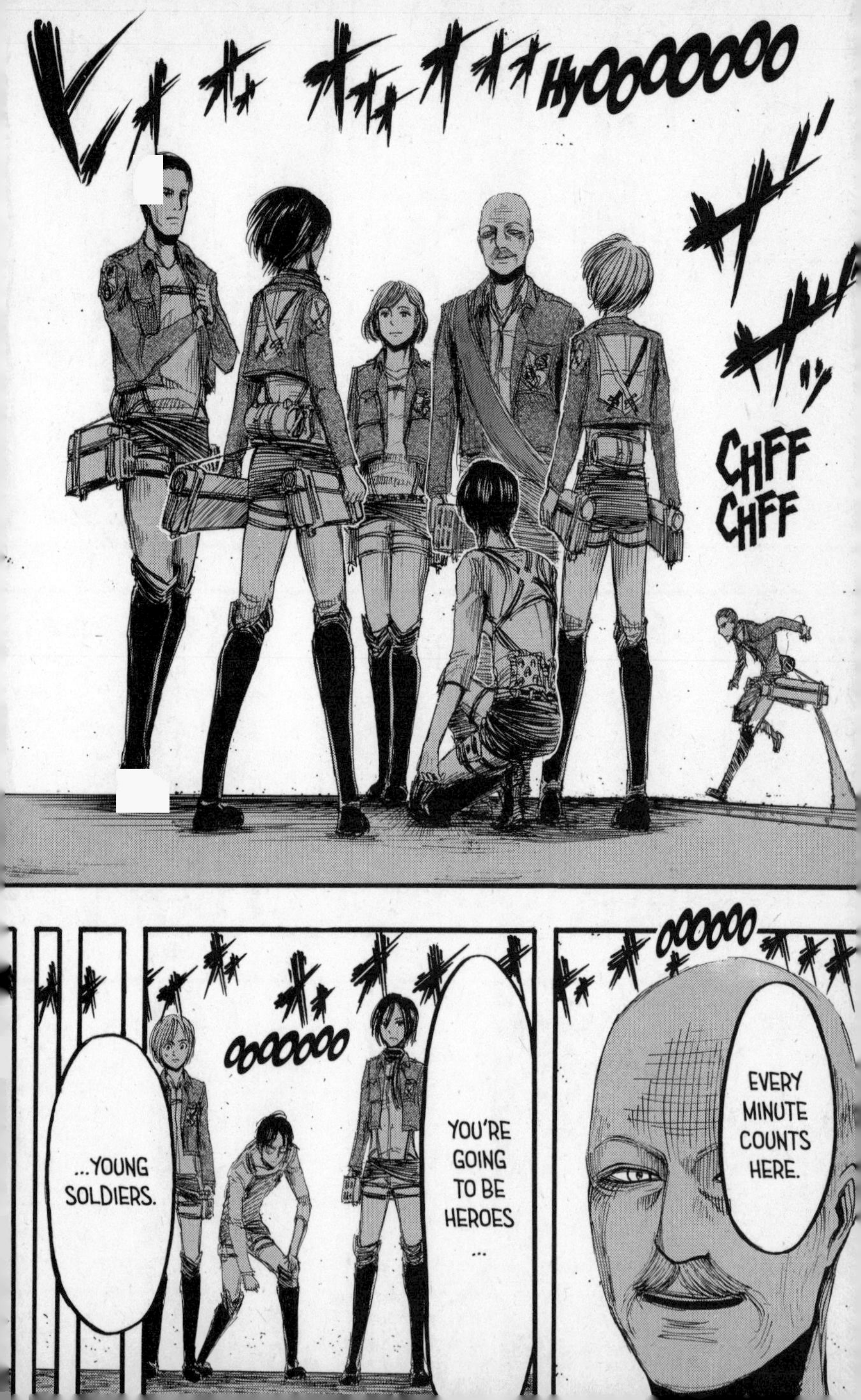
HYOOOOOOO
CHFF
CHFF
OOOOOO
EVERY MINUTE COUNTS HERE.
OOOOOOO
YOU'RE GOING TO BE HEROES ...
...YOUNG SOLDIERS.

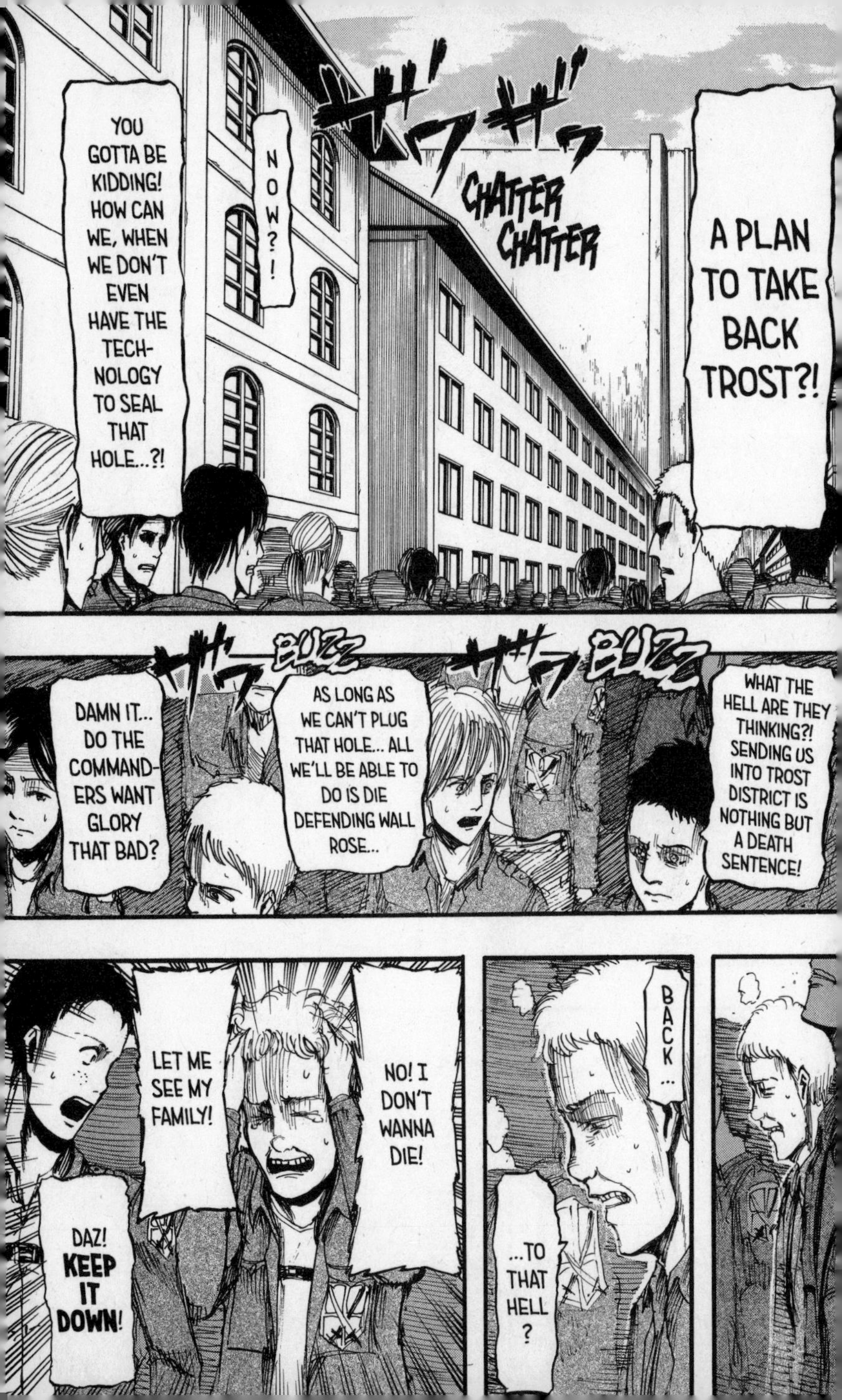
A PLAN TO TAKE BACK TROST?!
ザワザワ
CHATTER CHATTER
NOW?!
YOU GOTTA BE KIDDING! HOW CAN WE, WHEN WE DON'T EVEN HAVE THE TECH-NOLOGY TO SEAL THAT HOLE...?!
WHAT THE HELL ARE THEY THINKING?! SENDING US INTO TROST DISTRICT IS NOTHING BUT A DEATH SENTENCE!
ザワ
BUZZ
ザワ
BUZZ
AS LONG AS WE CAN'T PLUG THAT HOLE... ALL WE'LL BE ABLE TO DO IS DIE DEFENDING WALL ROSE...
DAMN IT... DO THE COMMAND-ERS WANT GLORY THAT BAD?
BACK...
...TO THAT HELL?
NO! I DON'T WANNA DIE!
LET ME SEE MY FAMILY!
DAZ! **KEEP IT DOWN!**

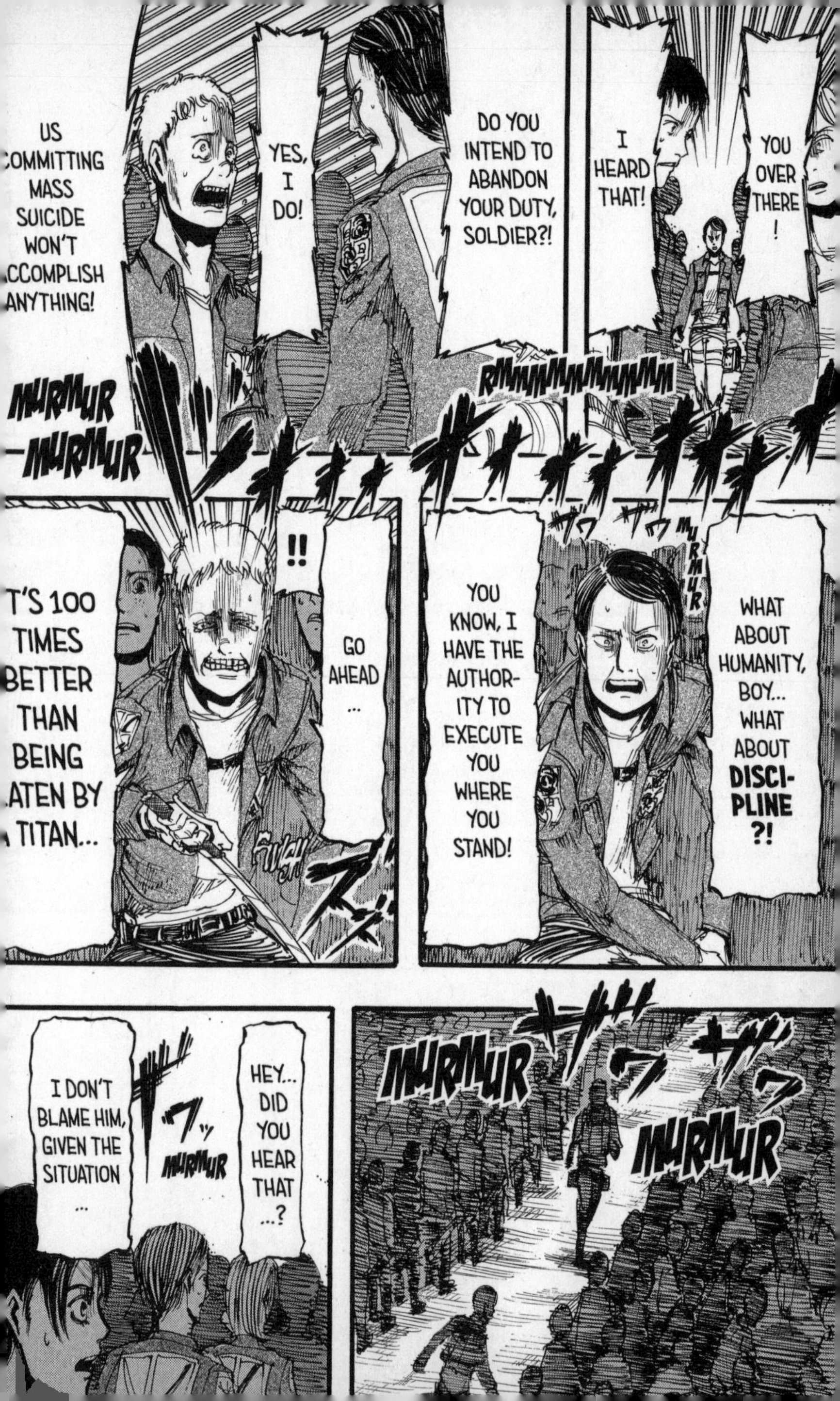
YOU OVER THERE!
I HEARD THAT!
DO YOU INTEND TO ABANDON YOUR DUTY, SOLDIER?!
YES, I DO!
US OMMITTING MASS SUICIDE WON'T CCOMPLISH ANYTHING!
RMMMMMMMMMMMM
MURMUR MURMUR
WHAT ABOUT HUMANITY, BOY... WHAT ABOUT DISCIPLINE?!
MURMUR
YOU KNOW, I HAVE THE AUTHORITY TO EXECUTE YOU WHERE YOU STAND!
GO AHEAD...
!!
T'S 100 TIMES BETTER THAN BEING ATEN BY TITAN...
MURMUR
MURMUR
HEY... DID YOU HEAR THAT...?
MURMUR
I DON'T BLAME HIM, GIVEN THE SITUATION...

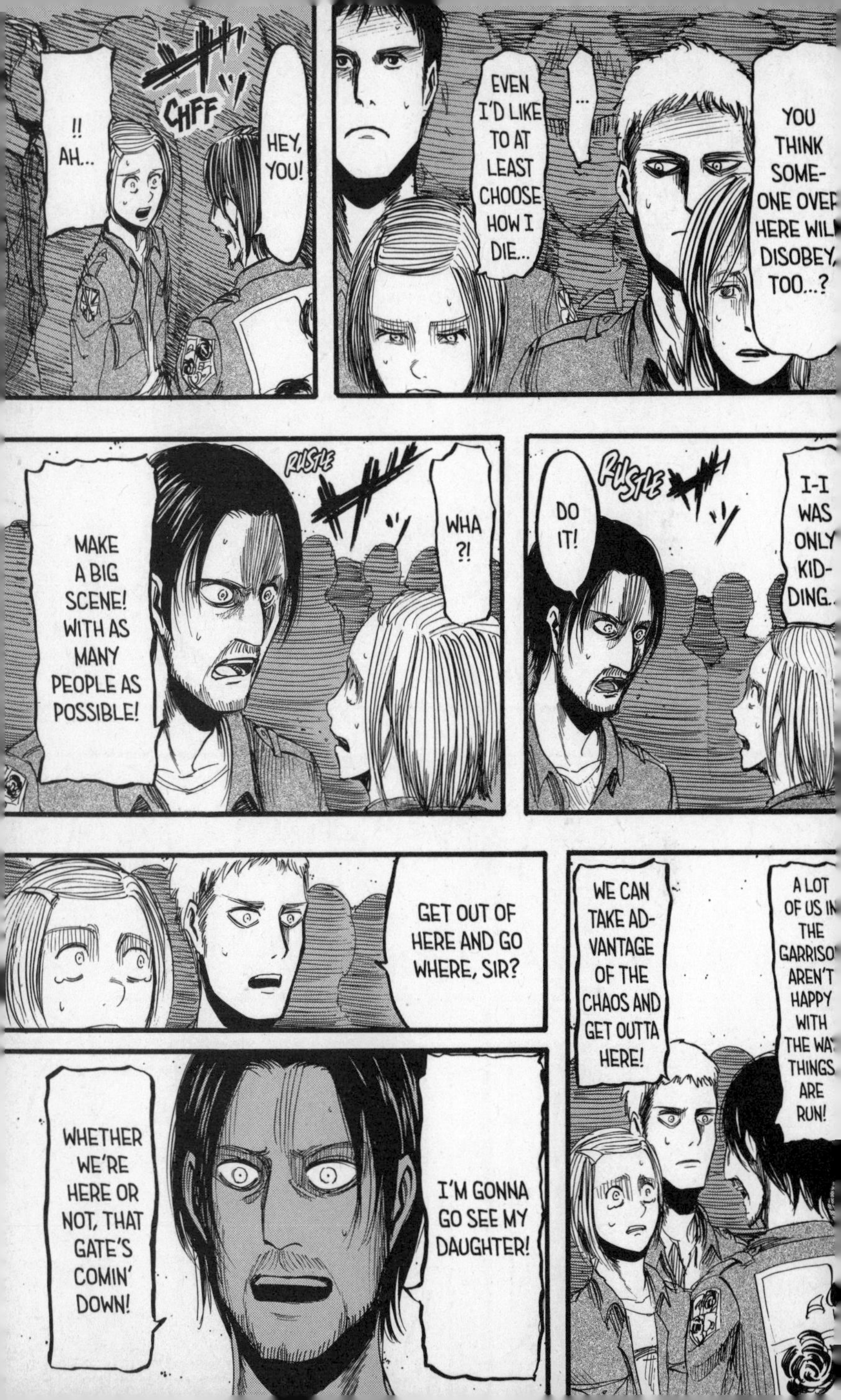
YOU THINK SOME-ONE OVER HERE WILL DISOBEY, TOO...?
...
EVEN I'D LIKE TO AT LEAST CHOOSE HOW I DIE...
HEY, YOU!
CHFF
!! AH...
I-I WAS ONLY KID-DING...
RUSTLE
DO IT!
WHA ?!
RUSTLE
MAKE A BIG SCENE! WITH AS MANY PEOPLE AS POSSIBLE!
A LOT OF US IN THE GARRISO AREN'T HAPPY WITH THE WA THINGS ARE RUN!
WE CAN TAKE AD-VANTAGE OF THE CHAOS AND GET OUTTA HERE!
GET OUT OF HERE AND GO WHERE, SIR?
I'M GONNA GO SEE MY DAUGHTER!
WHETHER WE'RE HERE OR NOT, THAT GATE'S COMIN' DOWN!

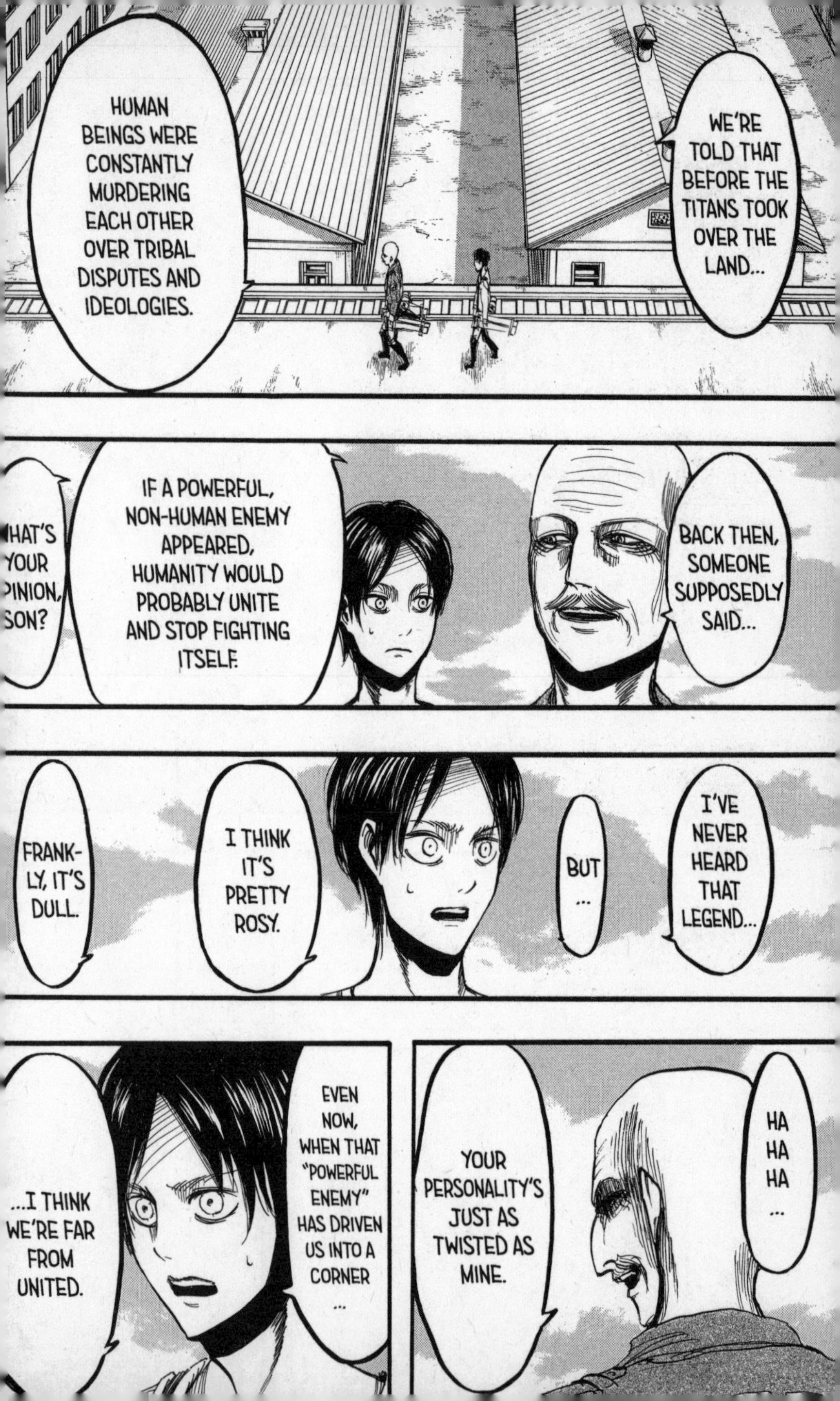
WE'RE TOLD THAT BEFORE THE TITANS TOOK OVER THE LAND...
HUMAN BEINGS WERE CONSTANTLY MURDERING EACH OTHER OVER TRIBAL DISPUTES AND IDEOLOGIES.
BACK THEN, SOMEONE SUPPOSEDLY SAID...
IF A POWERFUL, NON-HUMAN ENEMY APPEARED, HUMANITY WOULD PROBABLY UNITE AND STOP FIGHTING ITSELF.
HAT'S YOUR PINION, SON?
I'VE NEVER HEARD THAT LEGEND...
BUT ...
I THINK IT'S PRETTY ROSY.
FRANK-LY, IT'S DULL.
HA HA HA ...
YOUR PERSONALITY'S JUST AS TWISTED AS MINE.
EVEN NOW, WHEN THAT "POWERFUL ENEMY" HAS DRIVEN US INTO A CORNER ...
...I THINK WE'RE FAR FROM UNITED.

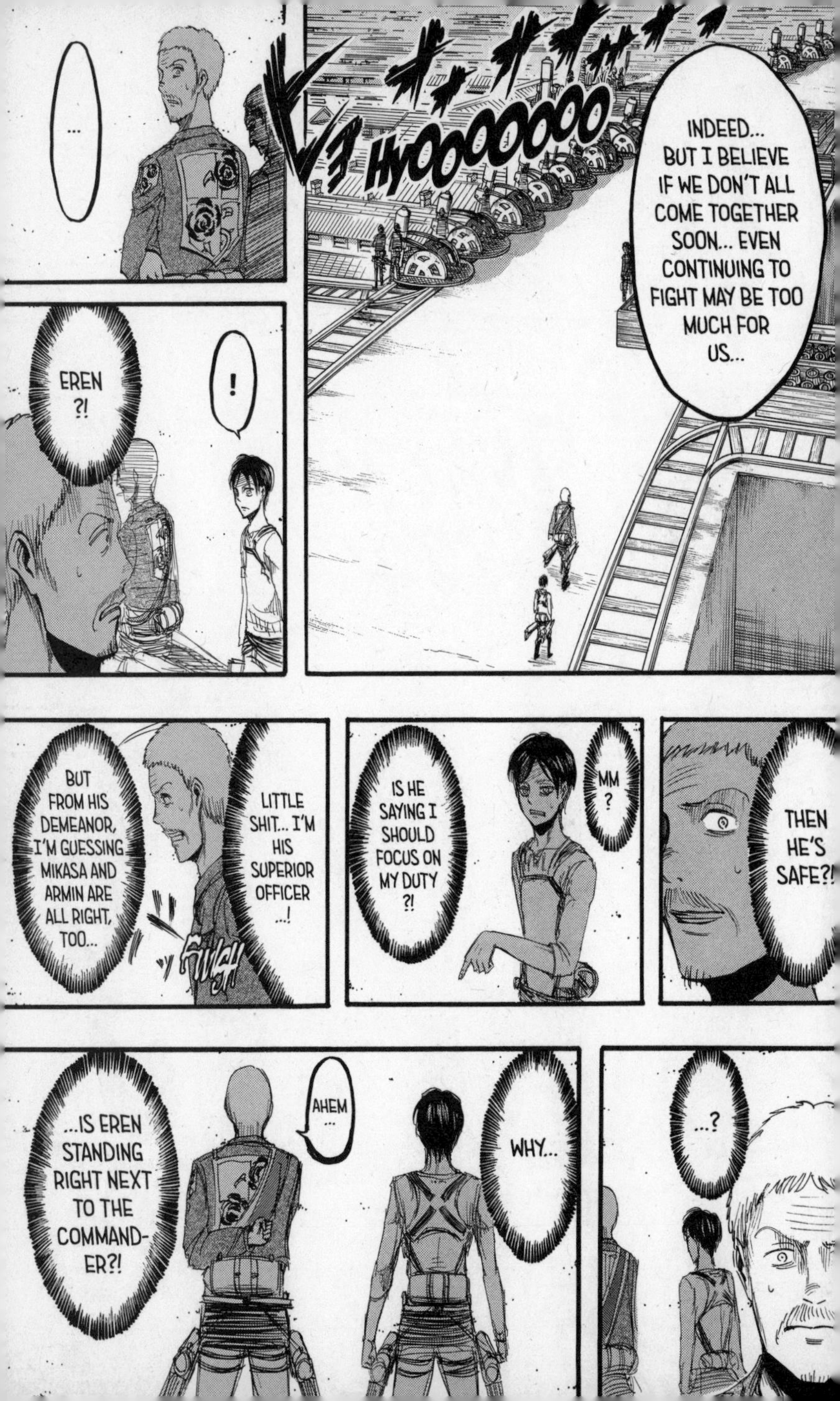
HYOOOOOOO
INDEED... BUT I BELIEVE IF WE DON'T ALL COME TOGETHER SOON... EVEN CONTINUING TO FIGHT MAY BE TOO MUCH FOR US...
...
!
EREN ?!
THEN HE'S SAFE?!
MM ?
IS HE SAYING I SHOULD FOCUS ON MY DUTY ?!
LITTLE SHIT... I'M HIS SUPERIOR OFFICER ...!
FWISH
BUT FROM HIS DEMEANOR, I'M GUESSING MIKASA AND ARMIN ARE ALL RIGHT, TOO...
...?
WHY...
AHEM ...
...IS EREN STANDING RIGHT NEXT TO THE COMMANDER?!

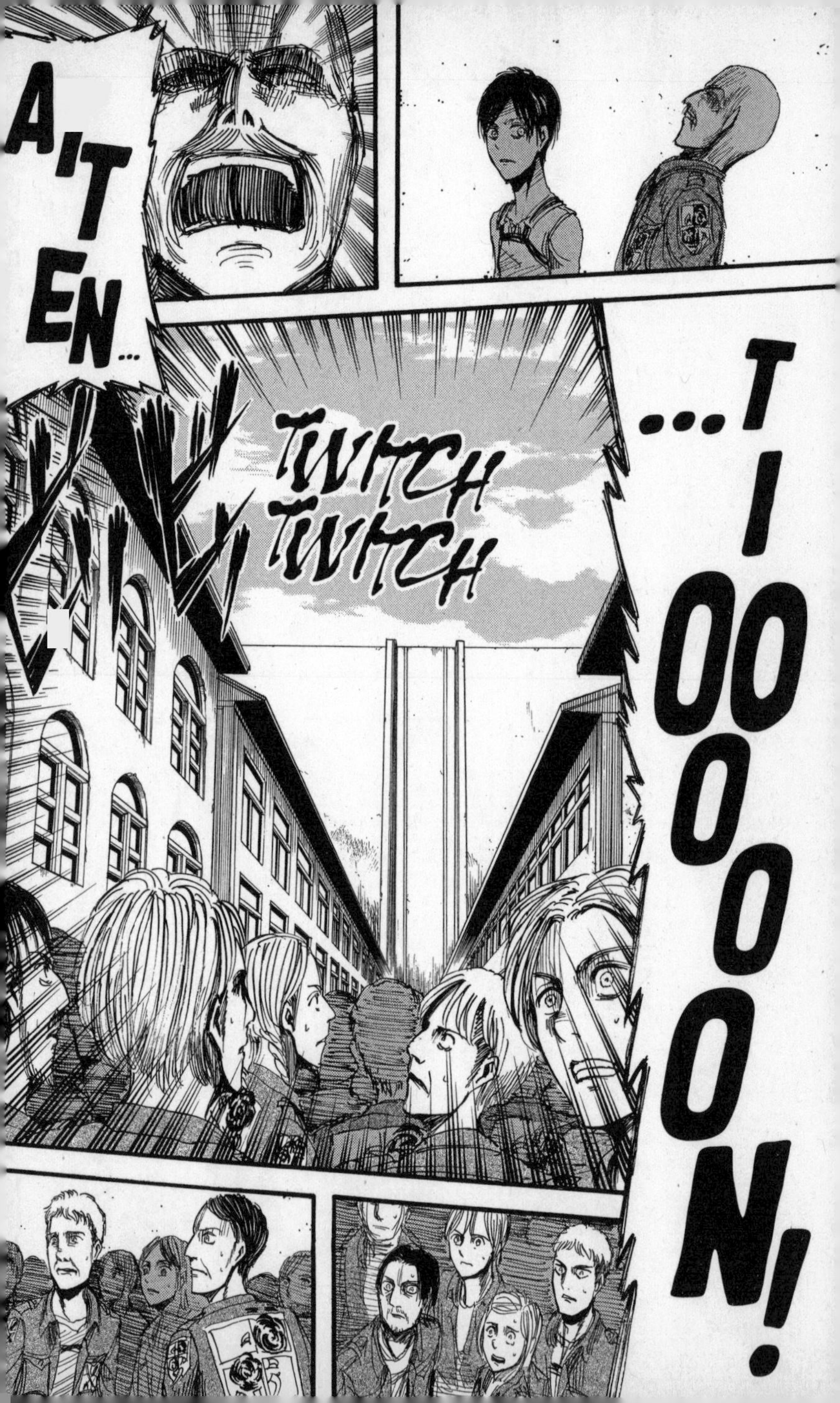

AITEN...
TWITCH TWITCH
...TIOOOOOON!

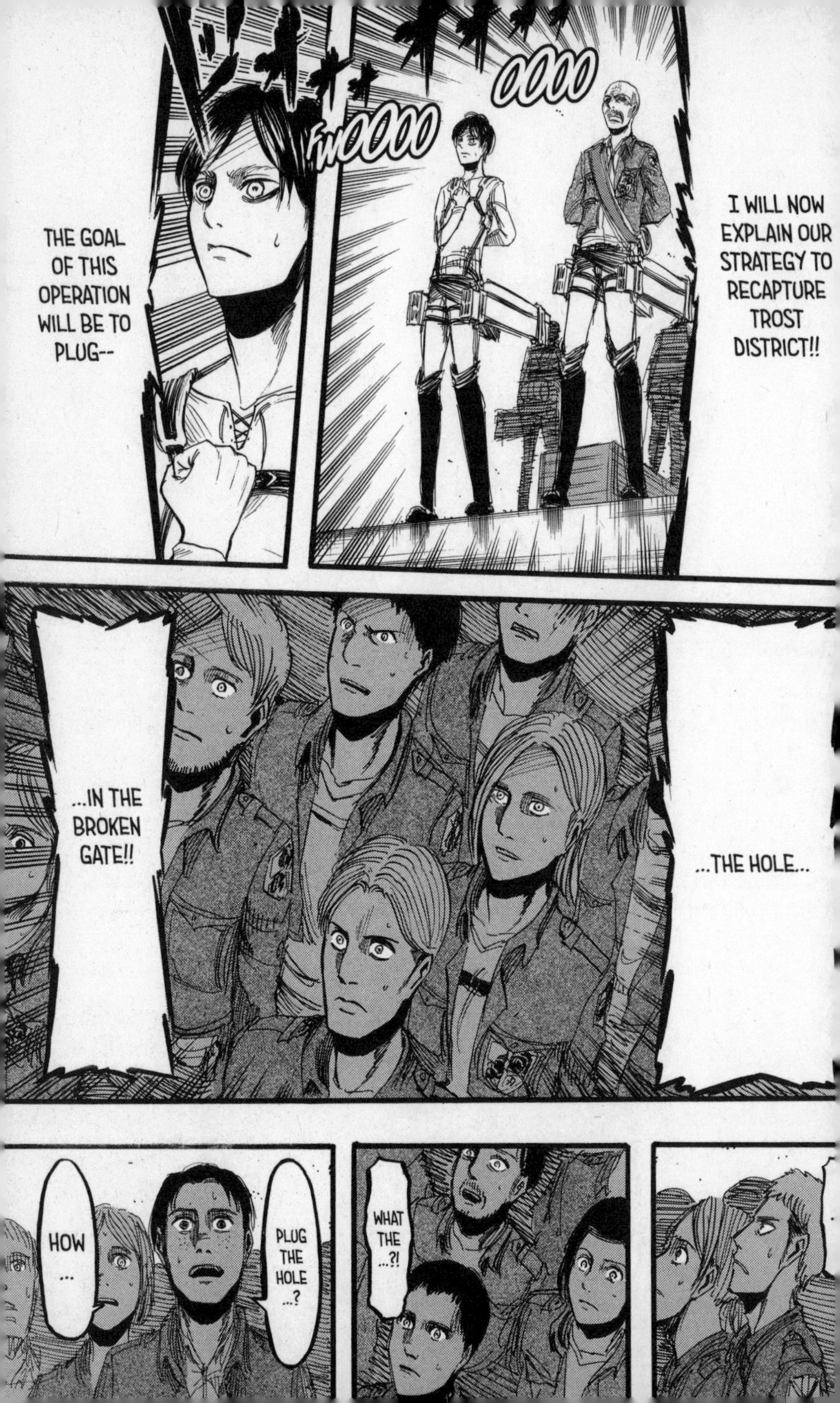
I WILL NOW EXPLAIN OUR STRATEGY TO RECAPTURE TROST DISTRICT!!
FwOOOO OOOO
THE GOAL OF THIS OPERATION WILL BE TO PLUG--
...THE HOLE...
...IN THE BROKEN GATE!!
WHAT THE ...?!
PLUG THE HOLE ...?
HOW ...

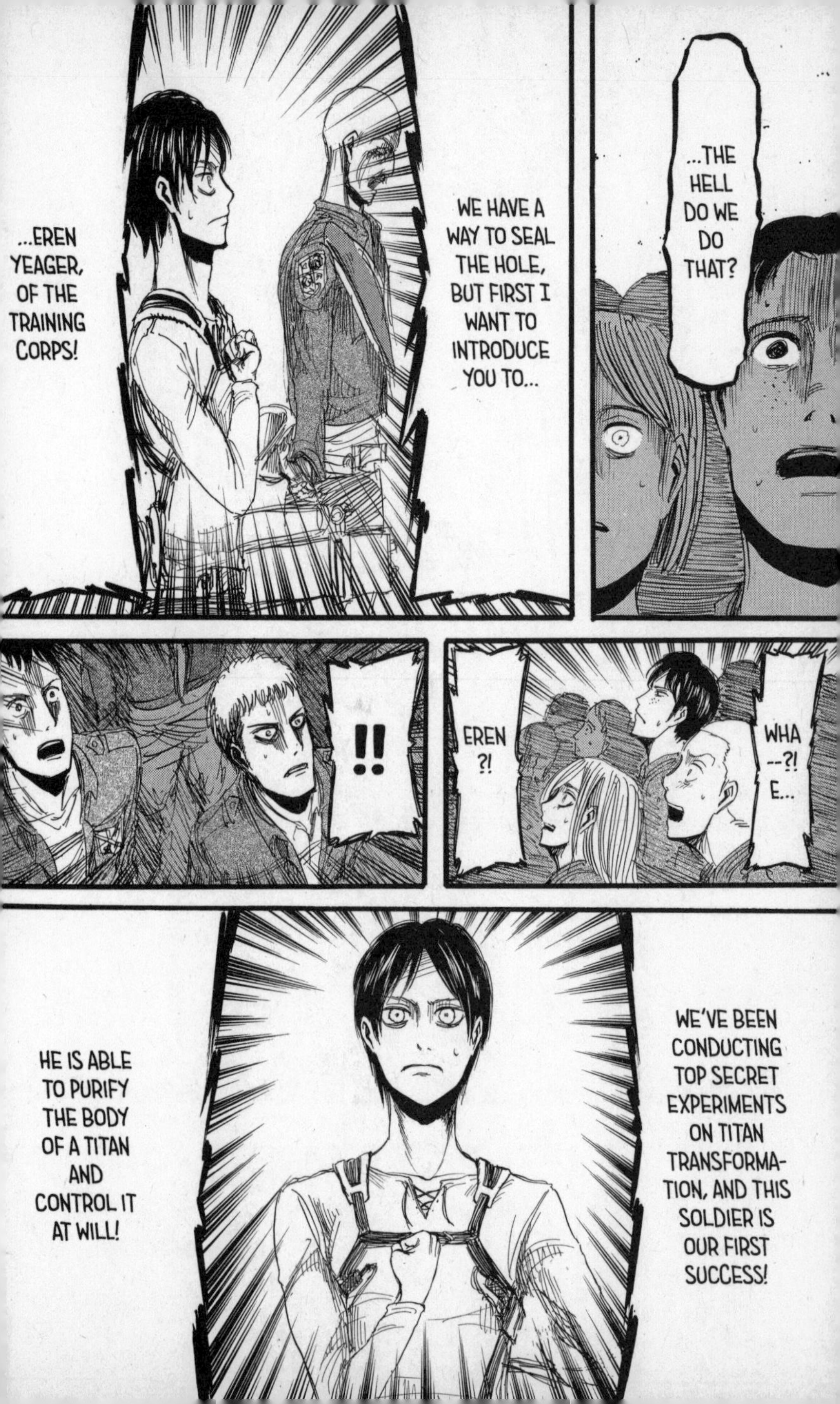
...THE HELL DO WE DO THAT?
WE HAVE A WAY TO SEAL THE HOLE, BUT FIRST I WANT TO INTRODUCE YOU TO...
...EREN YEAGER, OF THE TRAINING CORPS!
WHA--?! E...
EREN?!
!!
WE'VE BEEN CONDUCTING TOP SECRET EXPERIMENTS ON TITAN TRANSFORMATION, AND THIS SOLDIER IS OUR FIRST SUCCESS!
HE IS ABLE TO PURIFY THE BODY OF A TITAN AND CONTROL IT AT WILL!

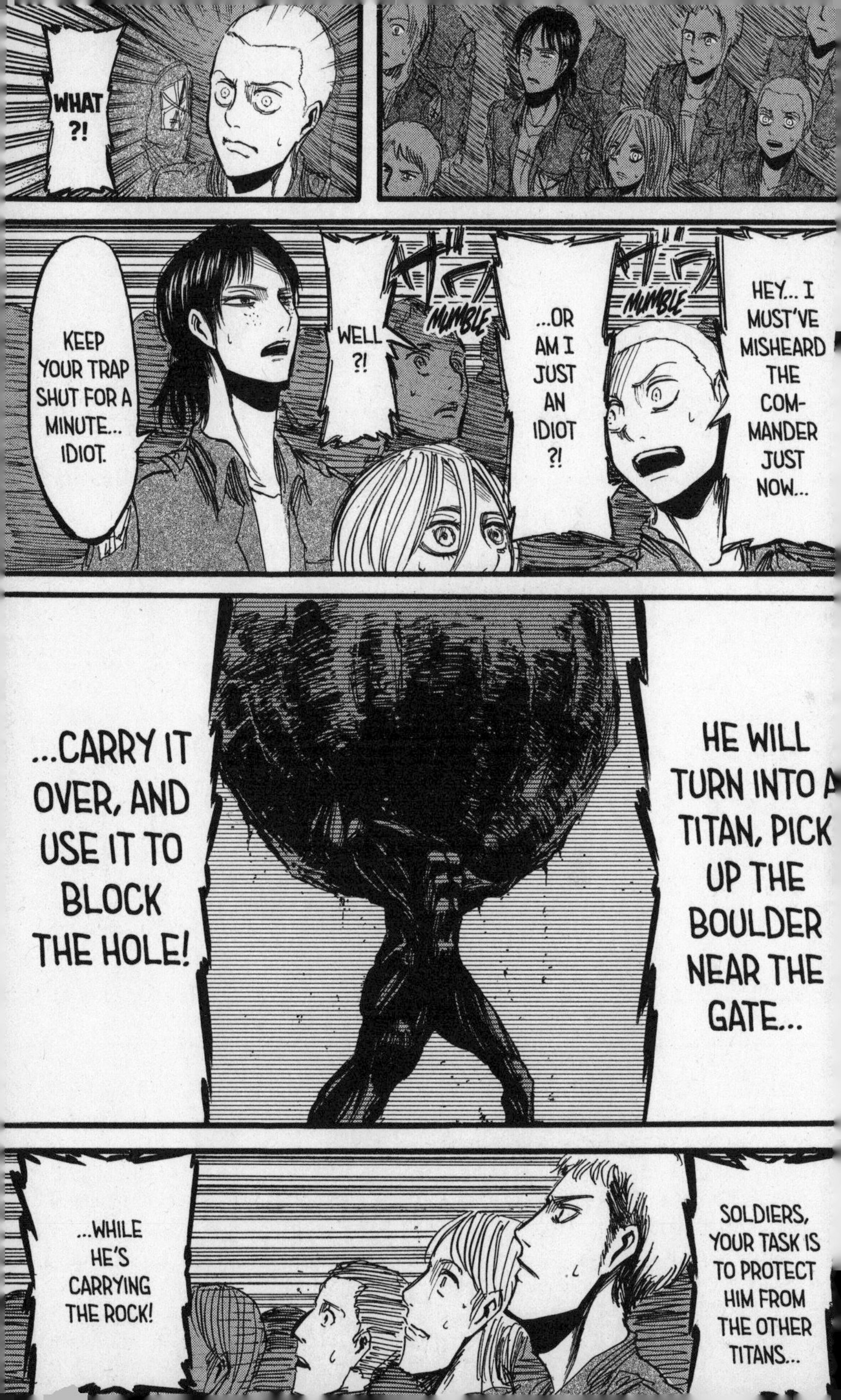
WHAT ?!
HEY... I MUST'VE MISHEARD THE COMMANDER JUST NOW...
MUMBLE
...OR AM I JUST AN IDIOT ?!
MUMBLE
WELL ?!
KEEP YOUR TRAP SHUT FOR A MINUTE... IDIOT.
HE WILL TURN INTO A TITAN, PICK UP THE BOULDER NEAR THE GATE...
...CARRY IT OVER, AND USE IT TO BLOCK THE HOLE!
SOLDIERS, YOUR TASK IS TO PROTECT HIM FROM THE OTHER TITANS...
...WHILE HE'S CARRYING THE ROCK!

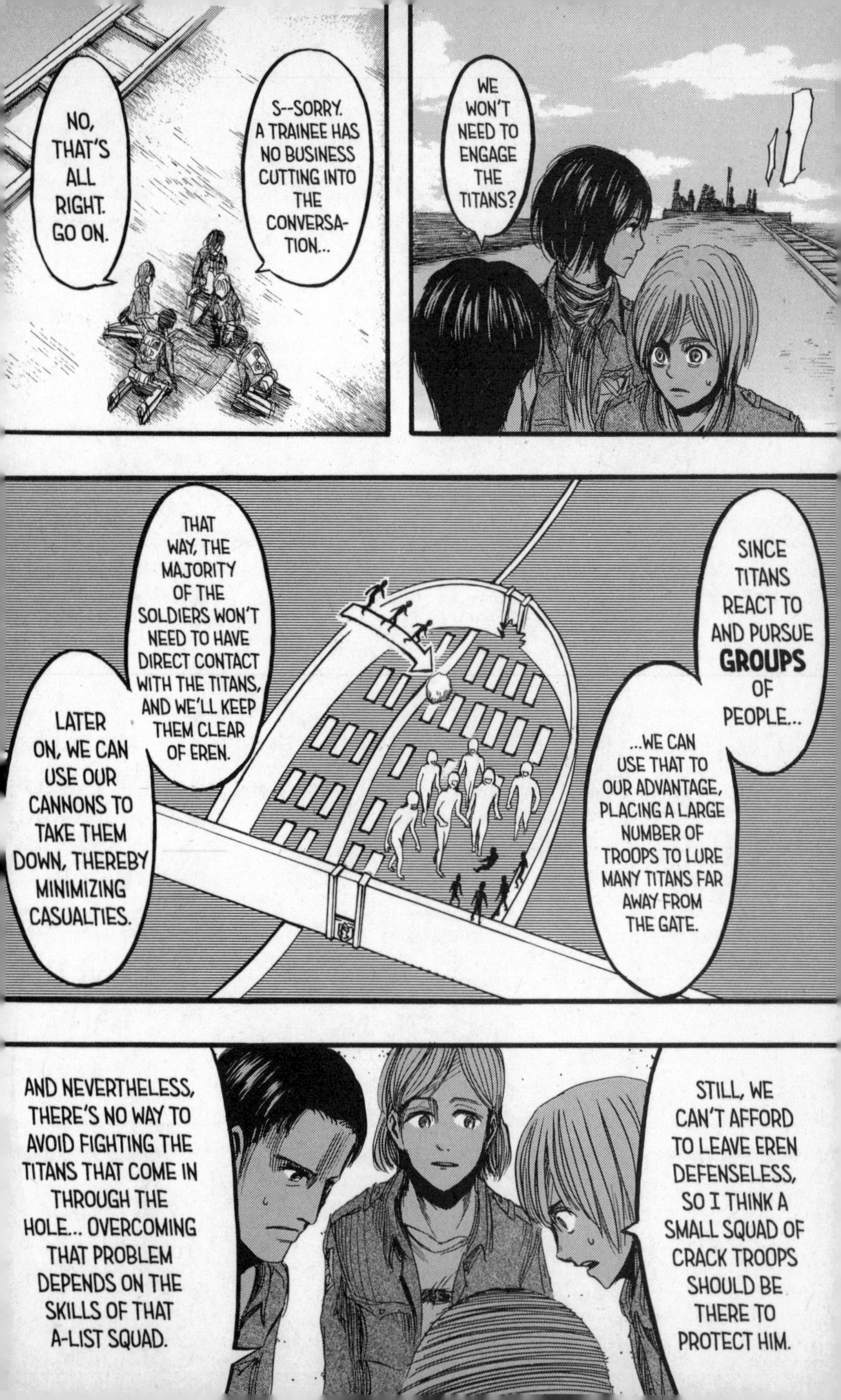
WE WON'T NEED TO ENGAGE THE TITANS?
S--SORRY. A TRAINEE HAS NO BUSINESS CUTTING INTO THE CONVERSA-TION...
NO, THAT'S ALL RIGHT. GO ON.
SINCE TITANS REACT TO AND PURSUE **GROUPS** OF PEOPLE...
...WE CAN USE THAT TO OUR ADVANTAGE, PLACING A LARGE NUMBER OF TROOPS TO LURE MANY TITANS FAR AWAY FROM THE GATE.
THAT WAY, THE MAJORITY OF THE SOLDIERS WON'T NEED TO HAVE DIRECT CONTACT WITH THE TITANS, AND WE'LL KEEP THEM CLEAR OF EREN.
LATER ON, WE CAN USE OUR CANNONS TO TAKE THEM DOWN, THEREBY MINIMIZING CASUALTIES.
STILL, WE CAN'T AFFORD TO LEAVE EREN DEFENSELESS, SO I THINK A SMALL SQUAD OF CRACK TROOPS SHOULD BE THERE TO PROTECT HIM.
AND NEVERTHELESS, THERE'S NO WAY TO AVOID FIGHTING THE TITANS THAT COME IN THROUGH THE HOLE... OVERCOMING THAT PROBLEM DEPENDS ON THE SKILLS OF THAT A-LIST SQUAD.

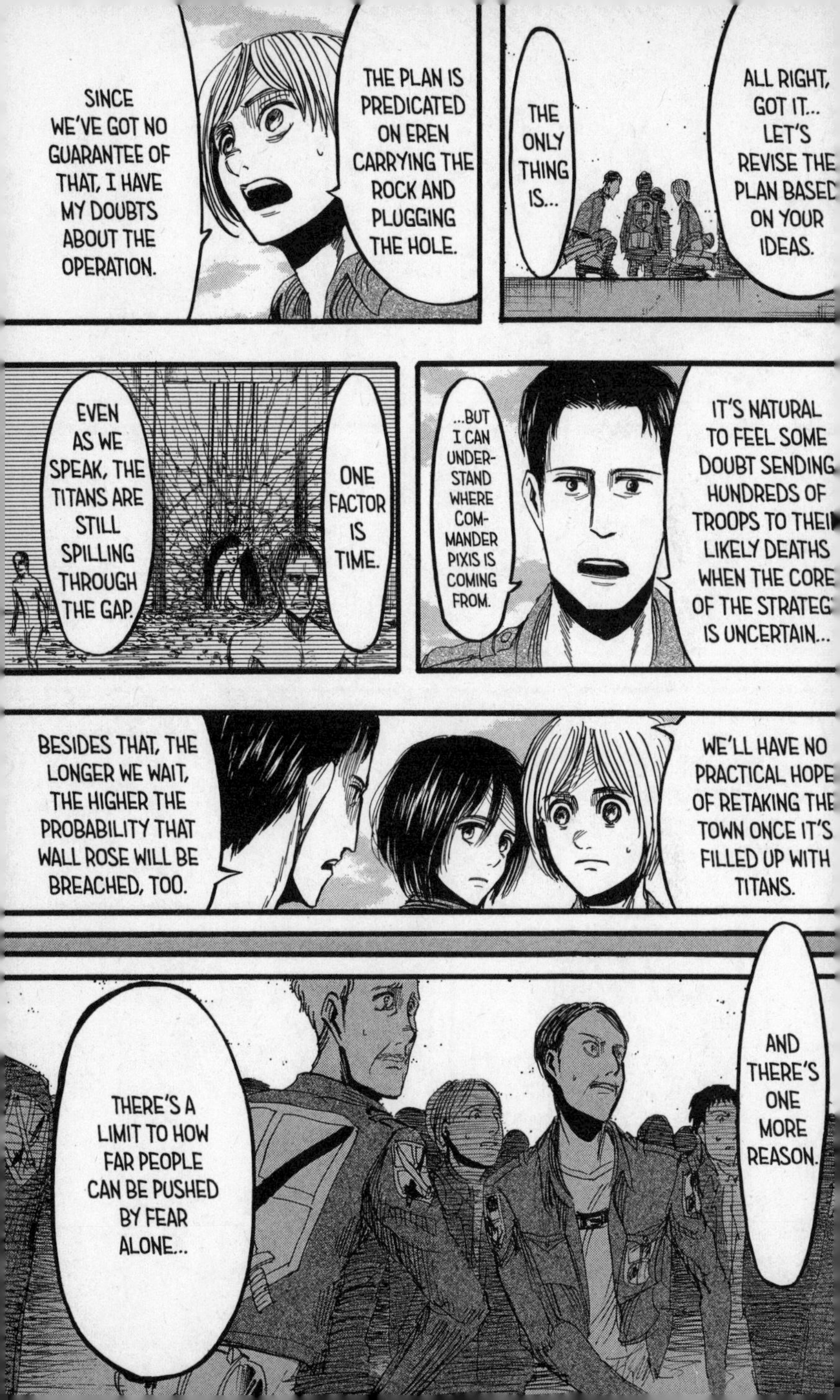
ALL RIGHT, GOT IT... LET'S REVISE THE PLAN BASED ON YOUR IDEAS.
THE ONLY THING IS...
THE PLAN IS PREDICATED ON EREN CARRYING THE ROCK AND PLUGGING THE HOLE.
SINCE WE'VE GOT NO GUARANTEE OF THAT, I HAVE MY DOUBTS ABOUT THE OPERATION.
IT'S NATURAL TO FEEL SOME DOUBT SENDING HUNDREDS OF TROOPS TO THEI LIKELY DEATHS WHEN THE CORE OF THE STRATEG IS UNCERTAIN...
...BUT I CAN UNDER-STAND WHERE COM-MANDER PIXIS IS COMING FROM.
ONE FACTOR IS TIME.
EVEN AS WE SPEAK, THE TITANS ARE STILL SPILLING THROUGH THE GAP.
WE'LL HAVE NO PRACTICAL HOPE OF RETAKING THE TOWN ONCE IT'S FILLED UP WITH TITANS.
BESIDES THAT, THE LONGER WE WAIT, THE HIGHER THE PROBABILITY THAT WALL ROSE WILL BE BREACHED, TOO.
AND THERE'S ONE MORE REASON.
THERE'S A LIMIT TO HOW FAR PEOPLE CAN BE PUSHED BY FEAR ALONE...

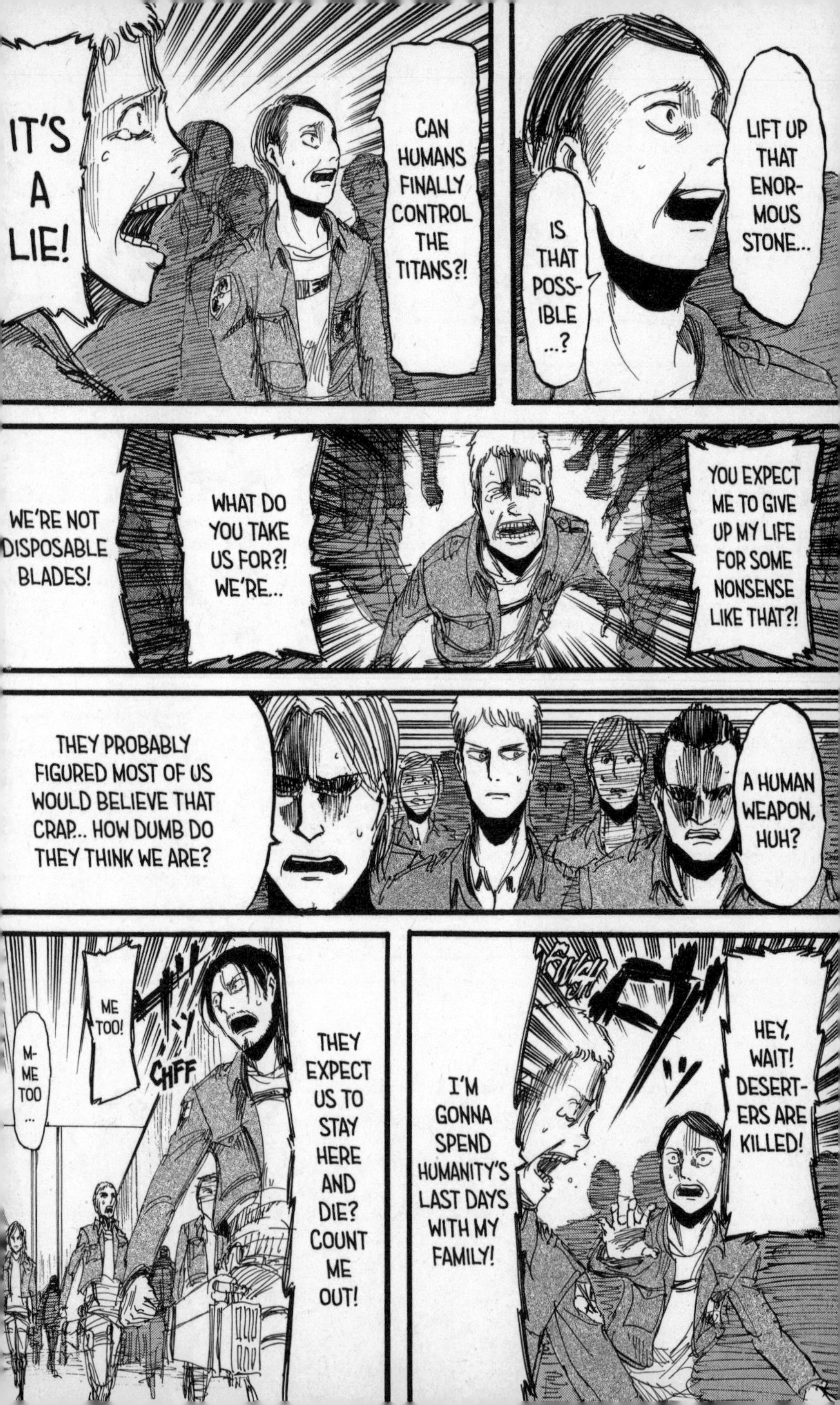
LIFT UP THAT ENORMOUS STONE...
IS THAT POSSIBLE...?
CAN HUMANS FINALLY CONTROL THE TITANS?!
IT'S A LIE!
YOU EXPECT ME TO GIVE UP MY LIFE FOR SOME NONSENSE LIKE THAT?!
WHAT DO YOU TAKE US FOR?! WE'RE...
WE'RE NOT DISPOSABLE BLADES!
A HUMAN WEAPON, HUH?
THEY PROBABLY FIGURED MOST OF US WOULD BELIEVE THAT CRAP... HOW DUMB DO THEY THINK WE ARE?
HEY, WAIT! DESERTERS ARE KILLED!
I'M GONNA SPEND HUMANITY'S LAST DAYS WITH MY FAMILY!
THEY EXPECT US TO STAY HERE AND DIE? COUNT ME OUT!
ME TOO!
CHFF
M-ME TOO...

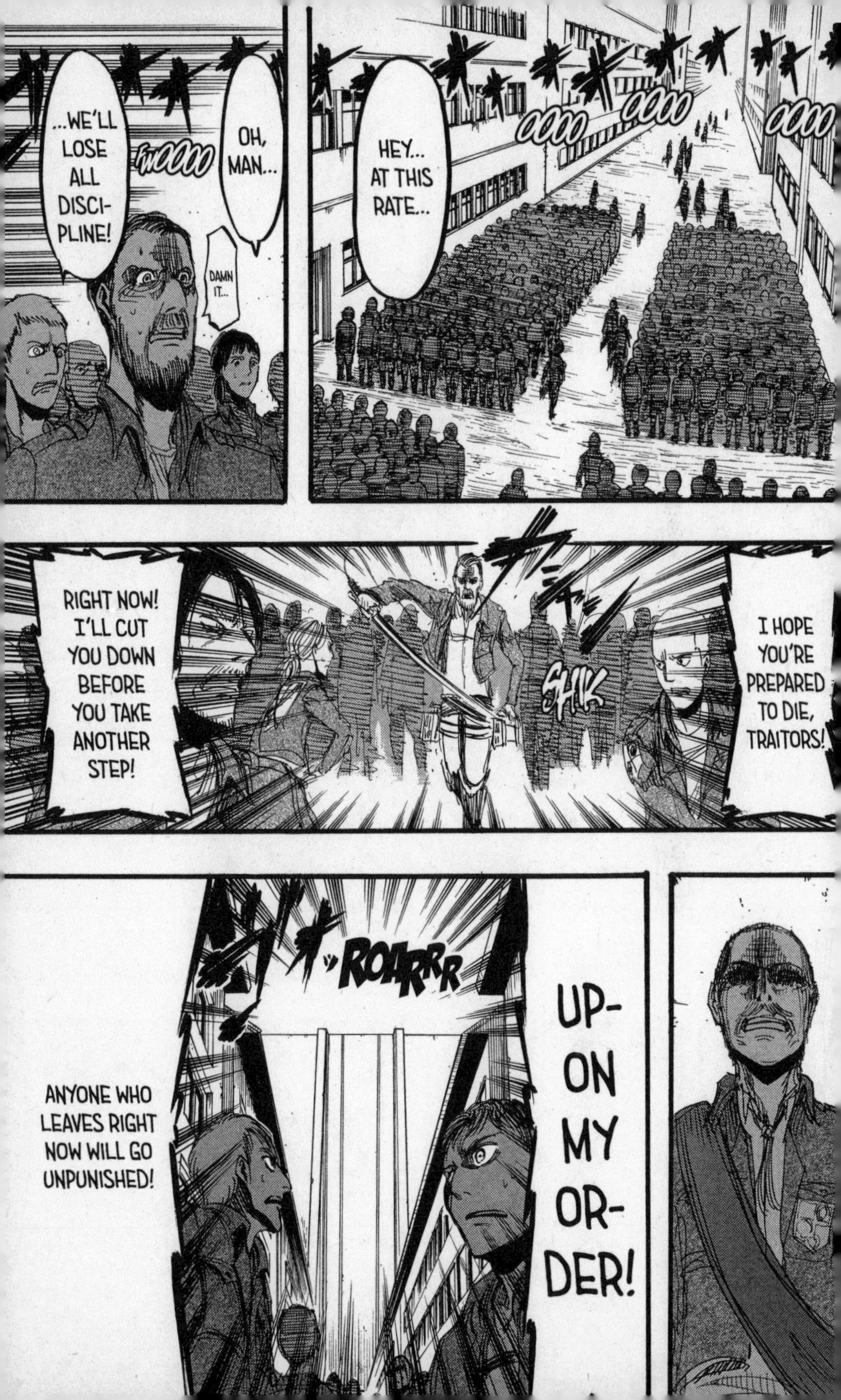
OOOO
OOOO
OOOO
HEY... AT THIS RATE...
OH, MAN...
FWOOOO
...WE'LL LOSE ALL DISCI-PLINE!
DAMN IT...
I HOPE YOU'RE PREPARED TO DIE, TRAITORS!
SHK
RIGHT NOW! I'LL CUT YOU DOWN BEFORE YOU TAKE ANOTHER STEP!
ROARRR
UP-ON MY OR-DER!
ANYONE WHO LEAVES RIGHT NOW WILL GO UNPUNISHED!

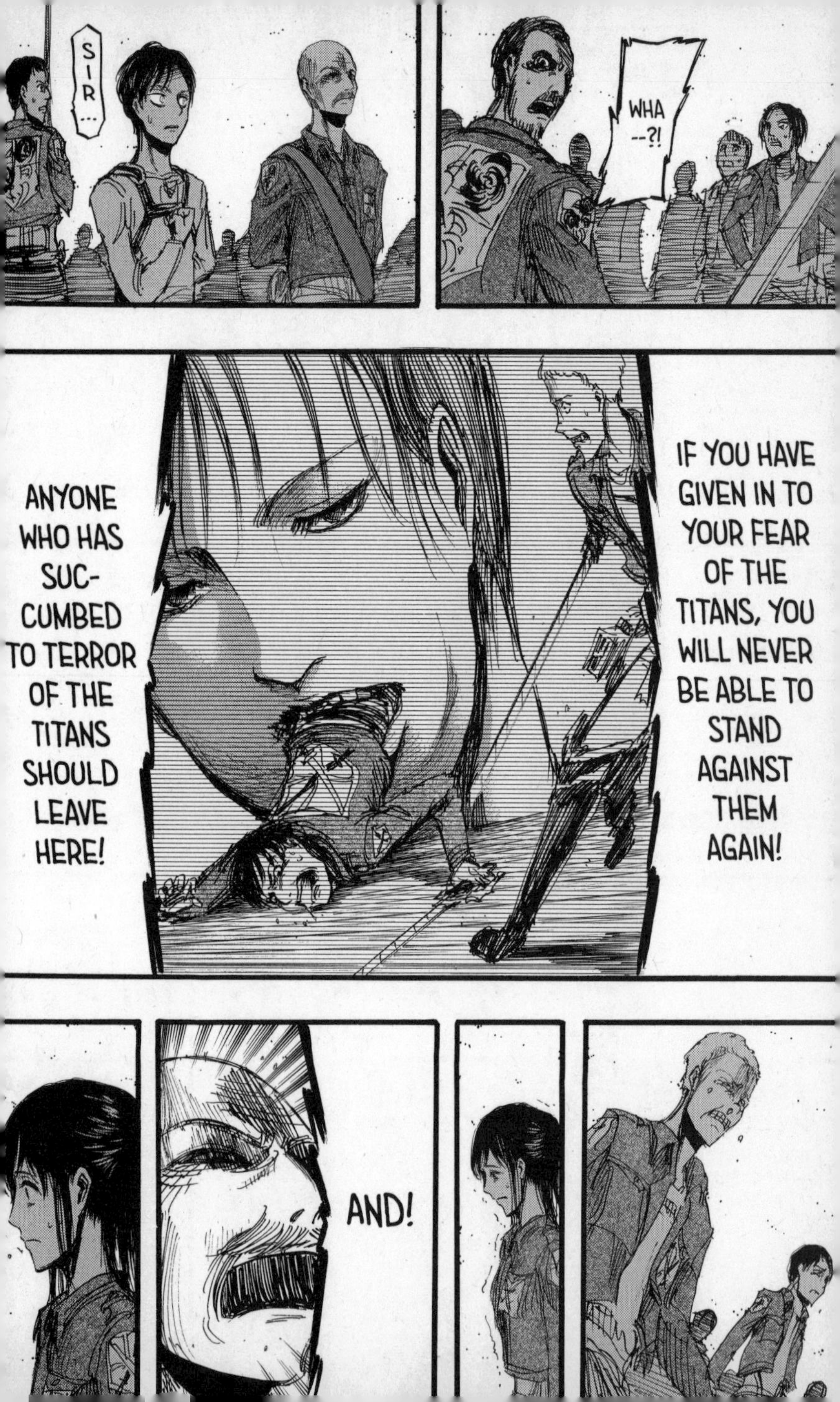
WHA--?!
SIR...
IF YOU HAVE GIVEN IN TO YOUR FEAR OF THE TITANS, YOU WILL NEVER BE ABLE TO STAND AGAINST THEM AGAIN!
ANYONE WHO HAS SUC-CUMBED TO TERROR OF THE TITANS SHOULD LEAVE HERE!
AND!

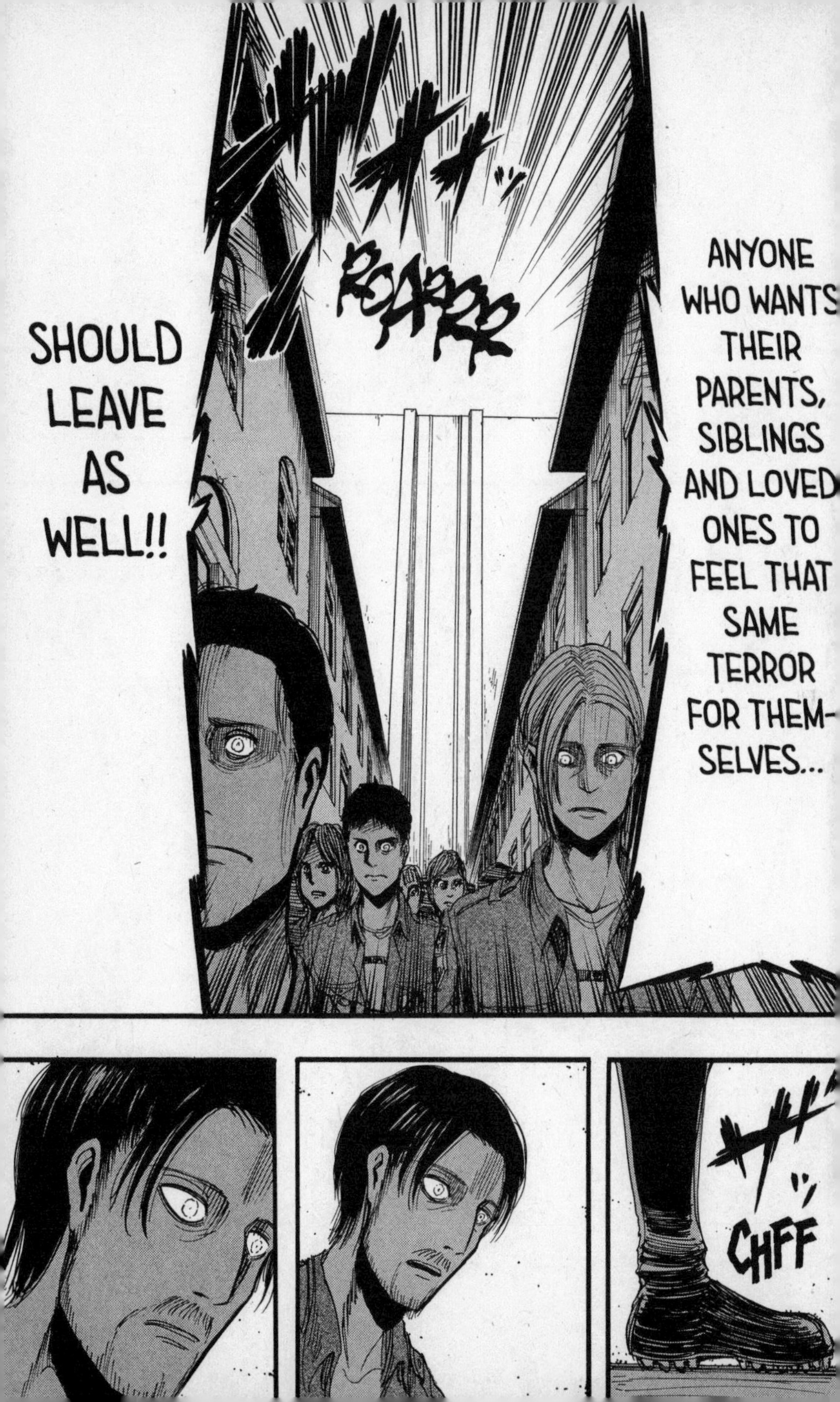
ROARRR
ANYONE WHO WANTS THEIR PARENTS, SIBLINGS AND LOVED ONES TO FEEL THAT SAME TERROR FOR THEM-SELVES...
SHOULD LEAVE AS WELL!!
CHFF

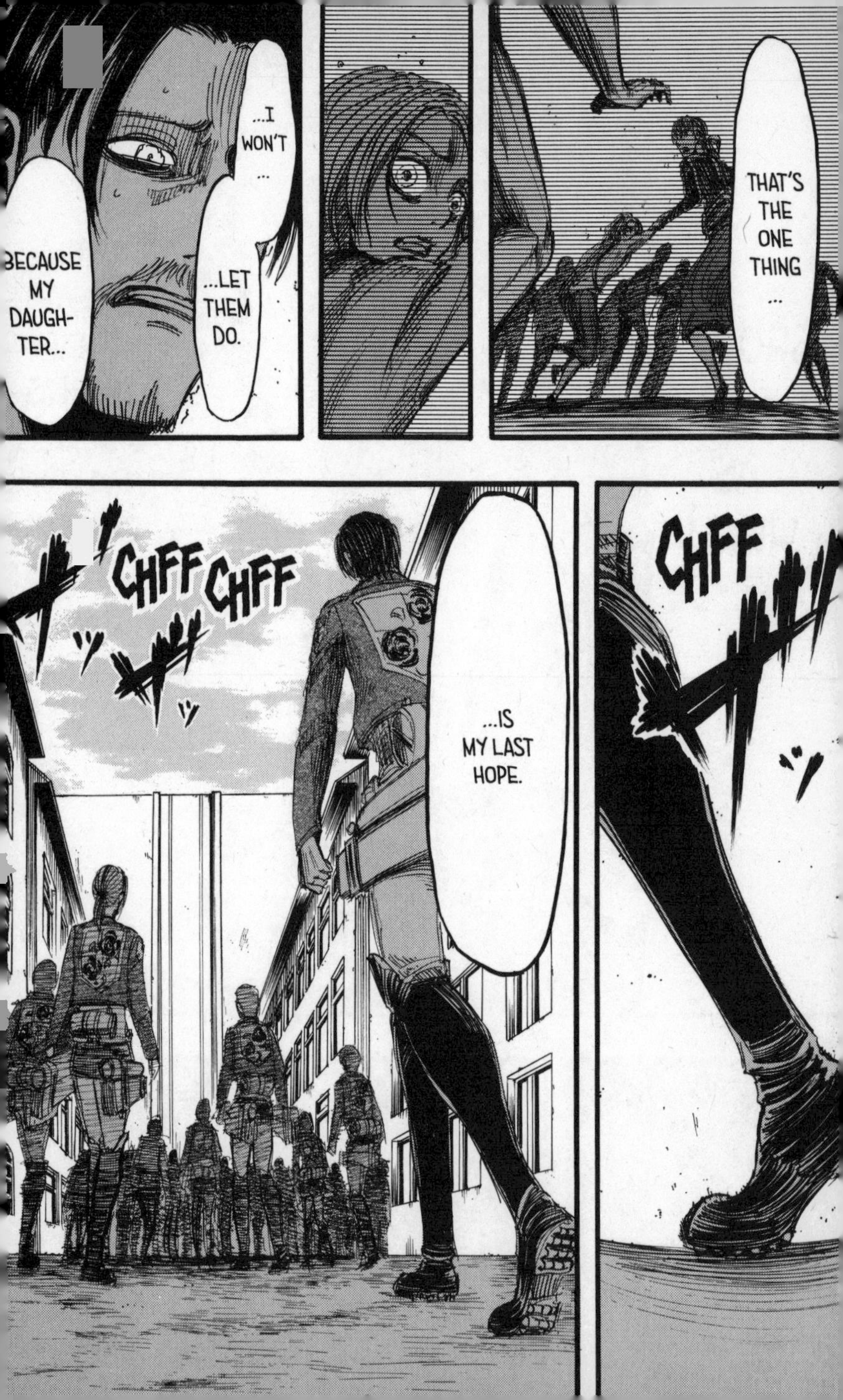
THAT'S THE ONE THING ...
...I WON'T ...
...LET THEM DO.
BECAUSE MY DAUGHTER...
CHFF
...IS MY LAST HOPE.
CHFF CHFF

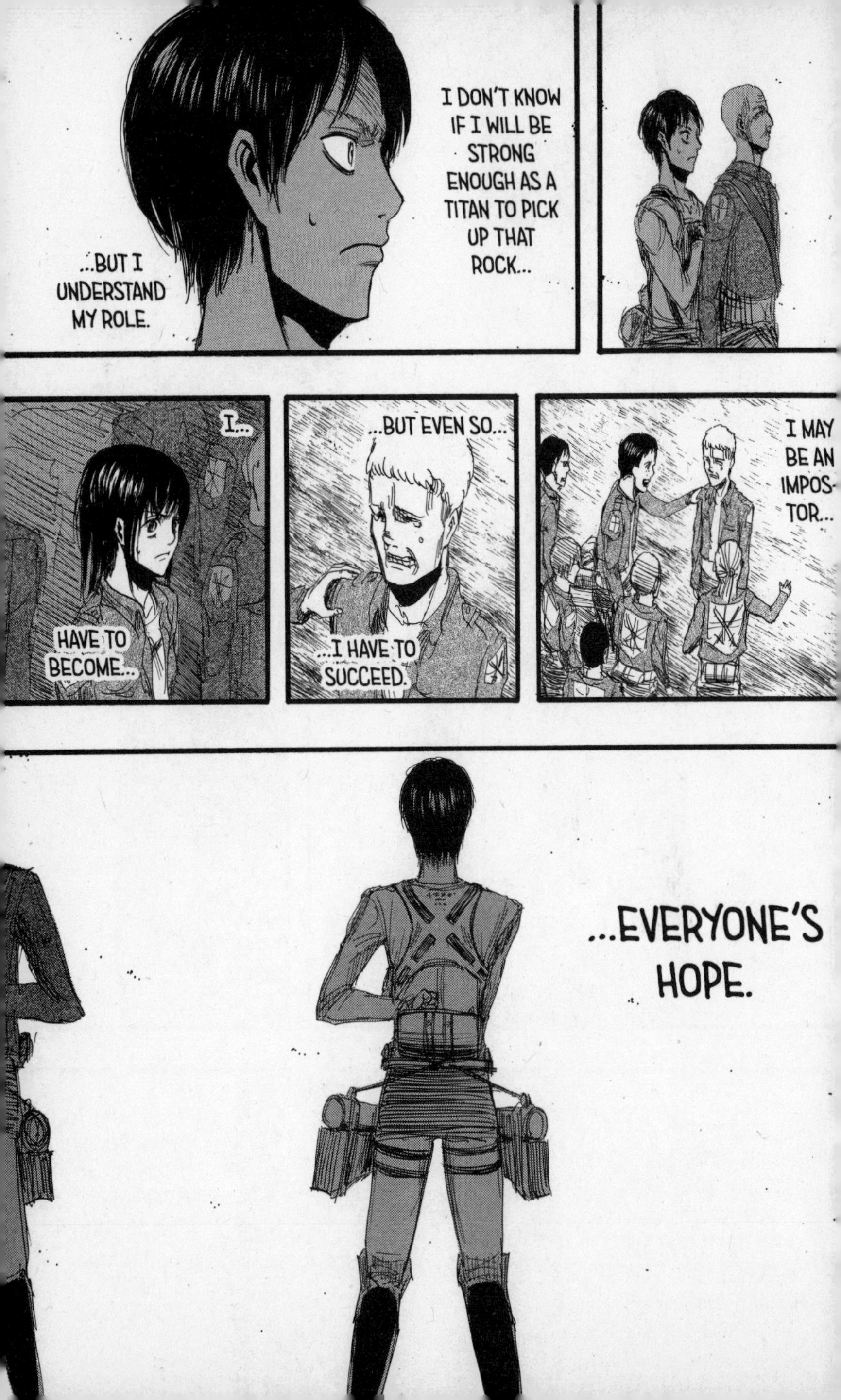
I DON'T KNOW IF I WILL BE STRONG ENOUGH AS A TITAN TO PICK UP THAT ROCK...
...BUT I UNDERSTAND MY ROLE.
I MAY BE AN IMPOS-TOR...
...BUT EVEN SO...
...I HAVE TO SUCCEED.
I...
HAVE TO BECOME...
...EVERYONE'S HOPE.

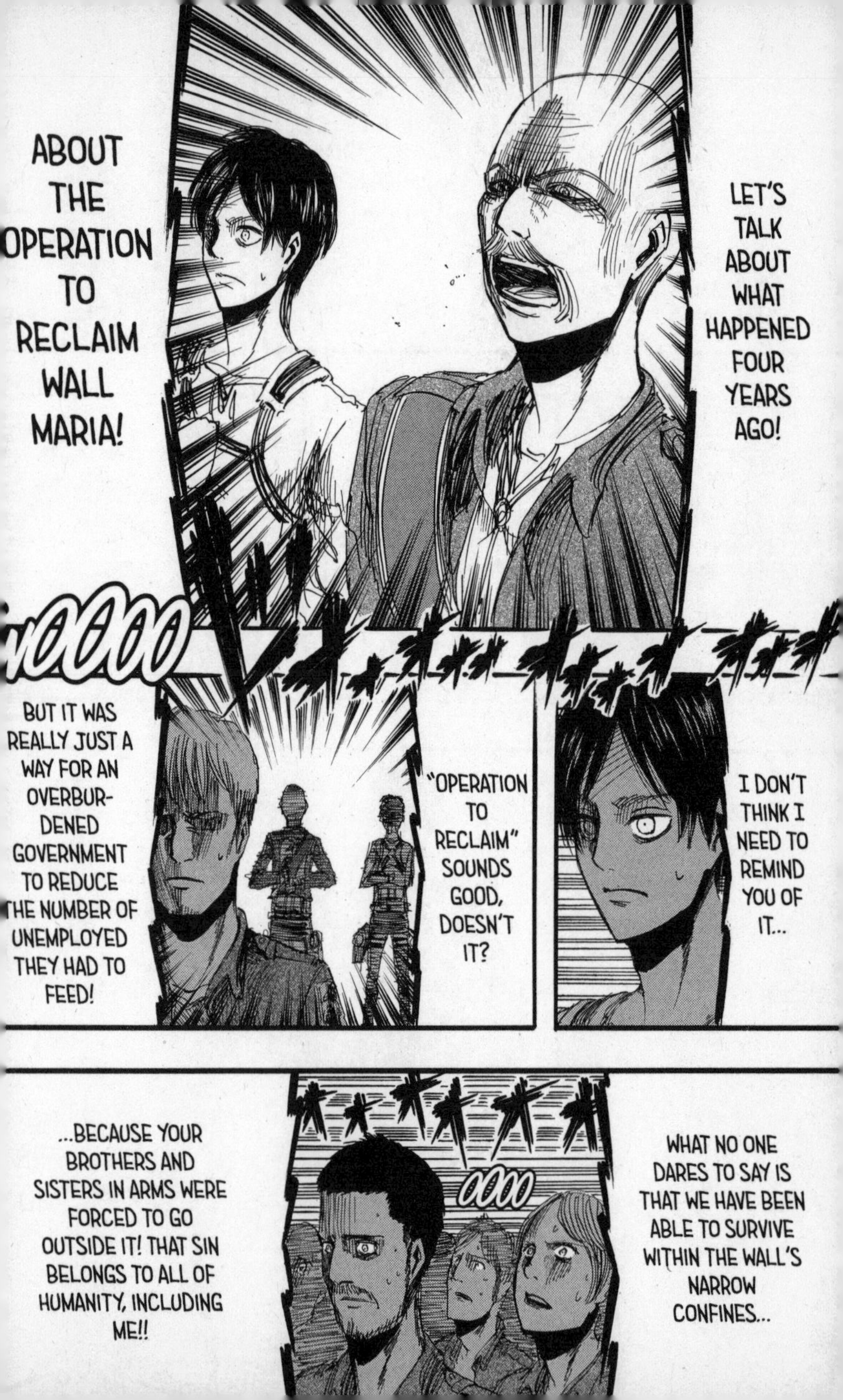
LET'S TALK ABOUT WHAT HAPPENED FOUR YEARS AGO!
ABOUT THE OPERATION TO RECLAIM WALL MARIA!
OOOO
I DON'T THINK I NEED TO REMIND YOU OF IT...
"OPERATION TO RECLAIM" SOUNDS GOOD, DOESN'T IT?
BUT IT WAS REALLY JUST A WAY FOR AN OVERBURDENED GOVERNMENT TO REDUCE THE NUMBER OF UNEMPLOYED THEY HAD TO FEED!
WHAT NO ONE DARES TO SAY IS THAT WE HAVE BEEN ABLE TO SURVIVE WITHIN THE WALL'S NARROW CONFINES...
OOOO
...BECAUSE YOUR BROTHERS AND SISTERS IN ARMS WERE FORCED TO GO OUTSIDE IT! THAT SIN BELONGS TO ALL OF HUMANITY, INCLUDING ME!!

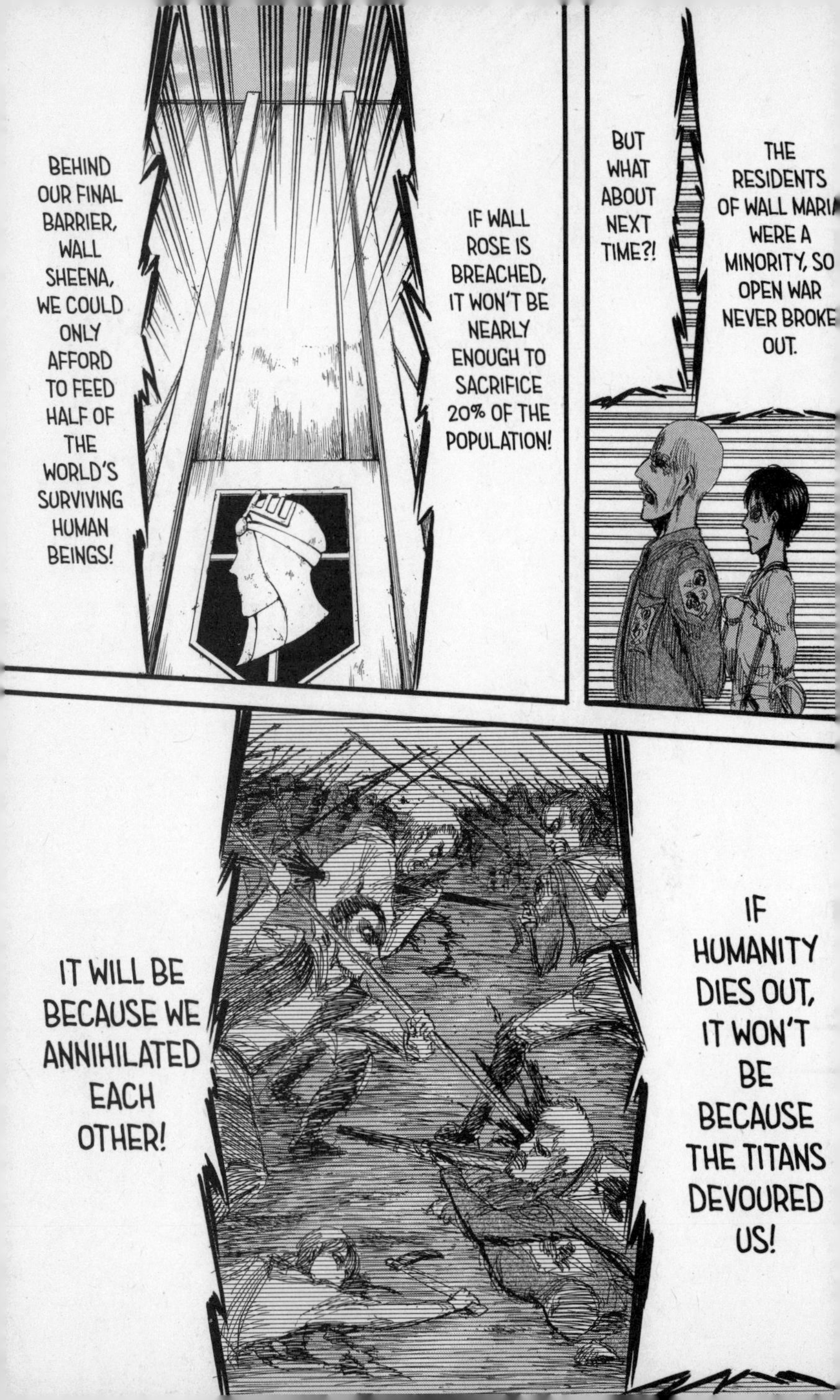
THE RESIDENTS OF WALL MARI WERE A MINORITY, SO OPEN WAR NEVER BROKE OUT.
BUT WHAT ABOUT NEXT TIME?!
IF WALL ROSE IS BREACHED, IT WON'T BE NEARLY ENOUGH TO SACRIFICE 20% OF THE POPULATION!
BEHIND OUR FINAL BARRIER, WALL SHEENA, WE COULD ONLY AFFORD TO FEED HALF OF THE WORLD'S SURVIVING HUMAN BEINGS!
IF HUMANITY DIES OUT, IT WON'T BE BECAUSE THE TITANS DEVOURED US!
IT WILL BE BECAUSE WE ANNIHILATED EACH OTHER!

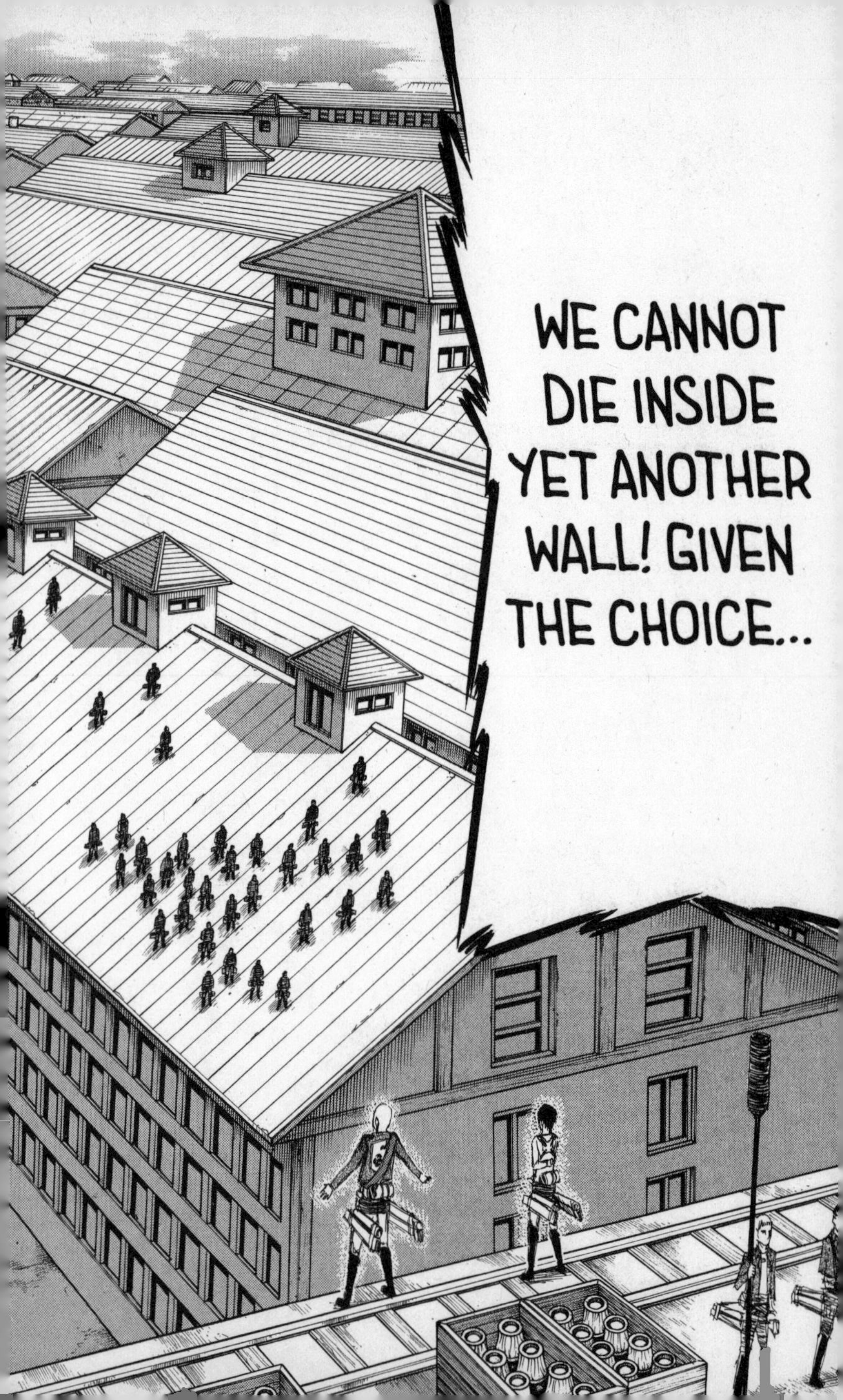
WE CANNOT DIE INSIDE YET ANOTHER WALL! GIVEN THE CHOICE...

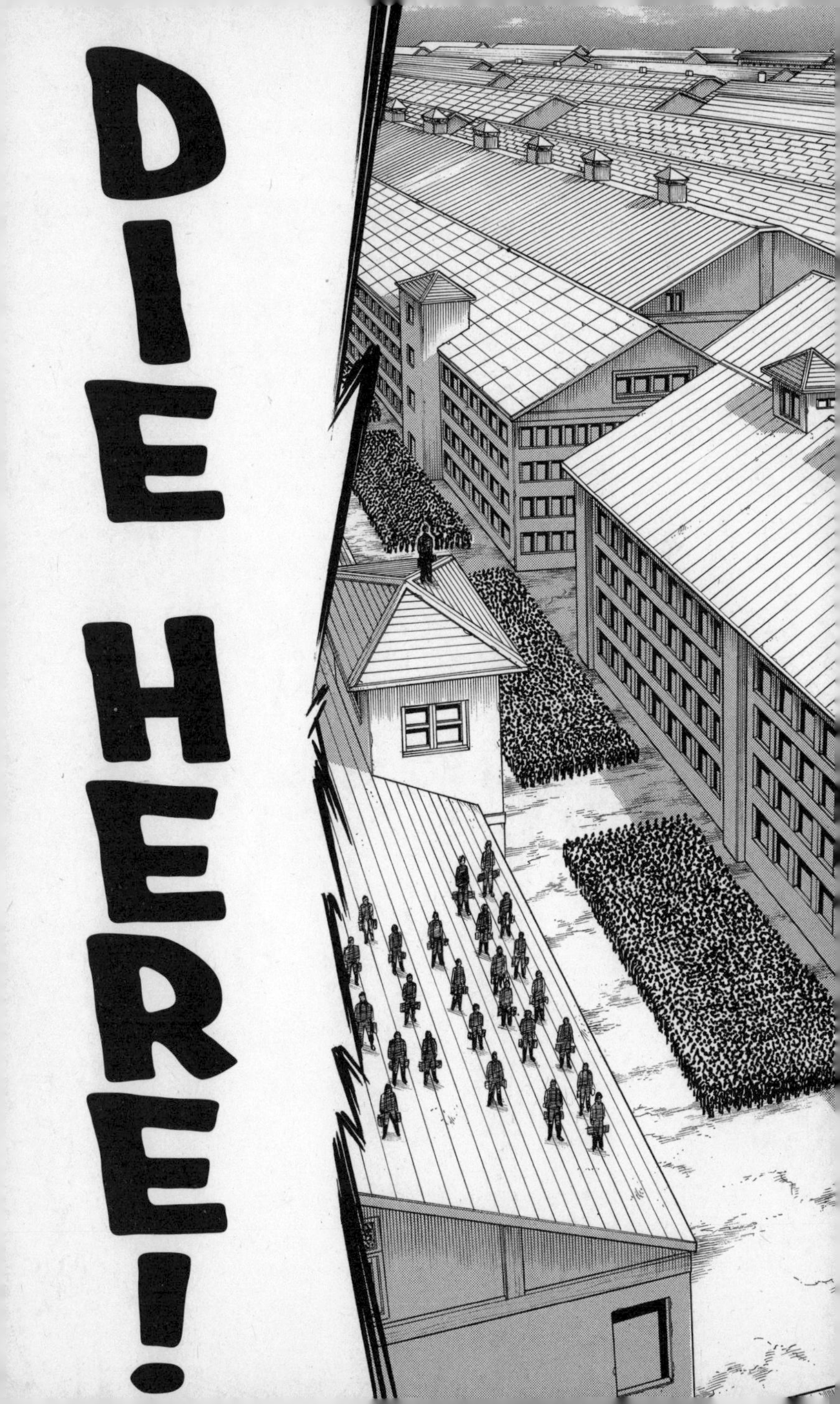
DIE HERE!

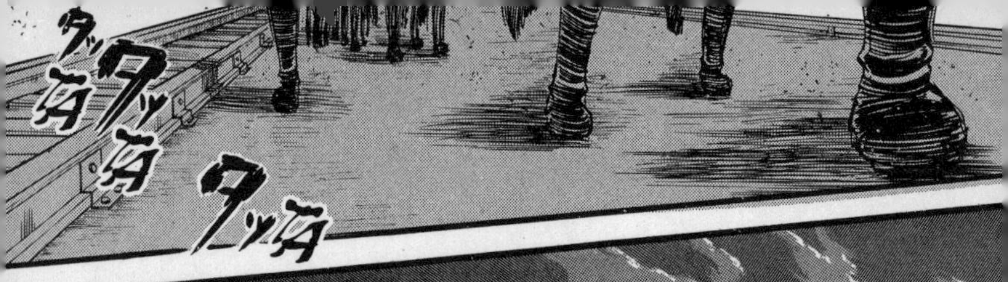
タッタ
タッタ
タッタ
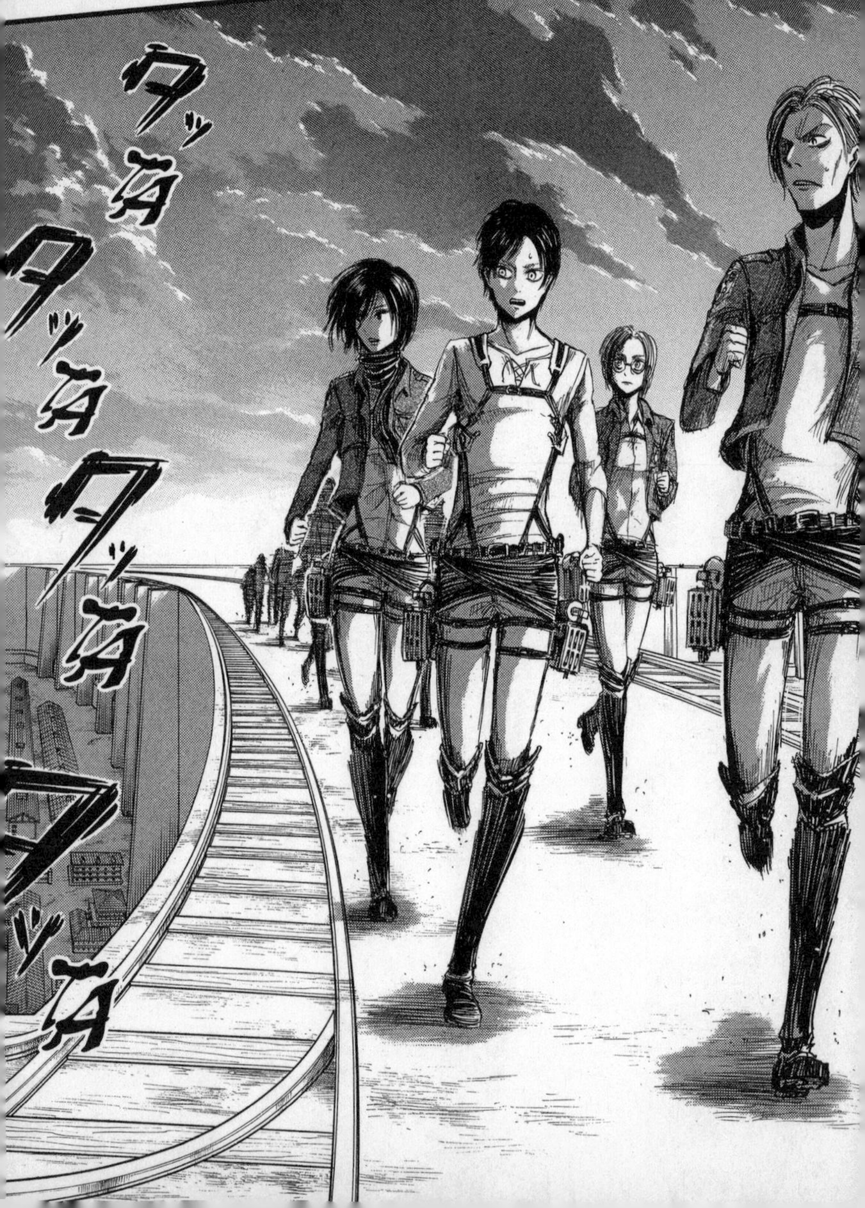
タッタ
タッタ
タッタ
タッタ

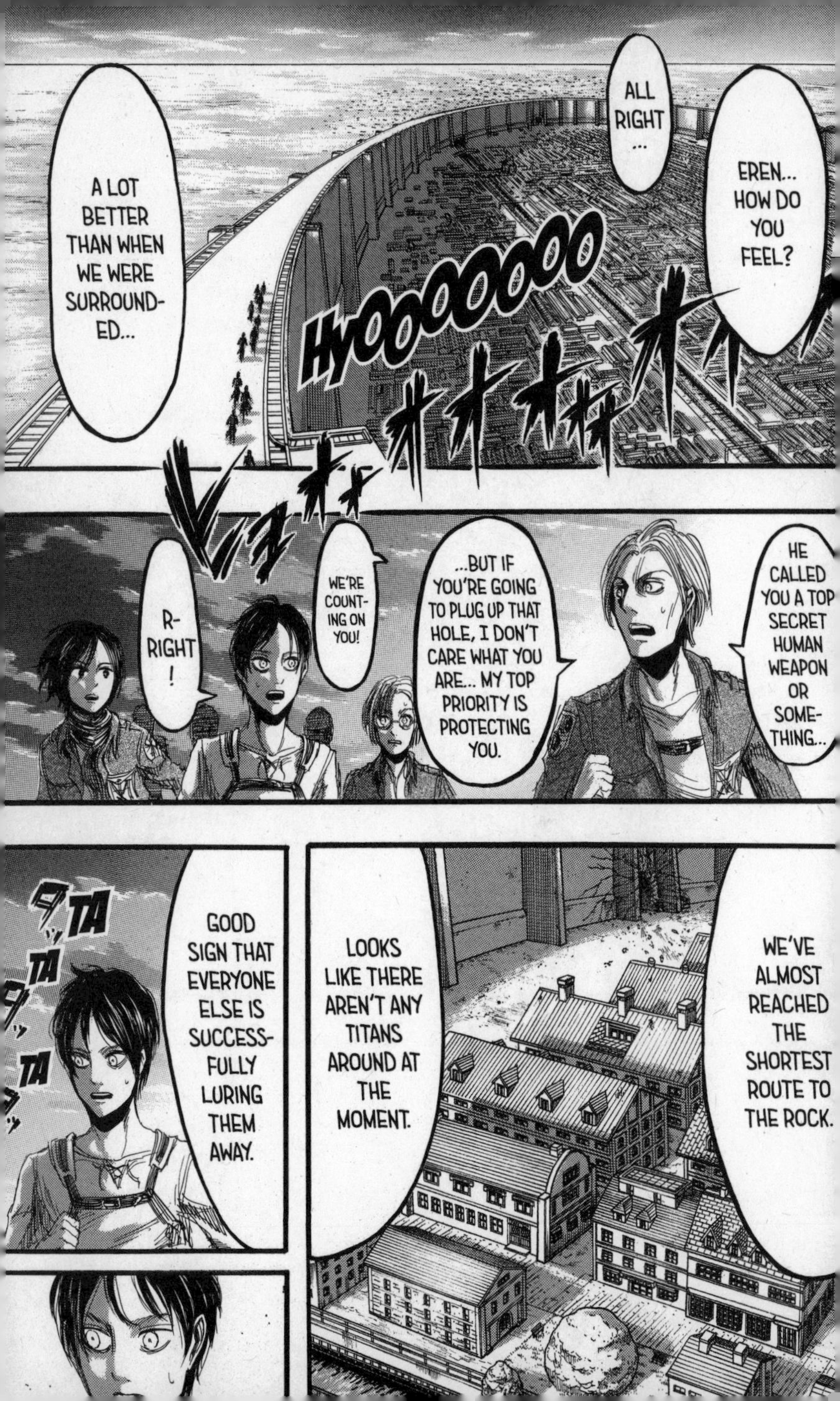
EREN... HOW DO YOU FEEL?
ALL RIGHT...
HYOOOOOOO
A LOT BETTER THAN WHEN WE WERE SURROUND-ED...
HE CALLED YOU A TOP SECRET HUMAN WEAPON OR SOME-THING...
...BUT IF YOU'RE GOING TO PLUG UP THAT HOLE, I DON'T CARE WHAT YOU ARE... MY TOP PRIORITY IS PROTECTING YOU.
WE'RE COUNT-ING ON YOU!
R-RIGHT!
WE'VE ALMOST REACHED THE SHORTEST ROUTE TO THE ROCK.
LOOKS LIKE THERE AREN'T ANY TITANS AROUND AT THE MOMENT.
GOOD SIGN THAT EVERYONE ELSE IS SUCCESS-FULLY LURING THEM AWAY.
TA
TA
TA

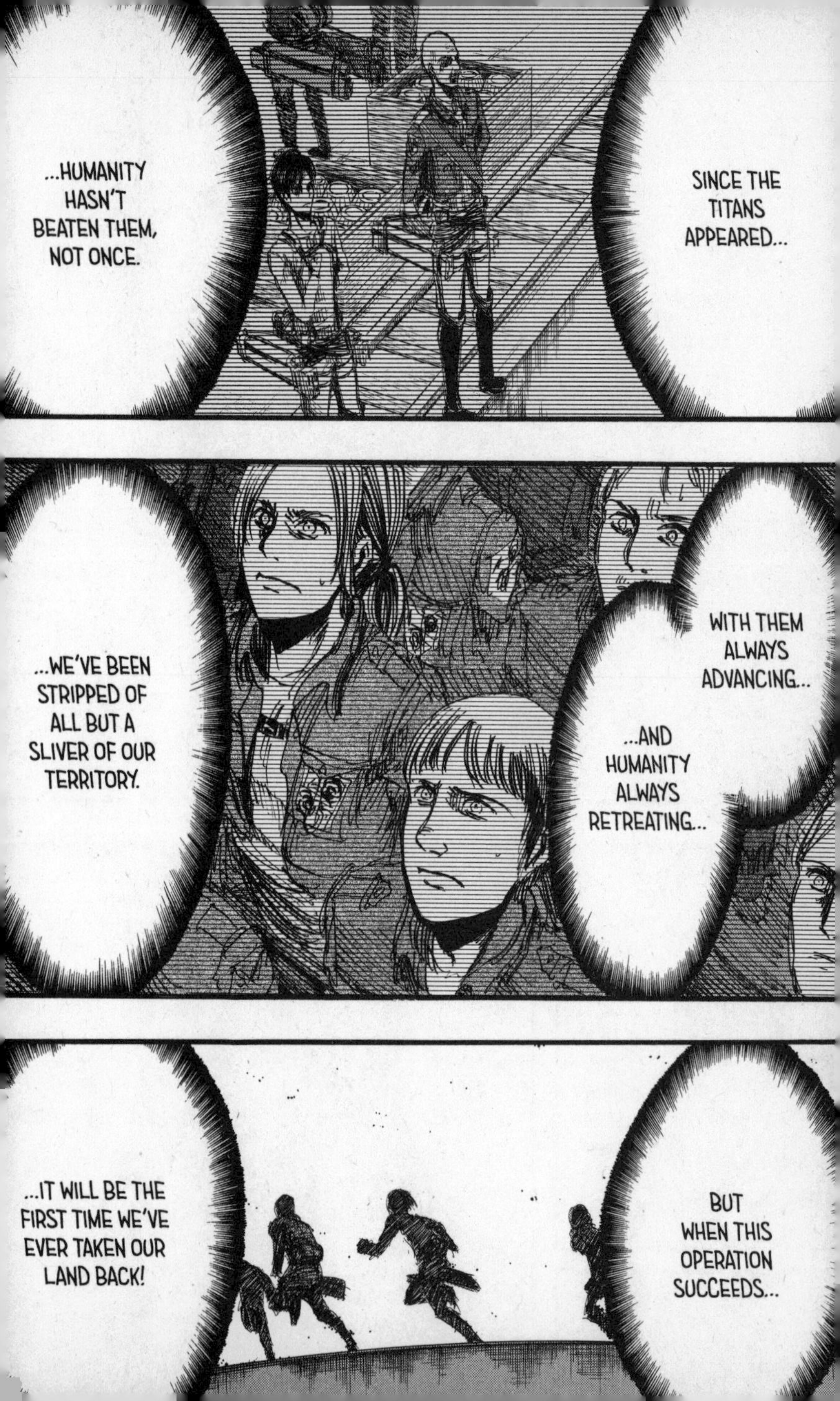

SINCE THE TITANS APPEARED...
...HUMANITY HASN'T BEATEN THEM, NOT ONCE.
WITH THEM ALWAYS ADVANCING...
...AND HUMANITY ALWAYS RETREATING...
...WE'VE BEEN STRIPPED OF ALL BUT A SLIVER OF OUR TERRITORY.
BUT WHEN THIS OPERATION SUCCEEDS...
...IT WILL BE THE FIRST TIME WE'VE EVER TAKEN OUR LAND BACK!

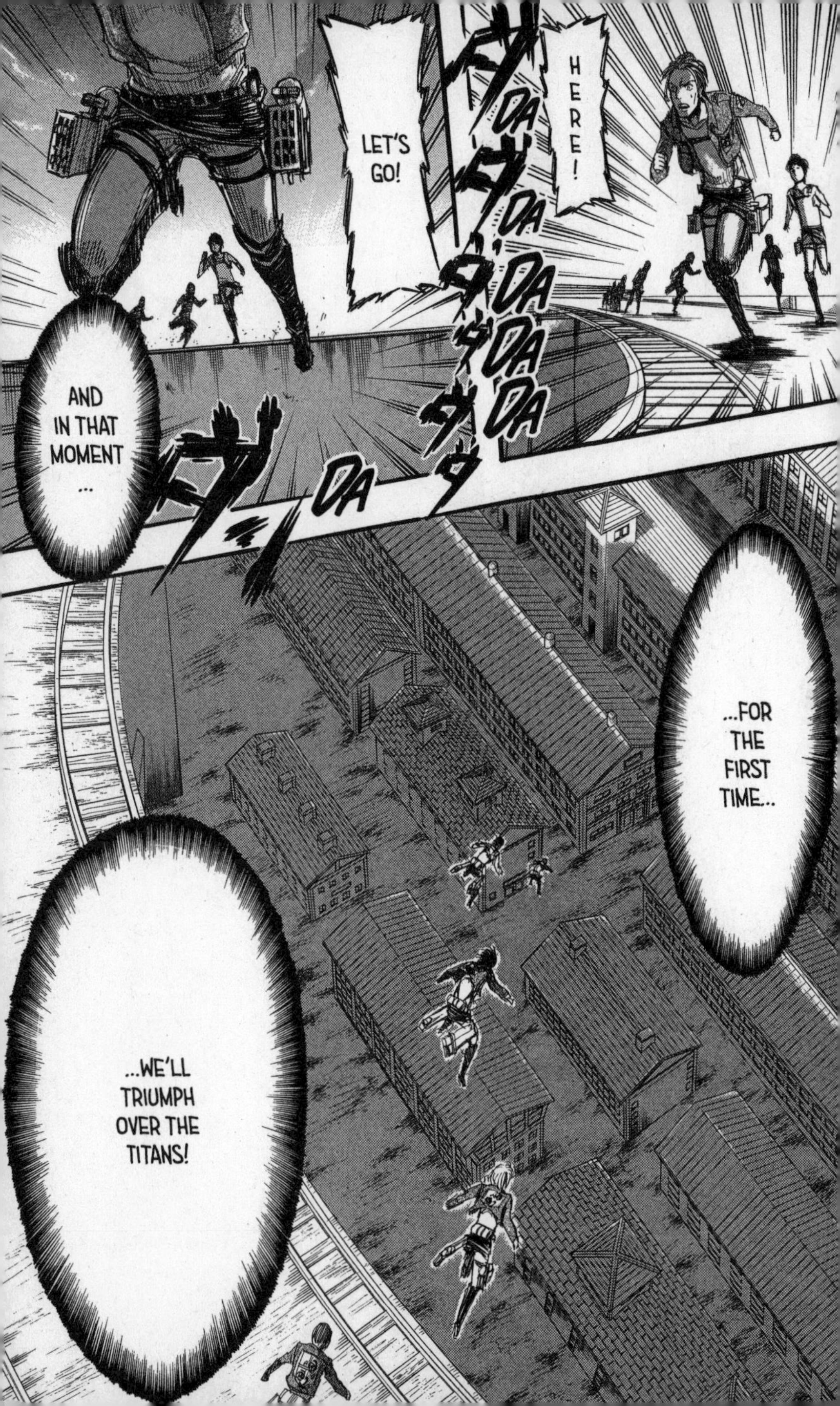
HERE!
LET'S GO!
DA DA DA DA DA DA
DA
AND IN THAT MOMENT ...
...FOR THE FIRST TIME...
...WE'LL TRIUMPH OVER THE TITANS!

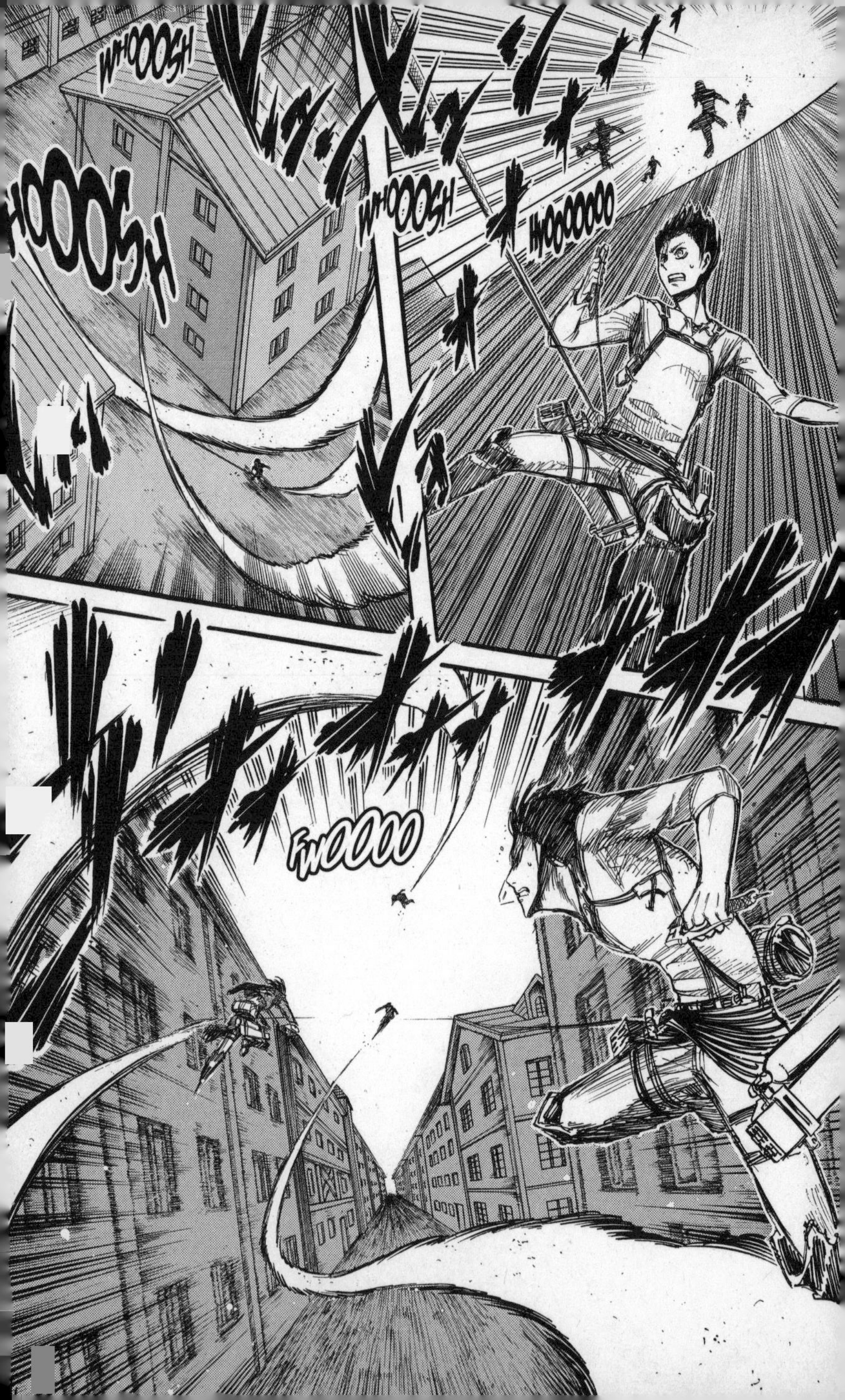
WHOOOOOO
WHOOOSH
WHOOOSH
HOOOSH
FWOOOO

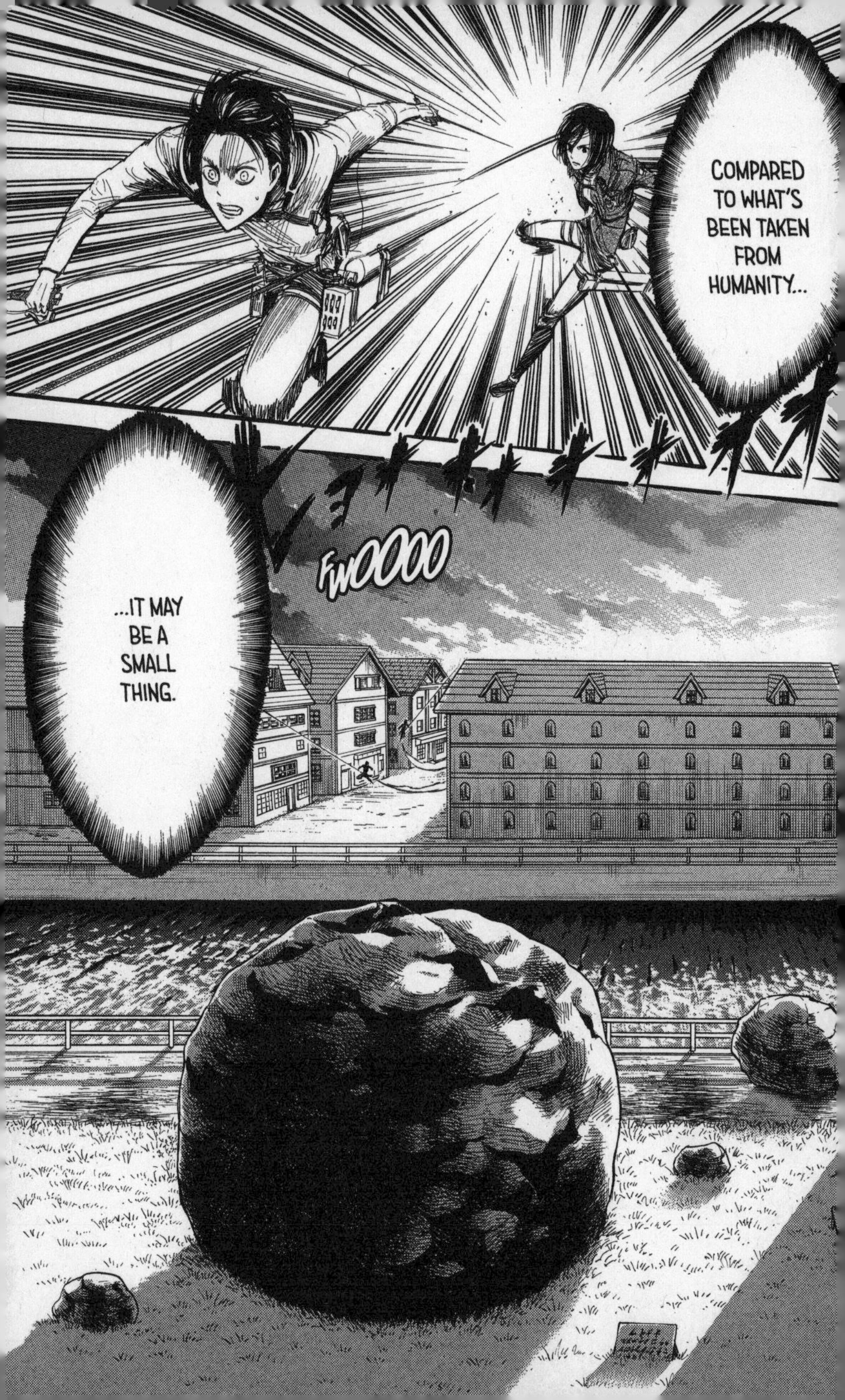
COMPARED TO WHAT'S BEEN TAKEN FROM HUMANITY...
...IT MAY BE A SMALL THING.
FWOOOO

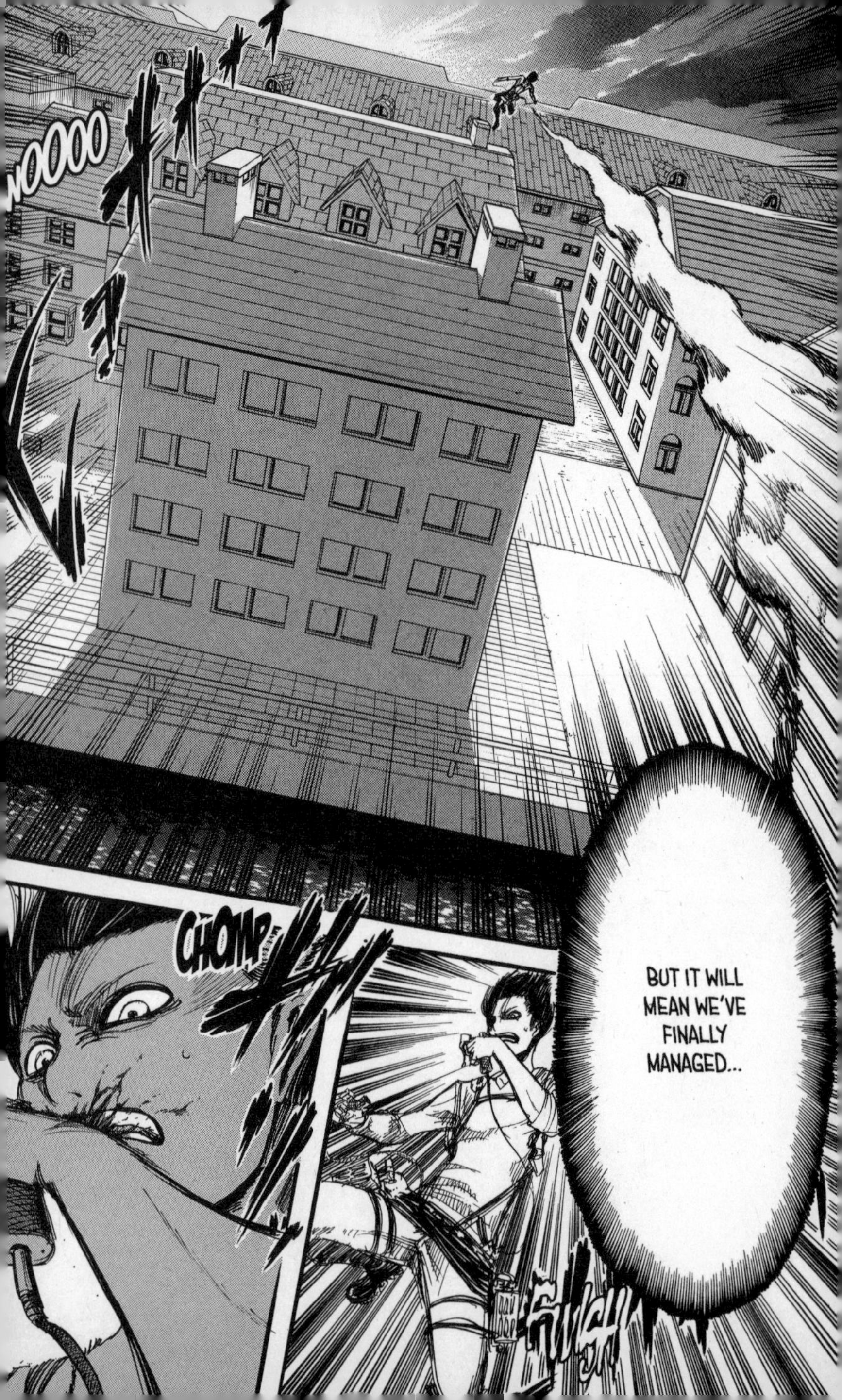
WOOOO
BUT IT WILL MEAN WE'VE FINALLY MANAGED...
FSSH
CHOMP

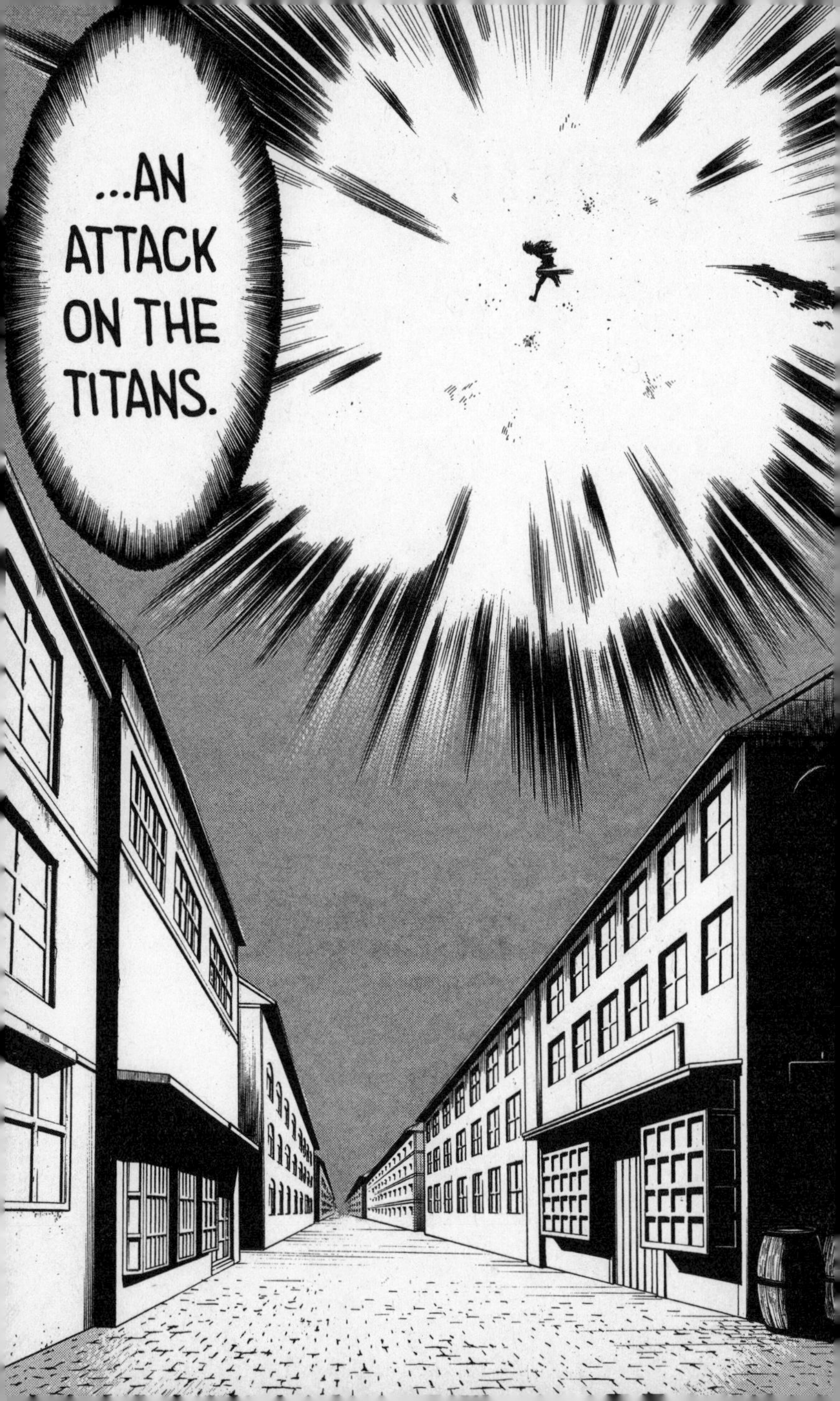
...AN ATTACK ON THE TITANS.

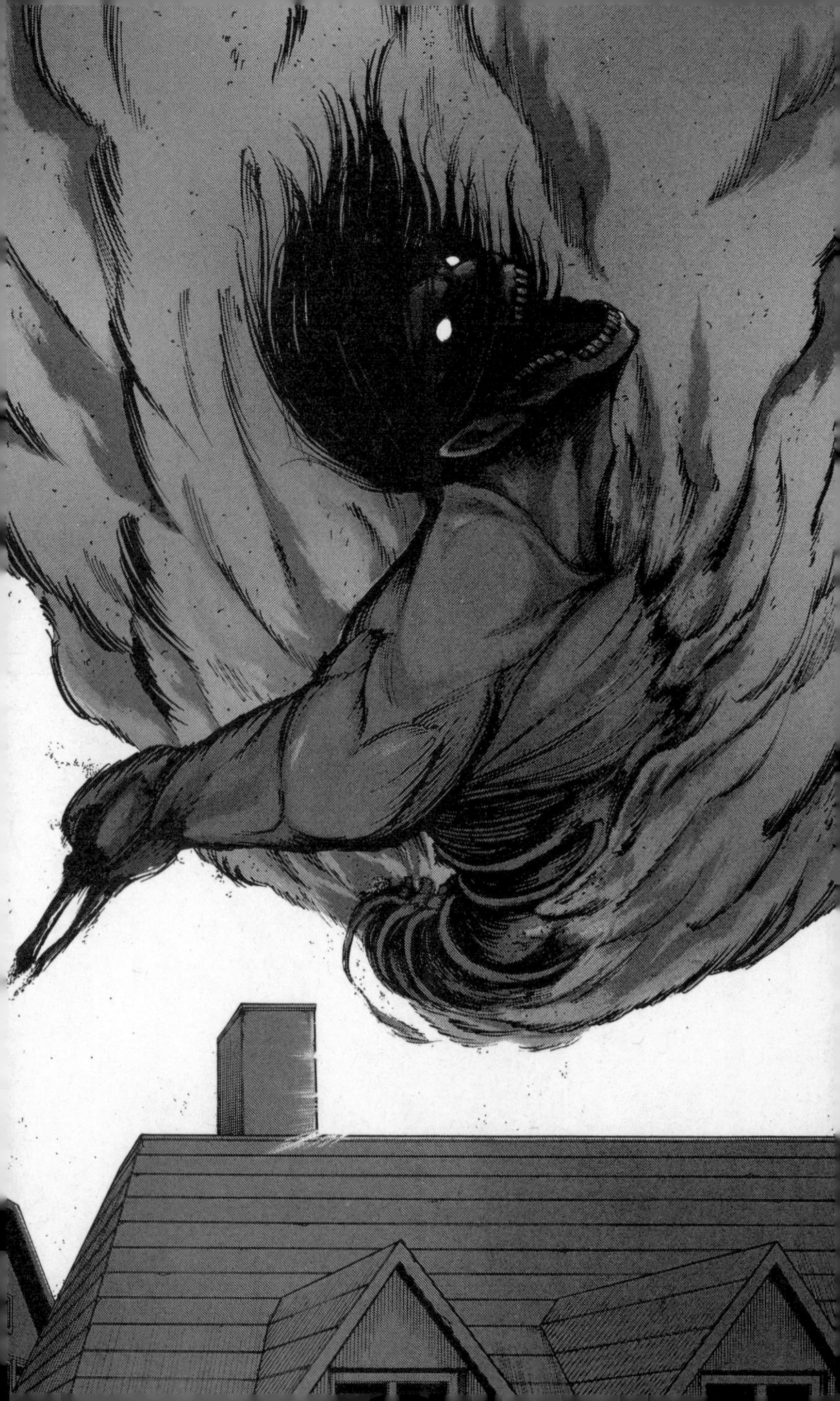

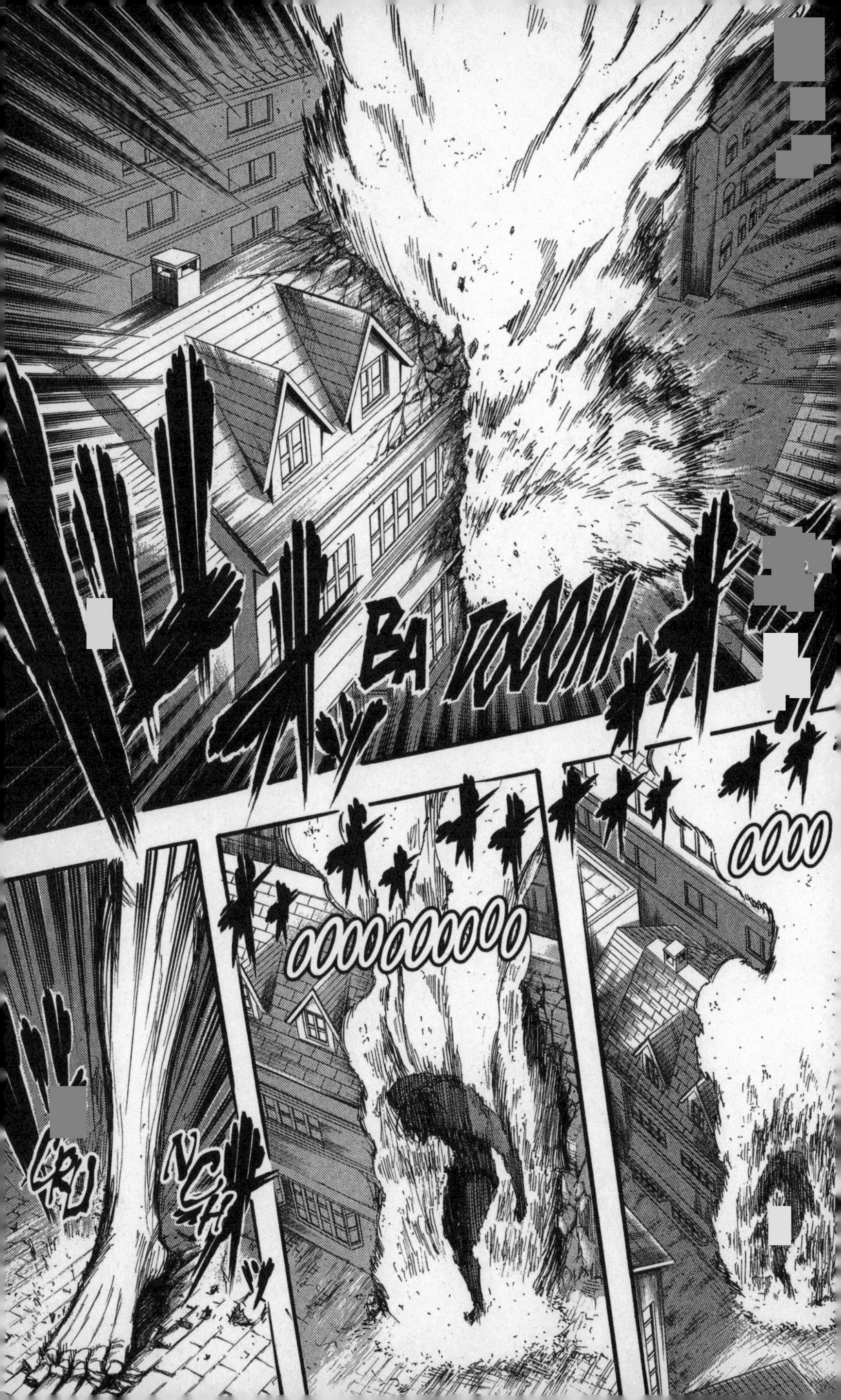
BA DOOOM
OOOO
OOOOOOOOOO
CRU
NCH

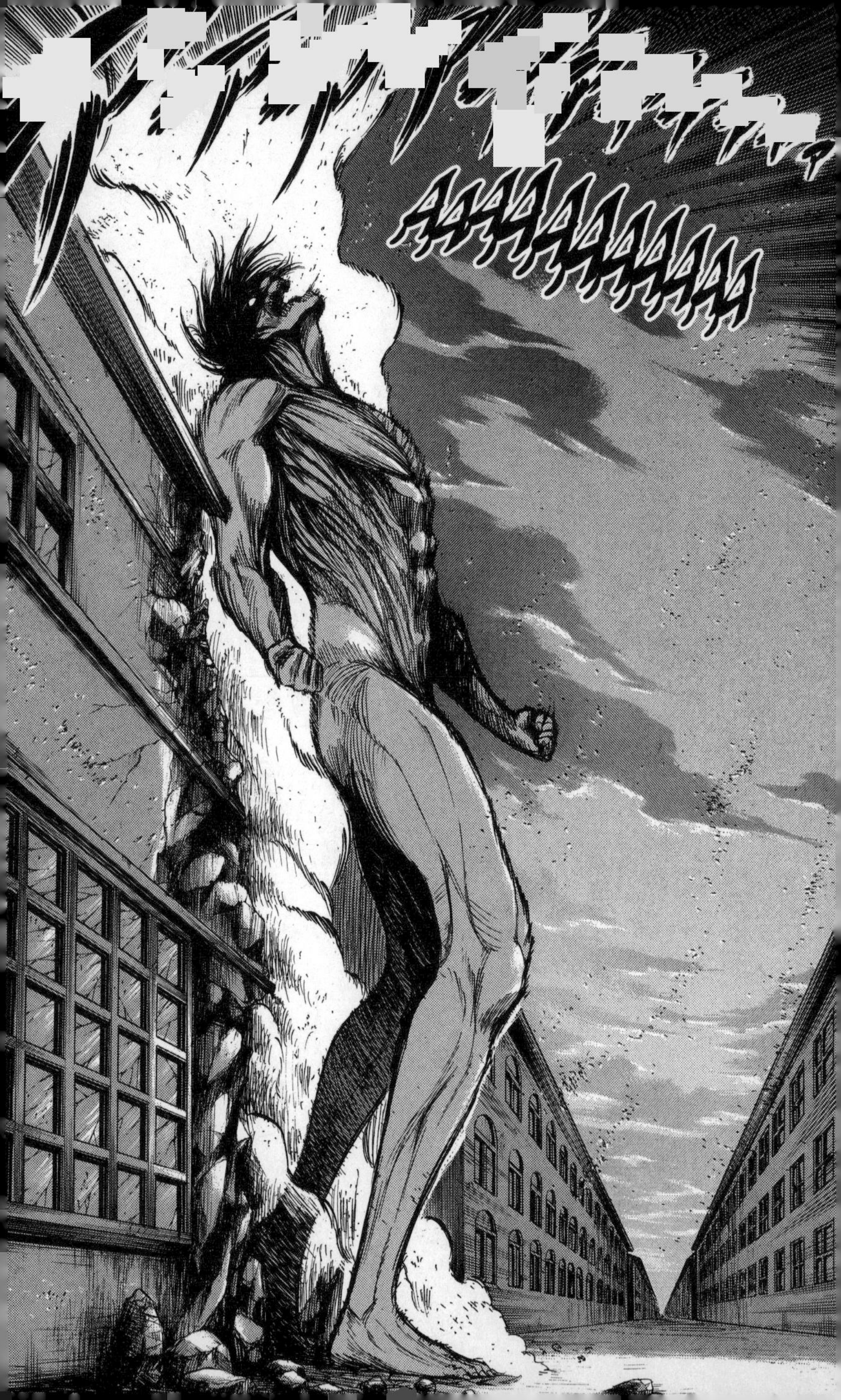
AAAAAAAAAAA

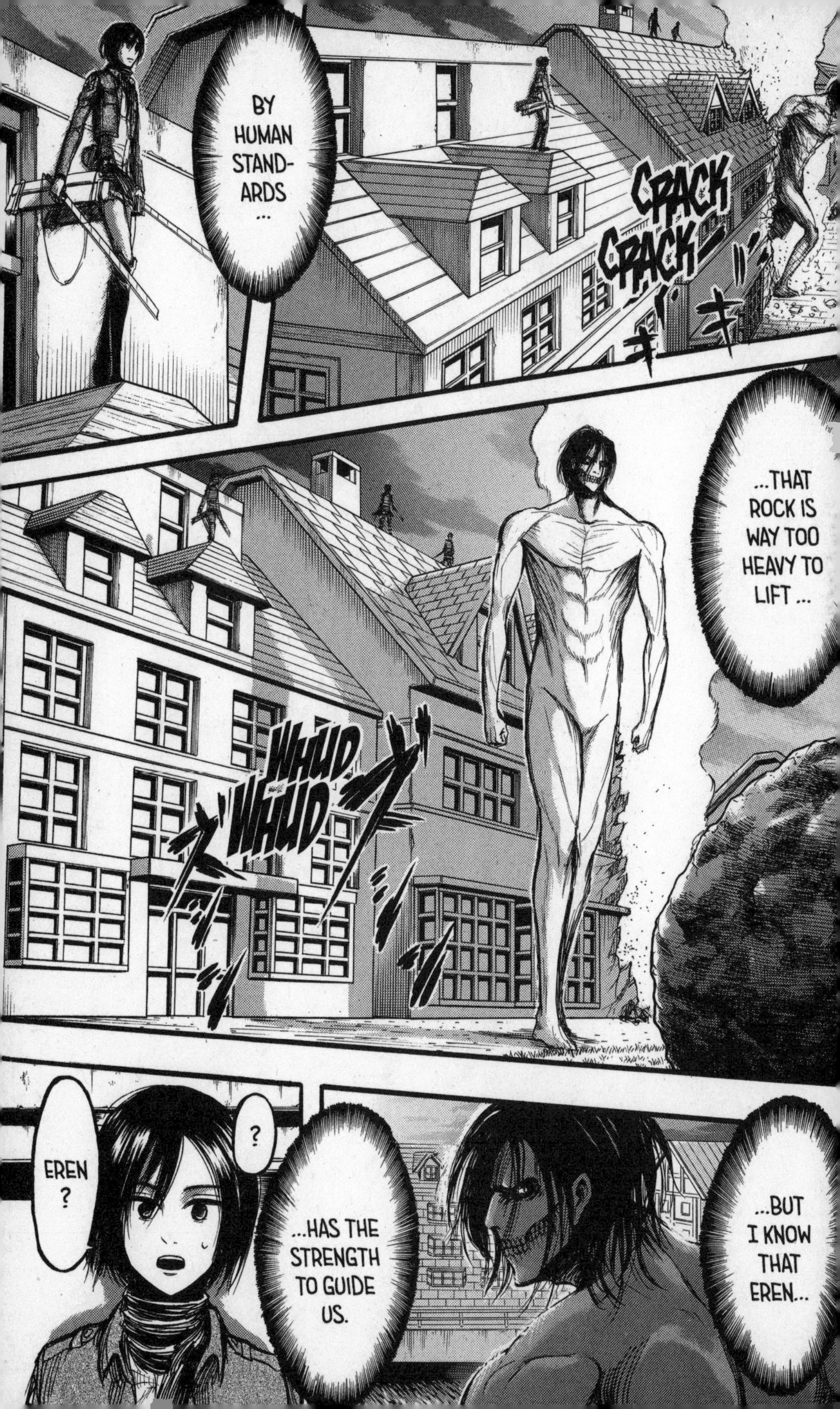
CRACK CRACK
BY HUMAN STANDARDS...
...THAT ROCK IS WAY TOO HEAVY TO LIFT...
WHUD WHUD
...BUT I KNOW THAT EREN...
...HAS THE STRENGTH TO GUIDE US.
?
EREN ?

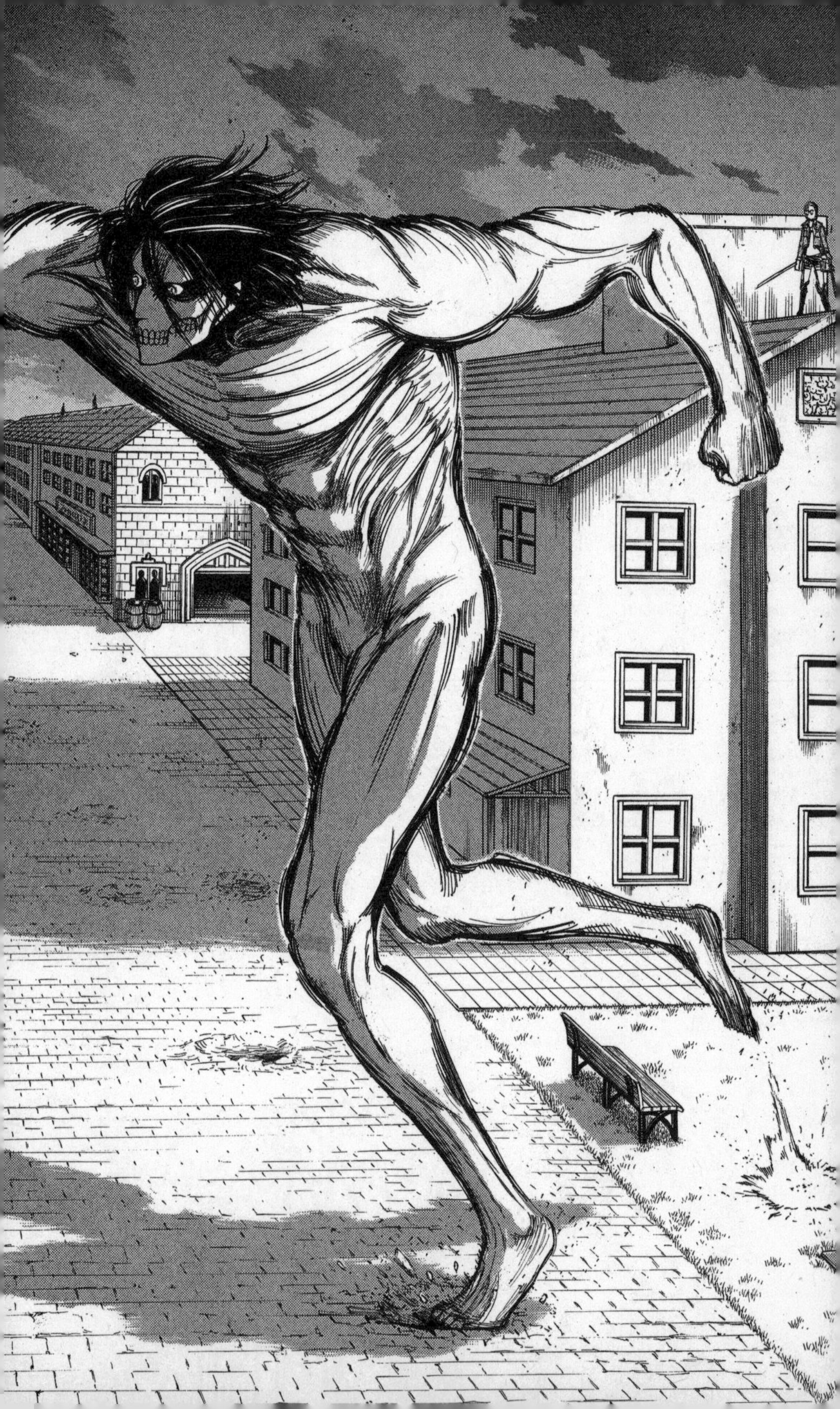

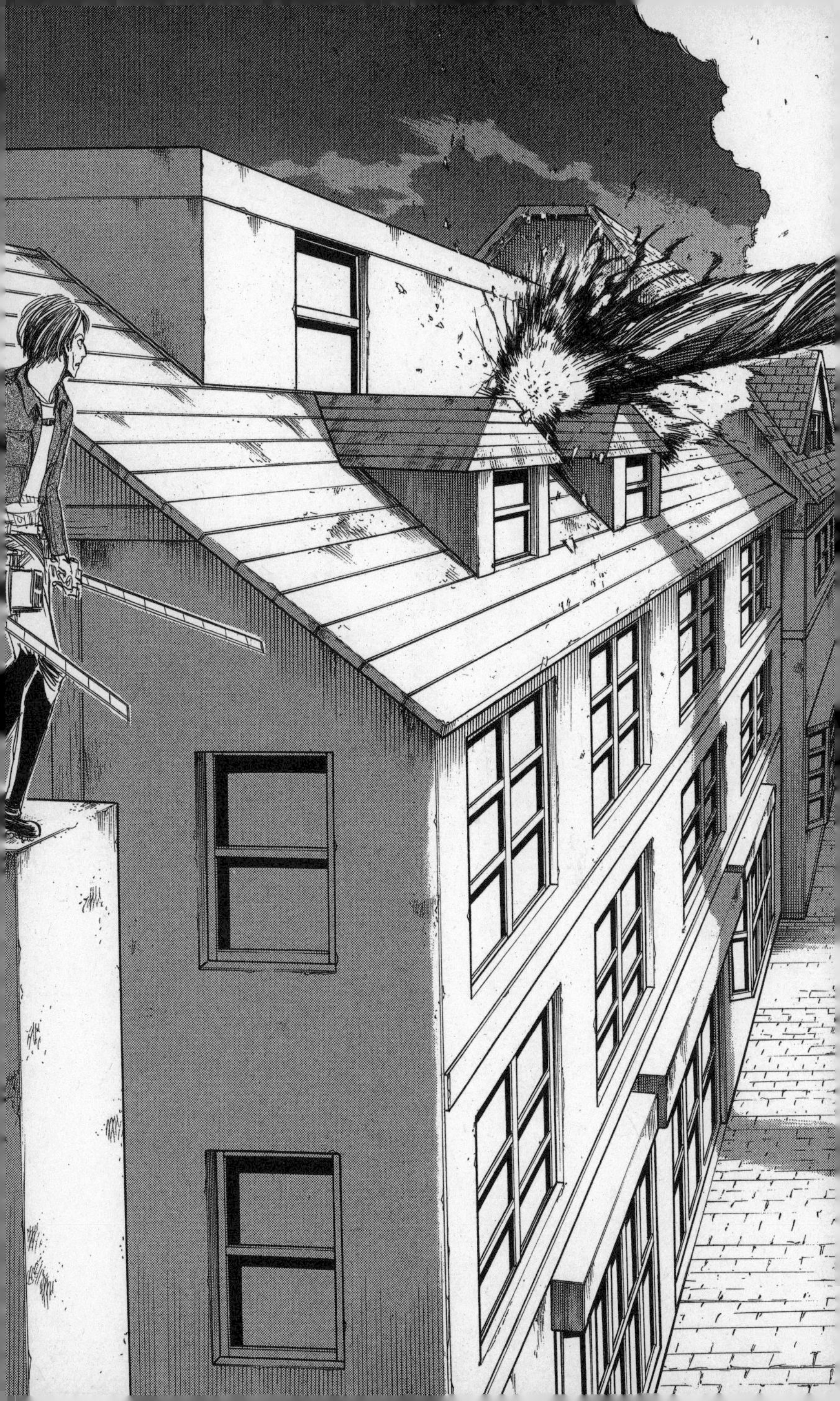

ATTACK on TITAN

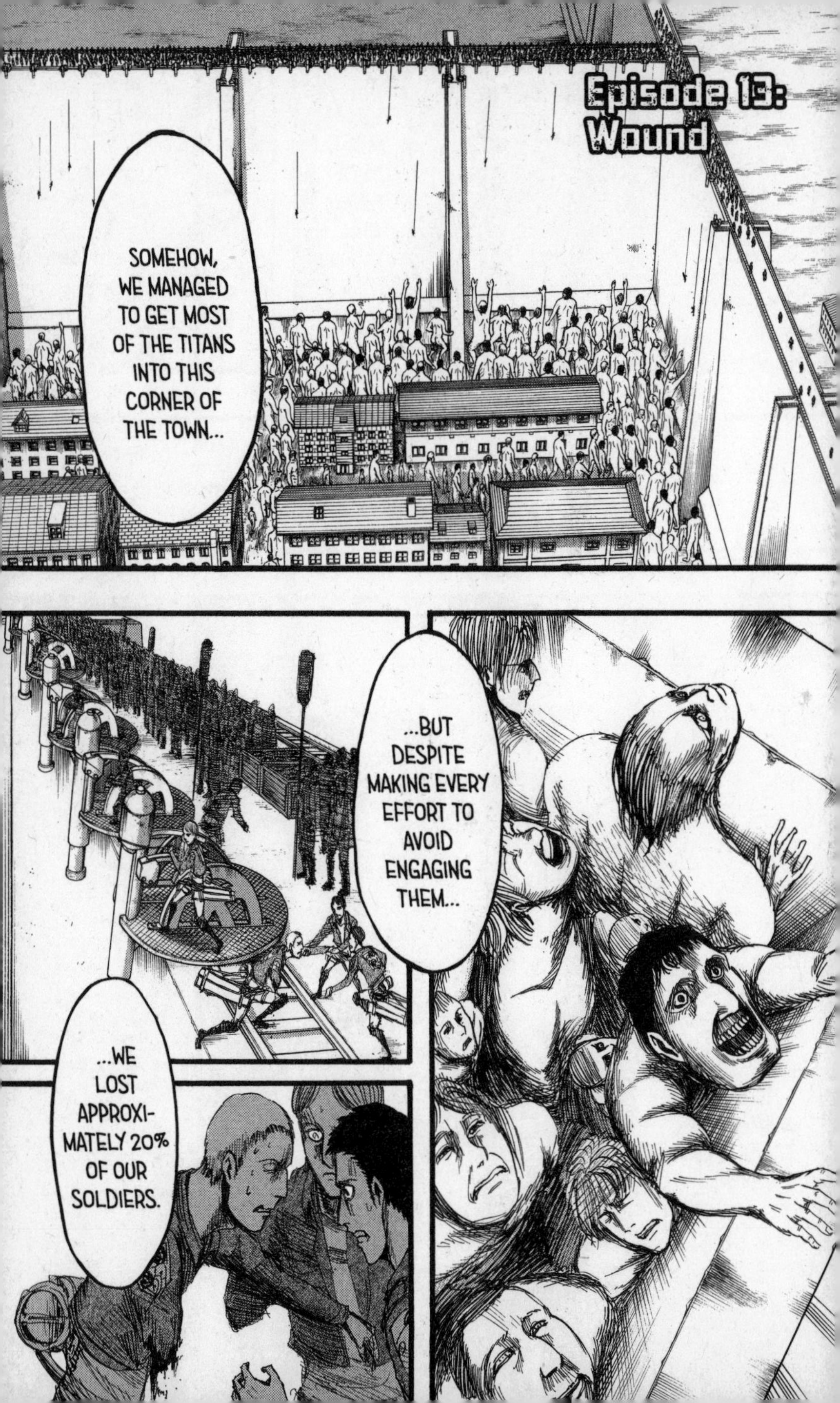
Episode 13: Wound
SOMEHOW, WE MANAGED TO GET MOST OF THE TITANS INTO THIS CORNER OF THE TOWN...
...BUT DESPITE MAKING EVERY EFFORT TO AVOID ENGAGING THEM...
...WE LOST APPROXI-MATELY 20% OF OUR SOLDIERS.

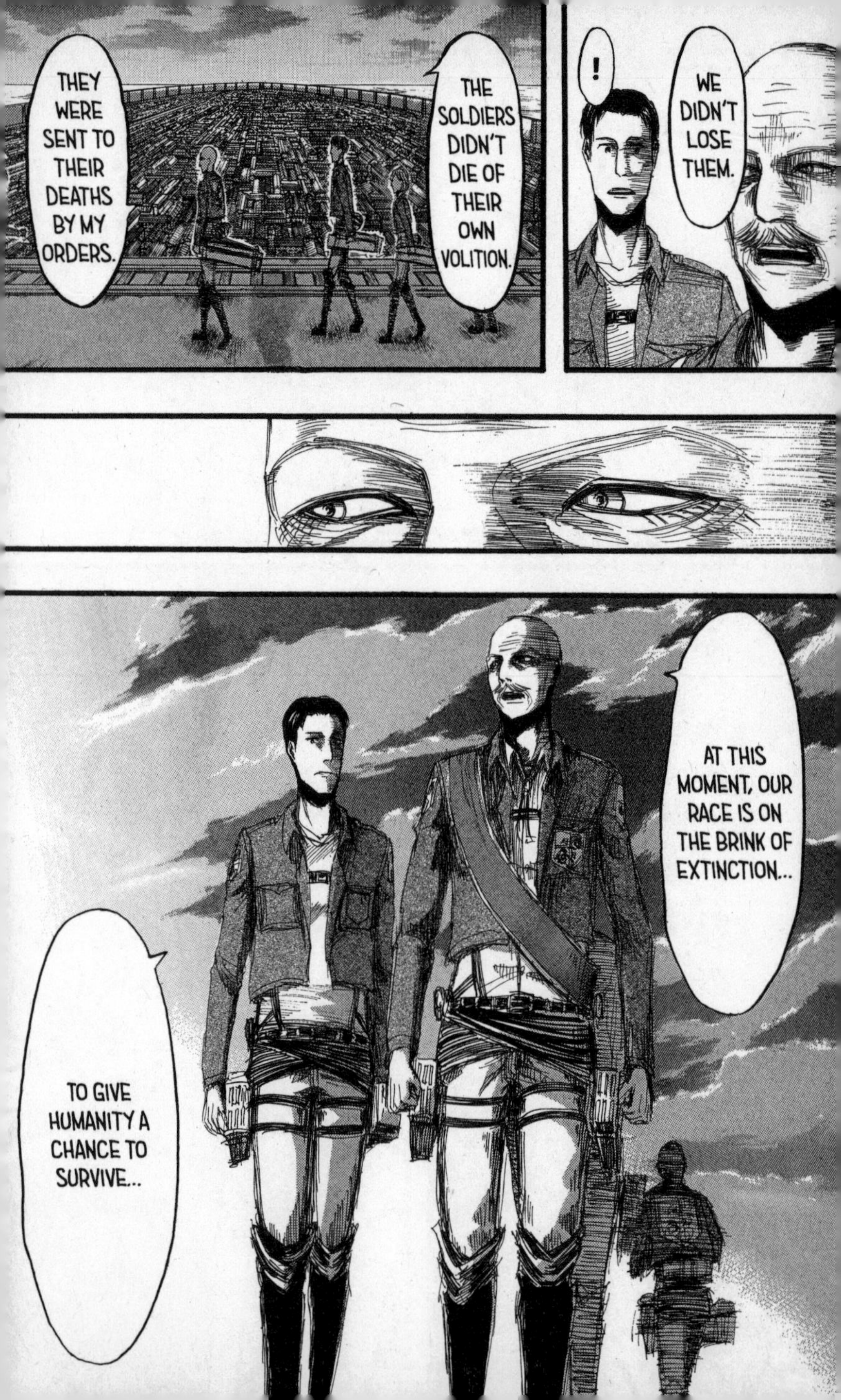
!
WE DIDN'T LOSE THEM.
THE SOLDIERS DIDN'T DIE OF THEIR OWN VOLITION.
THEY WERE SENT TO THEIR DEATHS BY MY ORDERS.
AT THIS MOMENT, OUR RACE IS ON THE BRINK OF EXTINCTION...
TO GIVE HUMANITY A CHANCE TO SURVIVE...

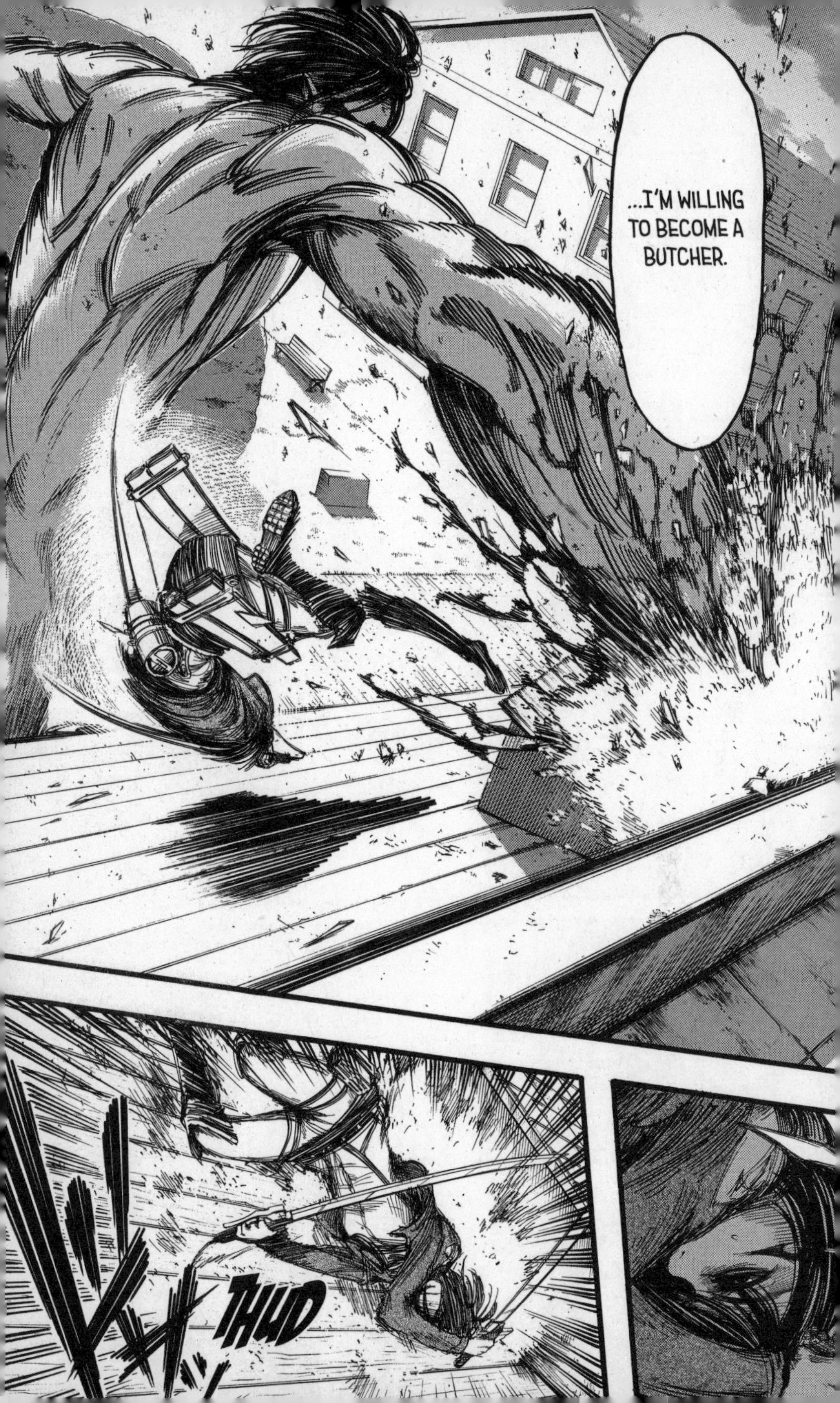
...I'M WILLING TO BECOME A BUTCHER.
THUD

FWOOOO

...?!

DASH

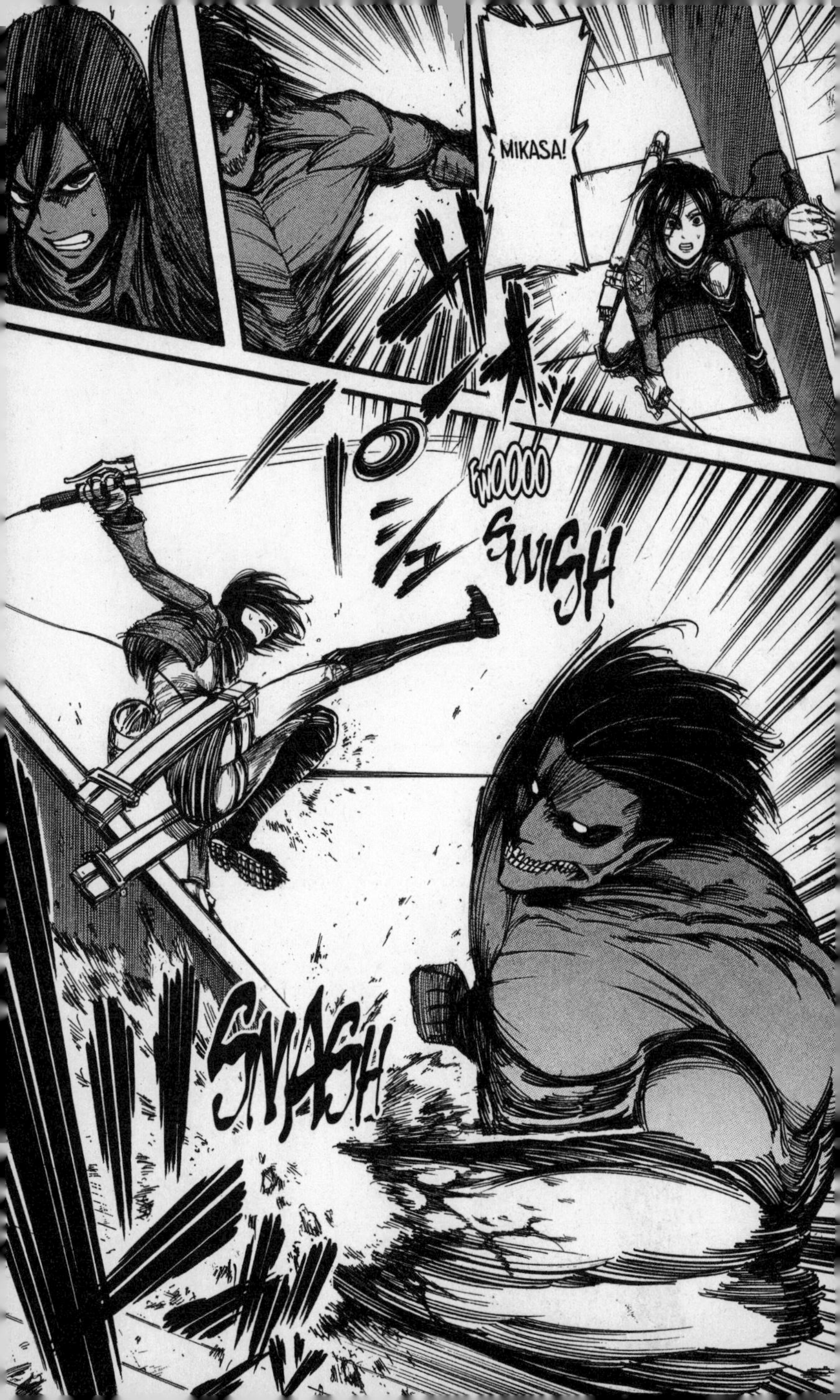
MIKASA!
FWOOOO
SWISH
SMASH!

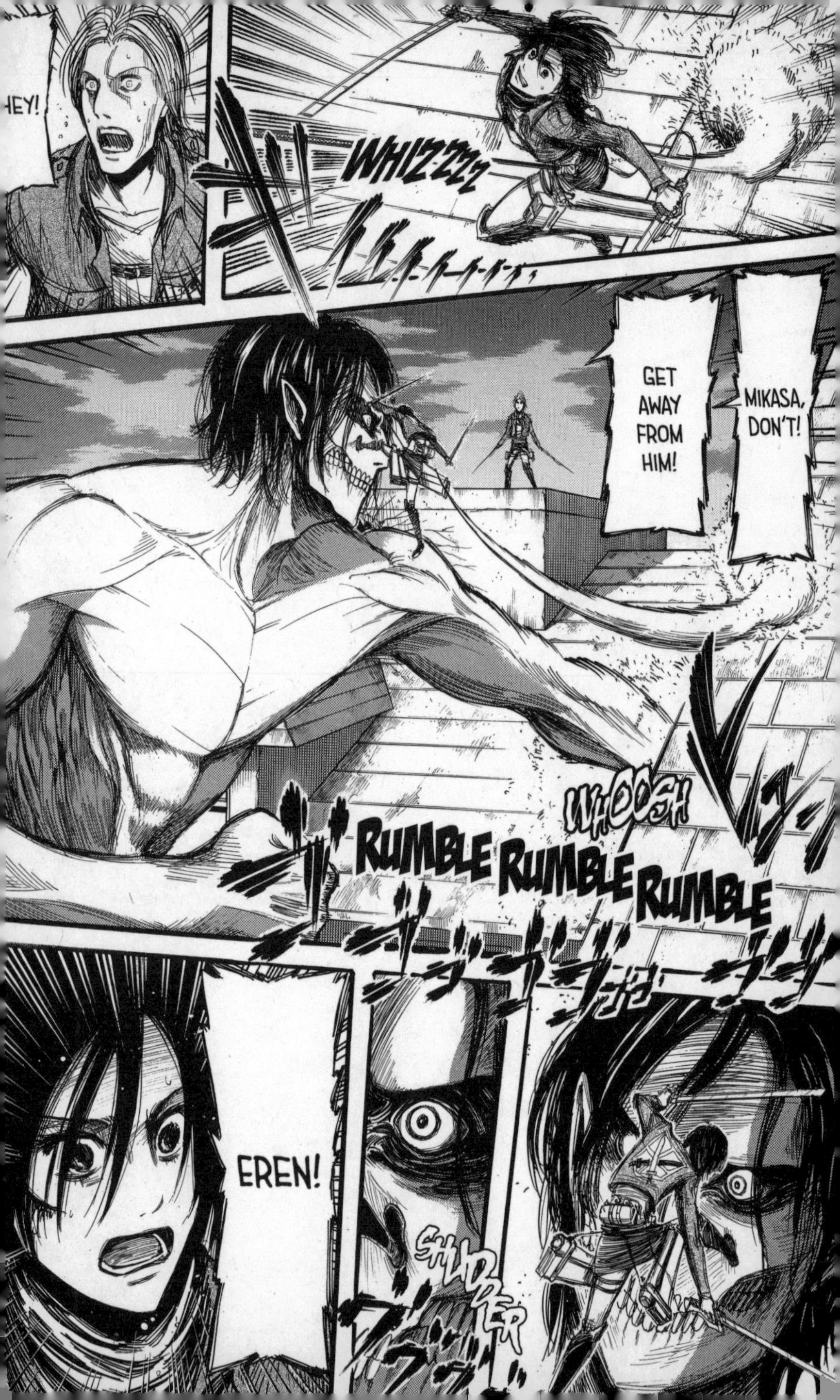
WHIZ-ZZZ
HEY!
MIKASA, DON'T!
GET AWAY FROM HIM!
WHOOSH
RUMBLE RUMBLE RUMBLE
SHUDDER
EREN!

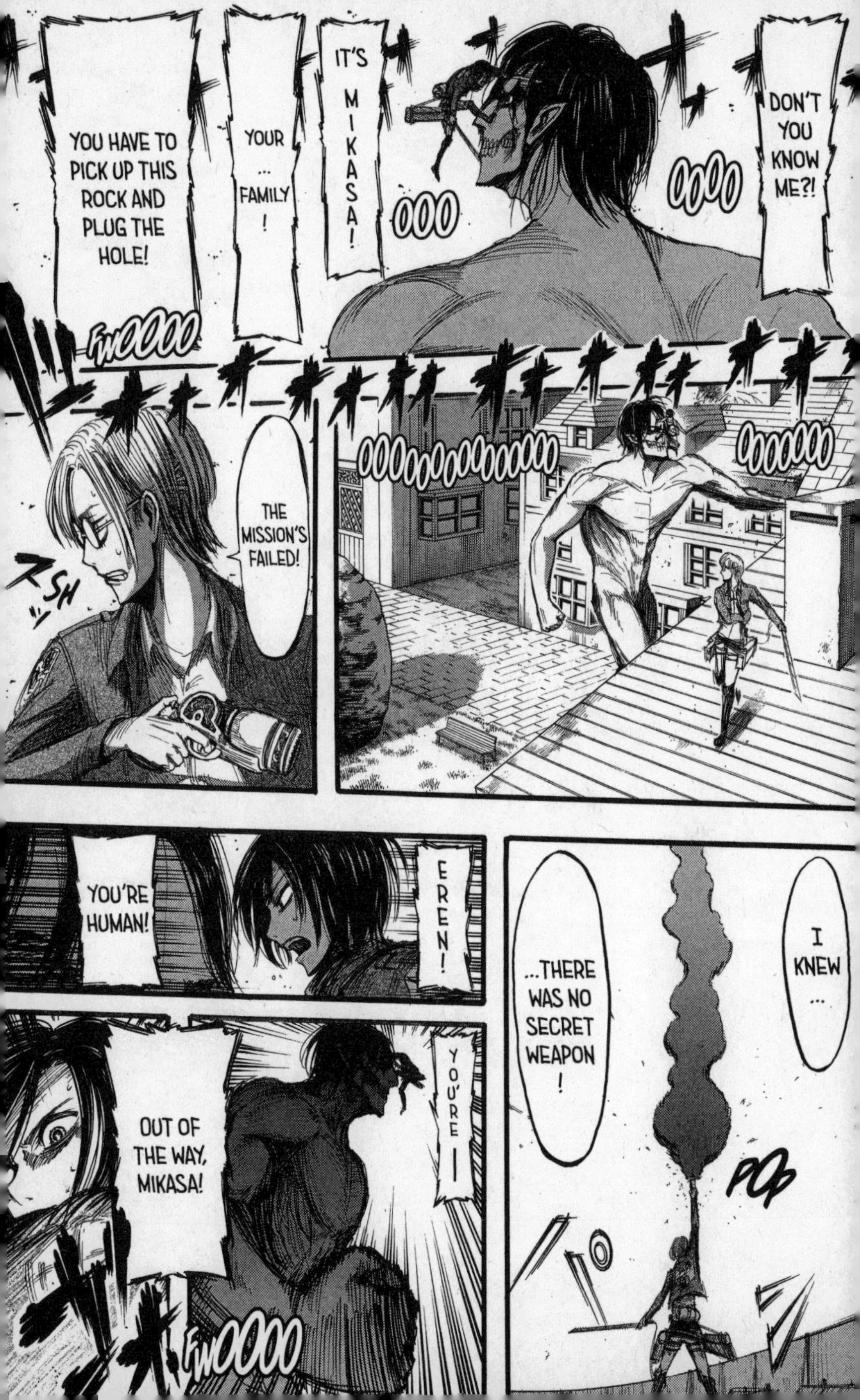

DON'T YOU KNOW ME?!
OOOO
OOO
IT'S MIKASA!
YOUR ... FAMILY!
YOU HAVE TO PICK UP THIS ROCK AND PLUG THE HOLE!
FWOOOO
OOOOOOO
OOOOOOOOOOOOOOO
THE MISSION'S FAILED!
SH
I KNEW ...
...THERE WAS NO SECRET WEAPON!
POP
EREN!
YOU'RE HUMAN!
YOU'RE—
OUT OF THE WAY, MIKASA!
FWOOOO

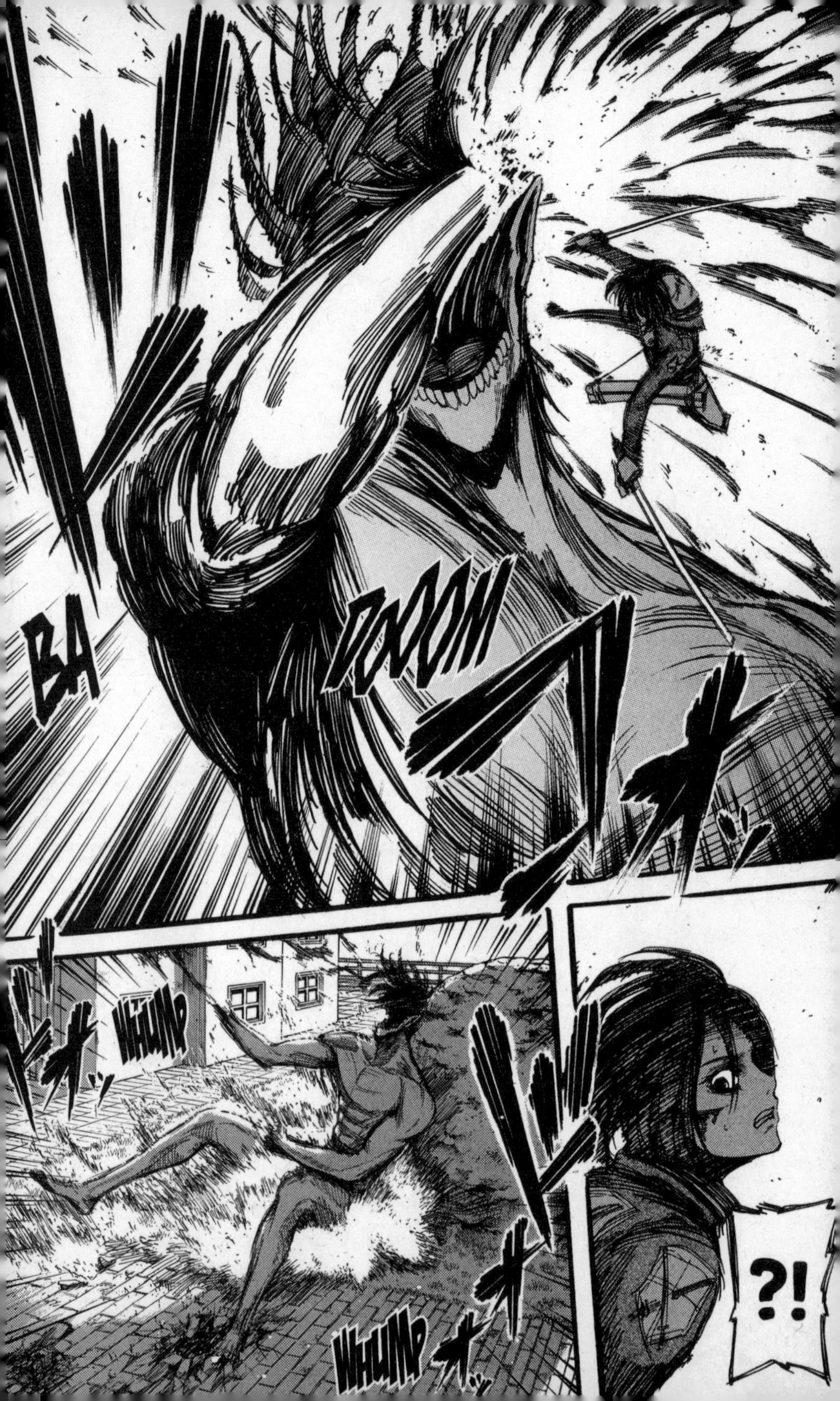
BA
DOOOM
?!
WHUMP
WHUMP

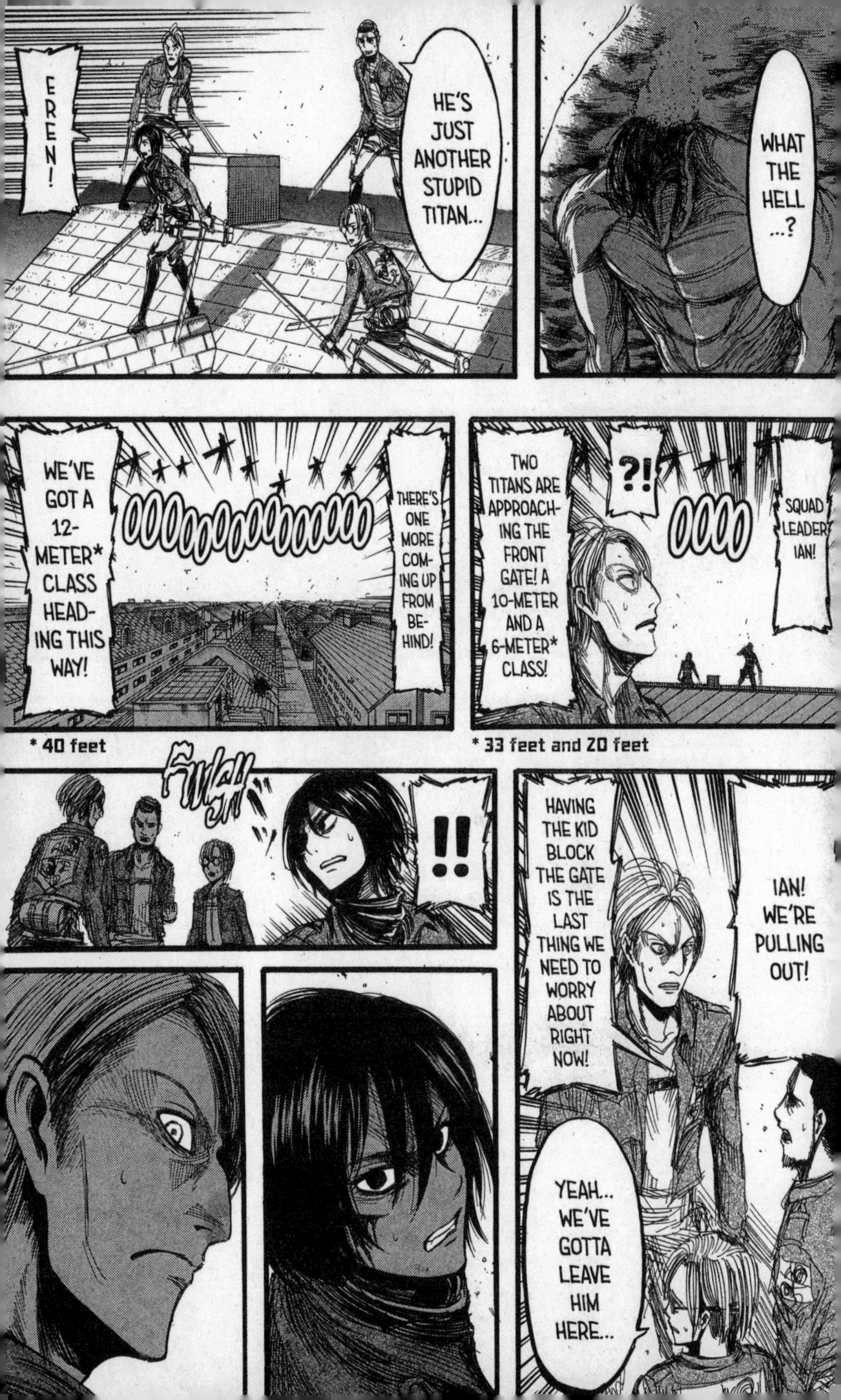
WHAT THE HELL ...?
HE'S JUST ANOTHER STUPID TITAN...
EREN!
SQUAD LEADER IAN!
OOOO
?!
TWO TITANS ARE APPROACHING THE FRONT GATE! A 10-METER AND A 6-METER* CLASS!
* 33 feet and 20 feet
THERE'S ONE MORE COMING UP FROM BEHIND!
OOOOOOOOOOOOOOO
WE'VE GOT A 12-METER* CLASS HEADING THIS WAY!
* 40 feet
IAN! WE'RE PULLING OUT!
HAVING THE KID BLOCK THE GATE IS THE LAST THING WE NEED TO WORRY ABOUT RIGHT NOW!
YEAH... WE'VE GOTTA LEAVE HIM HERE...
!!

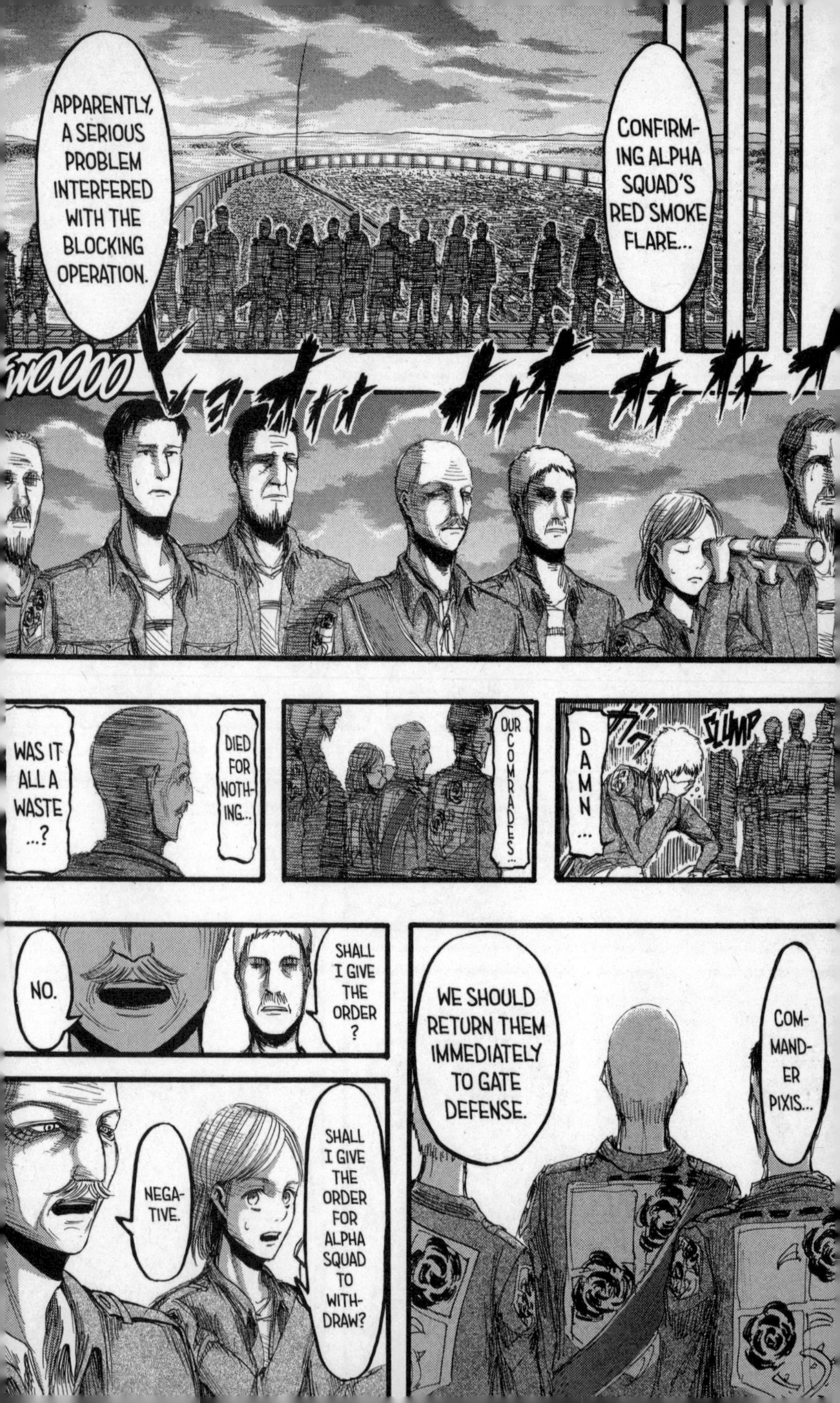
CONFIRMING ALPHA SQUAD'S RED SMOKE FLARE...
APPARENTLY, A SERIOUS PROBLEM INTERFERED WITH THE BLOCKING OPERATION.
WOOOOO
SLUMP
DAMN...
OUR COMRADES...
DIED FOR NOTHING...
WAS IT ALL A WASTE...?
COMMANDER PIXIS...
WE SHOULD RETURN THEM IMMEDIATELY TO GATE DEFENSE.
SHALL I GIVE THE ORDER?
NO.
SHALL I GIVE THE ORDER FOR ALPHA SQUAD TO WITHDRAW?
NEGATIVE.

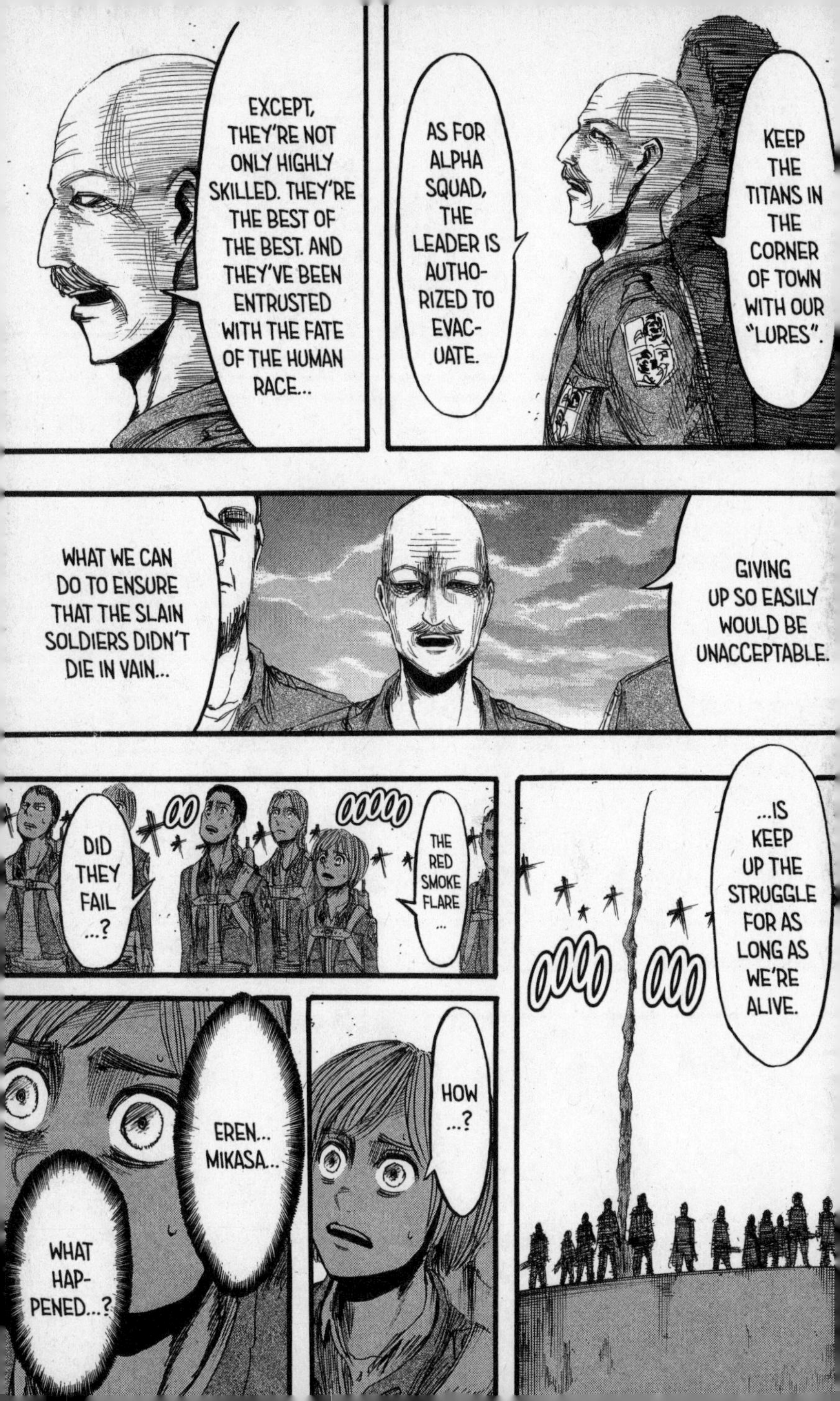
KEEP THE TITANS IN THE CORNER OF TOWN WITH OUR "LURES".
AS FOR ALPHA SQUAD, THE LEADER IS AUTHORIZED TO EVACUATE.
EXCEPT, THEY'RE NOT ONLY HIGHLY SKILLED. THEY'RE THE BEST OF THE BEST. AND THEY'VE BEEN ENTRUSTED WITH THE FATE OF THE HUMAN RACE...
GIVING UP SO EASILY WOULD BE UNACCEPTABLE.
WHAT WE CAN DO TO ENSURE THAT THE SLAIN SOLDIERS DIDN'T DIE IN VAIN...
...IS KEEP UP THE STRUGGLE FOR AS LONG AS WE'RE ALIVE.
THE RED SMOKE FLARE...
DID THEY FAIL...?
HOW...?
EREN... MIKASA...
WHAT HAPPENED...?

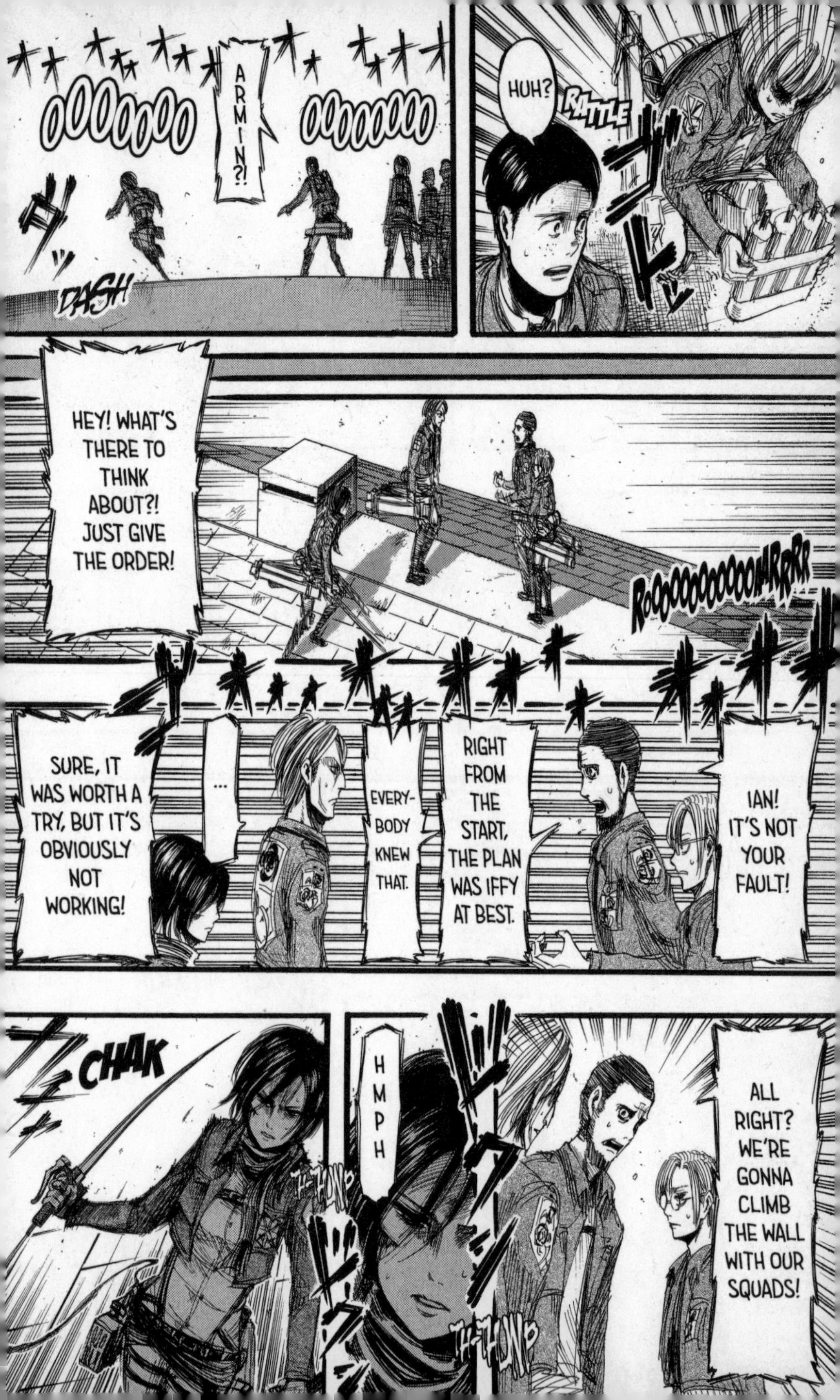
HUH?
RATTLE
OOOOOOOO
ARMIN?!
OOOOOOO
DASH
HEY! WHAT'S THERE TO THINK ABOUT?! JUST GIVE THE ORDER!
ROOOOOOOOOOOARRRR
IAN! IT'S NOT YOUR FAULT!
RIGHT FROM THE START, THE PLAN WAS IFFY AT BEST.
EVERY-BODY KNEW THAT.
...
SURE, IT WAS WORTH A TRY, BUT IT'S OBVIOUSLY NOT WORKING!
ALL RIGHT? WE'RE GONNA CLIMB THE WALL WITH OUR SQUADS!
HMPH
THUMP
THUMP
CHAK

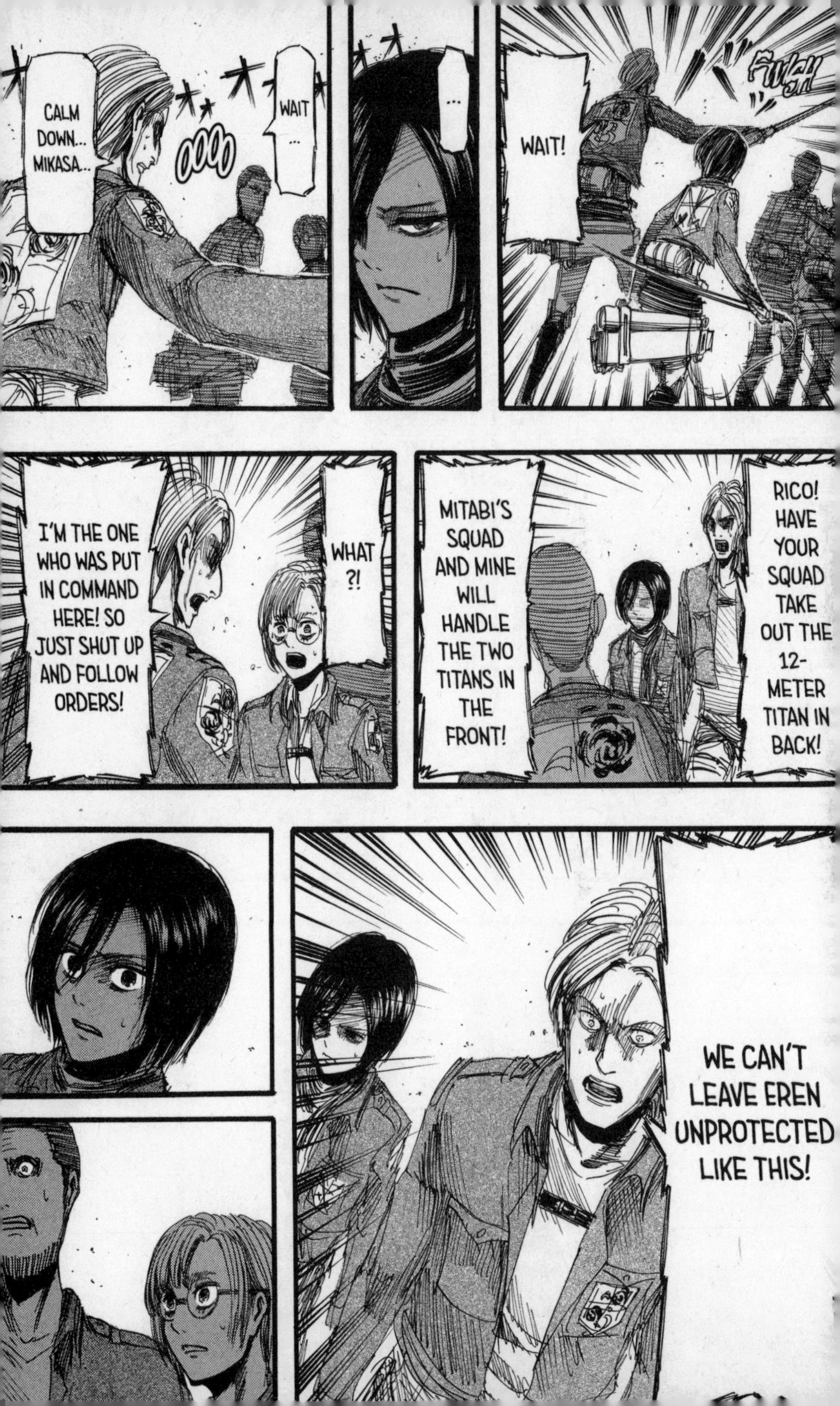
WAIT!
FWISH
...
WAIT ...
CALM DOWN... MIKASA...
RICO! HAVE YOUR SQUAD TAKE OUT THE 12-METER TITAN IN BACK!
MITABI'S SQUAD AND MINE WILL HANDLE THE TWO TITANS IN THE FRONT!
WHAT ?!
I'M THE ONE WHO WAS PUT IN COMMAND HERE! SO JUST SHUT UP AND FOLLOW ORDERS!
WE CAN'T LEAVE EREN UNPROTECTED LIKE THIS!

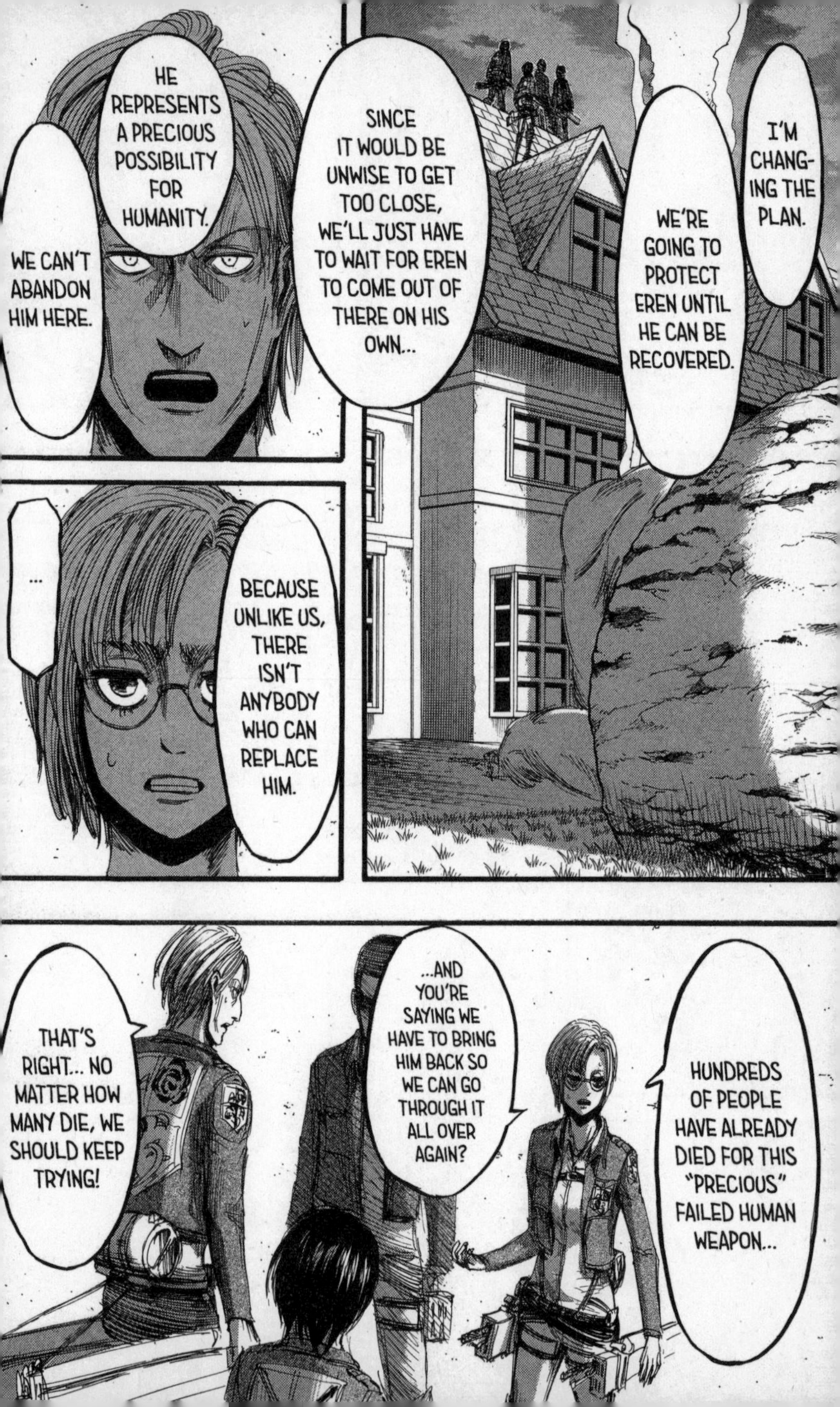
I'M CHANGING THE PLAN.
WE'RE GOING TO PROTECT EREN UNTIL HE CAN BE RECOVERED.
SINCE IT WOULD BE UNWISE TO GET TOO CLOSE, WE'LL JUST HAVE TO WAIT FOR EREN TO COME OUT OF THERE ON HIS OWN...
HE REPRESENTS A PRECIOUS POSSIBILITY FOR HUMANITY.
WE CAN'T ABANDON HIM HERE.
BECAUSE UNLIKE US, THERE ISN'T ANYBODY WHO CAN REPLACE HIM.
...
HUNDREDS OF PEOPLE HAVE ALREADY DIED FOR THIS "PRECIOUS" FAILED HUMAN WEAPON...
...AND YOU'RE SAYING WE HAVE TO BRING HIM BACK SO WE CAN GO THROUGH IT ALL OVER AGAIN?
THAT'S RIGHT... NO MATTER HOW MANY DIE, WE SHOULD KEEP TRYING!

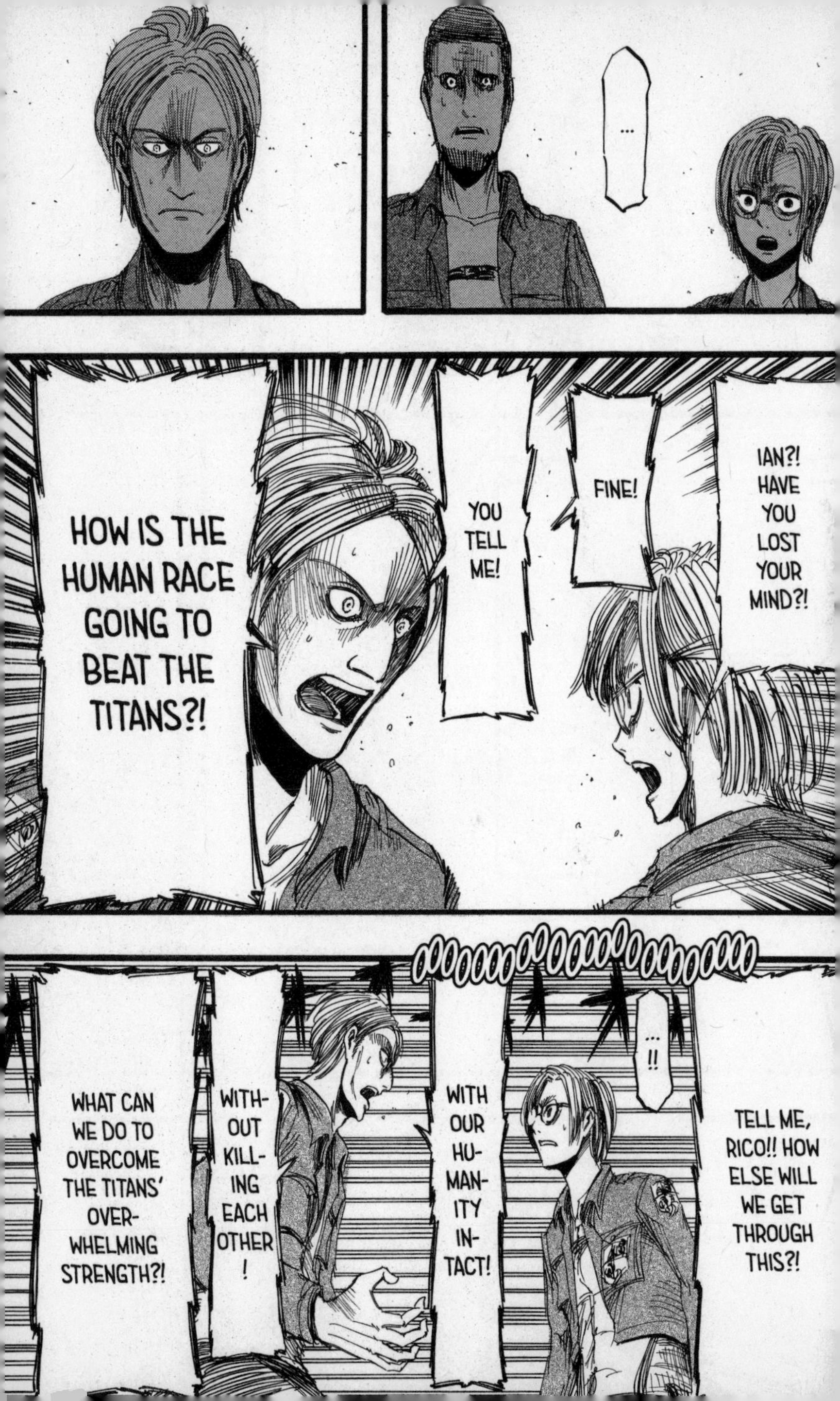
...
IAN?! HAVE YOU LOST YOUR MIND?!
FINE!
YOU TELL ME!
HOW IS THE HUMAN RACE GOING TO BEAT THE TITANS?!
OOOOOOOOOOOOOOOOOOOOOO
TELL ME, RICO!! HOW ELSE WILL WE GET THROUGH THIS?!
... !!
WITH OUR HUMANITY INTACT!
WITHOUT KILLING EACH OTHER!
WHAT CAN WE DO TO OVERCOME THE TITANS' OVERWHELMING STRENGTH?!

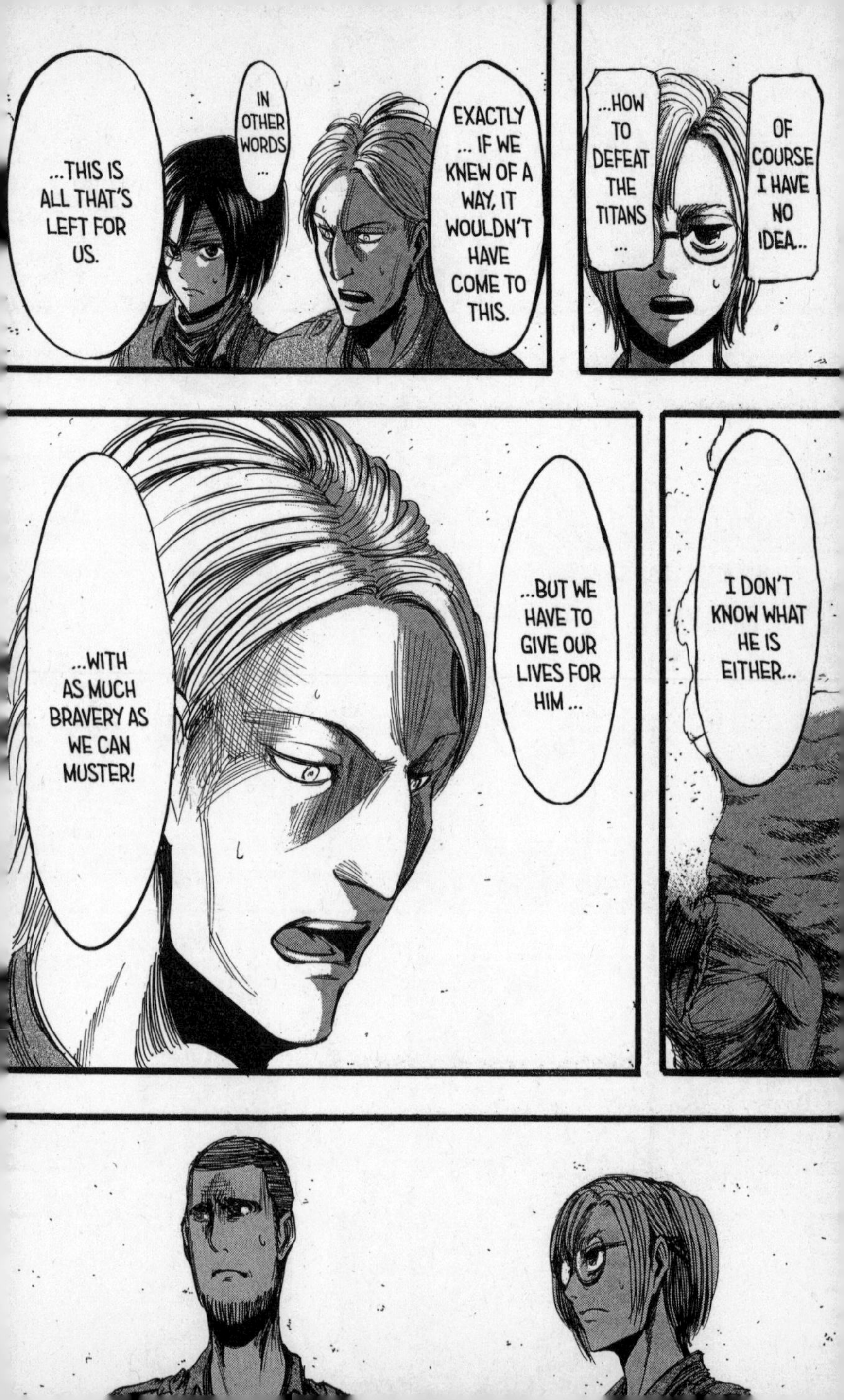
OF COURSE I HAVE NO IDEA...
...HOW TO DEFEAT THE TITANS ...
EXACTLY ... IF WE KNEW OF A WAY, IT WOULDN'T HAVE COME TO THIS.
IN OTHER WORDS ...
...THIS IS ALL THAT'S LEFT FOR US.
I DON'T KNOW WHAT HE IS EITHER...
...BUT WE HAVE TO GIVE OUR LIVES FOR HIM ...
...WITH AS MUCH BRAVERY AS WE CAN MUSTER!

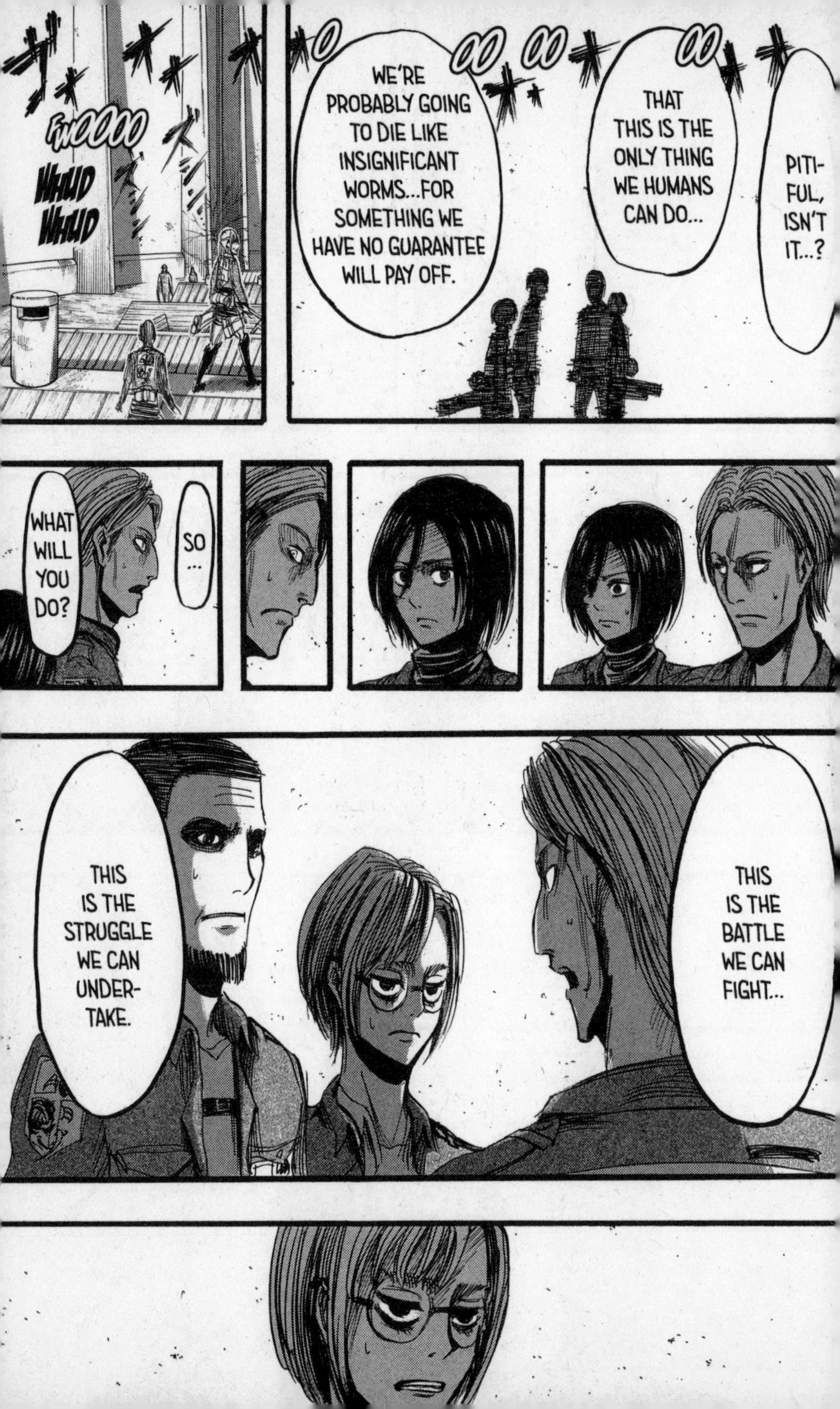

PITIFUL, ISN'T IT...?
THAT THIS IS THE ONLY THING WE HUMANS CAN DO...
WE'RE PROBABLY GOING TO DIE LIKE INSIGNIFICANT WORMS...FOR SOMETHING WE HAVE NO GUARANTEE WILL PAY OFF.
FWOOOO
WHUD WHUD
SO ...
WHAT WILL YOU DO?
THIS IS THE BATTLE WE CAN FIGHT...
THIS IS THE STRUGGLE WE CAN UNDERTAKE.

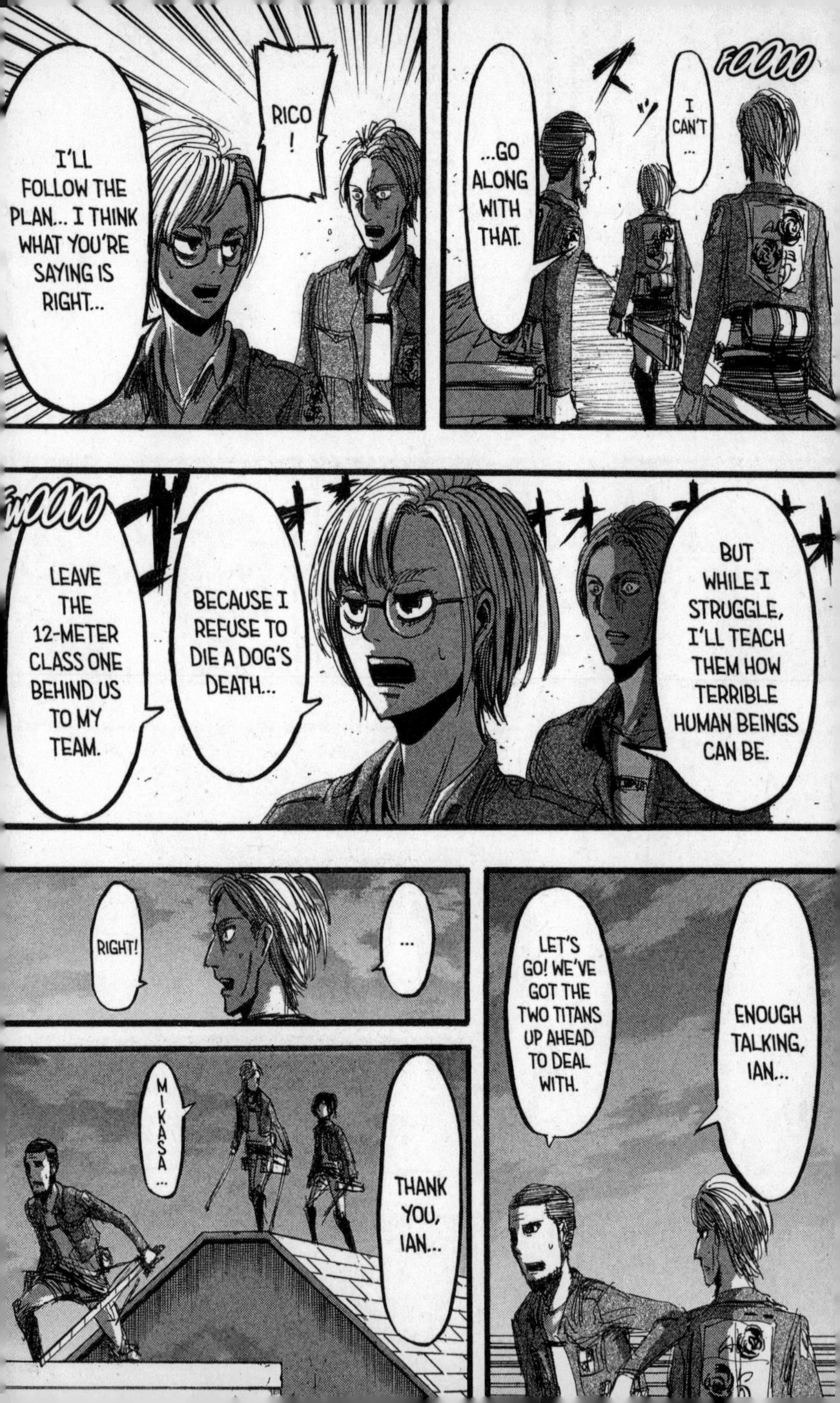
FOOOO
I CAN'T ...
...GO ALONG WITH THAT.
RICO!
I'LL FOLLOW THE PLAN... I THINK WHAT YOU'RE SAYING IS RIGHT...
BUT WHILE I STRUGGLE, I'LL TEACH THEM HOW TERRIBLE HUMAN BEINGS CAN BE.
BECAUSE I REFUSE TO DIE A DOG'S DEATH...
LEAVE THE 12-METER CLASS ONE BEHIND US TO MY TEAM.
FWOOOO
ENOUGH TALKING, IAN...
LET'S GO! WE'VE GOT THE TWO TITANS UP AHEAD TO DEAL WITH.
...
RIGHT!
THANK YOU, IAN...
MIKASA...

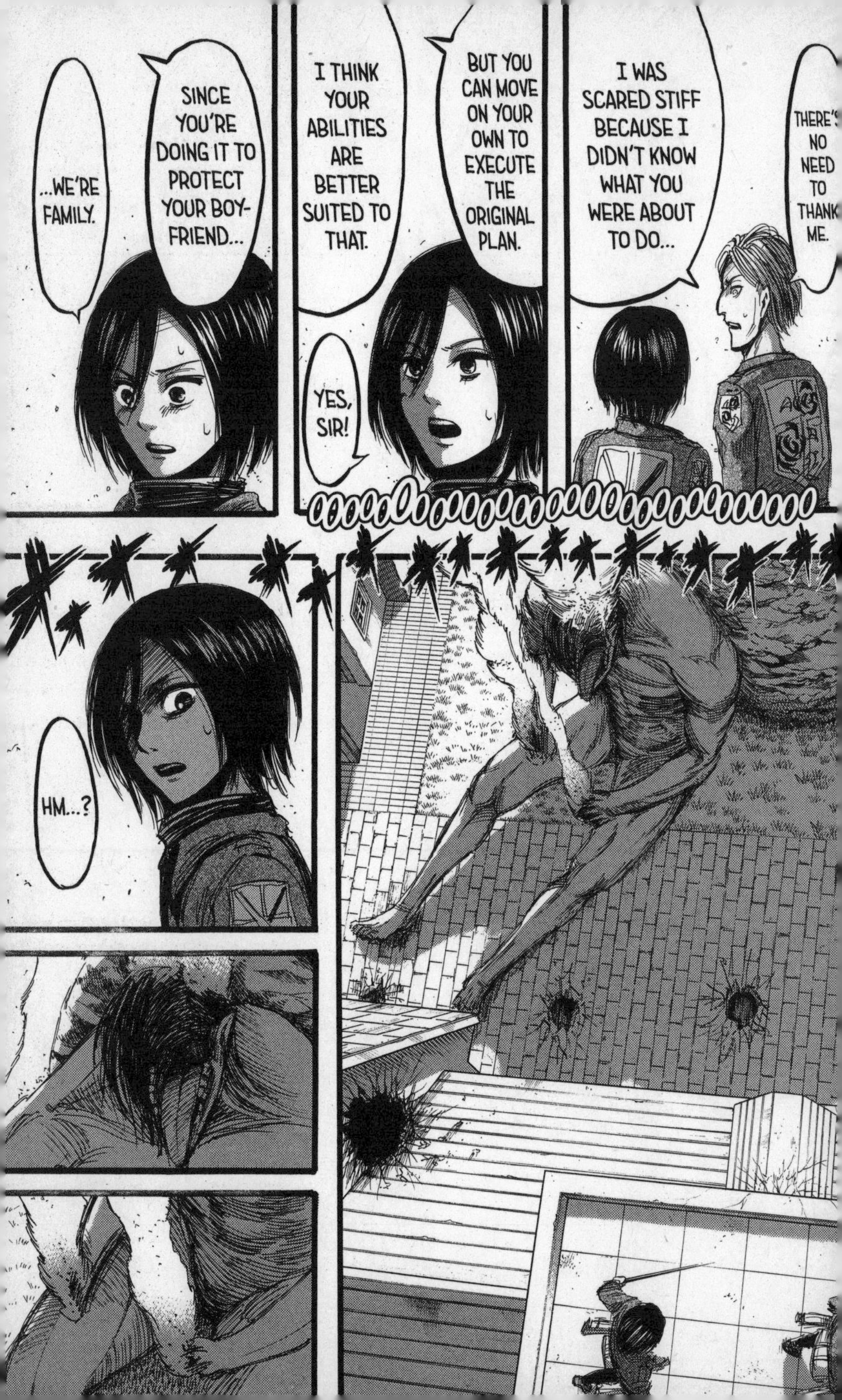
THERE'S NO NEED TO THANK ME.
I WAS SCARED STIFF BECAUSE I DIDN'T KNOW WHAT YOU WERE ABOUT TO DO...
BUT YOU CAN MOVE ON YOUR OWN TO EXECUTE THE ORIGINAL PLAN.
I THINK YOUR ABILITIES ARE BETTER SUITED TO THAT.
YES, SIR!
SINCE YOU'RE DOING IT TO PROTECT YOUR BOY-FRIEND...
...WE'RE FAMILY.
OOOOOOOOOOOOOOOOOOOOOOOOOOOOOOOOOOOO
HM...?

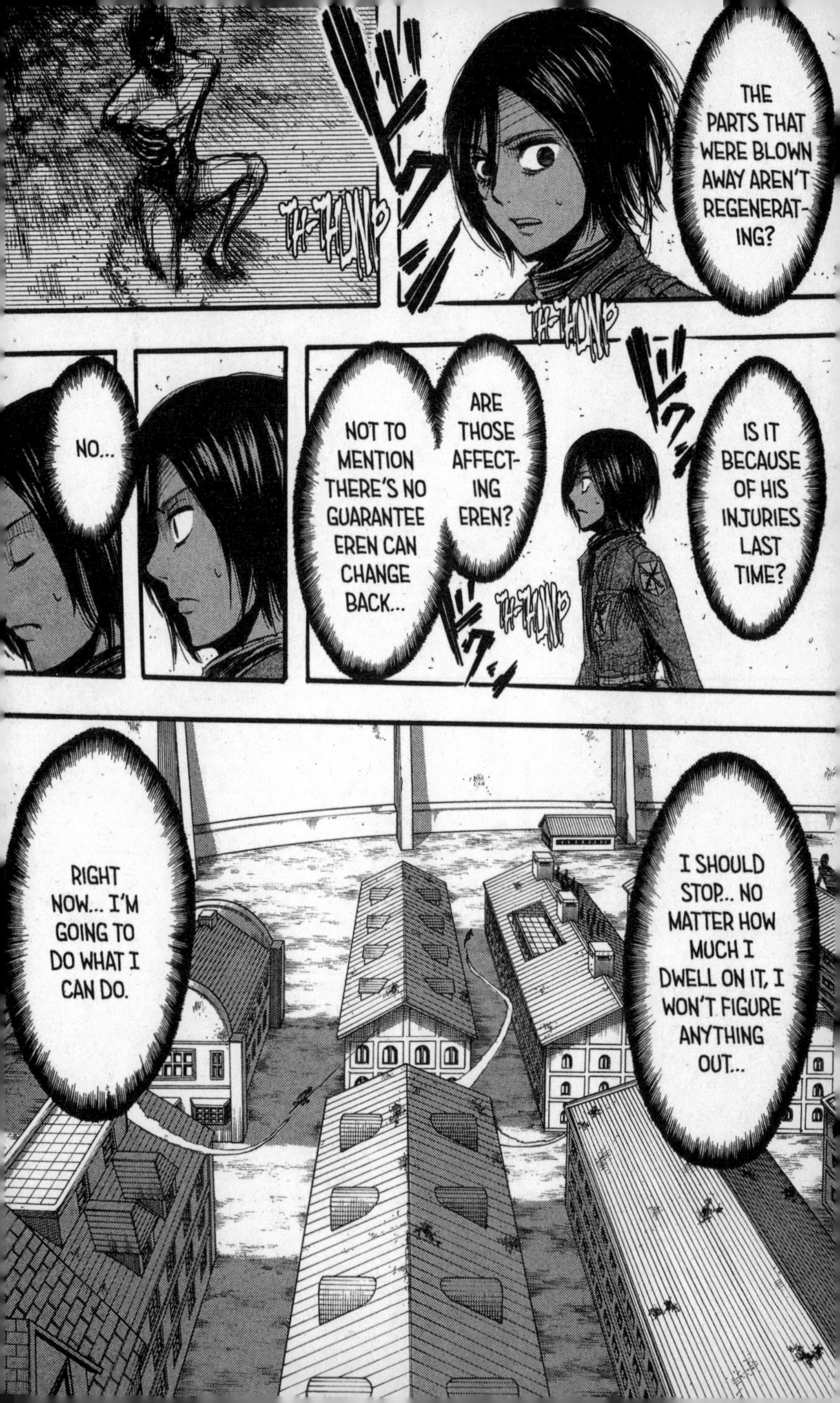
THE PARTS THAT WERE BLOWN AWAY AREN'T REGENERAT-ING?
TH-THUMP
TH-THUMP
IS IT BECAUSE OF HIS INJURIES LAST TIME?
ARE THOSE AFFECT-ING EREN?
NOT TO MENTION THERE'S NO GUARANTEE EREN CAN CHANGE BACK...
TH-THUMP
NO...
I SHOULD STOP... NO MATTER HOW MUCH I DWELL ON IT, I WON'T FIGURE ANYTHING OUT...
RIGHT NOW... I'M GOING TO DO WHAT I CAN DO.

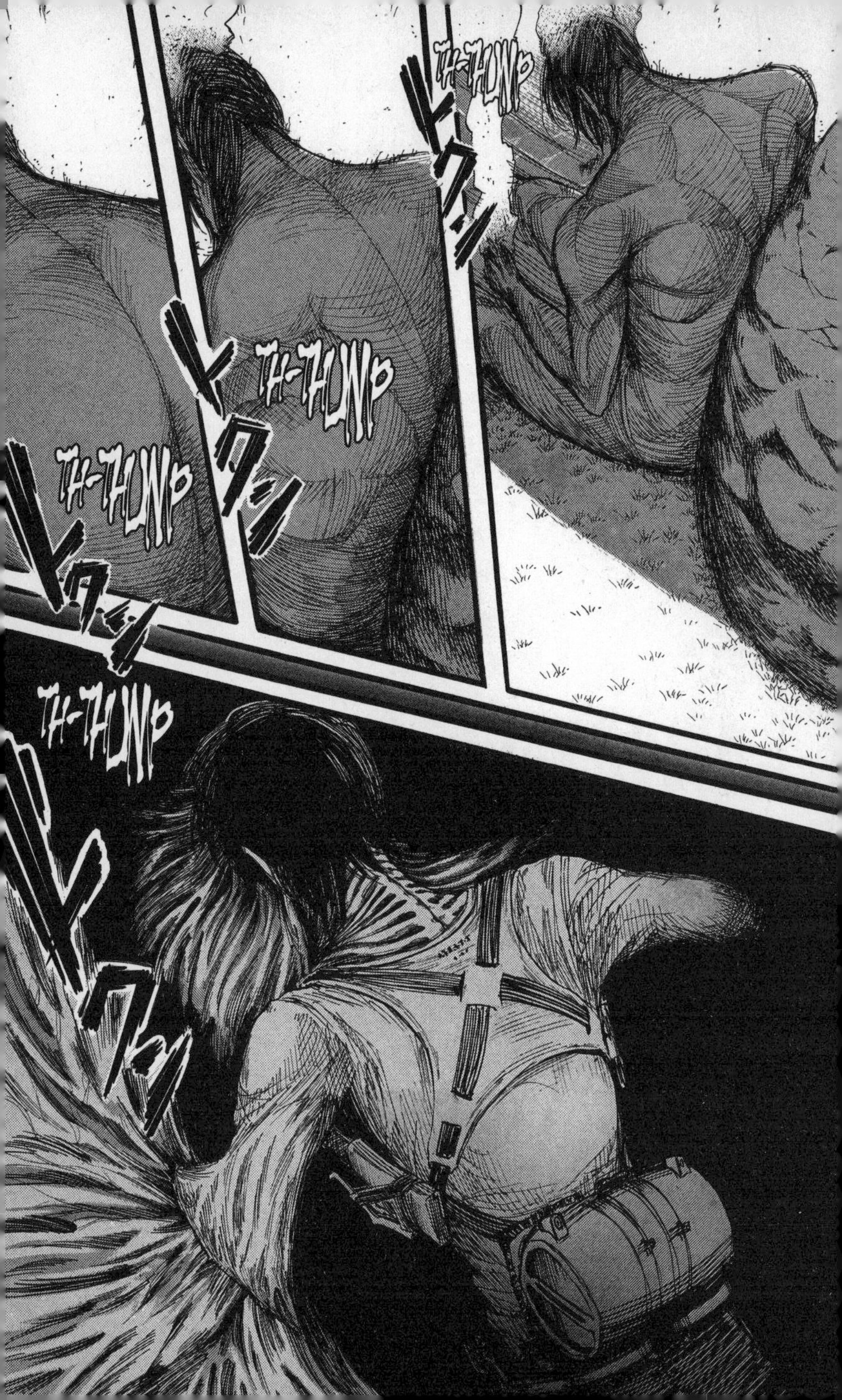
TH-THUMP
ドクン
TH-THUMP
ドクン
TH-THUMP
ドクン
TH-THUMP
ドクン

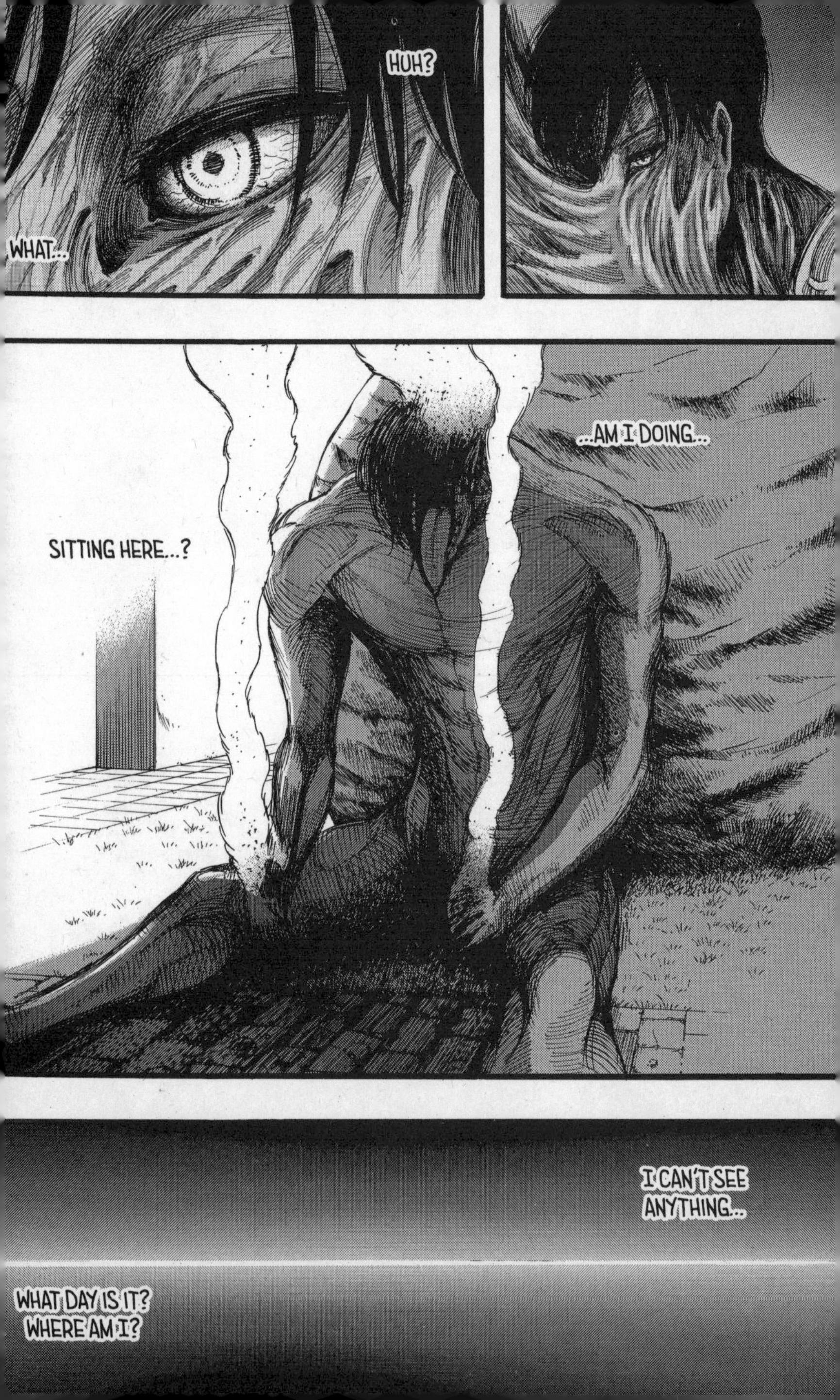
HUH?
WHAT...
...AM I DOING...
SITTING HERE...?
I CAN'T SEE ANYTHING...
WHAT DAY IS IT? WHERE AM I?

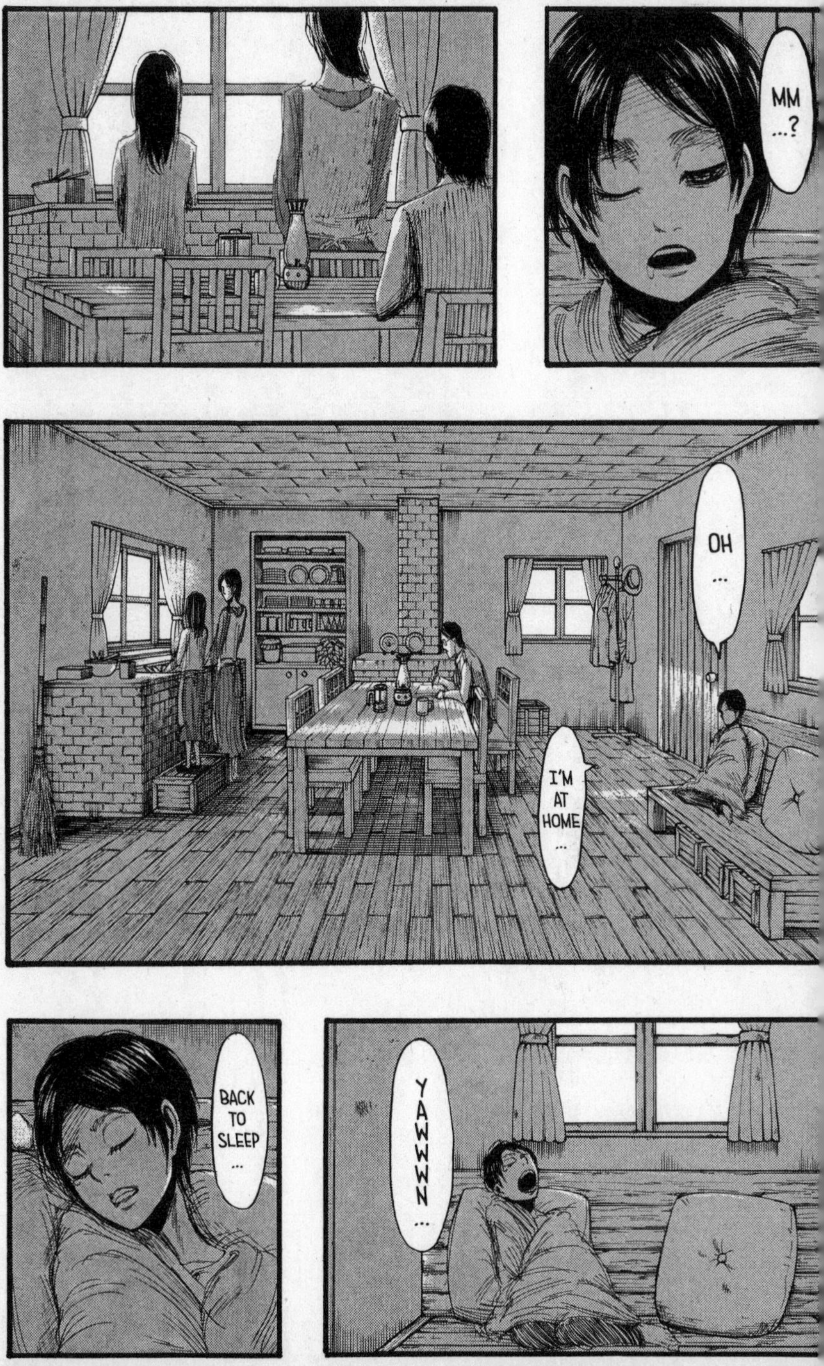
MM ...?
OH ...
I'M AT HOME ...
YAWWWN ...
BACK TO SLEEP ...

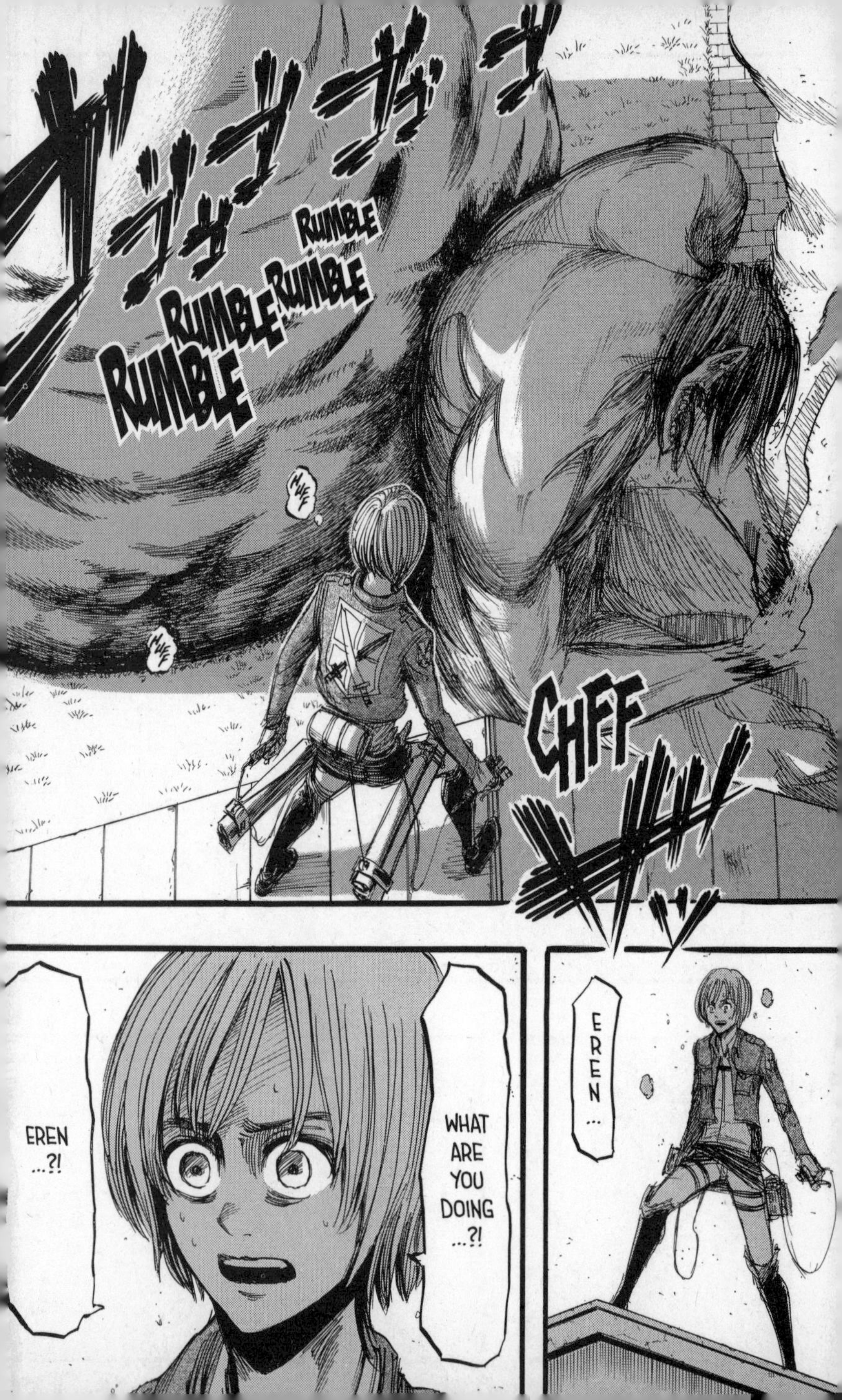
RUMBLE
RUMBLE RUMBLE
RUMBLE
HUFF
HUFF
CHFF
EREN ...
WHAT ARE YOU DOING ...?!
EREN ...?!

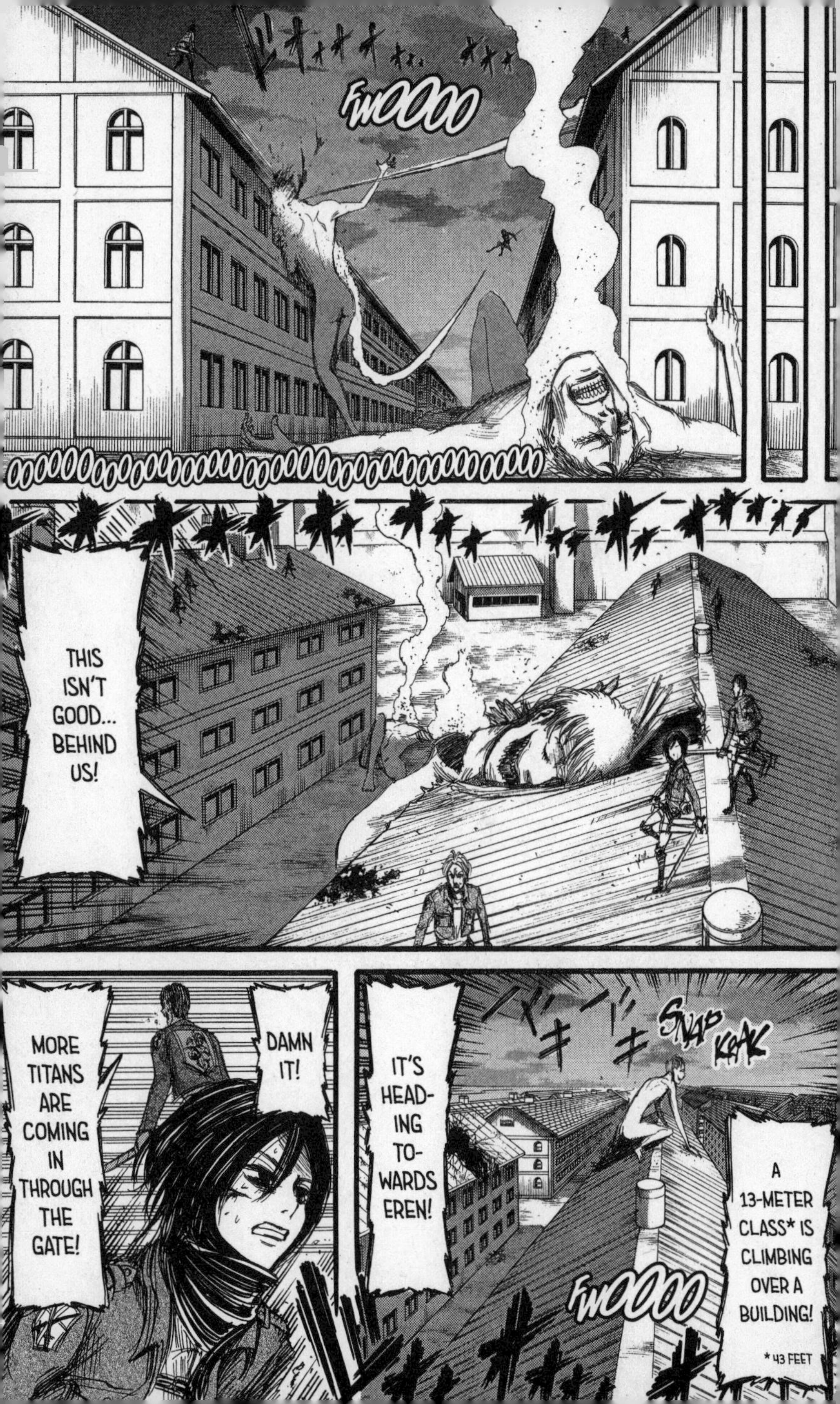
FWOOOO
OOOOOOOOOOOOOOOOOOOOOOOOOOOOOOOOOOO
THIS ISN'T GOOD... BEHIND US!
SNAP KRAK
A 13-METER CLASS* IS CLIMBING OVER A BUILDING!
IT'S HEADING TOWARDS EREN!
FWOOOO
* 43 FEET
DAMN IT!
MORE TITANS ARE COMING IN THROUGH THE GATE!

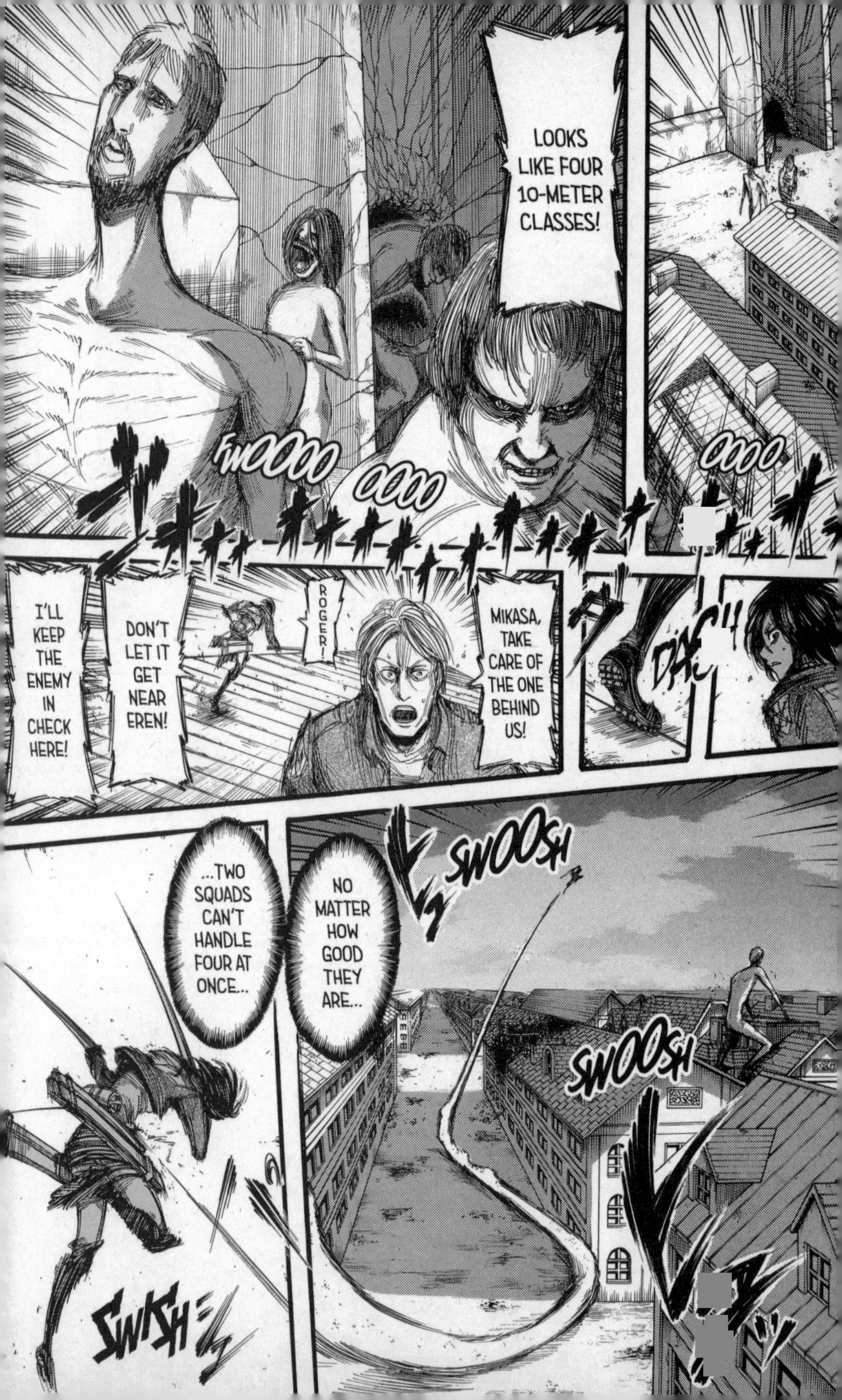
OOOO
LOOKS LIKE FOUR 10-METER CLASSES!
OOOO
FWOOOO
MIKASA, TAKE CARE OF THE ONE BEHIND US!
ROGER!
DON'T LET IT GET NEAR EREN!
I'LL KEEP THE ENEMY IN CHECK HERE!
SWOOSH
NO MATTER HOW GOOD THEY ARE...
...TWO SQUADS CAN'T HANDLE FOUR AT ONCE...
SWOOSH
SWISH

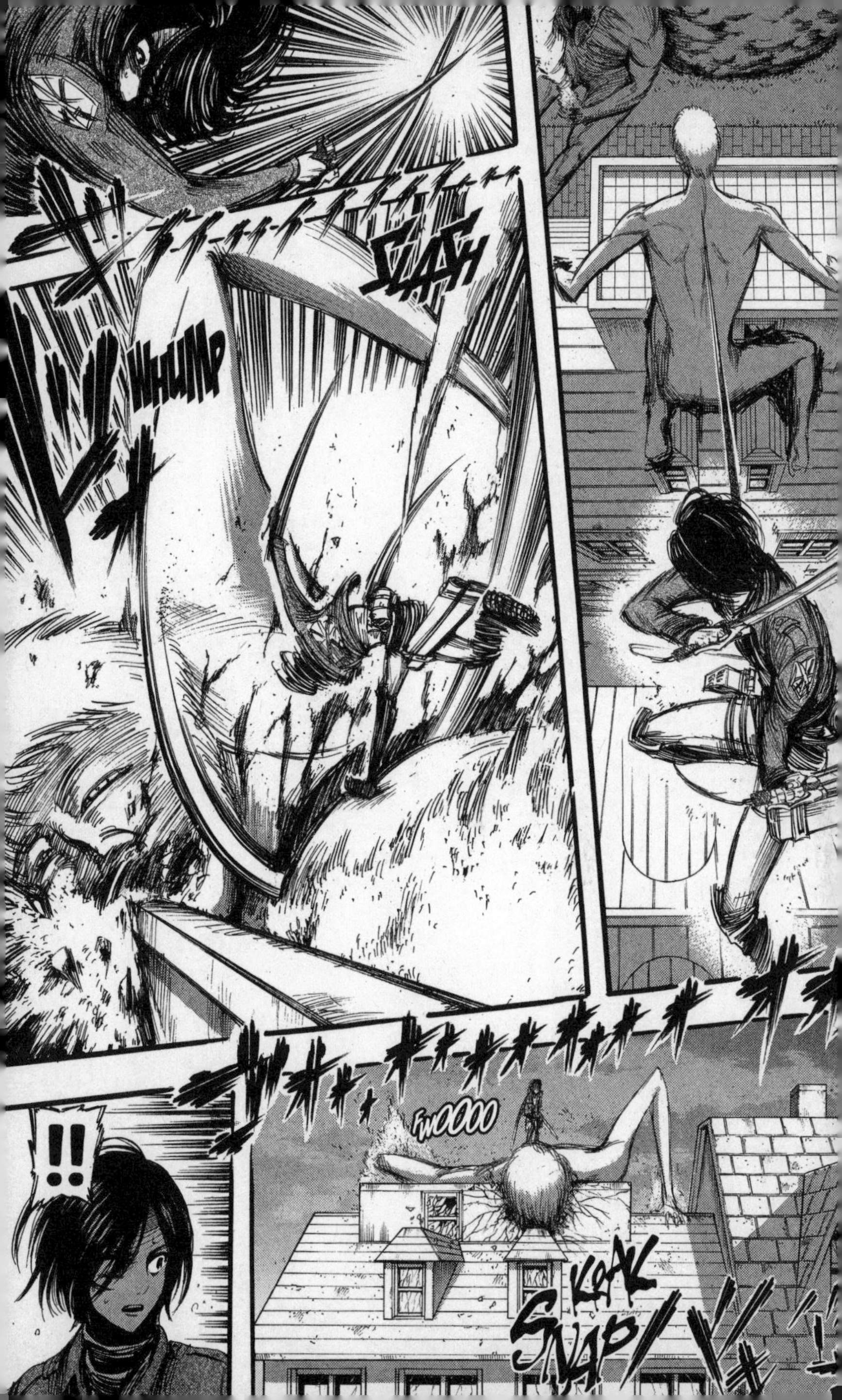
SLASH
WHUMP
FWOOOO
KRAK
SNAP
!!

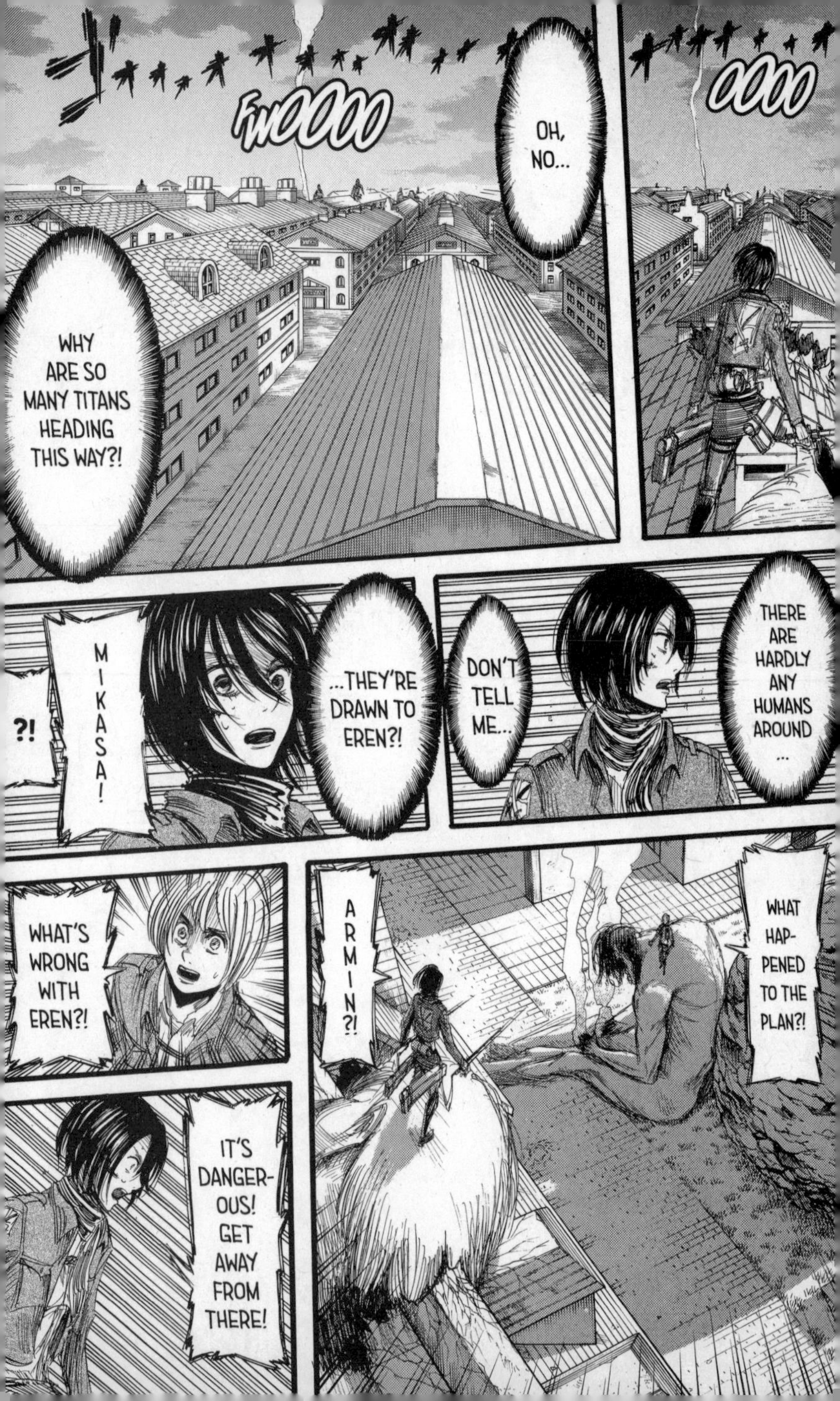
OOOO
OH, NO...
FWOOOO
WHY ARE SO MANY TITANS HEADING THIS WAY?!
THERE ARE HARDLY ANY HUMANS AROUND...
DON'T TELL ME...
...THEY'RE DRAWN TO EREN?!
MIKASA!
?!
WHAT HAP-PENED TO THE PLAN?!
ARMIN?!
WHAT'S WRONG WITH EREN?!
IT'S DANGER-OUS! GET AWAY FROM THERE!

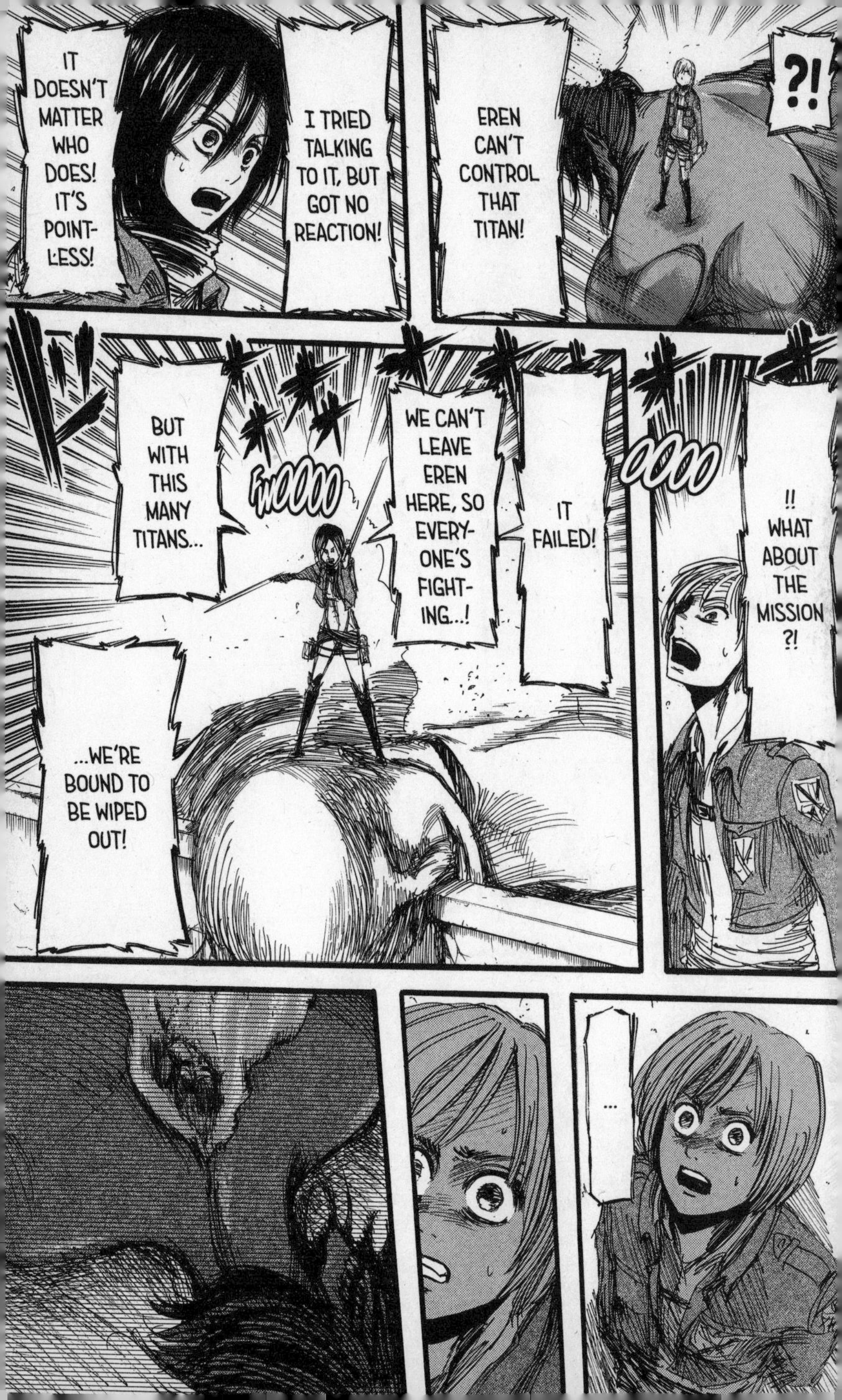
?!
EREN CAN'T CONTROL THAT TITAN!
I TRIED TALKING TO IT, BUT GOT NO REACTION!
IT DOESN'T MATTER WHO DOES! IT'S POINT-LESS!
OOOO
!! WHAT ABOUT THE MISSION ?!
IT FAILED!
WE CAN'T LEAVE EREN HERE, SO EVERY-ONE'S FIGHT-ING...!
FWOOOO
BUT WITH THIS MANY TITANS...
...WE'RE BOUND TO BE WIPED OUT!
...

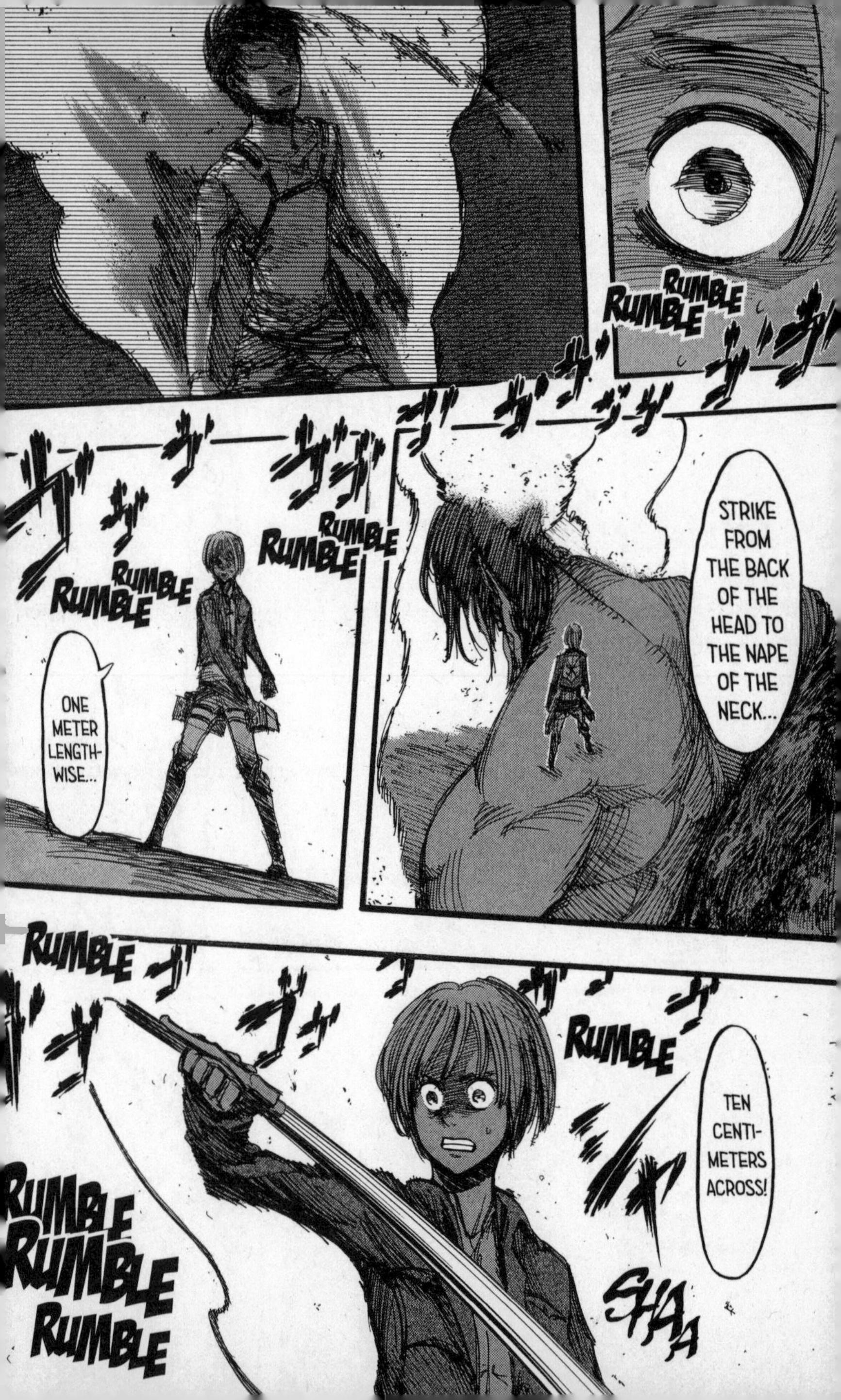

RUMBLE RUMBLE
STRIKE FROM THE BACK OF THE HEAD TO THE NAPE OF THE NECK...
RUMBLE RUMBLE
RUMBLE RUMBLE
ONE METER LENGTH-WISE...
RUMBLE
RUMBLE
TEN CENTI-METERS ACROSS!
SHAA
RUMBLE RUMBLE RUMBLE

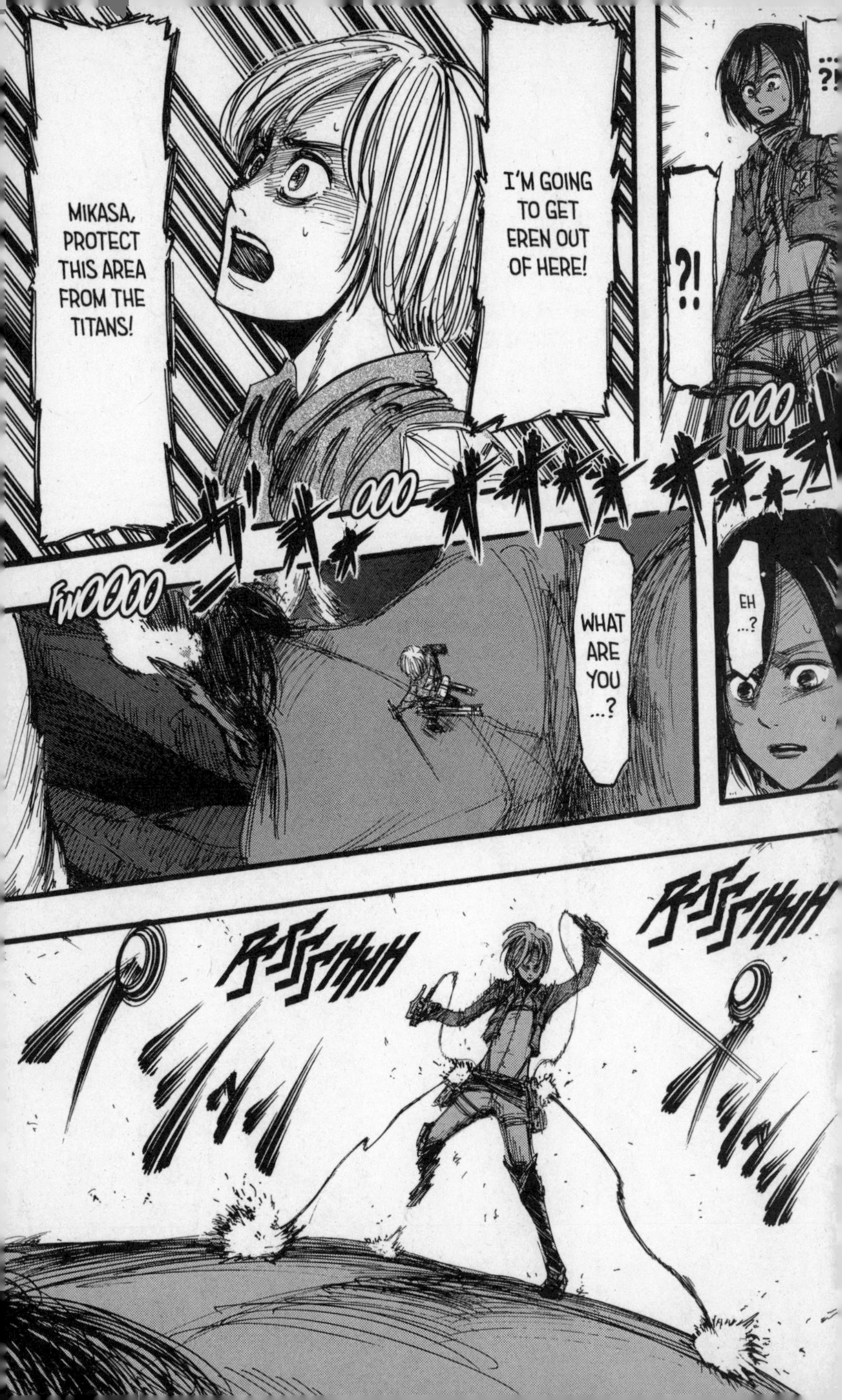

...?!
?!
OOO
I'M GOING TO GET EREN OUT OF HERE!
MIKASA, PROTECT THIS AREA FROM THE TITANS!
OOO
FWOOOO
EH ...?
WHAT ARE YOU ...?
R-SSHHH
R-SSHHH

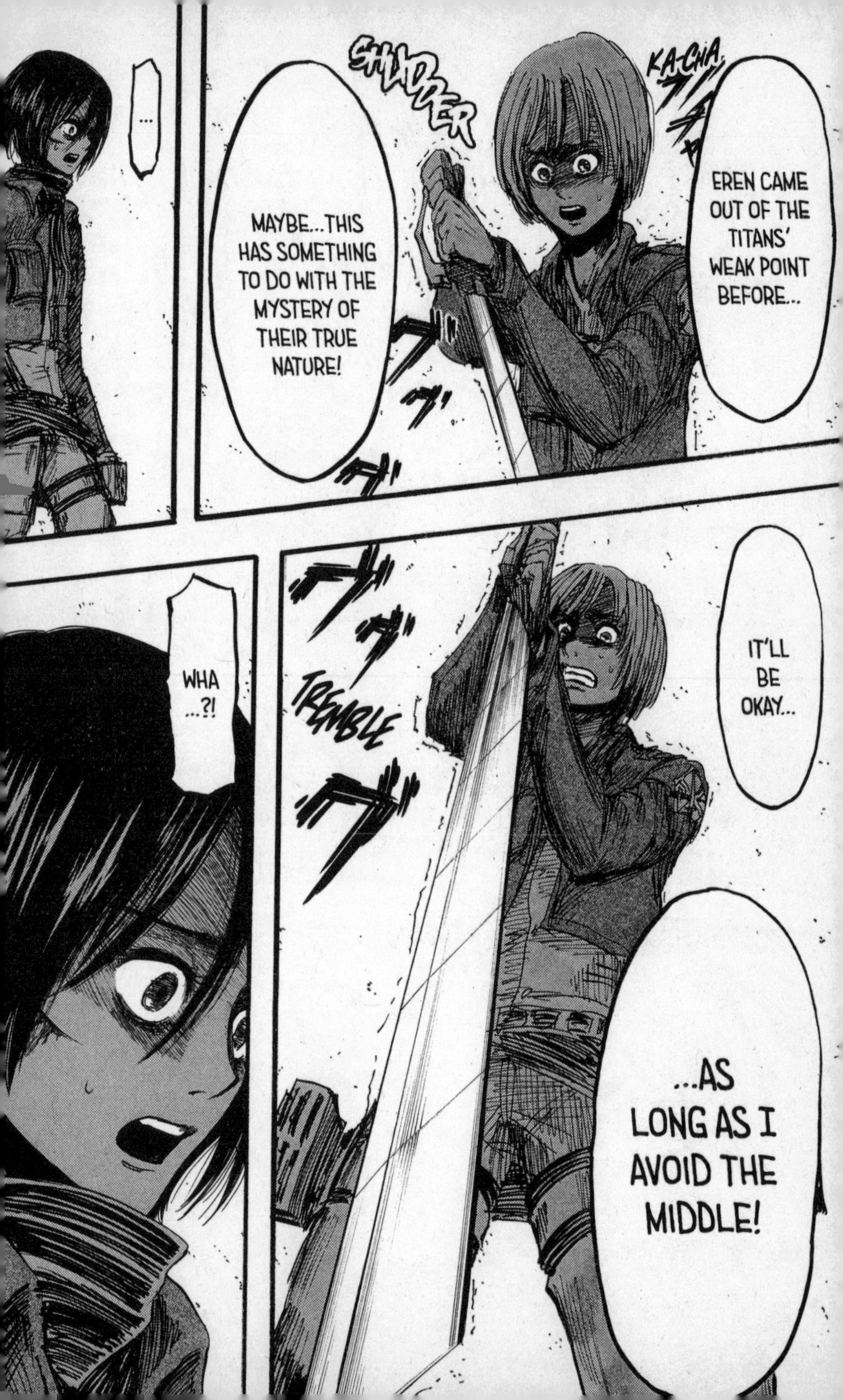

KA-CHA
EREN CAME OUT OF THE TITANS' WEAK POINT BEFORE...
SHUDDER
MAYBE...THIS HAS SOMETHING TO DO WITH THE MYSTERY OF THEIR TRUE NATURE!
...
IT'LL BE OKAY...
...AS LONG AS I AVOID THE MIDDLE!
TREMBLE
WHA ...?!

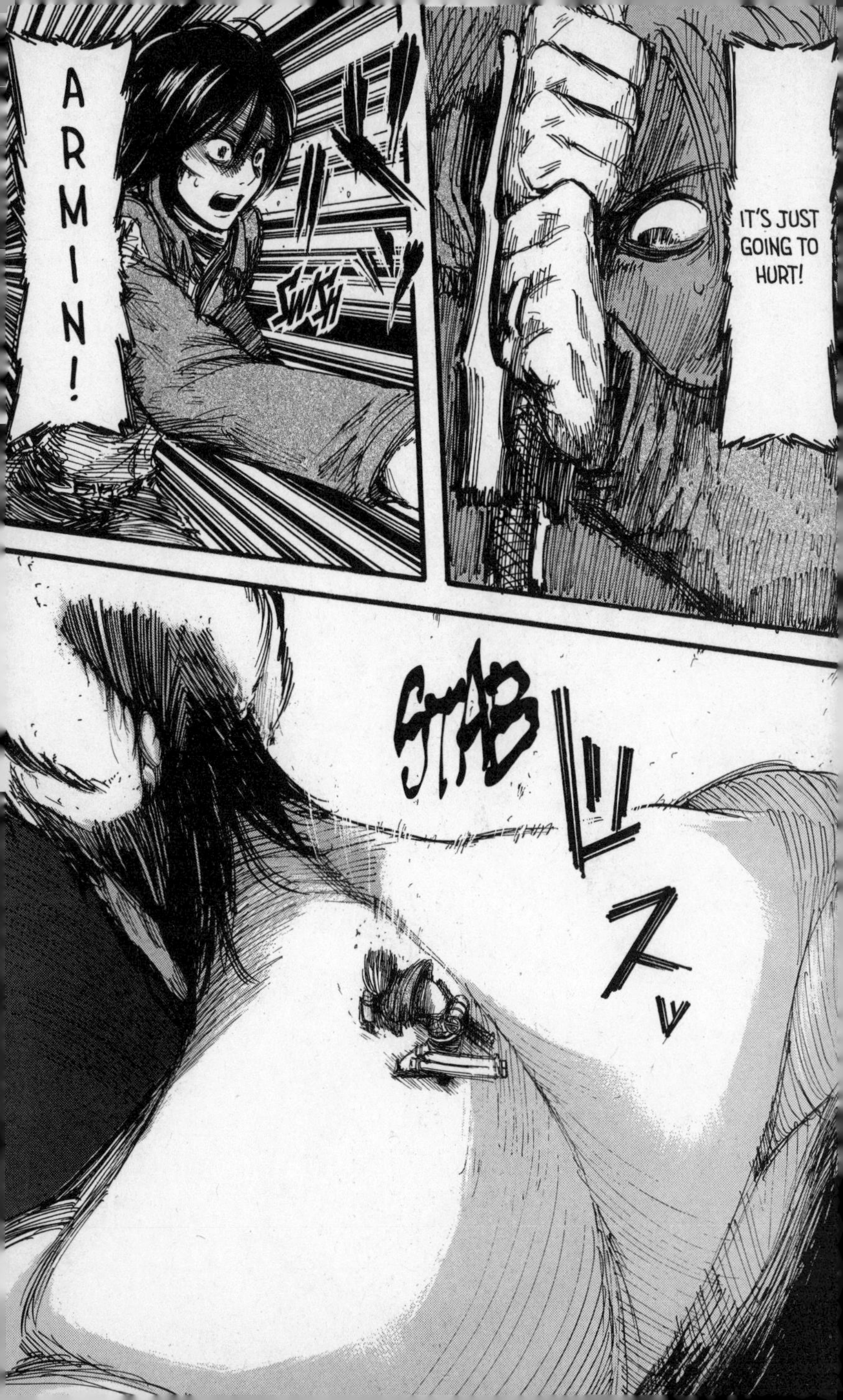
IT'S JUST GOING TO HURT!
ARMIN!
SWISH
STAB

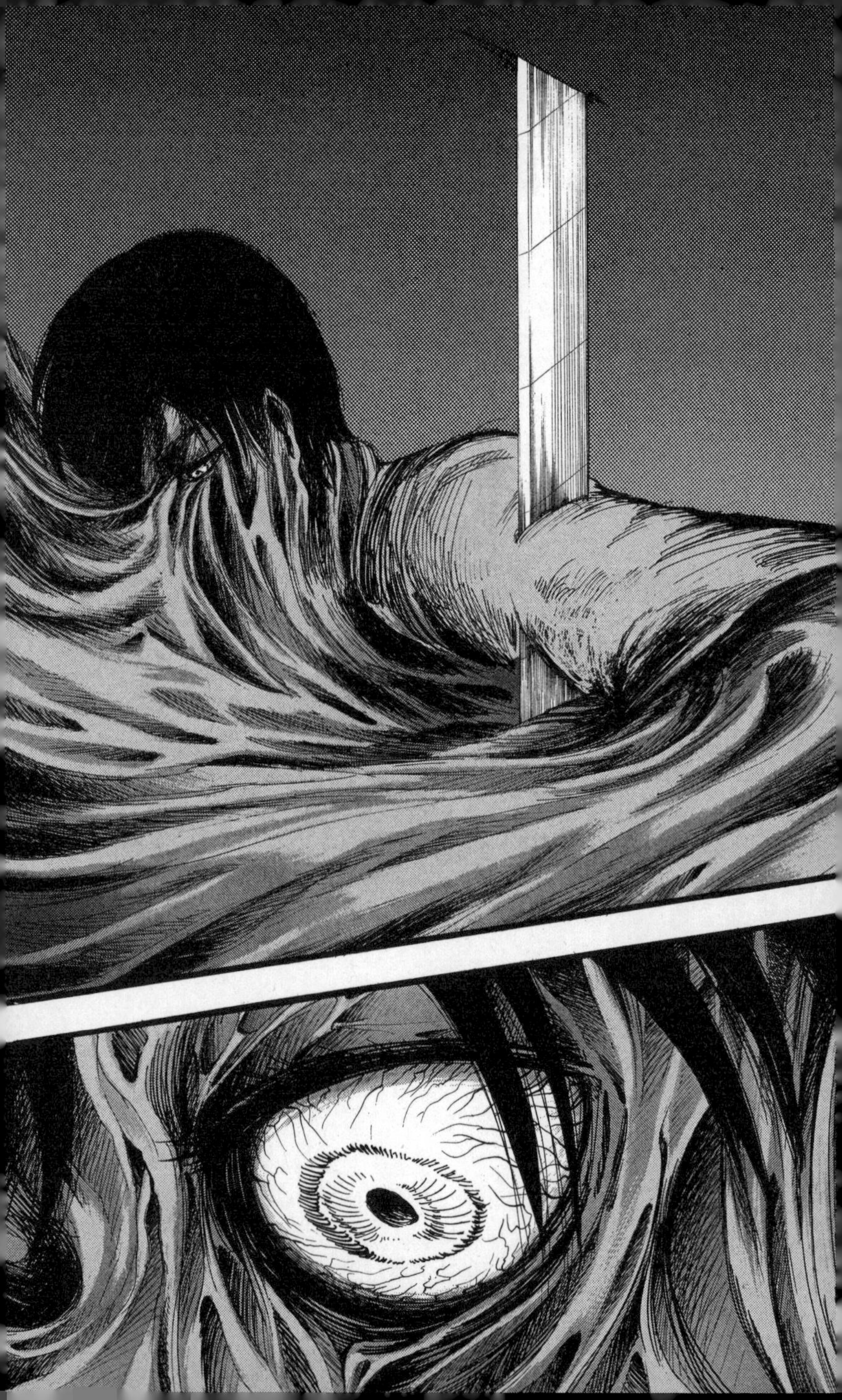

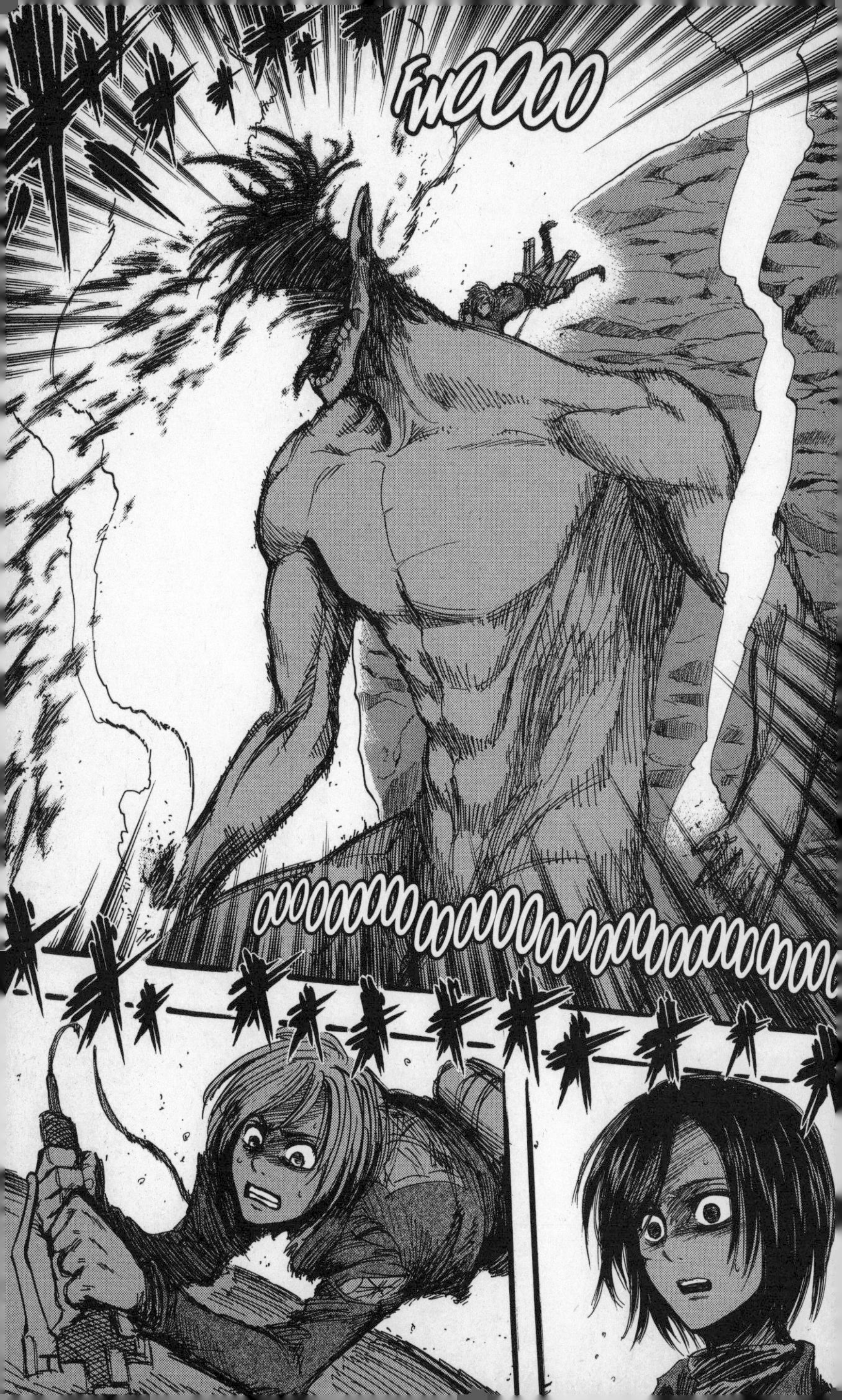
FWOOOOO
OOOOOOOOOOOOOOOOOOOOOOOOOOOOOOO

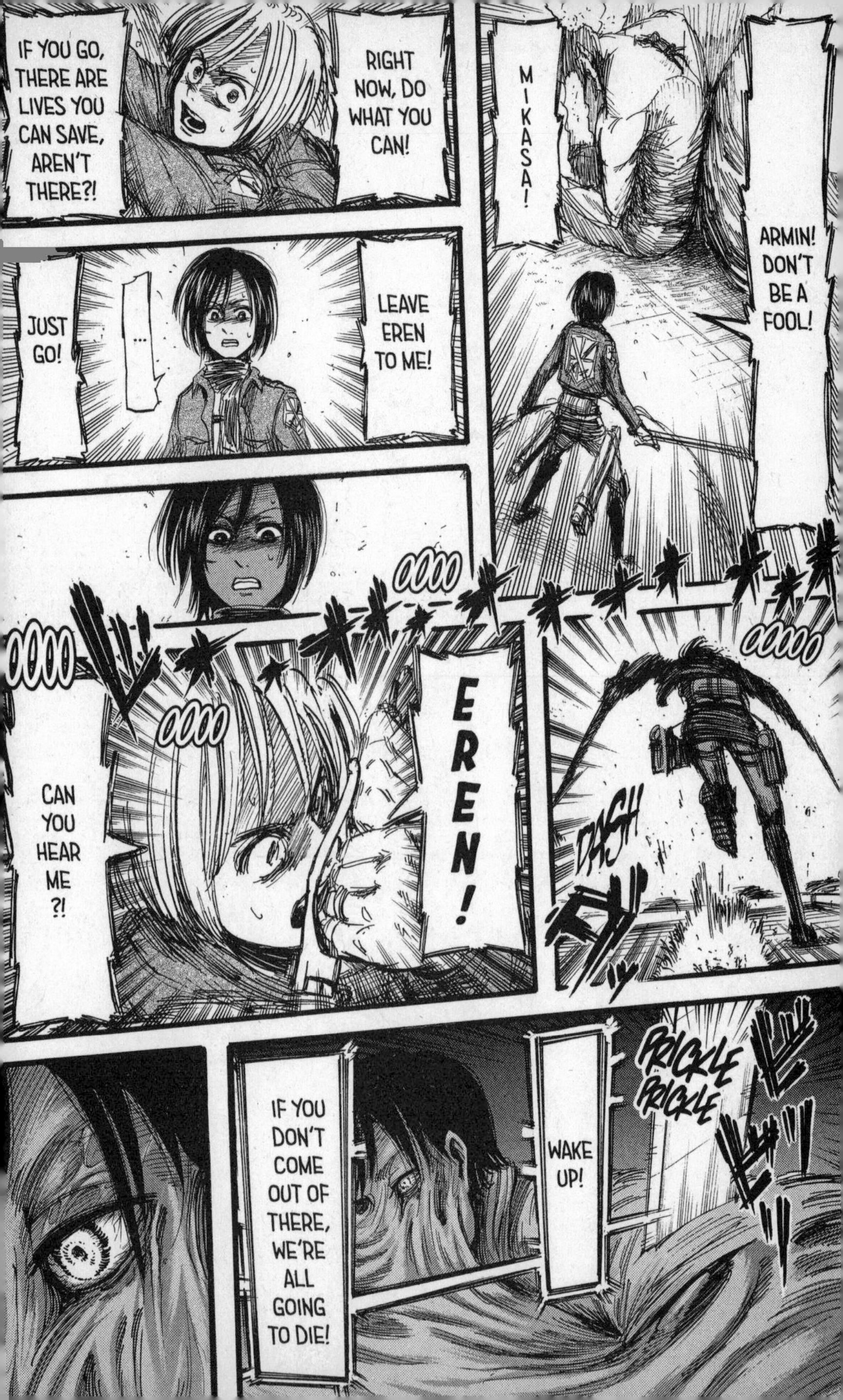
M I K A S A!
ARMIN! DON'T BE A FOOL!
RIGHT NOW, DO WHAT YOU CAN!
IF YOU GO, THERE ARE LIVES YOU CAN SAVE, AREN'T THERE?!
LEAVE EREN TO ME!
…
JUST GO!
OOOO
OOOOO
DASH
EREN!
OOOO
OOOO
CAN YOU HEAR ME ?!
PRICKLE PRICKLE
WAKE UP!
IF YOU DON'T COME OUT OF THERE, WE'RE ALL GOING TO DIE!

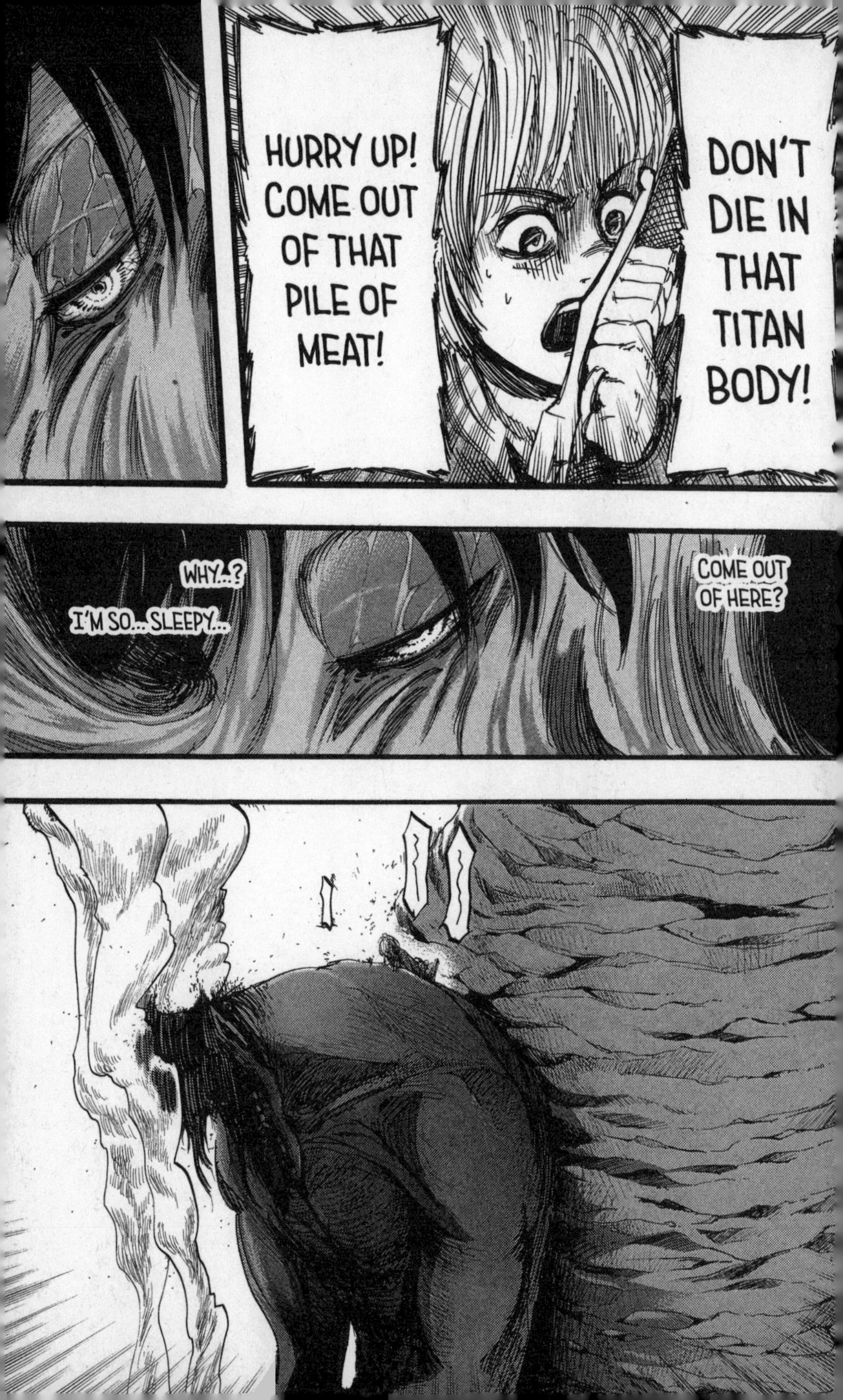
DON'T DIE IN THAT TITAN BODY!
HURRY UP! COME OUT OF THAT PILE OF MEAT!
COME OUT OF HERE?
WHY...?
I'M SO... SLEEPY...

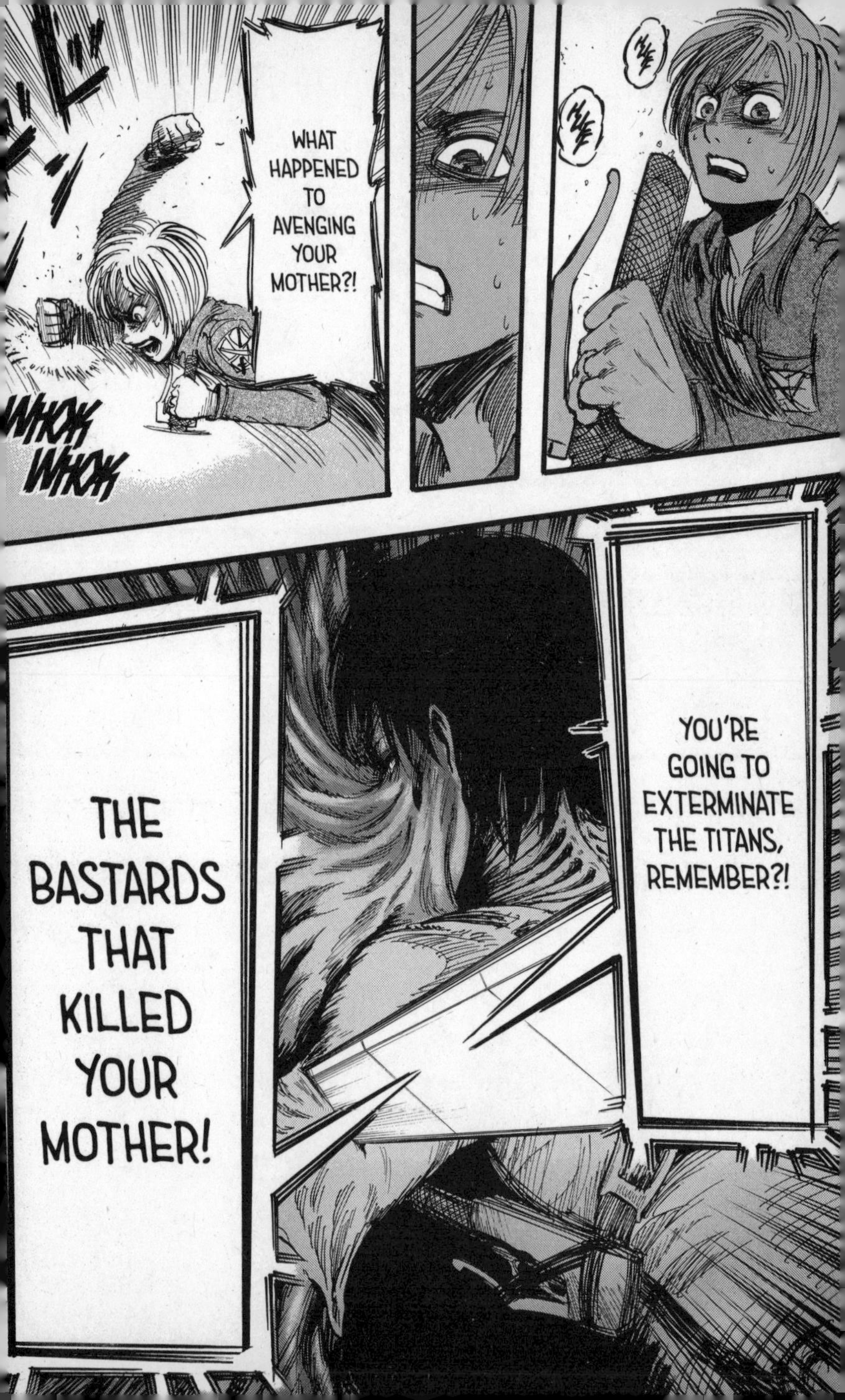
WHAT HAPPENED TO AVENGING YOUR MOTHER?!
WHOK WHOK
YOU'RE GOING TO EXTERMINATE THE TITANS, REMEMBER?!
THE BASTARDS THAT KILLED YOUR MOTHER!

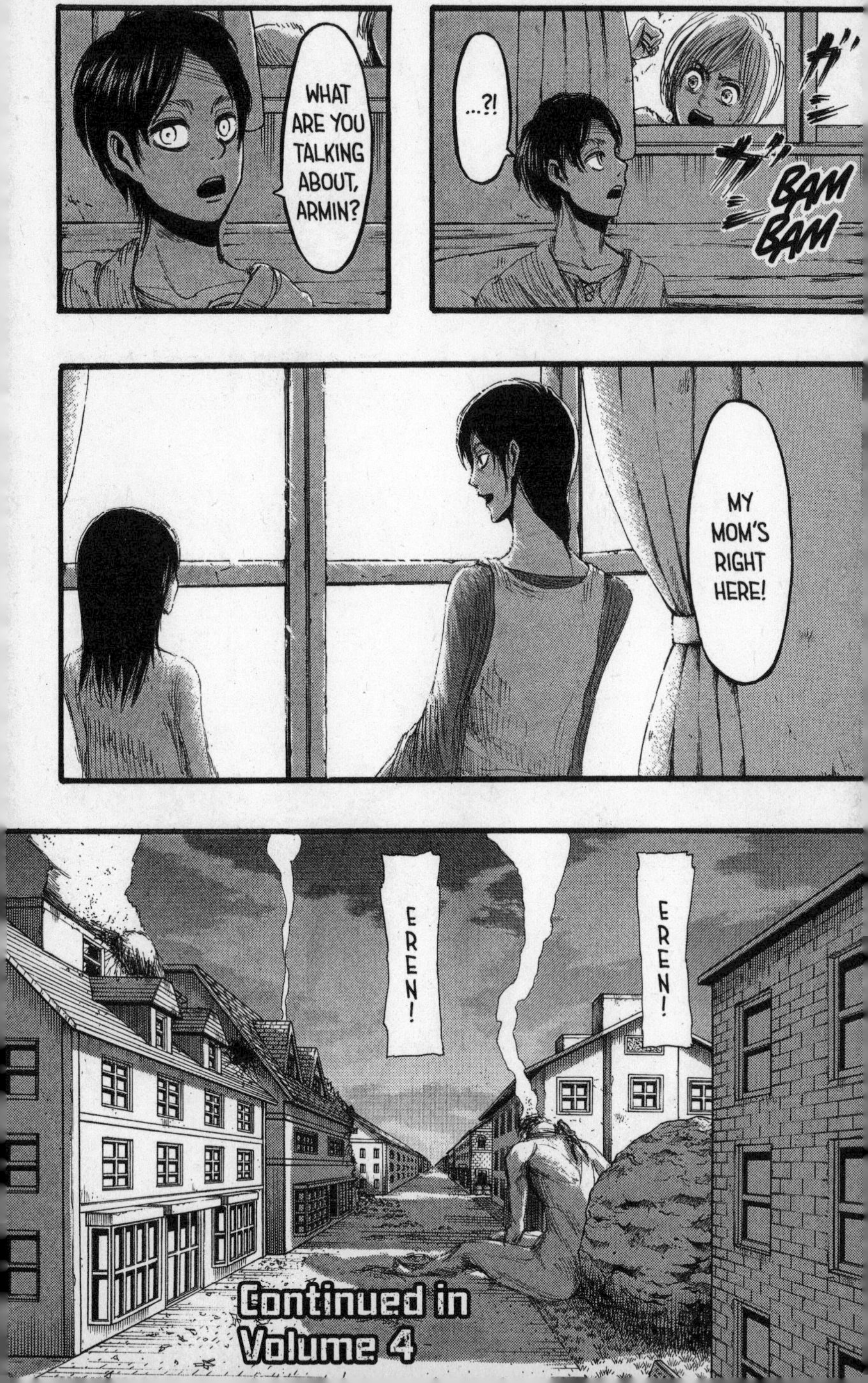
...?!
ガ ガ
BAM BAM
WHAT ARE YOU TALKING ABOUT, ARMIN?
MY MOM'S RIGHT HERE!
EREN!
EREN!
Continued in Volume 4

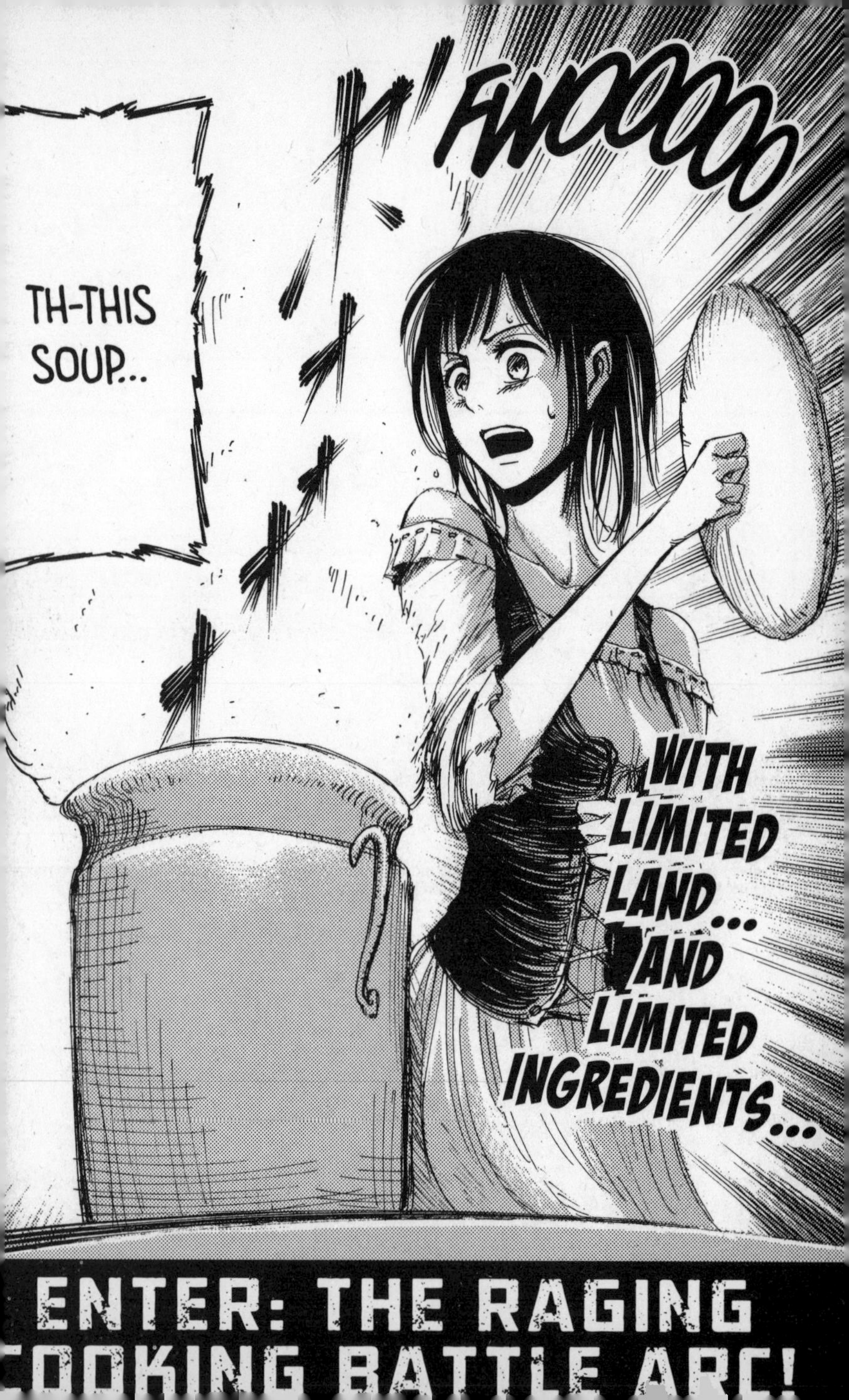
FWOOOOOO
TH-THIS SOUP...
WITH LIMITED LAND... AND LIMITED INGREDIENTS...
ENTER: THE RAGING COOKING BATTLE ARC!

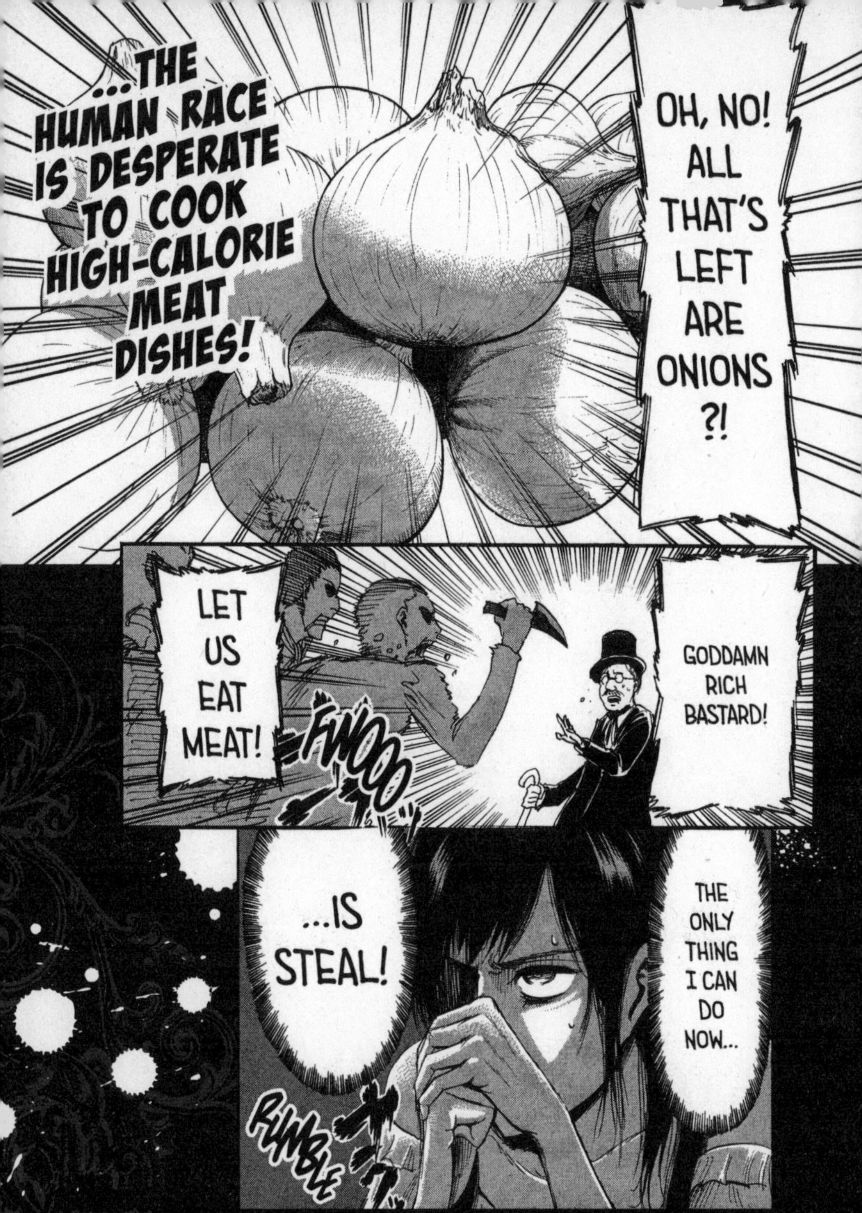
OH, NO! ALL THAT'S LEFT ARE ONIONS?!
...THE HUMAN RACE IS DESPERATE TO COOK HIGH-CALORIE MEAT DISHES!
GODDAMN RICH BASTARD!
FWOOO
LET US EAT MEAT!
THE ONLY THING I CAN DO NOW...
...IS STEAL!
RUMBLE

* Real preview is on the following page

Preview of Volume 4!

Preview of
Attack on Titan,
volume 4

We're pleased to present you a preview from **Attack on Titan,** volume 4. Please check our website (www.kodanshacomics.com) to see when this volume will be available.

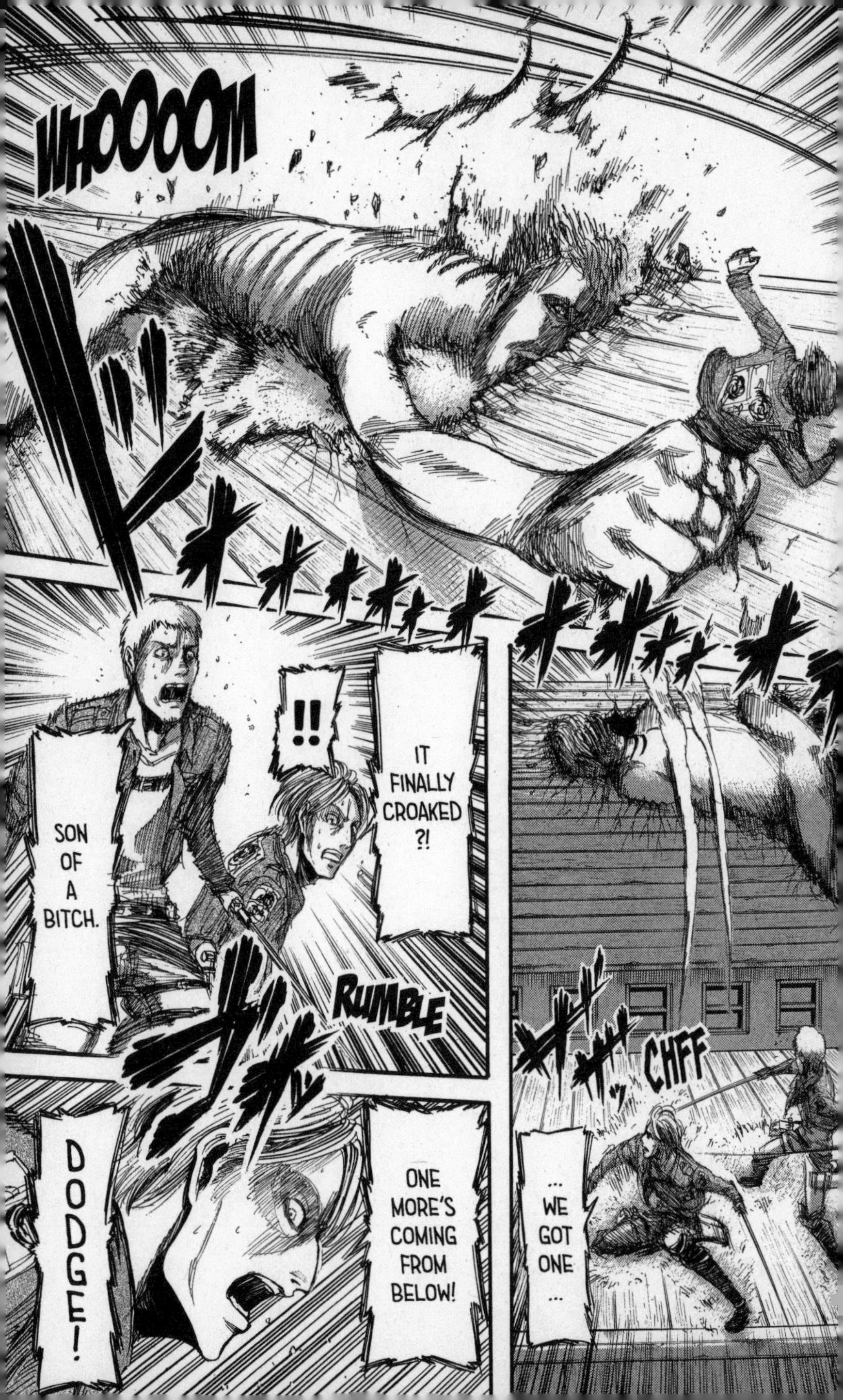
WHOOOOM
CHFF
... WE GOT ONE ...
IT FINALLY CROAKED ?!
!!
SON OF A BITCH.
RUMBLE
ONE MORE'S COMING FROM BELOW!
DODGE!

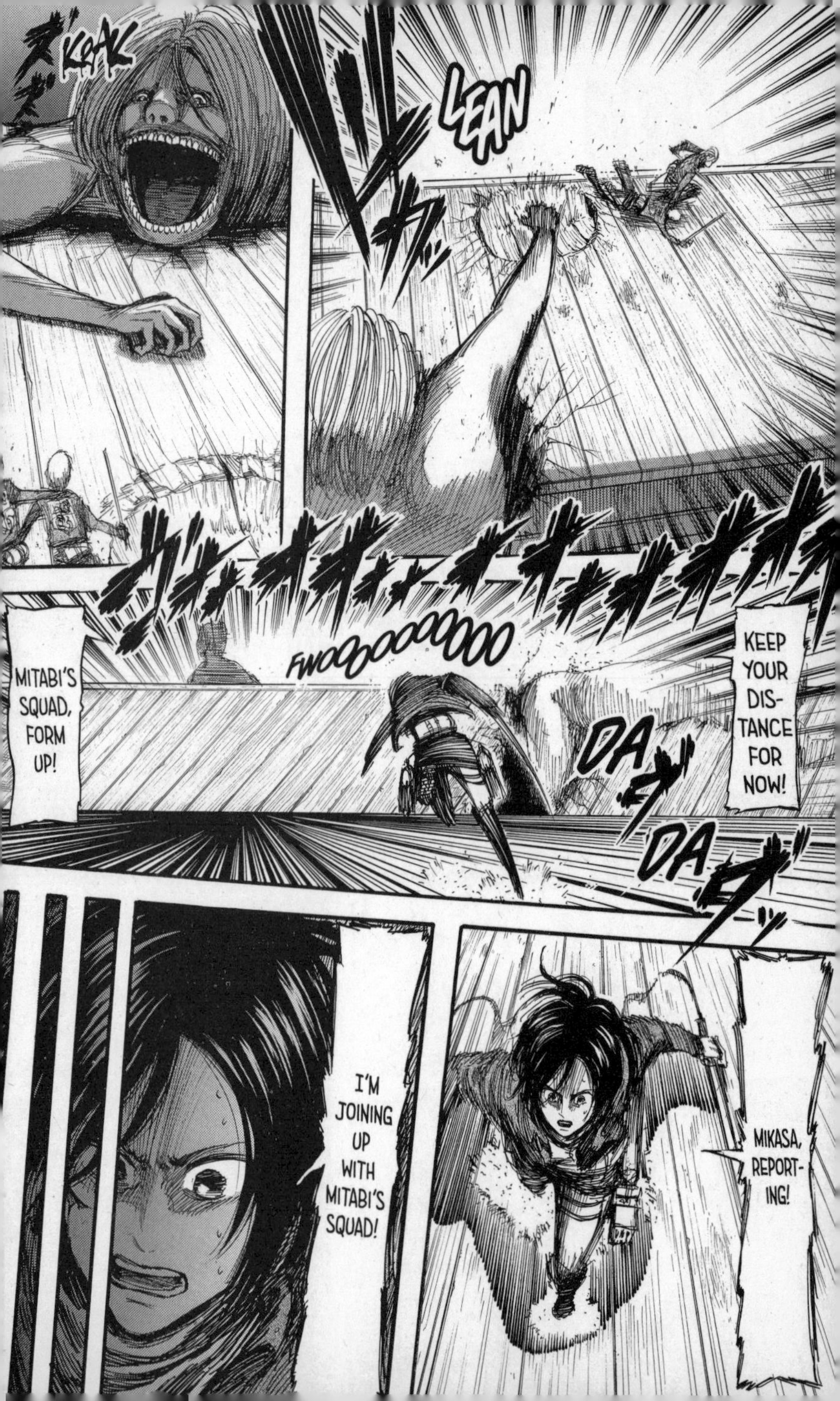
LEAN
KRAK
FWOOOOOOOOOO
KEEP YOUR DIS-TANCE FOR NOW!
DA
DA
MITABI'S SQUAD, FORM UP!
MIKASA, REPORT-ING!
I'M JOINING UP WITH MITABI'S SQUAD!

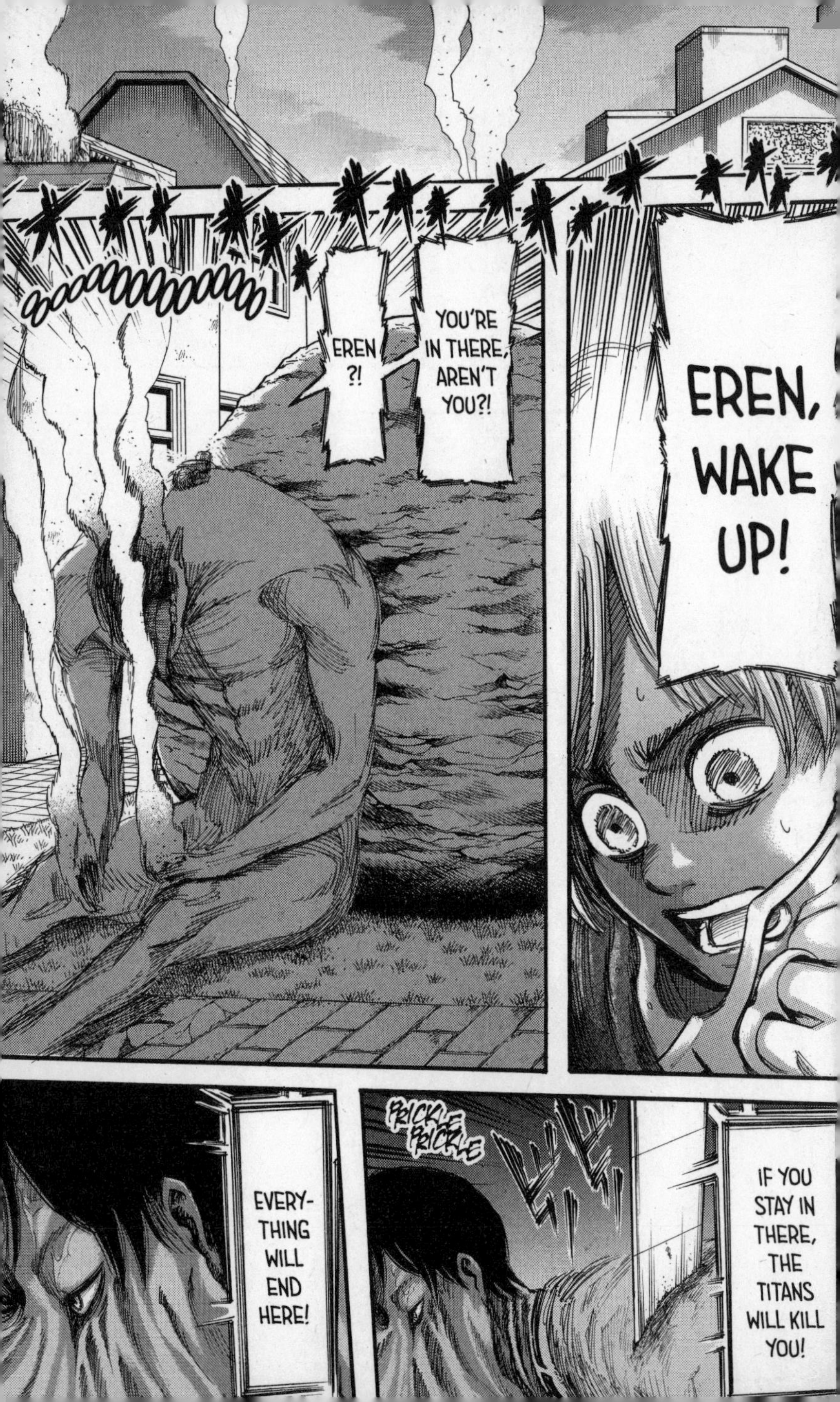
EREN, WAKE UP!
YOU'RE IN THERE, AREN'T YOU?!
EREN ?!
OOOOOOOOOOOOOO
PRICKLE PRICKLE
IF YOU STAY IN THERE, THE TITANS WILL KILL YOU!
EVERY-THING WILL END HERE!

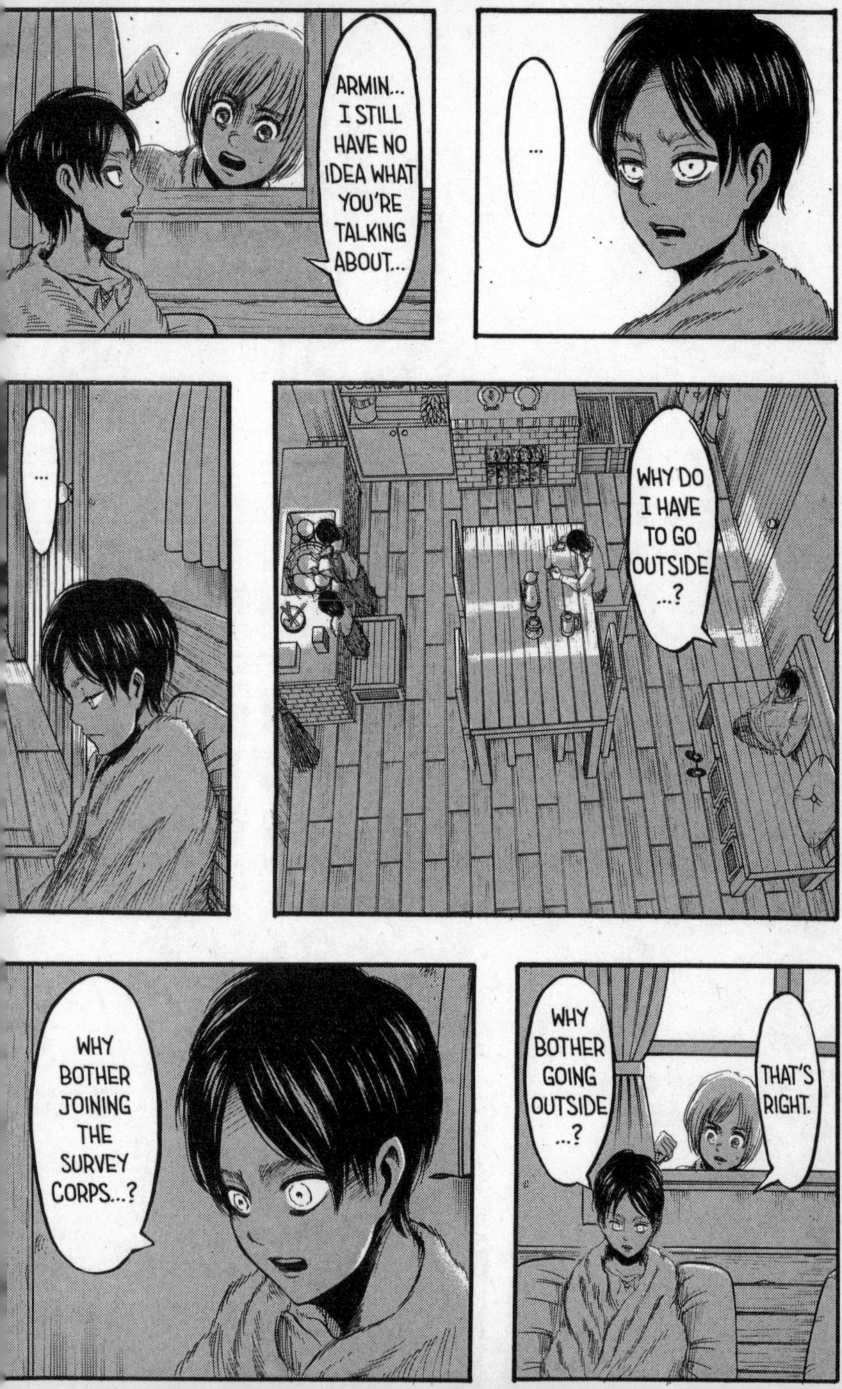
...
ARMIN... I STILL HAVE NO IDEA WHAT YOU'RE TALKING ABOUT...
WHY DO I HAVE TO GO OUTSIDE ...?
...
THAT'S RIGHT.
WHY BOTHER GOING OUTSIDE ...?
WHY BOTHER JOINING THE SURVEY CORPS...?

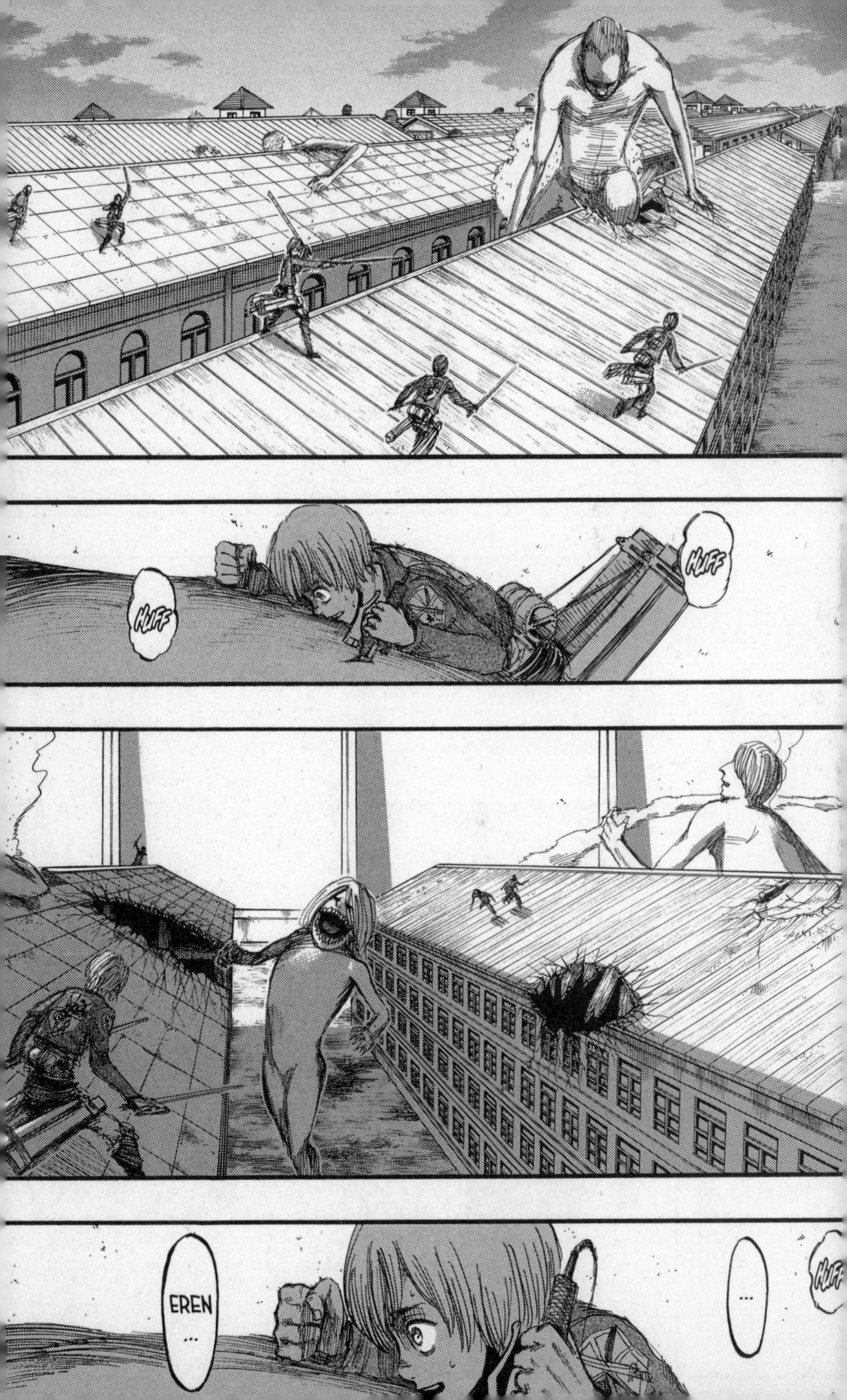
HUFF
HUFF
HUFF
...
EREN ...

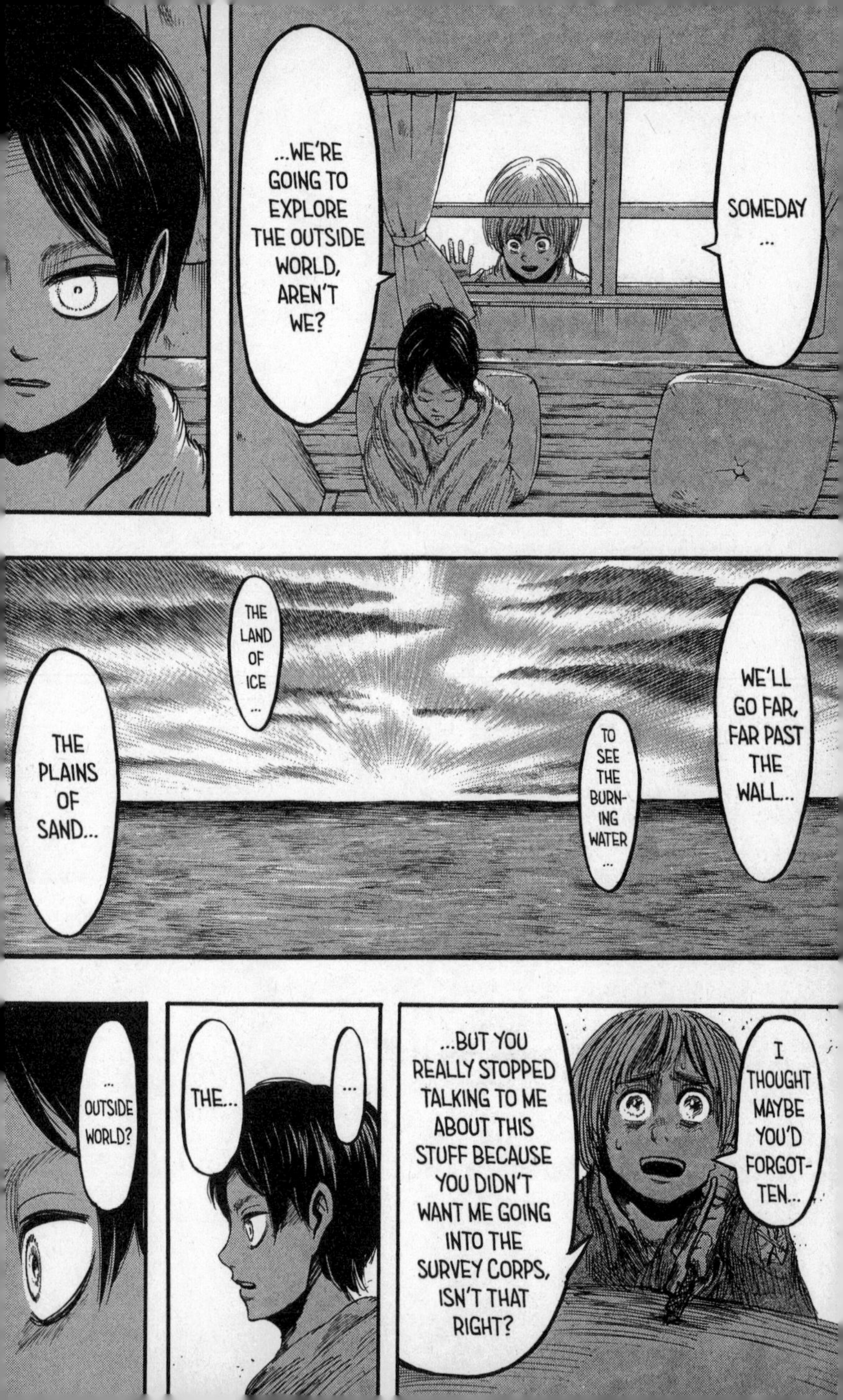
SOMEDAY ...
...WE'RE GOING TO EXPLORE THE OUTSIDE WORLD, AREN'T WE?
WE'LL GO FAR, FAR PAST THE WALL...
TO SEE THE BURN-ING WATER ...
THE LAND OF ICE ...
THE PLAINS OF SAND...
I THOUGHT MAYBE YOU'D FORGOT-TEN...
...BUT YOU REALLY STOPPED TALKING TO ME ABOUT THIS STUFF BECAUSE YOU DIDN'T WANT ME GOING INTO THE SURVEY CORPS, ISN'T THAT RIGHT?
...
THE...
... OUTSIDE WORLD?

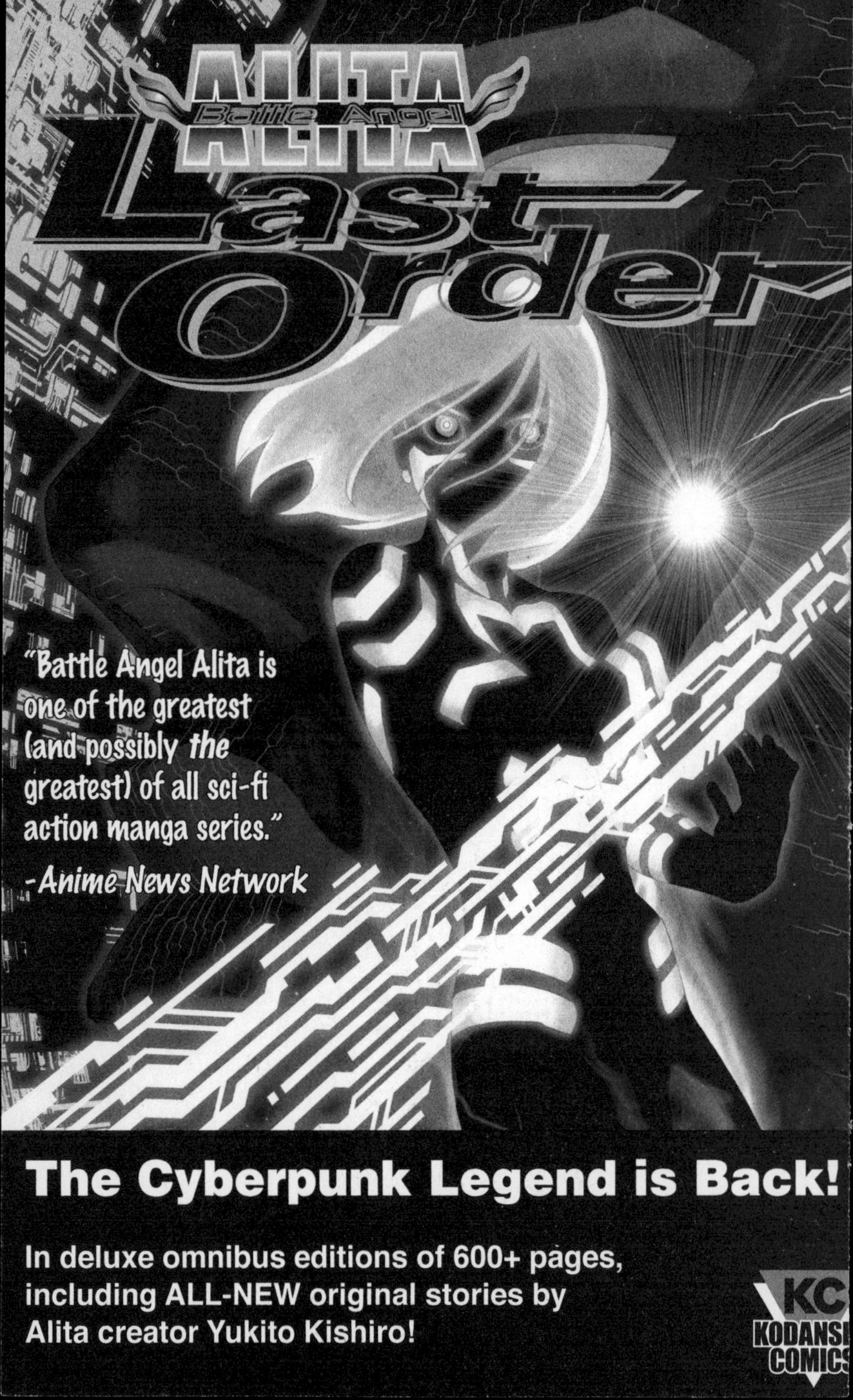
ALITA Battle Angel
Last Order
"Battle Angel Alita is one of the greatest (and possibly *the* greatest) of all sci-fi action manga series."
-Anime News Network
The Cyberpunk Legend is Back!
In deluxe omnibus editions of 600+ pages, including ALL-NEW original stories by Alita creator Yukito Kishiro!
KC KODANSHA COMICS

MARDOCK

マルドゥック・スクランブル

SCRAMBLE

Created by
Tow Ubukata

✕

Manga by
Yoshitoki Oima

"I'd rather be dead."

Rune Balot was a lost girl with nothing to live for. A man named Shell took her in and cared for her...until he tried to murder her. Standing at the precipice of death Rune is saved by Dr. Easter, a private investigator, who uses an experimental procedure known as "Mardock Scramble 09." The procedure grants Balot extraordinary abilities. Now, Rune must decide whether to use her new powers to help Dr. Easter bring Shell to justice, or if she even has the will to keep living a life that's been broken so badly.

Ages: 16+

Attack on Titan volume 3 is a work of fiction. Names, characters, places, and incidents are the products of the author's imagination or are used fictitiously. Any resemblance to actual events, locales, or persons, living or dead, is entirely coincidental.

A Kodansha Comics Trade Paperback Original
Attack on Titan volume 3 copyright © 2010 Hajime Isayama
English translation copyright © 2012 Hajime Isayama

Published in the United States by Kodansha Comics, an imprint of Kodansha USA Publishing, LLC, New York.

Publication rights for this English edition arranged through Kodansha Ltd, Tokyo.

First published in Japan in 2010 by Kodansha Ltd., Tokyo as Shingeki no Kyojin, volume 3.

ISBN 978-1-61262-026-8

Original cover design by Takashi Shimoyama (Red Rooster)

Printed in the United States of America.

www.kodanshacomics.com

9 8 7 6 5
Translation: Sheldon Drzka
Lettering: Steve Wands
Editing: Ben Applegate

You are going the *wrong way!*

Manga is a *completely* different type of reading experience.

To start at the *BEGINNING,* go to the *END!*

That's right! Authentic manga is read the traditional Japanese way--from right to left, exactly the opposite of how American books are read. It's easy to follow: just go to the other end of the book, and read each page--and each panel--from the right side to the left side, starting at the top right. Now you're experiencing manga as it was meant to be.